Corporate Planning and
Policy Design

Corporate Planning and Policy Design: A System Dynamics Approach

James M. Lyneis

Pugh-Roberts Associates, Inc.
Five Lee Street
Cambridge, Massachusetts

Third printing, August 1988

This book was set in Times Roman by Grafacon, Inc. and printed and bound by Halliday Lithograph in the United States of America.

Library of Congress Cataloging in Publication Data

Lyneis, James M.
    Corporate planning and policy design.

    (Pugh-Roberts Associates, Inc. Five Lee Street Cambridge, MA)
    Includes bibliographies and index.
    1. Corporate planning. I. Title.
HD30.28.L93   658.4'012   80-15996
ISBN 0-262-12083-6

To Debra

Contents

An Introductory Policy Design Example 3

Part II
Dynamics of Production and Employment Instability

Dynamics of Inventory Systems 4

**Dynamics Created by Interactions with
Customer and Competitors**   **8**

**Using a Model to Evaluate Financial
Performance**   **9**

**Dynamics Created by Financial
Control**   **10**

**Part III
Dynamics of Corporate Growth**

**Dynamics Created by Capacity
Expansion**

11

**Dynamics Created by Financial
Constraints**

12

**Dynamics Created by Professional
Resource Expansion**

13

Preface

This text evolved from the material used in a one-term introductory course on industrial dynamics given in the Alfred P. Sloan School of Management at MIT. The course attempted to familiarize the class with basic principles of system dynamics as applied to corporate planning: (1) the behavior of organizations is determined by the structure and policies of the organization in its interaction with the environment, (2) a computer model can be used to understand behavior and to design different policies that improve behavior, and (3) one important role of corporate management in such understanding and policy design.

The core material of the course consisted of readings and discussions of the basic principles and computer problems and case studies which provided a hands-on experience in the use of system dynamics. Supplementing it were readings and lectures on the system dynamics methodology and on additional managerial applications of system dynamics.

A background in the system dynamics methodology is not essential to using this text; an overview is contained in chapter 3 and appendixes A and B. Nevertheless, additional background material is helpful in studying part I of this book. Specific lectures and background readings used in the course were

1. Introduction to System Dynamics (chapters 1, 3, and 4 of *Principles of Systems* and chapters 1, 3, 4, and 6 of *Industrial Dynamics*),[1]
2. Overview of Modeling Process (chapters 5, 6, 7, 8, and 9 of *Princi-

1. Jay W. Forrester, *Principles of Systems* (Cambridge, Mass.: The MIT Press, 1968); Jay W. Forrester, *Industrial Dynamics* (Cambridge, Mass.: The MIT Press, 1961).

ples of Systems, chapter 9 of *Industrial Dynamics*, and chapter 1 and exercises 1 and 3 of *Study Notes in System Dynamics*),[2]
3. First-Order Systems (chapters 2.1, 2.2, and 10 of *Principles of Systems* and chapters 2 through 5 and exercises 2 through 8 of *Study Notes in System Dynamics*),
4. Delays (chapter 9 and appendixes E, G, and H of *Industrial Dynamics*).

With this background students are adequately prepared to study parts II and III of the book in depth. A more superficial study of the use of system dynamics in planning would not require this supplemental reading.

Corporate Planning and Policy Design is divided into three parts. Part I discusses the use of system dynamics in planning and policy design. First, motivation for the use of system dynamics is provided by describing how system dynamics addresses some common causes of planning failures: (1) an inability to calculate the behaviors created by interactions among functional areas within the company, and between the company and the environment, and (2) an inability to test the response of different policies under different assumptions about the environment. An overview of the application of system dynamics to planning and policy design at a major manufacturer of capital equipment follows. Then a simple policy design example is presented. The example carries out the five steps in a system dynamics study: (1) identify the problem behavior, (2) model the structure and policies creating the behavior, (3) develop an understanding of how the structure and policies create the behavior, (4) design policies that improve behavior, and (5) test policy response to different scenarios or assumptions about the environment.

Parts II and III address two important classes of problem behavior: production and employment instability and corporate growth. Each chapter within these parts describes how a specific set of interactions among functional areas or between the company and the environment contributes to these problem behaviors, in each case carrying out the five steps in a system dynamics study. Thus the book develops building blocks of common corporate structures that can be used as a starting point for applied corporate modeling projects. However, other

2. Michael R. Goodman, *Study Notes in System Dynamics* (Cambridge, Mass.: The MIT Press, 1975).

than identifying and executing the steps, the book does not describe the process of constructing models.

Within each chapter the model developed builds on the model developed in the preceding chapter. Thus, while the additional effort required to learn a new model is small, the book must be read in sequence.

The structures and policies described herein are typical of many companies but do not describe any particular company. Consequently to give the class an exposure to the types of models developed in an actual application and to illustrate the diversity of problem behaviors studied, additional readings can be assigned. One excellent source for these readings is Robert's *Managerial Applications of System Dynamics*.[3]

3. Edward R. Roberts, (ed.) *Managerial Applications of System Dynamics* (Cambridge, Mass.: The MIT Press, 1978).

Editor's note: A manual of suggested solutions to the cases and problems, including enlargements of selected figures and notes suitable for preparing transparencies, is available from The MIT Press. Please write for details.

A set of additional materials is available from the author at Pugh-Roberts Associates, Inc., 5 Lee Street, Cambridge, Mass. 02139. This includes (1) listings of the models used in each chapter and the rerun changes needed to make each run, (2) a tape containing the models used in each chapter, and (3) introductory notes on system dynamics suitable for preparing transparencies.

Acknowledgments

Jay W. Forrester provided the impetus for this book through his encouragement of my participation in system dynamics and by developing the many industrial applications on which it is based. I am grateful for his help and support.

Many past and present members of the System Dynamics Group at MIT also contributed to the Industrial Dynamics research program. I can only single out for special mention those that reviewed the many drafts of this book: David F. Andersen, Willard R. Fey, Gilbert Low, John D. W. Morecroft, and William A. Shaffer. The students in my classes at MIT also provided helpful comments.

The problems and cases included in this text have for the most part evolved over many years with many individuals working on them. John D. W. Morecroft and Peter M. Senge deserve special mention, however, as they developed new material and polished up some old.

Finally I would like to thank Geraldine Bourke who typed several drafts of the book and Diane Leonard-Senge who developed the enumerable figures.

Part I
Using System Dynamics in
Planning and Policy Design

A System Dynamics
Perspective of Corporate Planning
and Policy Design

1

1.1 Introduction

Strategic planning is the process of translating corporate objectives into the policies and resource allocations that will achieve those objectives. The process usually entails (1) establishing corporate goals and objectives, (2) assessing likely trends in the economic, political, technical, and competitive environment, (3) identifying potential opportunities and threats, and (4) developing strategies, policies, and resource allocations to cope with the threats and take advantage of the opportunities.

Unfortunately many companies do not meet performance expectations because the planning process uses tools that are particularly inadequate for our present-day environment of complexity and rapid change. Planning often boils down to setting goals arbitrarily and then taking actions based on intuition and experience to achieve these goals. Planning by means of intuition and experience, however, yields variable results. Some companies are very successful while the performance of others is mediocre or poor; also company performance often changes over time in response to changes in the business environment—what was a successful plan in one environment becomes unsuccessful in another.

Such variable performance is a consequence of complex corporate systems. The myriad interactions among functional areas within a company, and between a company and its environment, preclude consistently effective planning based solely on intuition. The human mind is incapable of evaluating the implications of more than a few such interactions. As a result performance suffers when unanticipated interactions among parts of the company or changes in the environment defeat the efforts of corporate plans.

Current planning efforts most often lead to underperformance because resource allocations and policies are designed in isolation. Budgets and operating policies are isolated by functional area. Yet the composite performance of functional areas determines corporate performance. Further, resource allocations and policies are isolated from the establishment of corporate goals and objectives in the sense that few companies explicitly calculate how the allocations and policies will achieve the goals. Without an explicit calculation there is no way of knowing if the goals are too high (creating stress from continued underperformance), too low (creating complacency and underperformance), or inconsistent (creating fluctuating performance). Finally, budgeting and policy design are often isolated from any analysis of alternative environmental scenarios. Plans are based on the most likely, and generally most recent, scenario. But changes in business conditions affect corporate performance as much as corporate actions.

Planning efforts also lead to underperformance because planning focuses more on the allocation of resources than on the design of policies. As used here, policy is broader than resource allocation. A policy is a set of generally informal and unwritten guidelines that determines resource allocation requests as well as actual allocations. A functional area may receive its entire requested allocation, but this may turn out to be insufficient because the policy guidelines that produced the request are inadequate. For example, a company may continually experience capacity problems even though all requests for additional capacity were approved. For such a company the problem lies in the policy guidelines through which information about customer demand, utilization rates, interest rates, and availability of financial resources are translated into capacity requests.

A policy can also be a set of guidelines that influences how resource allocations are used. For example, research allocations may be used more for product improvement than for new product development. Such a policy can produce short-run benefits but long-run costs. Effective corporate planning must evaluate policy guidelines, as the guidelines determine the requests, approval, and use of resources. To the extent that planning is only budgeting, it does not help the company understand why problems occur nor help it cope with change.

1.2 Examples of Underperformance

The following case summaries serve to illustrate corporate underperformance that results from a breakdown in the translation of corporate objectives into a set of policies and resource allocations designed to achieve those objectives. The examples are of necessity sketchy. Greater detail is contained in the references at the end of the chapter. Examples of similar underperformance are described by Hobbs and Heany (1977).

Underperformance Resulting from Policy Design Isolated by Functional Area

In a major U.S. manufacturing firm the policies of engineering, production, and capacity expansion interacted to cause a loss of market share. Engineering frequently introduced product modifications in response to the corporate objective of good customer service; production changed the assembly rate to match changes in customer orders in response to the corporate objectives of good customer service (quick delivery) and minimum inventory (alternatively, quick delivery could be made from a finished product inventory); capacity expansion was planned to minimize the degree of underutilization during business downturns because of the high costs of capacity.

Each of these policies looked at in isolation is reasonable. However, together they contribute to declining performance. Product modifications make obsolete current product design, thereby contributing to the desire to avoid finished inventories and necessitating changes in production rate to match changes in customer orders. But such changes are feasible only if sufficient capacity exists to increase production. Without sufficient capacity customer orders exceed production so that backlogs build and delivery times increase, resulting in lost orders. The manufacturer's capacity expansion policies, by minimizing underutilization in downturns, also caused insufficient capacity in upturns. The interactions among engineering, production, and capacity policies caused a loss of market share during peaks of business activity. The best policy or action plan for each functional area was not the best policy set for the company as a whole.

Poor performance frequently results when different functional areas attempt to achieve conflicting goals. For example, a Canadian retailer set sales revenue and profit margin goals for individual stores (Roberts et al. 1968). Corporate headquarters used changes in advertising to achieve the goals; individual stores used "specials" (equivalent to a price change). Because the goals are conflicting, attempts to improve sales revenue came at the expense of profit margin, and vice versa.

Because two corporate areas were taking actions to achieve the conflicting goals, the company experienced regular fluctuations in revenue and margins. When sales revenue was below target, stores first offered some specials, and headquarters later increased advertising (because of longer delays in getting information about store performance and changing advertising). The increased specials tended to correct most of the revenue problem so that the advertising change caused revenue to overshoot target. Unfortunately both actions reduced profit margins. In response to reduced margins and increased revenue, fewer specials were offered and later advertising reduced. These actions increased profit margins but reduced sales revenue. In attempting to achieve these conflicting goals through policies of different functional areas, the company experienced fluctuating performance.

As another example, research, marketing, and acquisitions in a large conglomerate all strived to achieve an earnings-per-share growth goal (Peters 1971). Based on a discrepancy between forecast earnings per share and the goal, the company adjusted research, development, and selling expenditures and made acquisitions. For example, when earnings-per-share fell below goal, research, development, and selling expenses were cut, while acquisitions were increased. But this control process produced both annual and three-year fluctuations in performance; the actions by three functional areas tended to cause performance to overshoot the goal in the short run (one year) but to undershoot the goal in the long run, as the effects of lower research and marketing budgets and the growth of overhead associated with acquisitions were felt. Actions to counteract the decline in performance perpetuated the cycles.

Policy design by functional area has been the only means of coping with the complexity of corporate systems. While top management attempts to coordinate the policies of functional areas, intuition alone is insufficient for consistently effective policy design. Even top companies experience performance below potential.

Underperformance Resulting from Policy Design Isolated from Establishment of Goals

When goals are established apart from policy design, and particularly when the effort required to achieve the objectives is not explicitly calculated, corporate performance is likely to deviate from objectives. Often objectives are set above those achievable with a reasonable allocation of resources. For example, after years of profitable but declining rate of growth, a producer of consumer goods undertook a major product development and marketing program to increase substantially growth in sales revenue (Richmond 1976). As expected, the development and marketing expenditures necessary to achieve the growth goal reduced profit margins. Unfortunately, to market successfully the new products, expenditures had to be increased well above original estimates. After several years profit margins had declined so much that actions to improve growth rate had to be reduced significantly. The company tried to achieve a growth rate goal inconsistent with reasonable profit margins. The initial resource allocations were insufficient to develop and market the products successfully; consequently allocations were increased in an attempt to salvage the development expenditures. Even the additional allocations proved insufficient. Resource allocations based on intuition and experience were inadequate for satisfaction of the conflicting goals.

In addition to problems created by goals set above reasonable resource allocations, the isolation of policy design from goal setting can lead to fluctuating performance. One example was the Canadian retailer just described. In setting the profit margin and sales revenue goals, the company did not evaluate the feasibility of jointly achieving those goals. Because the goals were conflicting, policies set up to achieve them caused fluctuations in performance.

Often companies classify product lines without thinking out the consequences of the classification. For example, a product line is classified as a growth business. Such a classification engenders goals like "Introduce three new products a year." Unfortunately no one thinks out how the new products will influence a company's competitive position. Will the new products adversely affect the sales of existing products? Will the proliferation of products adversely affect manufacturing capacity so that delivery times increase? Or, will the pressures to get out new products cause insufficient testing and thereby poor quality? Similar problems affect products classified as a "harvest" business. The classification can cause little capacity expansion and a reduction in cost-cutting research. Such actions lead to aging facilities and high operating costs that force higher prices and lost market share, or lower profits if prices are not raised. Either way the company can cause the forecast of slow or negative growth rate to be fulfilled by company actions, without the profit harvest.

In many companies the design of policies is left to people in positions too low in the organization. For example, a major manufacturing firm had an objective of maintaining adequate inventories of parts and materials but did not translate the term ''adequate'' into an operating goal for inventory or into rules for ordering parts. This function was left to the discretion of the several hundred parts planners. Unintentionally management exerted pressures on the planners only when the inventory became too high. On perceiving the negative consequences of holding too much inventory, management's goal of adequate inventory was translated into ''Avoid excess inventory at all costs.'' Actions by parts planners produced stockouts and shortages as a consequence of striving for minimum inventory.

The establishment of corporate goals is often isolated from the policies necessary to achieve those goals. Such an isolation can cause goals that are too high, too low, conflicting, or different at operating levels fron those desired by management. Performance below potential results.

Underperformance Resulting from Policy Design Isolated from Environmental Analysis

Poor performance can result if the company fails to make the policy robust, able to handle changing conditions. A land developer had a growth policy that worked wonders as long as demand grew rapidly but led to disaster when demand fell (Richmond 1976). Through heavy reliance on debt, the policy produced a corporate condition that could only be sustained in a growth market. A more robust policy might have produced less rapid growth but averted disaster in a temporary downturn. Similarly a publishing firm pursued a strategy that produced growth and profits until the market saturated, at which point the strategy caused decline and bankruptcy (Richmond 1976). A manufacturing firm followed a diversification strategy based on a forecast of declining growth rate in their major business. When more rapid growth rather than decline ensued, the strategy resulted in high debt levels, cash flow problems, and lost market share.

Causes of Underperformance

The underperformance of the companies described was not exclusively caused by bad management. In most cases management was attempting to solve problems using currently accepted practices and techniques. Nevertheless, the solutions were either causing or contributing to the problem. Such a breakdown of standard practice results from the nature of corporate systems:

1. Corporate behavior is affected by many interactions between parts of the company and the company and the environment.
2. Interactions tend to be more important than components—policy design by functional area is not always effective.
3. Long-term may differ from short-term results—actions taken to correct an immediate problem may make matters worse in the future.

Management requires a tool to supplement intuition and experience that provides a means of handling interactions and calculating long-term as well as short-term effects.

1.3 The System Dynamics View

System dynamics provides three elements essential to effective corporate planning and policy design: an emphasis on understanding how behavior results from corporate structure and policies, a theory of behavior, and the use of computer modeling to aid planning. When a company understands all aspects of its corporate behavior, it can bridge the gap between goals and policy design. Rather than first arbitrarily setting goals and then selecting resource allocations and policies suggested by intuition and experience to achieve the goals, the company can evaluate goals and policies together. This first contribution of system dynamics is more one of philosophy than technique: a philosophy that the role of management is one of controlling corporate behavior by first understanding what causes that behavior and then designing policies to improve behavior.

Computer modeling provides the tools for implementing the philosophy. The computer model of the company is constructed, based on the system dynamics theory of causes of dynamic behavior. Simulation of the model traces out the behavioral consequences of different policies. Management thus has a laboratory for designing improved corporate policies.

Understanding How Behavior Results from Corporate Structure and Policies

No company sits still. Sales, profits, and market share all change over time. For example, figure 1.1 illustrates several different sales patterns

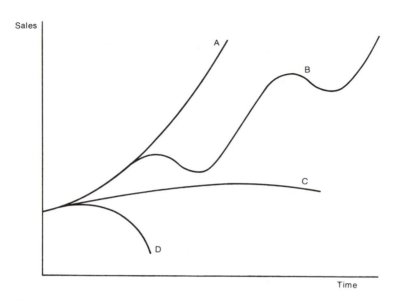

Figure 1.1   Examples of dynamic behavior

that a company might experience: curve *A* depicts the rare, smoothly growing company, curve *B* the company that grows with a series of reversals, curve *C* the company that stagnates, and curve *D* the company that declines. Dynamic behavior is the movement of a company from one condition to another over a period of time.

Dynamic behavior results from three distinct factors: actions by the company; actions of competitors, for example, price or product changes that alter competitive positions; and changes in the environment, for example, business cycles, population trends, or government regulations. System dynamics provides a means whereby dynamic behavior can be understood and controlled. Corporate policies and resource allocations are designed that are capable of achieving corporate goals (and perhaps identifying inconsistent or unachievable goals) and minimize the adverse impacts of, or capitalize on, environmental changes and competitor actions.

The system dynamics approach yields an understanding of dynamic behavior by focusing on the behavioral forces and dynamic interrelationships that cause change. Ordinarily decision processes operate on the straightforward, problem-action-result basis illustrated in figure 1.2a: the company detects a problem or opportunity, allocates resources, and anticipates a result. For example, in figure 1.2b sales revenue growth below the goal causes the action "increases sales

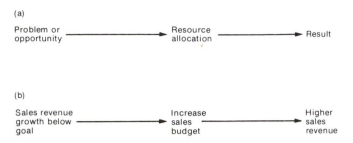

Figure 1.2   Problem-action-result sequence

budget,'' an action that eventually increases sales revenue. The problem-action-result sequence is, however, only one of the dynamic interrelationships that causes change. Feedbacks and interactions between functional areas also bring about change.

Figure 1.3 shows a slightly expanded problem-action-result system. One important element in figure 1.3 is feedback. Feedback occurs whenever a problem gives rise to an action that in turn achieves a result, and the result alleviates the problem. As shown in figure 1.3 by arrow 1, higher sales revenue alleviates the problem of sales growth below goal and therefore halts further increases in the sales budget, all other things remaining equal. Feedback interrelationships underlie all dynamic behavior: problems lead to actions that produce results, perhaps eliminating problems and thus stopping further action.

But feedback interactions connect other elements of the corporate system. For example, an increase in sales budget potentially creates a problem of shortage of financial resources, as indicated by arrow 2 in figure 1.3. The company might respond to such a problem by reducing inventory accumulation, with the result of reduced product availability. But the reduced product availability tends to reduce sales revenue and thereby stimulates action to increase further the sales budget, worsen the shortage of financial resources, and reduce inventory accumulation. A downward spiral potentially develops.

Many other feedback interactions could be added to figure 1.3. Nevertheless, the figure serves to illustrate how change—dynamic behavior—is created by feedback interactions involving company policies. Different policies create different behavior. For example, rather than reducing inventory accumulation, the company might raise price. Such an action initiates many feedback interactions whose outcome might differ from the previously described downward spiral.

A complete model of the causal forces inducing change might also

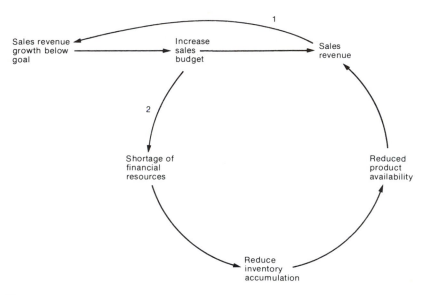

Figure 1.3 Expanded problem-action-result sequence

include competitor actions and changes in the environment. Figure 1.4 provides a framework for incorporating these additional forces and organizing the company's internal forces. In figure 1.4 corporate policies guide the acquisition and allocation of resources. Corporate policies state how resources will be acquired, allocated, and used in an effort to keep corporate performance in line with corporate goals. As discrepancies between goal and performance occur, resources are deployed to alleviate the discrepancy. In turn resources affect a company's competitive variables, its aggregate product attractiveness, market share, customer orders, and profits, cash flow, and other measures of performance. Performance feeds back to affect the future acquisition and allocation of resources. Competitor actions also affect a company's dynamic behavior through competitor product attractiveness. Finally, changes in the environment such as market demand might influence dynamic behavior.

Of the factors determining dynamic behavior, the company has direct control only over corporate policies and goals. The function of corporate planning should be therefore the design of policies that yield acceptable performance independent of competitor actions and market changes. Corporate planning should first ensure that company policies are not creating poor behavior, as was the case in many of the examples described earlier. Then planning should design policies capable of

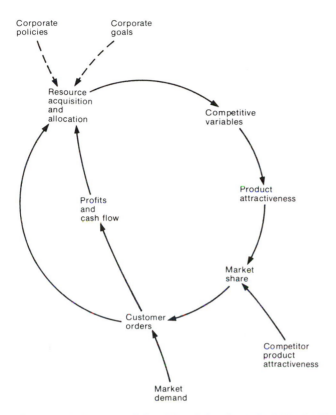

Figure 1.4   Framework for determining dynamic behavior and evaluating policies

responding to, or taking advantage of, changes in the market or competitor actions. The framework illustrated in figure 1.4 provides a
method of relating corporate policies to dynamic behavior and thereby
designing effective corporate policies. The framework provides a
means of handling interrelationships within the company and between
the company and the market and of evaluating the short- and long-term
results of a policy. The competitive variable and resource elements of
the framework will be described in detail.

A company's incoming order rate is a function of the attractiveness
of its products relative to the attractiveness of competing products.
Any differences in attractiveness result, other things equal, in an increased flow of orders (increased market share) to the more attractive
product. Such a flow continues until actions by the company or by
competitors equalize the attractiveness of competing products.

The net attractiveness of a company's product is a composite deter-

Table 1.1
Some determinants of product attractiveness

Price
Delivery delay (availability)
Quality
Product newness
Sales effort
Service

Table 1.2
Typical corporate resources

Production
Workforce
Capital equipment
Floor space
Raw materials

Financial
Cash flow
Debt capacity
Stock price

Professional Personnel
Marketing and sales
Research and development
Management

mined by the competitive variables that distinguish two products. Table 1.1 lists some of these competitive variables: price, delivery delay, quality, product newness (technological differentiation), sales effort, and service. The market (customers) weigh these competitive variables in arriving at a composite attractiveness. As a result two products can have the same net attractiveness but differ in the individual competitive variables. For example, higher price may offset higher quality.

A company's resources have an important effect on product attractiveness. The company that acquires and utilizes resources to maintain a superior product attractiveness will, other things equal, grow faster and more smoothly than competing companies.

Table 1.2 lists and classifies these resources into three broad categories: production, financial, and professional resources. Production resources are the means by which a company makes and services its products. Financial resources provide the cash for acquiring production and professional resources. Finally, professional resources manage, market, and design and engineer the flow of products provided by a company.

A system dynamics model represents the causal feedback interactions that guide the acquisition and allocation of resources, the determination of competitive position based on these resources, and the response of the market to relative competitive positions. As a result the model becomes a vehicle for understanding the causes of company behavior and for designing policies to improve that behavior.

Using a Computer Model to Aid Planning

Experience from working with managers in many corporations indicates that they are generally able to specify the detailed relationships among corporate policies, resources, competitive variables, and company performance. However, managers are unable to determine accurately the dynamic behavior implied by these relationships. Human intuition is ill-suited for calculating the consequences of thousands of interactions over time. But the computer is highly efficient at carrying out such calculations.

The system dynamics approach to corporate planning and policy design combines the strengths of managers with the strength of the computer. The manager aids by specifying relationships within the corporate system; the computer then calculates the dynamic consequences of these relationships.

Construction of the model offers the company four benefits. First, the model allows the company to take into account a greater number of factors than can be considered with intuition alone. Rather than developing policies for parts of the company, a best set of policies for a larger portion of the company can be designed. A set of policies, each of which in isolation may appear less than optimal, can jointly improve overall performance.

Second, the model provides a means of explicitly calculating the effect of different goals and policies on corporate behavior. Because the model traces out time paths of behavior through role playing of causal interactions within the company system, the effect of policy changes on behavior are easily obtained.

Third, the model is a vehicle for testing the response of company policies to different economic, competitive, and environmental scenarios. For example, rapid inflation, material shortages, depression, and competitor technological breakthroughs have different impacts on company performance. While the model cannot predict if these events will occur, it can give management a feel for the consequences of their occurrence. Then management can design policies and contingency plans for the occurrence of potentially damaging events.

And finally, construction of the model forces managers to step back from the day-to-day pressures of operating decisions and examine the company as a whole, question current practices and policies, and take a longer-run view of the company and its environment.

1.4 Summary

Successful corporate planning and policy design require that the company carefully coordinate the actions of the different functional areas, weigh short- and long-run costs and benefits, and evaluate the impact of changes in the business environment. These requirements preclude consistently effective planning based solely on managerial intuition and experience. Particularly in times of rapid change, the manager must supplement intuition and experience with planning tools capable of addressing these requirements.

System dynamics provides one tool that allows a company to improve performance through the design of better policies. System dynamics contributes three elements essential to effective corporate planning:

1. Philosophy of management—the role of management is one of controlling corporate behavior by first understanding what causes that behavior and then designing policies to improve behavior.
2. Theory of causes of dynamic behavior—within companies behavior is caused by feedback interactions among policies for the acquisition and allocation of resources, the determination of competitive position based on these resources, and market response to relative competitive positions.
3. Use of computer model—a computer model allows the company to consider many interactions, calculate explicitly the behavioral consequences of policies, and test policy response to different competitive, economic, and environmental scenarios.

References

Forrester, Jay W. 1961. *Industrial Dynamics*. Cambridge, Mass.: The MIT Press.

Hobb, John M., and Donald F. Heany. 1977. Coupling Strategy to Operating Plans. *Harvard Business Review*. 55:119.

Peters, Donald H. 1971. The Impact of Financial Control on Financial Performance. Mimeographed.

Richmond, Barry. 1976. Profiles in Corporate Growth Pathology. Mimeographed.

Roberts, Edward B., Henry B. Weil, and Dan I. Abrams. 1968. A Systems Study of Policy Formulation in a Vertically Integrated Firm. *Management Science*. 14:674–694.

Roberts, Edward B. 1976. *Managerial Applications of System Dynamics.* Cambridge, Mass.: The MIT Press.

A System Dynamics
Case Study of Corporate Planning
and Policy Design

2

2.1 Introduction

A system dynamics model is being used by a major manufacturer of industrial equipment as a tool for corporate planning and policy design. The model provides the company with an explicit means of translating corporate objectives into the policies capable of achieving those objectives. Moreover the model is a vehicle for testing the effect of changes in the economic, competitive, or regulatory environment on corporate policy. As such, the model is also an important tool in the company's strategic planning process.

A system dynamics model is constructed for the purpose of understanding the causes of such corporate problems as employment instability and/or slow growth and for designing policies to alleviate the problems. In this case the company faced several problems:

1. gradual loss of market share,
2. declining profitability,
3. production and employment instability.

While corporate performance was still generally good, it was below expectations and capabilities.

The underperformance was not caused by bad management or by changing external conditions. Rather it resulted from a selection of operating goals and policies that, while eminently reasonable in isolation, in combination interacted over time to cause declining performance. The complexity of corporate systems often forces such isolated policy design. Corporations have difficulty designing a set of policies that act together to achieve desired goals.

2.2 Corporate Goals and Policies Causing Problem Behavior

The manufacturing company under discussion is a leading producer of industrial equipment; the gradual decline in market share and profitability was suffered over a ten- to fifteen-year period. A significant cause of the declining performance was the interaction among several operating policies designed to improve corporate performance. But this was not the only cause of the company's problems. A diversification program, supplier delays, and wage-price controls were additional contributing factors. Nevertheless, company policies substantially affected performance. A well-designed set of policies should enable the company to respond to such external shocks without suffering loss of market share, liquidity problems, or declining profitability (at least relative to competitors).

The company developed a corporate strategy (objectives and operating policies) intended to produce good financial performance in the face of a changing environment. The objectives of the company could be inferred as follows:

1. Maintain a high responsiveness to customers by keeping pace with technological change through frequent engineering and product design changes and providing a broad range of product options on demand.
2. Minimize investment in assets, because of rapid technological and economic change.
3. Minimize delivery times on orders.

These objectives were translated into the following operating policies:

1. Production rate—because of the large number of product options and frequent product changes no finished inventory was held; thus production schedules were based on actual customer orders, and aggregate production rates were changed as quickly as possible to maintain minimum delivery times in the face of variable customer demand.
2. Parts ordering—ordering was based on averages of past usage rates; the parts planners further tried to maintain low levels of inventory because of the desire to minimize investment in assets.
3. Capacity expansion—the cyclical nature of the industry, coupled with the seemingly high cost of capital, dictated caution in capacity expansion; the company wanted to be sure increases in demand were permanent before investing in fixed assets.

4. Pricing—because of a higher quality product a slightly higher price was maintained than that of the competition.

5. Engineering change—major and minor product design changes were allowed as a matter of course.

When looked at individually, the objectives and associated policies seem reasonable if not optimal. Many companies have similar policies. Yet the combination contributed to a decline in market share and profitability.

A system dynamics model was constructed by a team of consultants and client personnel to show how the combination of policies created problem behavior. Early in the modeling project a working hypothesis was established that the loss of market share was caused not by low quality or high prices (since both were competitive with or better than those of competitors) but by long lead times, erratic delivery, and inability to meet demand at peaks in the sales cycle. Development and analysis of the model demonstrated that the decline in market share could have been caused by long delivery lead times.

The company had viewed its high-quality product as "custom designed," made to order for each customer. As a consequence there was no inventory of finished product, and responses to unexpected increase in demand were limited by the long lead time involved in ordering raw materials and capital equipment. When demand rose sharply, supply seldom was able to follow: the result was long lead times and allocation of the scarce product among customers. Business was thus deflected to competitors. Conversely unexpected declines in business were immediately reflected in abrupt production declines, causing instability in raw material control, service-parts production, and production itself.

Before the model was constructed, the company attributed loss of market share to product problems and the desire of customers for multiple suppliers. While delivery times were known to be important, company management could develop no convincing hypothesis as to why the company's lead times were longer than competitors, if in fact they were (company and competitors tended to be on allocation at the same time)—intuition suggested that availability was important, but evidence was contradictory. The computer simulation model provided a consistent hypothesis.

Figure 2.1 depicts the relationships that caused reduced product availability and the ensuing loss of market share. Simply stated, the

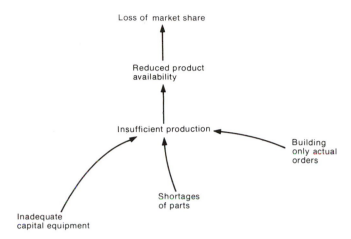

Figure 2.1   Relationships causing reduced product availability and ensuing loss of market share

product was unavailable because of insufficient production. Insufficient production in turn resulted from a combination of three factors:

1. Building only actual customer orders—production rate follows fluctuations in actual orders; as a result of the capacity constraint the company encounters periods when it is unable to produce sufficient product.

2. Shortages of parts—even given adequate capacity, shortages of parts slow the assembly line and cause incomplete assembly.

3. Inadequate capital equipment—capacity places an upper limit on production.

Each of these factors will be examined in more detail.

Production Rate Policy

Building only to actual customer orders and changing production rate to match changes in customer orders is an effective policy only if the company has sufficient capacity (including overtime) to follow such changes. Otherwise, as illustrated in figure 2.2, the company will experience periods of insufficient production and lost orders. Such was the experience at the company under discussion.

In figure 2.2 potential incoming order rate is shown to vary cyclically about a growth trend. Potential incoming order rate is the rate that

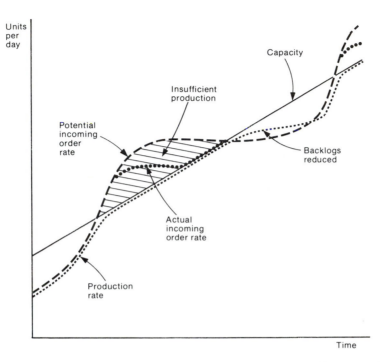

Figure 2.2   Building to actual customer orders causing insufficient production
with limited capacity

would prevail if a constant market share were maintained in a growing
market. Capacity is assumed to grow with the average of potential
incoming order rate. Consequently at times potential incoming order
rate increases above capacity. Production rate, however, cannot increase above capacity. As a result backlogs increase, thereby causing
actual orders to fall below potential orders as customers switch to
competitors offering more rapid delivery (company loses market
share). When orders fall below capacity, production rate remains
above incoming order rate until backlogs are reduced.

   To illustrate the concept of policy design, the performance of
another policy is examined. Given a condition of limited capacity, a
better policy may be to continue to produce at capacity, thereby building inventories during business downturns. The surplus can then be
used to fill customer orders in excess of capacity during business upturns. The cost of holding surplus inventory must be weighed against
the savings realized from smoother production and revenues provided

from achieving full potential sales (or even gaining market share if competitors fail to produce sufficient inventory).[1]

A production rate policy, however, must be more complex than "Always build at capacity." Such a simple policy implicitly assumes incoming order rate will always vary cyclically at the same magnitude. But what if orders should continue to decline rather than increase after a downturn? Or, what if the magnitude of the downturns increase? A production rate policy must specify production if these order rate patterns occur. How quickly should production be reduced as inventory builds? The quicker the reduction, the lower the inventory accumulation. Then if orders again increase, production must increase, although it may fall short of potential orders. The policy design process examines the performance of different policies in response to such order rate patterns and selects a policy that performs acceptably under a range of likely order rate patterns. A complete statement of production rate policy would generally include

1. how quickly to respond to changes in incoming order rate,
2. which, if any, forecasting procedures are used,
3. how desired levels of inventory are determined,
4. how quickly discrepancies between desired and actual inventory are corrected.

A similar policy design process was carried out for the company under study.

Parts-Ordering Policy

Parts shortages slow the assembly line and contribute to insufficient production. As shown in figure 2.3, two factors combine to create shortages: low levels of current parts inventory (parts used for assembly) and fluctuations in build rate.

1. One should be careful in assuming that an optimal production policy can be obtained by incorporating stockout costs in an optimization model. Besides the inherent difficulties in estimating the short-run loss of potential sales, the analyst must also estimate long-run effects. For example, will customers turned away in a business upturn return when business declines, or will they continue to order from competitors? Might competitors, on noting increased orders, expand more aggressively and continue to increase market share in the future? A simulation model that incorporates these effects, coupled with sensitivity tests, may yield a better policy than the supposedly optimal policy given by an optimization model that fails to incorporate the effects.

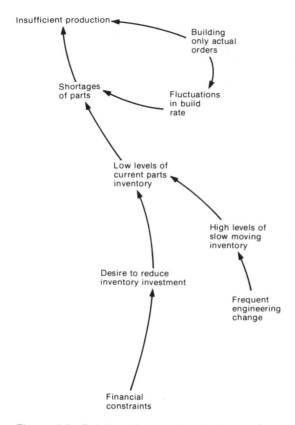

Figure 2.3 Relationships causing shortages of parts

In the company low levels of current parts inventory resulted from
some rather subtle interactions among various categories and mea-
surements of parts inventory. The two basic categories of parts are
current parts and slow-moving parts. Slow-moving parts are those used
only for service. Current parts become slow moving when an engineering design change renders them obsolete for assembly. Such obsoles-
cence dramatically lowers the usage rate. Thus, unless design change
and parts ordering are carefully coordinated, a thirty-day supply of
inventory can suddenly turn into a three-year supply. This occurred
frequently enough to cause high levels of slow-moving parts the company did not aggressively write off because of the adverse impact on
profits. (Even with careful coordination, frequent engineering change
causes larger inventory levels because of the larger number of service
parts.)

High levels of slow-moving parts caused low levels of current parts because the company desired to reduce inventory investment. The company's financial constraints produced considerable pressure for tight working capital management. Financial controllers continually monitored dollar value of inventory (inflated by high levels of slow-moving parts) and placed considerable pressure on parts planners to reduce inventory when dollar value grew too large. Since parts planners were not responsible for writing off obsolete inventory, they used the only effective control at their disposal to reduce inventory—which was to reduce levels of current parts. In summary frequent engineering change, insufficient write-off of slow-moving parts, and financial pressures based on total dollar inventory combined to cause low levels of current parts inventory.

In isolation carrying low parts inventory is not a bad policy. If inventory usage rate (production rate) is stable, the ordering, arrival, and usage of parts will remain in balance, and inventory will be needed only in cases of supplier problems. However, a company policy of building to actual orders introduces a second influence causing parts shortages.

Building to actual orders, which fluctuate considerably, results in fluctuations in inventory usage rate. As shown in figure 2.4, because of the delay in ordering (caused by averaging usage) and receiving parts from suppliers, parts arrival rate lags parts order rate. Consequently parts inventory falls until at point A parts arrival rate equals build rate. Parts inventory increases when parts arrival rate exceeds build rate, until at point B arrivals again equal usage. Such declines in inventory create potential inventory shortages, unless the company carries ample safety stocks. But here the company carries low inventory levels. Thus because of the production rate policy the company's inventory policy creates shortages of parts, insufficient production, and lost orders.

One inventory policy consistent with the production rate policy is to carry ample safety stocks. A second consistent inventory policy is to schedule production far enough in advance that parts arrive as they are used. But to do so requires even longer lead times, if the company builds only actual orders, or a finished inventory to buffer production from customer orders.

Capital Equipment-Ordering Policy

Figure 2.5 depicts the relationships causing inadequate capital equipment, or capacity. Inadequate capacity resulted from expansion less

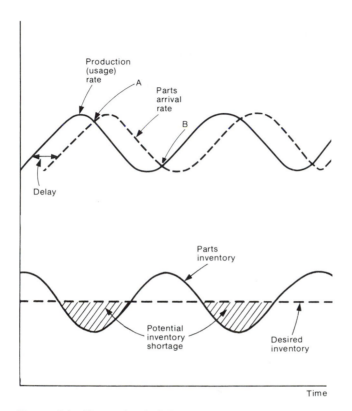

Figure 2.4 Fluctuating building rate causing a potential inventory shortage

than growth in market demand. Financial constraints, which contribute to parts shortages, are one factor limiting capacity expansion. Besides the lack of financing the company failed to expand sufficiently because of underestimates of demand—an incorrect forecast. Further, the company delayed or canceled orders during business downturns when the present factory was underutilized. Thus the capacity needed in the next upturn was not available.

Inadequate capacity creates insufficient production only if the company's production policies are inconsistent. Without a finished product inventory to buffer against capacity shortfalls, market share may be lost. Either the production or capacity expansion policy should be changed. If a finished product inventory is not carried, then a buffer of excess capacity to meet peak demand is the only consistent capacity policy.

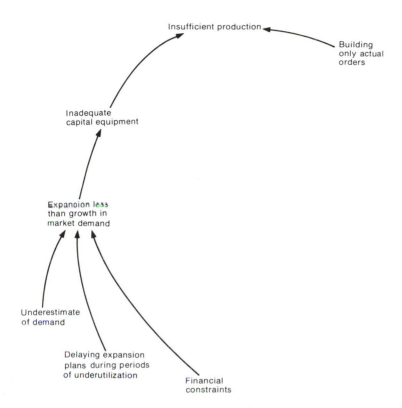

Figure 2.5   Relationships causing inadequate capital equipment

Financial Constraints as a Connecting Link

Figure 2.6 summarizes the interrelationships contributing to loss of market share, production instability, and low profits and shows that a connecting link among the three policy areas is financial constraints. In an upturn inadequate capital equipment and parts shortages are compensated by the use of large amounts of overtime and extra employees to fill promised orders. But overtime and extra employees reduce profits and cash flow, thereby increasing the need for additional debt and making equity financing more difficult and costly. As debt levels increase, financial constraints on current parts inventory and expansion of capital equipment become more and more severe. It becomes difficult for the company to break out of the downward spiral of even greater financial difficulty.

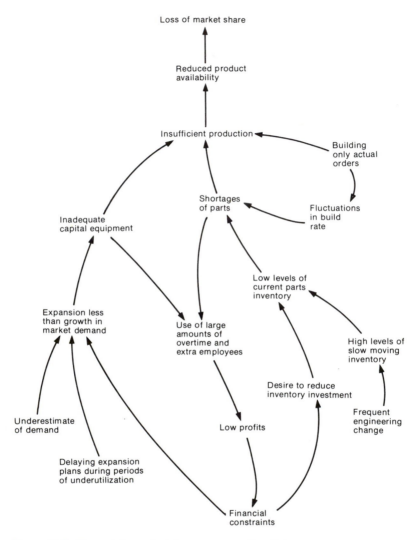

Figure 2.6   Financial constraints as a connecting link

Summary of Interrelationships

It is important to emphasize that at every decision point people were acting in what they felt to be the best interests of the company:

• Production rates were changed to follow incoming orders in an effort to satisfy customers but avoid finished inventories, such inventories being perceived as expensive and risky investments.
• Engineering changes were made to improve the product.
• Parts planners balanced conflicting manufacturing pressures for more inventory with financial and engineering change pressures to reduce inventory.
• Overtime and extra employees were used to satisfy customer orders.
• Financial constraints necessarily limited expansion.
• The high cost of capital equipment and the uncertian cyclical nature of business seemingly dictated caution in investment decisions.

The interrelationships among the policies, however, led to overall underperformance. The build rate policy is effective only if there is sufficient capacity and parts; the capacity expansion policy will work only if a finished product inventory is available to act as a buffer against an inaccurate forecast; the parts-ordering policy is valid only if build rate changes slowly.

2.3 The System Dynamics Model for Planning and Policy Design

A system dynamics model was used to demonstrate inconsistencies among policies and the adverse consequences of them. The model was also used to design a set of consistent policies that might improve company performance. The main elements of the model attempted to capture the interrelationships causing company problems:

1. Build rate—determined by the amounts of parts inventory, capital equipment, employment, and overtime.
2. Desired build rate—used in hiring, firing, and overtime decisions; depends on average incoming order rate and level of unfilled customer orders.
3. Parts-ordering and capital equipment-ordering policies.
4. Production policy and capacity of parts supplier—allow important restrictions on parts availability to be considered.
5. A complete representation of the company's financial and account-

ing structure—checks the profitability of various policies and expresses important financial constraints.

6. The most likely response of the market to the company's and competitors' product availability and prices.

7. The most likely production, capacity, and pricing policies of the competition—enable the company to examine the consequences of different competitor actions and reactions.

Once the model was constructed, several behavioral tests were conducted to compare its output with management experience. One test compared the model behavior with company behavior over a ten-year period. The only historical time-series data inputs to the model were total market demand and prices of such production factors as labor, capital, and raw materials. The model was initialized in 1965 and run without further updating by the modeler. The model generated market share, production rate, prices, and profits based on company and competitor production, capacity expansion, and pricing policies. Figure 2.7

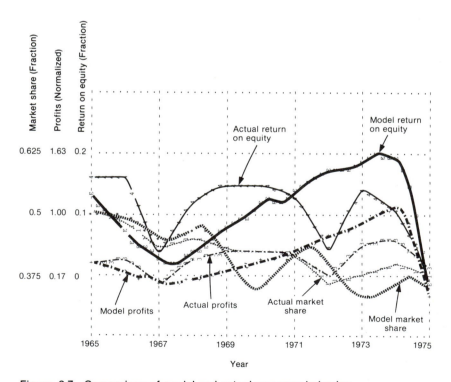

Figure 2.7 Comparison of model and actual company behavior

shows some sample output from this model simulation compared with actual corporate behavior. Model output and historical behavior are quite similar for the variables shown, as well as for most other model variables. Most discrepancies could be attributed to external events such as strikes (1972) and investments outside the major line of business that caused company profits to fall relative to model profits (1972 to 1974).

The interrelationships captured by the model, and the resulting model output, served to stimulate management thinking about alternative policies. The model had a number of direct and indirect impacts on corporate policies.

The model was then used to design some preliminary build rate, parts-ordering rate, and capacity expansion policies. Which of the consistent policies are the most profitable? Initial model results indicated that market share, stability, and profitability could be improved by the following policy changes:

1. Production rate—maintain a stable build rate near capacity and absorb differences between customer orders and production with a finished product inventory.

2. Parts ordering—plan production rate in advance of supplier lead time so that parts can be ordered and received before production changes.

3. Capacity expansion—plan for 10 percent above forecast as a buffer against an inaccurate forecast.

Figure 2.8 illustrates the types of improvements produced by these policy changes in the model company. The new policies reverse the loss of market share and decline in profitability.

These model results had direct and indirect effects on company decisions in several areas. First, during the 1970 business downturn the company maintained production and tried to build a finished product inventory. But the attempt to stock a finished product was defeated because every unit scheduled for stock was sold before it got there (just as the model indicated would happen). This production rate/stocking decision was estimated by one company manager to have earned the company $10 million in profits. (Note in figure 2.7 that model output for market share during 1970 was lower than actual market share because the model representation of company policies did not incorporate the attempt to stock a finished product in 1970.) A second area of model impact has been in capacity expansion decisions. The company

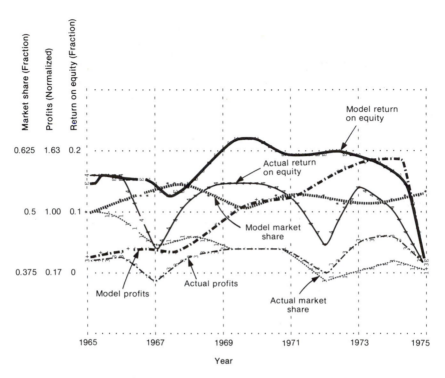

Figure 2.8 Comparison of model output with new policies to actual company behavior

now plans for some excess capacity as a buffer against forecasting errors.

The model indirectly influenced company policies concerning engineering change and product options. The model clearly demonstrated the adverse impact of frequent engineering change on parts inventory levels and thereby on production rate and availability. As a result the company has carefully examined the reasons behind the large number of engineering changes in an effort to reduce or at least bundle such changes. The model also demonstrated the advantages of carrying a stock of finished product. In checking the feasibility of carrying such a stock, the company discovered that relatively few product options comprised a large portion of company orders. Over time the demands of the market shifted toward specific options. Standardization, and a stock of finished product, became feasible.

The model was then used to design detailed production, parts-ordering, and capacity expansion policies (sometimes referred to as formal decision rules). The policy design approach was as follows:

1. Develop a set of policies that together improve company performance under the most common market demand patterns experienced by the company (growth, business cycle, random changes). Each policy specifies how information about customer order rate and production rates are used, how inventory goals are set, and how quickly discrepancies between goals and actual are corrected.

2. Test the policy set under a wider range of market demand patterns, for example, rapid growth or rapid decline. Sometimes the policy set must be changed to accommodate the wider range of market demand. Some compromise may need to be made. For example, a policy that carries a large excess of capacity relative to forecast demand may be best in a growth market but disastrous in a declining market. An alternative policy of less excess capacity coupled with a higher goal for finished product inventory could provide an improved performance in a decline. Here the consequences of another depression, rapid inflation, and resource shortages were of particular concern to management.

3. Test the performance of the policy set under other assumptions about competitor and customer response. The model contains assumptions about competitor capacity expansion, production, and pricing policy. Variations in these assumptions are easy to test. For example, what if the competitor introduces a production process that lowers unit costs? If he lowers price, will his normal expansion policy increase capacity sufficiently to match any increases in orders? If not, the company may lose some orders in the short run but regain them as customers become dissatisfied with competitor delivery times. Or, if the company matches the competitor's price decrease, will it be saving customers now only to lose them in the future because profits are too low to allow expansion?

The policies are being implemented at the company on a gradual basis for reasons discussed in Lyneis et al. (1977).

2.4 Summary

A system dynamics model is a useful tool for corporate planning and policy design. First, with such a model the company can consider a greater number of factors than with intuition alone. The analyst is able to work with a larger portion of the company and design a best set of policies rather than individual best policies for each part. Policies that in isolation may appear less than optimal can as a set improve overall performance. Second, in constructing the model, managers are forced to step back from day-to-day operating decisions, examine the company as a whole, question current practices and policies, and take a longer-run view of the company and its environment. And third, by simulating the model the company can test the responses of proposed policies to different economic, competitive, and environmental scenarios.

Each of these benefits accrued to the company examined in this chapter. A system dynamics model demonstrated the problem behavior created by interactions among inconsistent production, parts-ordering, and capacity expansion policies. The model was then used to develop a consistent set of policies that improved behavior. In providing an overview of the interactions among the parts of the company, the model brought to the attention of management the adverse consequences of engineering change and product option policies. The model was then used to test policy response to different economic, competitive, and environmental scenarios.

Reference

Lyneis, James M., David W. Peterson, and Brooke E. Tuttle. 1977. Implementing the Results of Computer Based Models: Lessons from a Case Study. System dynamics group working paper D-2674. Alfred P. Sloan School of Management, Massachusetts Institute of Technology, Cambridge, Mass.

An Introductory Policy Design Example

3

3.1 Introduction

Chapter 2 provided an overview of the types of problems addressed by a system dynamics model and the general approach to constructing a model and designing improved policies. Chapter 2 was of necessity lacking in detail regarding the structure and behavior of a model.

Chapter 3 moves to the other extreme. Starting from the description of a simple inventory control problem, a detailed system dynamics model is developed and analyzed. Construction and analysis of such a detailed model serves two purposes: it demonstrates the connection between corporate structure, policies, and behavior, and it places the contents of this book within the framework of the total system dynamics approach.

A fundamental tenet of system dynamics is that corporate behavior results directly from corporate structure and policies. Improvement of corporate behavior therefore requires an understanding of the relationship between structure, policies, and behavior.

Improved corporate behavior comes after better policies are implemented in the corporate system. Generally such implementation occurs only after a long process of defining a company's problem behavior, structuring a model of the forces creating that problem, understanding the causes of the problem, developing management confidence in the model as a vehicle for understanding the causes, and designing better policies. While construction of the model in this chapter may appear deceptively simple, in real companies it seldom is. Much practice is required to develop the necessary skills.

Consequently, rather than teach the reader how to build models, the reader is guided to an understanding of how corporate structures and policies create dynamic behavior and thus how structures and policies can be designed to improve behavior and insulate the corporation from external shocks. This exposure can improve the reader's intuition about corporate behavior, thereby improve decision making, and it can serve as the foundation for constructing corporate models using model-building skills learned elsewhere.

3.2 Overview of the System Dynamics Approach

The system dynamics approach to designing corporate policies starts with an identification of some corporate behavior that might be improved. Modes of dynamic behavior include growth, alternating growth and decline, stagnation, decay, and cyclical variation. In industry symptoms of problem behavior or underperformance include loss of market share, declining profitability, declining productivity, and fluctuating production and employment.

The purpose of a system dynamics analysis is to understand and improve corporate behavior. It is essential therefore for the analysis to begin with some statement of the type of behavior the model should exhibit. As shown in later chapters, certain types of corporate structures exhibit characteristic behaviors. Consequently a clear statement of the behavior mode of interest, coupled with an understanding of the connection between corporate structure and behavior, provides guidelines for relationships and factors that might be included in a model.

The second step in a system dynamics analysis is to identify and describe the nature of, and relationships between, the factors deemed important to the behavior being studied. Such a description includes the feedback loops, accumulations, delays, and corporate policies hypothesized to cause corporate behavior. The description serves as a basis for the construction of a computer model which is used to simulate the operation of the actual system.

The third step in a system dynamics analysis aims to develop an understanding of the relationship between structure and behavior. The step is an iterative process of simulating the model, comparing simulated behavior to corporate behavior, revising model structure in an effort to achieve correspondence between model and corporate behavior, resimulating the model, and so on. The process is most efficient when the modeler understands why a particular structure produces the simulated behavior. If understanding is achieved, subsequent revisions will correct errors in model behavior, thus facilitating the design of better policies.

The final step in a system dynamics analysis is the design of better policies. The step consists of two phases: the modeler identifies policies that alleviate the problem behavior, and then the proposed policies are tested under a wide range of external conditions, or scenarios. The proposed policies are developed assuming a particular market demand pattern, competitor actions and responses, and supplier actions. But these assumptions may be incorrect. The policies may need to be revised to accommodate other external conditions.

The system dynamics approach can be summarized as

1. identify problem behavior,
2. construct a computer model of the relationships believed to cause the behavior,
3. develop an understanding of the relationship between structure and behavior,
4. design policies that improve behavior.

3.3 Description of Problem Behavior

The company described in chapter 2 experienced alternating periods of parts inventory shortages and excesses (although the shortages tended to be more frequent and severe than the excesses).[1] Also parts-ordering rate fluctuated more than production rate. After the system dynamics model was constructed, the company recognized that fluctuations in production rate contributed to both the inventory shortages and excesses while engineering change contributed to the dominance of shortages. Nevertheless, inventory and parts ordering seemed to fluctuate more than indicated by fluctuations in production rate.

In this company parts ordering was the responsibility of several hundred parts planners (the company used several thousand parts). Once a month each planner would receive a report giving the usage over the past month and the average usage over the prior three months of the parts for which he/she was responsible. Planners were also in contact with manufacturing regarding the status of inventory shortages and with finance regarding aggregate inventory levels. Based on average usage and perceptions of inventory shortage or excess, planners would send orders to suppliers: if planners perceived a shortage, they would order above usage; if they perceived an excess, they would

1. Jay W. Forrester and David W. Peterson developed earlier versions of this example.

order below usage. Parts would arrive from suppliers after an average
of three months.

The experienced model builder, on perceiving this corporate structure, would immediately identify several factors that might cause parts
ordering to fluctuate more than production rate and inventory to fluctuate more than necessary:

1. the long delay between the time orders are placed and received,
2. the delay created by averaging usage rate over three months,
3. no consistent method of detecting and correcting inventory shortages or excesses—each planner identified the degree of excess or shortage and proceeded with an appropriate response.

3.4 Structure Creating Problem Behavior

A system's structure consists of accumulations of physical quantities,
flows that alter the accumulations, policies that govern the flows, and
flows of information used in the policies. A model attempts to capture
those elements of structure that create the problem behavior in the real
system.

Physical accumulations and flows are usually the easiest to identify
and model. In the inventory system described in section 3.3 several
flows and accumulations interact. The first of these represented in the
model is fundamental to any parts inventory: parts inventory is increased by parts arrival rate and decreased by production rate. In a
system dynamics model accumulations such as parts inventory are
represented by rectangles, as shown in figure 3.1, and are referred to as
levels. Think of the rectangle as representing a box that accumulates or
stores things: when a part arrives, parts inventory increases by one;
when a part is used, parts inventory decreases by one. Flows of material, such as the parts arrival rate, are represented by heavy arrows.

The second relationship in the model deals with parts arrival rate:

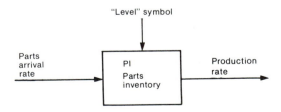

Figure 3.1   Relationship describing changes in parts inventory

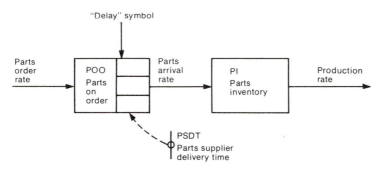

Figure 3.2   Relationship defining parts arrival rate

parts arrive about three months after they are ordered. Three months is the average lead time on parts ordered by the company. In the computer simulation the three-month delay between parts-ordering and parts arrival rates behaves much as in real life: some parts arrive before three months, others later than three months. But on the average it takes about three months for parts to arrive after they have been ordered. Figure 3.2 shows the flow of parts order rate through a delay, represented by a rectangle with internal markings, to become parts arrival rate. Parts supplier delivery time defines the length of the delay, here taken to equal three months.[2]

In a system dynamics notation flows, or rates, are labeled with a valvelike symbol, as shown in figure 3.3. The irregular, cloudlike shapes at the far ends of the diagram simply indicate that the parts come from and eventually go to levels outside this particular model. Figure 3.3 shows that production rate depletes parts inventory, parts order rate increases parts on order, and parts arrival rate depletes parts on order and builds parts inventory. By convention, valvelike symbols are not shown for rates flowing from delays because such a rate is the natural consequence of the delay and therefore not subject to control.

Figure 3.3 gives a flow diagram of the physical accumulations and flows in the parts inventory system. A complete model of the system also includes equations describing how the accumulations and flows are calculated.

Equation 2 specifies the calculation of parts inventory PI. Since PI represents an accumulation or level, equation 2 is a level equation, as

2. The structure and behavior of different types of delays are described in appendix B. Readers new to system dynamics are urged to read appendixes A and B after the basic model is described.

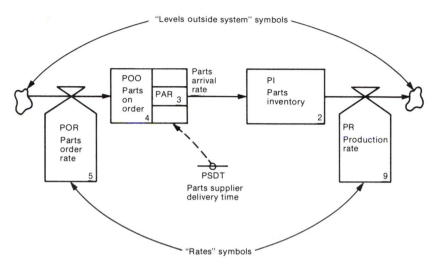

Figure 3.3   Symbols for rates and levels outside the system

indicated by the "2, L" at the right. All level variables are given initial
values. PI is initialized by equation 2.1, N to equal desired days parts
inventory DDPI multiplied by constant production rate CPR. In this
example DDPI equals 20 days and CPR equals 400 units per day.
Therefore PI initially equals 8,000 units.

PI.K = PI.J + (DT)(PAR.JK − PR.JK)   2, L
PI = DDPI * CPR   2.1, N

where
PI   = parts inventory (units)
DT   = delta time, simulation solution interval (days)
PAR   = parts arrival rate (units/day)
PR   = production rate (units/day)
DDPI = desired days parts inventory (days)
CPR   = constant production rate (units/day).

All equations in this book are written in the DYNAMO computer
language described briefly in appendix A.† All level equations have the
format given in equation 2. Equation 2 states that the level of parts
inventory at the current time PI.K is calculated by adding to the level
of parts inventory at the past time PI.J the flows into and out of parts

—————
†Editor's note: Spaces are introduced around operation symbols for
readability. These spaces do not appear in the actual computer model.

inventory over the interval from J to K: parts arrival rate PAR.JK and production rate PR.JK. The interval from J to K is of length DT; so the total change in PI is found by multiplying the flow rates by DT. For example, if PR equals 400 units per day, and DT equals one day, 400 units are subtracted from PI each solution.

Equation 3 specifies the calculation of parts arrival rate PAR (equation 3 is a rate equation, thus the "R"). Because delays are frequently used in system dynamics models, DYNAMO contains a built-in delay function DELAY3 described in appendix B. Equation 3 states that parts arrival rate equals a third-order delay of parts order rate POR. The length of the delay is given by parts supplier delivery time PSDT, equation 3.1 (a constant, or C, equation). PSDT equals 60 days (3 months times 20 working days per month).

PAR.KL = DELAY3(POR.JK,PSDT)   3, R
PSDT = 60   3.1, C

where
PAR   = parts arrival rate (units/day)
DELAY3 = dynamo macro for calculating third-order delay
POR   = parts order rate (units/day)
PSDT   = parts supplier delivery time (days).

The contents of the delay are the parts on order not yet received from the supplier. The amount of parts on order POO is calculated in equation 4. POO accumulates the difference between parts order rate POR and parts arrival rate PAR and therefore is a level equation.

POO.K = POO.J + (DT)(POR.JK − PAR.JK)   4, L
POO = PSDT * CPR   4.1, N

where
POO = parts on order (units)
DT   = delta time, simulation solution interval (days)
POR = parts order rate (units/day)
PAR = parts arrival rate (units/day)
PSDT = parts supplier delivery time (days)
CPR   = constant production rate (units/day).

The relationships describing the physical flows and accumulations are straightforward but can cause some confusion. For example, assume that production rate is 400 units per day, meaning 400 units worth of parts per day. Further imagine that the flow of parts is in equilibrium. Equilibrium is defined as no change in system levels. Therefore, if parts are being used at 400 units per day, they are also being received at 400 units per day.

Question: How many parts are on order? The reader is encouraged to write down an answer before reading further.

Many people find the correct answer surprisingly high. It is 24,000 units worth of parts: 60 days worth of parts at 400 units per day = 24,000 units worth of parts. Assuming a 20-day supply of parts inventory, or 8,000 units, then the level of parts on order (or pipeline) contains three times more than parts inventory.

Another way of obtaining the correct answer is to let the computer simulate these relationships. The result is shown in figure 3.4, a computer output graph of the situation described for figure 3.3. The computer also calculates that there are 24,000 units worth of parts on order. As given at the right of the graph, parts on order POO is plotted as an *X* on a scale which extends from 18,000 to 30,000. As time progresses from left to right in the graph, POO remains constant.

Figure 3.4 also shows that parts inventory remains constant at 8,000 units and production rate at 400 units per day. The figure further indicates that parts order and arrival rates equal the production rate be-

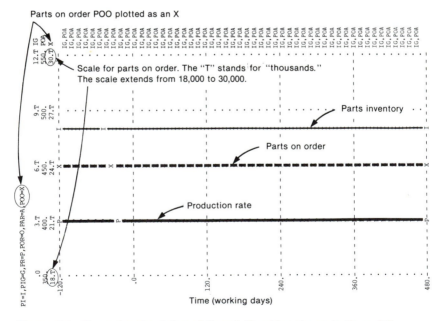

Figure 3.4 Computer simulation of the relationships shown in figure 3.3

cause they are all plotted with the same symbol. The abbreviations IG and POA at the top of the graph say I and G are plotted using I, and P, O, and A are plotted using P. Should P differ from O or A, they would be plotted with different symbols.

In order to complete the model, the relationships defining parts order rate and production rate must be specified. Production rate is determined by manufacturing; therefore for the purpose of this model it is exogenous to the parts inventory system. However, since production rate imposes changes on the parts inventory system—variations in production rate initiate variations in part order rate and parts inventory—production rate is an appropriate test input for comparing model behavior with company behavior and designing better policies.

System dynamics modelers use many different types of test inputs. The simplest of these are STEP changes, one-shot changes of a fixed magnitude, and RAMP changes, continual changes of a fixed magnitude. These simple test inputs are very helpful in understanding model behavior and therefore are used to analyze the behavior of the parts inventory system.

Equation 9 defines production rate PR to equal constant production rate CPR multiplied by a STEP change in production rate SPR and by a RAMP change in production rate RPR.

PR.KL = CPR * SPR.K * RPR.K   9, R
CPR = 400   9.1, C

where
PR   = production rate (units/day)
CPR = constant production rate (units/day)
SPR = STEP change in production rate (dimensionless)
RPR = RAMP change in production rate (dimensionless).

Equations 10 and 11 use internal DYNAMO STEP and RAMP functions to generate STEP change in production rate SPR and RAMP change in production rate RPR. The height and slope arguments are self-explanatory; the time arguments specify the starting time of the change.

SPR.K = 1 + STEP(SH1, ST1) + STEP(SH2, ST2)   10, A
SH1 = 0/ST1 = 0/SH2 = 0/ST2 = 0   10.1, C

where
SPR   = STEP change in production rate (dimensionless)
STEP = DYNAMO macro for STEP function

SH1 = STEP height one (dimensionless)
ST1 = STEP time one (days)
SH2 = STEP height two (dimensionless)
ST2 = STEP time two (days);

RPR.K = 1 + RAMP(RS1/240,RT1)   11, A
RS1 = 0/RT1 = 0   11.1, C

where
RPR   = RAMP change in production rate (dimensionless)
RAMP = DYNAMO macro for RAMP function
RS1   = RAMP slope one (dimensionless)
RT1   = RAMP time one (days).

Parts order rate represents the actions of parts planners. The parts inventory system will be discussed in detail in the next section, as several different parts order rate policies are analyzed.

3.5 Understanding Problem Behavior

One of the simplest parts order rate policies states, "Parts order rate equals production rate." Figure 3.5 illustrates this policy. For example, if production rate is 400 units per day, then parts order rate is 400 units per day. In other words parts are reordered as those on hand are used for production. Equation 5 specifies calculation of parts order rate.

POR.KL = PR.JK   5, R

where
POR = parts order rate (units/day)
PR   = production rate (units/day).

With these relationships assembled into a computer model, the response of the parts inventory system to different test inputs can be analyzed. Suppose that the system starts out with a production rate of 400 units per day which makes parts order rate 400 units per day and parts arrival rate 400 units per day. Some 24,000 units worth of parts on order are in the pipeline, and 8,000 units worth of parts are in parts inventory. Now imagine that production increases suddenly by 10 percent, from 400 units per day to 440 units per day, and stays at the higher volume, as illustrated in figure 3.6. Such a test input is called a STEP increase in production rate.

Question: What happens to parts inventory? If it begins at 8,000 units

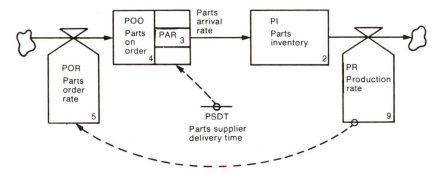

Figure 3.5 Relationships defining parts order rate: parts order rate equals production rate

worth of parts, how large will it be a year later? The reader is encouraged to think through a response and sketch the behavior of parts inventory on figure 3.6 before reading further.

Figure 3.7 shows the computer simulation run that answers the preceding question. At day zero, the production rate increases suddenly from 400 per day to 440 per day, as does parts order rate. But parts inventory declines from 8,000 to 5,600 units worth of parts. This seems paradoxical because a part was reordered for every one used—where did the missing 2,400 units go?

A close examination of figure 3.7 reveals that the missing parts appear as parts on order. The total number of parts ordered equals the total number of parts used, but the parts order rate has now increased. Therefore the pipeline must now contain more parts: specifically 40 more units per day multiplied by 60 days, or 2,400 more parts. Parts on order have increased at the expense of inventory.

The sharp and sudden increase in production rate in figure 3.7 is perhaps a bit artificial. It would certainly be unusual for production rate of a real part to stay as constant and change as abruptly at only one time. To get closer to reality, we might consider how the same relationships would react to a production rate that grows smoothly, as shown in figure 3.8. Production rate begins at 400 units per day, rises smoothly by 15 percent in the first year, and continues the straight-line growth indefinitely. Such a test input is called RAMP increase in production rate.

Question: What will parts inventory do? The reader should sketch in figure 3.8 an estimate of what will happen to parts inventory, which begins at 8,000 units worth of parts.

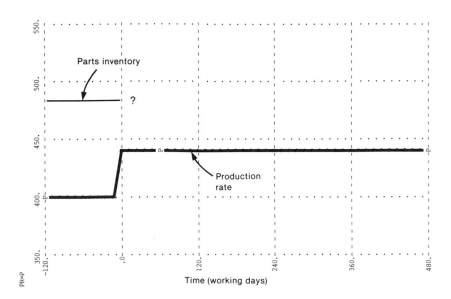

Figure 3.6   The 10 percent STEP increase in production rate

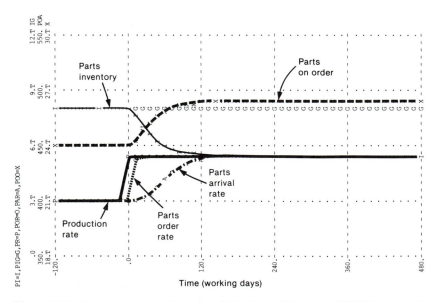

Figure 3.7   Behavior of parts inventory following a 10 percent STEP increase in production rate

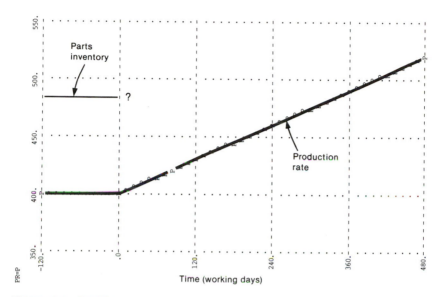

Figure 3.8   RAMP increase in production rate at 15 percent per year

Figure 3.9 shows that parts inventory never stops falling. Although parts order rate matches production rate exactly, parts arrival rate always lags parts order rate if production rate keeps increasing. For example, at the end of the first year shown in the figure (day 240) production rate and parts order rate are at 460 units per day, but parts arrival rate is still only about 445 units per day because the parts that are arriving at the end of the first year are those that were ordered 60 days earlier, when production rate was only 445 units per day. Since production rate exceeds parts arrival rate throughout the run, parts inventory falls and continues to fall without limit. When parts inventory nears zero, as it does toward the end of figure 3.9, lowered inventories would force down production, causing the production to lag behind customer orders. Hence parts inventory would level off short of disappearing entirely. But the main point of figure 3.9 remains valid: with increasing usage, ordering by usage will cause parts inventory to fall. Parts inventory will continue to fall until shortages restrict usage rate.

In this company, however, parts planners do not base parts order rate on current production rate but on a sixty-day average of production rate. Figure 3.10 illustrates the revised policy, with parts order rate now set equal to average production rate. Because averaging of information accumulates that information, an average in system dynamics is

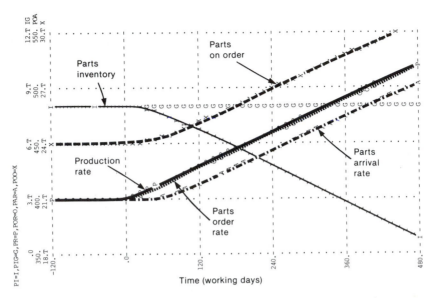

Figure 3.9 Response of parts inventory to RAMP increase in production rate

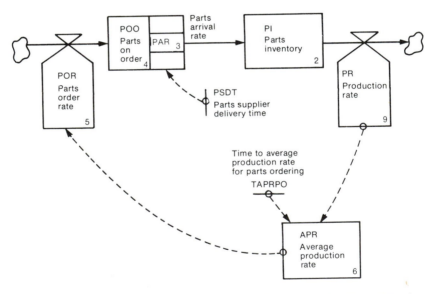

Figure 3.10 Parts inventory system with parts order rate equal to average production rate

represented by a rectangular symbol. Note that only information (dashed lines) and not physical quantitics (solid lines) flow into or out of the average. For more information on averages see appendix B.

The rewritten equation 5 specifies the calculation of parts order rate POR. POR equals average production rate APR.

$$POR.KL = APR.K \qquad\qquad\qquad 5,R$$

where
POR = parts order rate (units/day)
APR = average production rate (units/day).

Equation 6 defines average production rate APR. Because information averages are frequently used in system dynamics models, DYNAMO contains a built-in, SMOOTH function described in appendix B. Equation 6 states that APR is a first-order delay, or exponential average, of production rate PR. The averaging time is given by time to average production rate for parts ordering TAPRPO.[3]

$$APR.K = SMOOTH(PR.JK,TAPRPO) \qquad\qquad 6, A$$
$$TAPRPO = 5 \qquad\qquad\qquad 6.1, C$$

where
APR   = average production rate (units/day)
SMOOTH = DYNAMO macro for calculating first-order delay
PR   = production rate (units/day)
TAPRPO = time to average production rate for parts ordering
             (days).

Figure 3.11 shows the response of the revised policy to a 10 percent STEP increase in production rate. Inventory falls much lower here than in the policy without averaging, down to nearly 3,000 units. The greater loss of inventory is a result of the delay introduced by the averaging of information. In figure 3.11 parts order rate lags about 60 days behind production rate. Consequently parts inventory falls not only because parts arrival rate lags parts order rate but also because parts order rate now lags production rate.

With the revised policy, parts are no longer reordered for every unit produced. Thus, while inventory falls to nearly 4,800 units, parts on

---

3. Although an exponential average contains an accumulation, the equation is specified as an auxiliary, or A, equation because it does not have the same format as level equations. Auxiliary equations are technically part of rate equations but are defined separately for ease in constructing and explaining a model.

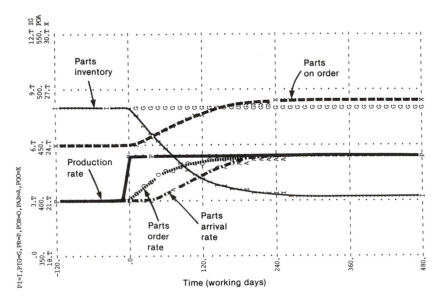

Figure 3.11 Response of parts inventory to STEP increase in production rate with ordering based on average production rate

order increases only 2,400 units. As with the policy in which parts order rate equaled production rate, parts order rate eventually increases by 40 units per day. The 40 units per day multiplied by the 60-day parts supplier delivery time gives an additional 2,400 units in parts on order.

The last three computer runs reveal an important insight regarding one connection between corporate structure and behavior: if a level's inflow rate responds only after a delay to an increase in the level's outflow rate, the level must fall; such a delayed response can be caused by either the averaging of information or delays in a physical flow channel.

In the preceding computer runs inventory never increases again because the parts order rate policy contains no feedback control. Feedback control exists whenever information about the level of an accumulation returns as an input to the decisions that effect the flow rates from the accumulation. One example of feedback control would involve basing parts order rate on the level of parts inventory—as parts inventory falls, parts order rate increases, eventually enlarging parts inventory and feeding back to reduce parts order rate. Another example of feedback control would involve the affect of parts inventory on produc-

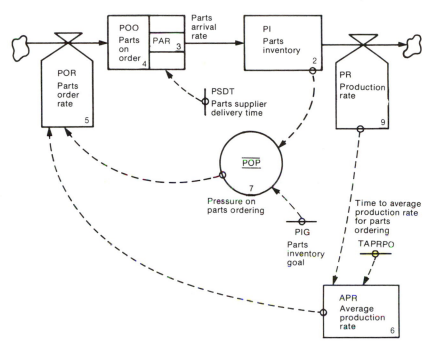

Figure 3.12 Relationship added describing pressures on parts-ordering rate from shortages and excesses of parts inventory

tion rate—as parts inventory falls, production rate is reduced by shortages, thereby slowing the decrease in parts inventory.

Feedback control is an intrinsic characteristic of company policies. In the problem description parts planners were said to increase or decrease parts order rate from average production rate in response to inventory levels. The model can be made more realistic by adding feedback control to parts order rate as shown in figure 3.12: excess parts inventory reduces parts order rate; parts inventory shortages increase parts order rate. This relationship describes the pressure on parts ordering that arises when parts inventories are too small or too large.

Figure 3.13 shows a specific interpretation of the relationship between parts inventory and order rate. Parts inventory is compared with a constant parts inventory goal of 8,000 units worth of parts. As long as the actual parts inventory equals its goal, parts order rate equals average production rate, as before. If parts inventory falls below the parts inventory goal, parts order rate exceeds average production rate. For

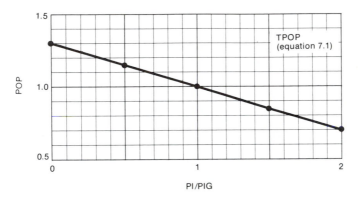

Figure 3.13   Precise interpretation of the relationship shown in figure 3.12

example, in the extreme case of no parts inventory, parts order rate equals 130 percent of the average production rate. Similarly, if parts inventory exceeds the parts inventory goal, parts order rate is depressed below average production rate. The right-hand end of the graph represents a parts inventory twice as large as the parts inventory goal, reducing parts order rate to 70 percent of average production rate. Such a relationship might represent the composite reaction of many parts planners to different levels. It might also represent the reaction of planners to pressures from management: from manufacturing, when inventory is too low, and finance, when inventory is too high.

Equation 5 is rewritten to incorporate pressure on parts ordering POP into the calculation of parts order rate POR. POR equals average production rate APR multiplied by POP.

POR.KL = APR.K * POP.K   5, R

where
POR = parts order rate (units/day)
APR = average production rate (units/day)
POP = pressure on parts ordering (dimensionless).

Pressure on parts ordering POP is a second auxiliary component of parts order rate. POP is defined in equation 7 as a TABLE function of parts inventory PI divided by parts inventory goal PIG. TABLE functions are DYNAMO functions that allow the modeler to specify relationships between variables, like that shown in figure 3.13. The relationship need not be linear. The equation format for TABLE functions is described in appendix A.

POP.K = TABLE(TPOP,PI.K/PIG.K,0,2,.5)   7, A
TROP = 1.3/1.15/1/.85/.7   7.1, T

where
POP   = pressure on parts ordering (dimensionless)
TPOP = table for pressure on parts ordering (dimensionless)
PI   = parts inventory (units)
PIG   = parts inventory goal (units).

Equation 8 defines parts inventory goal PIG to equal desired days parts inventory DDPI multiplied by constant production rate CPR. DDPI is arbitrarily set to 20 days.

PIG.K = DDPI * CPR   8, A
DDPI = 20   8.1, C

where
PIG   = parts inventory goal (units)
DDPI = desired days parts inventory (days)
CPR   = constant production rate (units/day).

With the relationship in figure 3.13 added, parts order rate will no longer necessarily equal average production rate. Now there is pressure on parts ordering to keep parts inventory in line—feedback control. Such feedback is called negative feedback because, as inventory increases, parts order rate decreases, and vice versa.

Question: Now what happens to parts inventory for a STEP increase in production rate? The reader should sketch in figure 3.14 the path parts inventory might follow.

Figure 3.15 shows the behavior of parts inventory in response to a STEP increase in production rate under the influence of pressure on parts ordering to control parts inventory. There are three interesting things to notice about the run:

1. In spite of the pressure introduced to prevent parts inventory from falling, it falls anyway.
2. Parts inventory not only falls but falls nearly as low as it did when there were no pressures whatsoever on parts order rate.
3. About one year after the upturn there is an excess of parts inventory.

In summary the efforts to increase parts inventory take nearly a year to succeed and then overshoot the mark.

The natural reaction to such a result is to recognize that the pressure

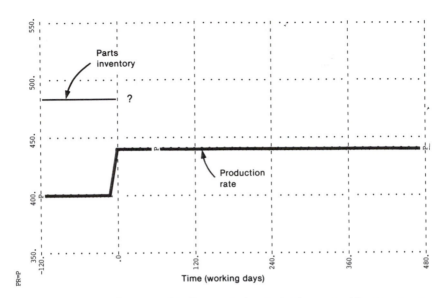

Figure 3.14   The 10 percent STEP increase in production rate with pressure on parts ordering, as shown in figure 3.13

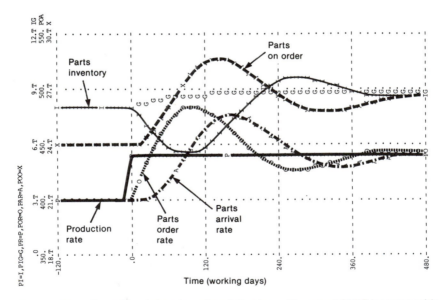

Figure 3.15   Behavior of parts inventory following a 10 percent STEP increase with parts order rate influenced by the relationship shown in figure 3.13

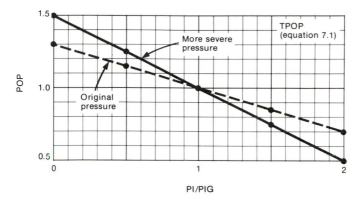

Figure 3.16   Relationship defining pressure on parts ordering changed to reflect more severe pressure to imbalances in inventory

on parts ordering was too mild to take effect in time. It might be unreasonable to expect that, if parts inventory were zero, the company would increase parts order rate to only 130 percent of average production rate. To verify or check whether more pressure on parts ordering will reduce the shortfall of parts inventory, the hypothetical relationship assumed in figure 3.13 is changed to a new more severe pressure on parts ordering shown in figure 3.16. Such pressure would represent a more drastic management reaction to parts inventory that differs from the parts inventory goal. In this case, if parts inventory should fall to zero, parts order rate is increased to 145 percent of average production rate.

Figure 3.17 shows the response of parts inventory to a STEP increase in production rate with more severe pressures on parts ordering. The fall in parts inventory has been reduced only slightly. But the steeper pressures on inventory have caused a more severe excess one year after the increase. Notice that during the excess of parts inventory parts order rate is well below production rate which indicates an attempt to correct the excess, but, instead of eliminating the excess, the extra effort creates a second shortage of parts inventory around day 480.

Making parts order rate responsive to pressures based on excesses or shortages in inventory prevents the permanent shortage of parts inventory that might result from a STEP increase. The different pressures on parts ordering do not, however, change the magnitude of the decrease in parts inventory after the STEP. The more vigorously management responds to the upturn by increasing parts order rate, the

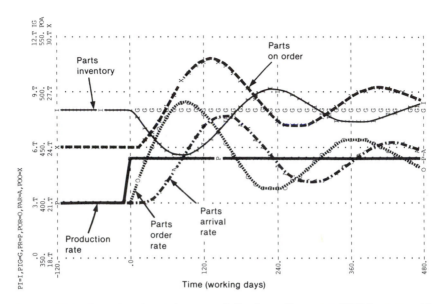

Figure 3.17 Behavior of parts inventory following a 10 percent STEP increase with more severe pressure on parts ordering, as defined in figure 3.16

sooner an excess appears after the upturn, and the more severe it becomes. But the fact that an upturn creates a fall in inventory is not affected by management policy or the severity of the policy's response.

The fall in inventory is an unavoidable consequence of the structure of the system. The delayed response of parts arrival rate to increases in production rate causes such a fall. Greater pressure from inventory shortage only seems to affect the timing and severity of the subsequent inventory excess. Since an inventory fall cannot be prevented by greater pressure, perhaps the excess can by less pressure. Less pressure should produce a lower parts order rate and consequently reduce the excess.

Figure 3.18 shows a pressure on parts ordering that responds less severely to excesses or shortages of parts inventory. For a given discrepancy between parts inventory and its goal, pressure on parts ordering will cause only one-half as much change in the parts order rate as the original policy of figure 3.13. Pressure will still be exerted to control parts inventory, but the resulting changes in the parts order rate will be more gradual.

Figure 3.19 shows the results of the slower, less severe pressure on parts-ordering policy to a STEP increase. Immediately after the in-

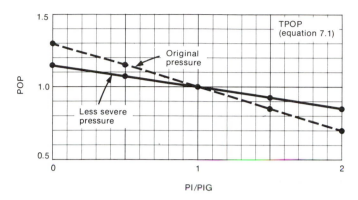

Figure 3.18   Relation defining pressure on parts ordering changed to reflect less pressure due to imbalances in parts inventory

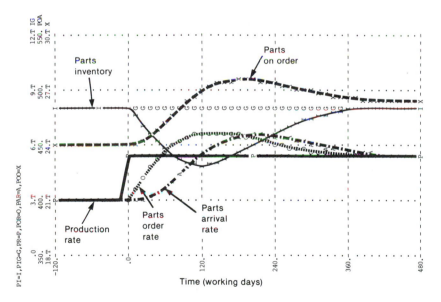

Figure 3.19   Behavior of parts inventory following a 10 percent STEP increase with less severe pressure on parts ordering, as defined in figure 3.18

crease parts inventory falls, as it inevitably must, but with the slower policy the trouble seen in previous computer runs is avoided: namely, the permanent shortage that results from ordering by production rate alone and the excesses that result from aggressively attempting to control parts inventory. A slightly increased parts order rate causes parts inventory to return smoothly and gradually to parts inventory goal. Unfortunately the improved behavior of parts order rate and parts inventory is not without cost—parts inventory falls lower and remains below the goal longer.

The computer simulation runs exhibit behavior consistent with that observed in the company—fluctuations in parts order rate that are greater than the fluctuations in production rate. In a more detailed analysis the modeler would also examine the behavior of the parts inventory system with a production rate more characteristic of an actual company rate (here regular fluctuations). The modeler would compare such relationships as the relative magnitude of parts order rate and inventory fluctuations and the relative timing of peaks in production and bottoms of inventory. The greater the correspondence between model output and company experience, the greater ones confidence in the model as a representation of the real system.

A model that exhibits behavior consistent with that observed in the company has now been developed. The next step in a system dynamics study is to design policies that improve that behavior. Policy design builds on the understanding of the relationships between structure and behavior: (1) some pressure on parts ordering (feedback control) is essential to maintaining inventory near desired levels; (2) the stronger the pressure, the greater the swings in parts order rate, see figure 3.20; (3) with weak pressure parts inventory remains below its goal for 360 days; and (4) some drop in parts inventory is unavoidable because of delays introduced by averaging information and supplier delivery times. The analysis so far indicates that, to avoid fluctuations in parts order rate and parts inventory, the company must suffer greater inventory shortages.

3.6 Policy Design for Improving Behavior

The relationship describing pressure on parts ordering might represent the aggregate response of parts planners (if parts inventory represents aggregate parts) or the response of one planner (if parts inventory represents a single part). Whichever, the relationship describes a pol-

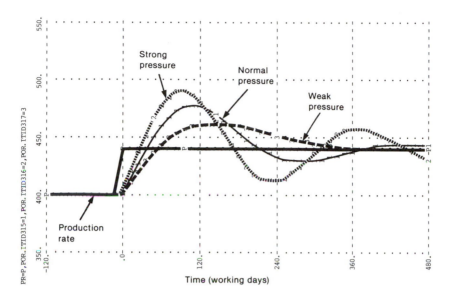

Figure 3.20 Comparison of parts order rate following a 10 percent STEP increase with different pressures on parts ordering

icy based on response to operating pressures. Such a policy has three characteristics:

1. No two people respond to pressures in the same way—some may overreact and create large fluctuations in parts order rate, while others underreact and create greater than desired shortages or excesses of inventory (as a result the company may experience shortages of some parts and excesses of others at the same time).
2. People will respond to the same pressures in different ways at different times—because they have no consistent rule for correcting, or even measuring, inventory imbalances, planners are likely to respond to the same inventory problem in different ways.
3. Management can exert no real control over inventory, other than try to change the pressures perceived by planners (with unpredictable results).

Consequently pressure-based policies can result in overreaction, inconsistency, and lack of control. Pressure-based policies are common in all corporate systems.

Based on the pressure-based policy simulations summarized in figure 3.20, a hypothesis of the cause of fluctuations might be overreaction on the part of planners: when inventory falls (as it must in response to an upturn), planners overreact and increase parts order rate more than is necessary to correct the shortage; then when inventory overshoots, planners cut back parts ordering too much.

One method of explicitly determining how much parts order rate should be changed to meet inventory goals is to make a calculation of the difference between parts inventory goal and parts inventory. This parts inventory correction PIC is then added to average production rate APR to determine parts order rate POR. POR is defined explicitly by the policy in equation 5 (see also figure 3.21).

$$POR.KL = APR.K + PIC.K \hspace{4cm} 5, R$$

where
POR = parts order rate (units/day)
APR = average production rate (units/day)
PIC = parts inventory correction (units/day).

Equation 7 defines parts inventory correction PIC to equal the difference between parts inventory goal PIG and parts inventory PI divided

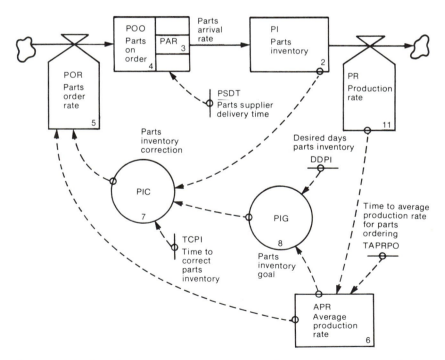

Figure 3.21   Parts inventory system with parts order rate based on explicit parts inventory correction

by time to correct parts inventory TCPI. TCPI is set at 60 days. In other words all parts planners would adjust any inventory discrepancies over a period of 60 days. The consequences, for system behavior, of different values for TCPI are examined in subsequent simulation runs.

PIC.K = (PIG.K − PI.K)/TCPI   7, A
TCPI = 60   7.1, C

where
PIC = parts inventory correction (units/day)
PIG = parts inventory goal (units)
PI   = parts inventory (units)
TCPI = time to correct parts inventory (days).

The parts order rate policy is complete with the specification of parts inventory goal. In most companies desired inventory levels change with the volume of business. Consequently equation 8 states that parts inventory goal PIG equals desired days parts inventory DDPI multiplied by average production rate APR. DDPI is arbitrarily set to 20 days (corresponding to the 8,000 units goal in the prior simulations).

PIG.K = DDPI * APR.K   8, A
DDPI = 20   8.1, C

where
PIG = parts inventory goal (units)
DDPI = desired days parts inventory (days)
APR = average production rate (units/day).

Figure 3.22 shows the response of the explicit parts order policy to a 10 percent STEP increase in production rate. Contrary to expectations the new policy performs no better than the old pressure-based policy even though an explicit inventory correction is calculated. Why does the policy increase ordering too much, only to cause inventory to rise above the goal? The answer lies in the parts on order pipeline.

In figure 3.22 the sudden change in production rate causes parts inventory to decrease. In response to the falling inventory and the increase in average production rate (not shown), parts order rate increases. Parts order rate rises above production rate because extra units must be ordered to rebuild inventory. The delays introduced by averaging, and the delays in the physical flow channels, cause parts inventory to decrease as production rate increases. As a consequence

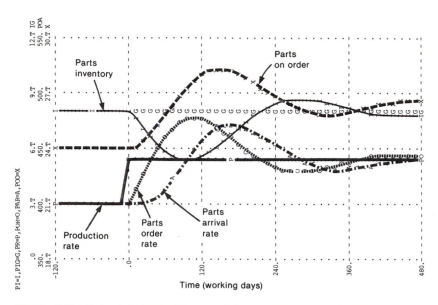

Figure 3.22 Behavior of parts inventory following a 10 percent STEP increase with parts order rate equal to average production rate and parts inventory correction

parts order rate must increase more than production rate to rebuild inventory.

In figure 3.22 parts arrival rate lags parts order rate because of the parts supplier delivery time. At day 84, when parts arrival rate crosses production rate, inventory bottoms. Parts order rate also peaks at day 84 because (1) average production rate (not shown) nearly equals production rate and (2) the parts inventory correction is at a maximum when inventory is at a minimum. But, because parts inventory is below its goal, the parts inventory correction is positive, and therefore parts order rate exceeds production rate.

After day 84 parts arrival rate exceeds production rate; thus parts inventory increases. At day 216 parts inventory equals parts inventory goal (plotted as *G*). Consequently parts inventory correction (not shown) equals zero, and parts order rate equals average production rate (which is the same as the production rate). But parts arrival rate still exceeds production rate so that after day 216 parts inventory rises above parts inventory goal.

Parts arrival rate exceeds production rate for the simple reason that the company ordered more parts for inventory than were necessary to correct the inventory discrepancy. But how can that be when the difference between parts inventory and parts inventory goal was calculated explicitly and used for ordering parts? The answer is that the company did not take into account those parts ordered but not yet received, the level of parts on order.

For example, suppose that production rate is constant and equal to parts order and arrival rates, and that parts inventory equals its goal. Then imagine a warehouse fire destroys 100 units of inventory. The difference between parts inventory goal and parts inventory now equals 100 units. For simplicity, assume the company corrects the difference in one day and orders 100 units per day above production rate. But the parts inventory discrepancy persists for 60 days until parts ordered arrive from suppliers. Based on the current parts order rate policy, the company continues to order 100 units per day above production rate even though sufficient units have already been ordered and are in the parts on order pipeline.

To resolve the overordering problem, the parts order rate policy must adjust for parts ordered but not yet received. A parts on order correction POC is added to the parts order rate equation (rewritten in equation 5). Figure 3.23 illustrates the complete parts inventory system.

$$POR.KL = APR.K + ISWT * PIC.K + PSWT * POC.K \qquad 5, R$$
$$ISWT = 1 \qquad 5.1, C$$
$$PSWT = 1 \qquad 5.2, C$$

where
POR = parts order rate (units/day)
APR = average production rate (units/day)
ISWT = inventory correction switch (dimensionless)
PIC   = parts inventory correction (units/day)
PSWT = parts on order correction switch (dimensionless)
POC = parts on order correction (units/day).

Parts on order correction POC, equation 9, is similar to parts inventory correction: the difference between parts on order goal POOG and parts on order POO is corrected over time to correct parts inventory TCPI.

$$POC.K = (POOG.K - POO.K)/TCPI \qquad 9, A$$

where
POC = parts on order correction (units/day)
POOG = parts on order goal (units)

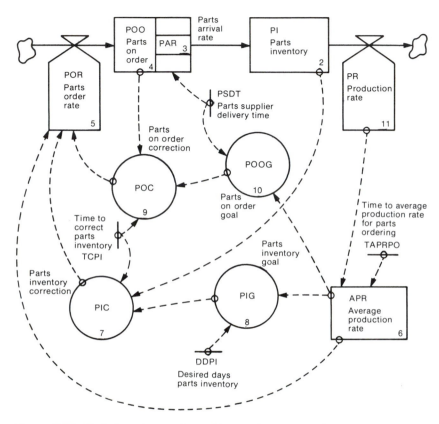

Figure 3.23 Parts inventory system with complete parts order rate policy

POO   = parts on order (units)
TCPI = time to correct parts inventory (days).

Parts on order goal POOG equals the normal level of orders the company would have at the supplier: parts supplier delivery time PSDT mutliplied by average production rate APR (see equation 10).

POOG.K = PSDT * APR.K   10, A

where
POOG = parts on order goal (units)
PSDT = parts supplier delivery time (days)
APR = average production rate (units/day).

Figure 3.24 shows the response of the revised parts order rate policy to a 10 percent STEP increase in production rate. The policy is suc-

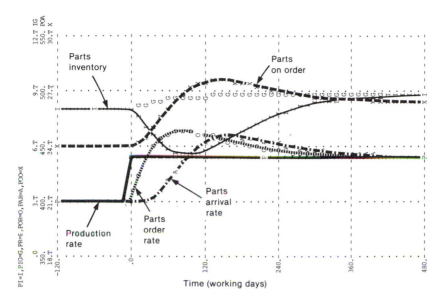

Figure 3.24 Behavior of parts inventory system following a 10 percent STEP increase with parts order rate equal to sum of average production rate, parts inventory correction, and parts on order correction

cessful in eliminating the overshoot in parts inventory and the corresponding undershoot in parts order rate.[4]

Notice in figure 3.24 the sudden change in production rate causes parts inventory to decrease. Parts order rate increases in response to

1. the increase in average production rate (not shown),
2. a positive parts inventory correction (not shown), which results from the decrease in inventory and increase in parts inventory goal,
3. a positive parts on order correction (not shown), which results from an increase in parts on order goal.

The increase occurs slightly faster than with the previous policy, figure 3.22, because of the parts on order correction. Parts order rate rises above production rate because again extra units must be ordered to rebuild inventory.

In contrast to the prior policy, however, parts order rate begins to level off and peak shortly after it crosses production rate. In fact the parts order rate peak now occurs before the bottom of parts inventory,

4. The reader is urged to verify that the revised policy would not overorder in the fire example.

even though the parts inventory correction is greatest at the bottom. The parts on order correction term recognizes that sufficient orders have already been placed to correct the inventory shortage and adjusts parts order rate accordingly. The new policy produces a gradual adjustment of parts inventory to its goal.

Nevertheless, parts order rate still overshoots production rate: a 10 percent change in production rate results in a 17 percent change in parts order rate. Underlying such amplification is the necessity of increasing parts order rate above production rate to fill depleted inventory (and partly to build inventory to a higher equilibrium level). Recall that inventory is depleted because delays introduced by averaging information and delays in the physical flow channels cause parts arrival rate to lag well behind production rate.

Figure 3.25 shows the components of parts order rate for the simulation of figure 3.24. (Inventory correction sums the parts inventory and parts on order corrections.) The amplification, parts order rate rising more than production rate, is seen to be a direct result of the inventory corrections.

Parts inventory in figure 3.24 falls to 70 percent of its goal and remains below the goal for nearly 360 days. Such behavior might be deemed unacceptable by many managers. In an effort to reduce the

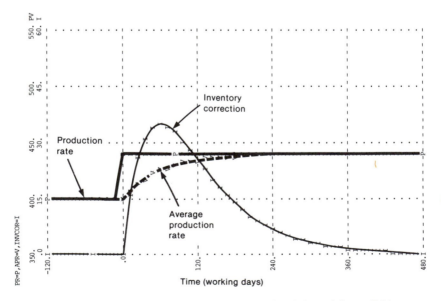

Figure 3.25   Components of parts order rate for simulation of figure 3.24

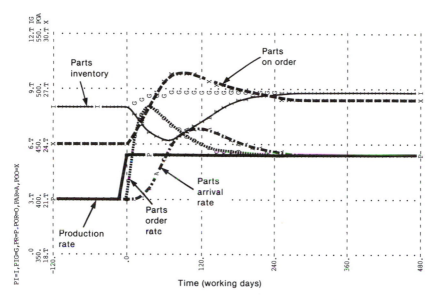

Figure 3.26 Parts inventory system response to a 10 percent STEP increase with TAPRPO and TCPI equal to 30 days

drop in inventory and the long period of recovery, the company might respond more quickly to changing conditions. Figure 3.26 shows the response of the parts inventory system when time to average production rate for parts ordering TAPRPO and time to correct parts inventory TCPI are both reduced from 60 to 30 days. Such changes imply that the company follows shifts in production more quickly and is more aggressive in correcting inventory discrepancies.

Figure 3.26 indicates that even with quick and aggressive actions parts inventory increases to its equilibrium value with no overshoot. With a properly designed policy a company can eliminate unintended fluctuations, even with aggressive actions.

Quick and aggressive actions are not without cost, however. The inventory shortfall is corrected by day 240, but the maximum shortage is reduced to only 78 percent of desired inventory (versus 70 percent with the original policy). The sixty-day parts supplier delivery time assures a significant inventory loss. In addition the degree of amplification has increased: a 10 percent increase in production rate results in a 22 percent increase in parts order rate. With more aggressive actions inventory corrections are substantially larger, as shown in figure 3.27.

Figure 3.28 illustrates the consequences of slower and less aggressive actions (TAPRPO and TCPI equal to 240 days). While the am-

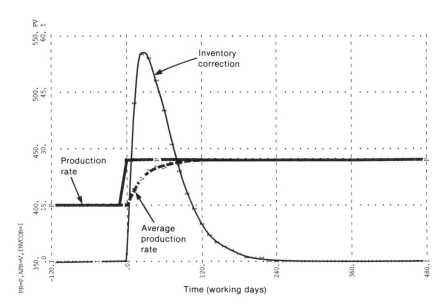

Figure 3.27 Components of parts order rate for simulation of figure 3.26

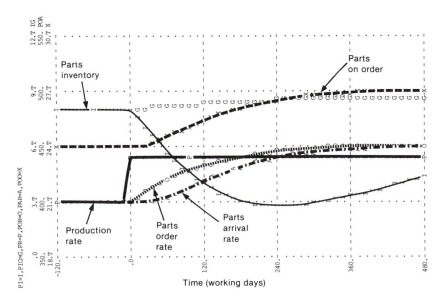

Figure 3.28 Parts inventory system response to a 10 percent STEP increase with TAPRPO and TCPI equal to 240 days

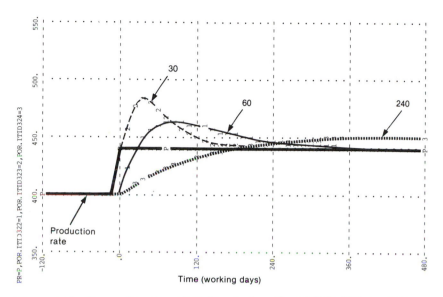

Figure 3.29 Comparison of parts order rate from figures 3.24, 3.26, and 3.28

plification has been reduced substantially, inventory falls to almost one-third of its desired value and recovers very slowly.

The last three simulations point out an apparent trade-off between the stabilities of parts order rate and inventory: the longer the averaging and correction times, the lower the amplification in parts order rate, figure 3.29, but the lower inventory falls and the longer it takes to reach its desired value, figure 3.30. A company must use either the parts order rate or parts inventory to absorb changes in production rate.

Thus far a policy that eliminates unintended fluctuations has been developed. The degree of trade-off between parts order rate and parts inventory stability has been identified. Selection of the best policy now depends on the relative costs of parts order rate and inventory stability. If fluctuations in inventory are more costly than fluctuations in parts order rate, the company would select a policy that reduces the swings in inventory, thus allowing the company to reduce the average level of inventory. If fluctuations in parts order rate are more costly, the company would select a policy that reduces swings in parts order rate. With such a policy a higher level of parts inventory would need to be carried to avoid stockouts.

The policy design process is, however, incomplete. The selection of a policy might depend on a number of other factors, for example,

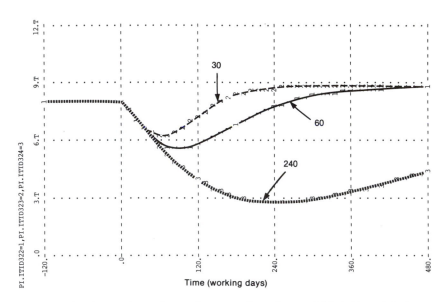

Figure 3.30 Comparison of parts inventory from figures 3.24, 3.26, and 3.28

1. the ability of suppliers to fill orders—a policy that minimizes parts inventory and allows parts order rate to vary substantially is of little good if suppliers have capacity constraints preventing deliveries;
2. other demand patterns the company might face—a policy that responds quickly to permanent changes may cause too much instability for temporary changes.

   Such factors can be considered in the design of a policy by testing policy response to different external inputs, or scenarios. Sometimes, however, the behavior of other factors depends on company policy: for example, the delivery time of suppliers often depends on the degree of fluctuations in parts order rate. An analysis of external factors can only be performed if the model boundary is expanded to include the actions of these factors. Examples of this type of analysis as well as more scenario analyses are given in later chapters of the book.

3.7 Testing Scenarios in Policy Design

The most common scenario tests evaluate the response of a policy to other demand variations a company has or might experience. Testing policy response to historical variations assures that the policy can cope with, and improve if necessary, company performance in normal market conditions. By testing policy response to other variations, the company can design policies resilient to changes in market conditions. In effect the company is prepared for changes and not merely reacting to them.

As an example of scenario testing suppose that the company experiences temporary as well as permanent STEP changes in production rate. A temporary STEP here entails a 10 percent increase in production rate from 400 to 440 units per day at day 0, followed by a similar decrease from 440 to 400 units per day at day 150.

Figure 3.31 compares the behavior of parts order rate for the three parameter sets in response to such a temporary upturn. The figure shows that the quicker the response, the greater the instability. With a quick, 30-day response parts order rate rises above production rate to rebuild inventory. But about the time inventory is rebuilt (as indicated by parts order rate leveling off at production rate), production rate decreases. Then parts order rate is cut back sharply to reduce inventory. In contrast with the slower-reacting, 240-day response parts order rate has not exceeded production rate when production rate steps down. Then because inventory has not been rebuilt, parts order rate does not need to decrease below production rate to reduce inventory—parts order rate is much more stable.

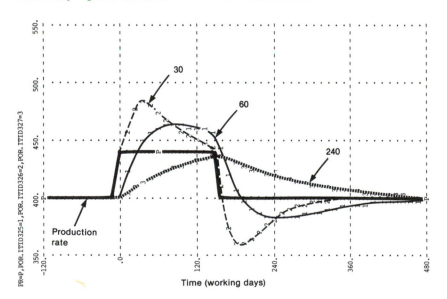

Figure 3.31   Comparison of parts order rate for three parameter sets in response to temporary STEP

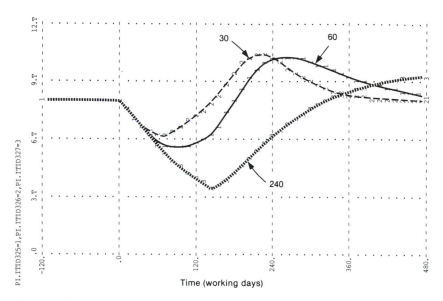

Figure 3.32 Comparison of parts inventory for three parameter sets in response to temporary STEP

Figure 3.32 compares the behavior of parts inventory for the three parameter sets. With the quick policy inventory is built up and then must be reduced. With the slow policy inventory falls farther but does not overshoot as much.

The variation in parts order rate produced by quick reactions in response to temporary changes is substantial. Whereas the variation may be tolerable if the change were permanent, it may not be if the change is temporary. Consequently the selection of a best policy must consider other possible demand inputs.

3.8 General Comments about Policy Design

In system dynamics a policy is distinguished from a decision. A policy is a general rule that states how decisions are made on the basis of available information: a policy might state how a company's dividend payments depend on earnings, earnings growth rate, return on equity, and cash availability. In contrast, a decision is the policy application to a specific set of information: it would be a decision to pay $2 per share in dividends if earnings per share is $3, earnings growth rate 3 percent per year, return on equity 10 percent, and cash equal to desired cash. A

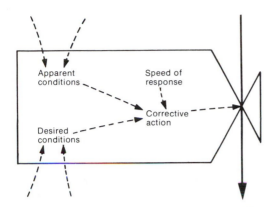

Figure 3.33   Components of a policy (adapted from Forrester 1961, figure 10.4)

system dynamics model provides a vehicle for testing the effects of various policies on the behavior of the overall system.

As shown in figure 3.33, every policy has four components: desired conditions or goals, apparent conditions, speed of response, and corrective action. Each component affects the performance of the company. Desired conditions and apparent conditions are the information inputs to a policy. In the parts-ordering example the inclusion of additional inventory and parts on order information affected system performance. Speed of response measures how quickly and aggressively management reacts to changing conditions. Changing management aggressiveness significantly affected system behavior in the parts-ordering example. A company can also take different actions in response to differences between desired and apparent conditions. For example, prices might be changed to correct inventory discrepancies.[5]

In policy design the process of selecting the goals, information, actions, and speed of response to improve company performance is conducted according to the four steps of the system dynamics approach given in section 3.2. In the remainder of this book different corporate problem behaviors are identified, models of relationships that cause these behaviors presented, an understanding of the connection between these relationships or structures and behavior developed, and extensive policy testing performed. The emphasis is on a cataloguing of common company structures and how these structures create the ob-

5. The interested reader can find a more detailed discussion of policy in Forrester (1961), chapter 10.

served behavior. The book does not discuss how to identify problem behavior and construct a model in an actual situation.

Rather the purposes of this book—(1) to illustrate the use of system dynamics in planning and policy design and (2) to provide the reader with an understanding of how corporate structures and policies create dynamic behavior, and how structures and policies can be designed to improve behavior and insulate the company from external shocks—are accomplished through the analysis of real corporate problems with models representative of the structures characteristic of real corporations. The model(s) are not intended to be complete model(s) of corporate structure but of certain aspects of corporate structure. Moreover, while the policy guidelines developed in subsequent chapters are useful for enhancing intuition, they should not be taken as universally applicable to every company in every situation.

Subsequent chapters develop a procedure, typical structures, and useful guidelines that should lead to an understanding of planning, corporate behavior, and system dynamics models. They do not develop the ideal model of a corporation and universal policy prescriptions. The problems of production, employment instability, and corporate growth, while important, are not the only dynamic problems experienced by companies. Nor are the structures developed the only structures responsible for stability or growth problems.

Reference

Forrester, Jay W. 1961. *Industrial Dynamics*. Cambridge, Mass.: The MIT Press.

Appendix 3.1: Equation Listing of Pressure-Based Policy Model ITID31

```
ITID31.DYNAMO
00001 *     PARTS-INVENTORY SYSTEM, PRESSURE-BASED POLICY
00002 NOTE
00003 NOTE     SIMPLE PARTS-INVENTORY SYSTEM MODEL -
00004 NOTE         PRESSURE-BASED ORDERING POLICY
00005 NOTE
00006 NOTE     MODEL USED IN CHAPTER 3 OF
00007 NOTE     'INTRODUCTION TO INDUSTRIAL DYNAMICS'
00008 NOTE      BY JAMES M. LYNEIS
00009 NOTE
00011 NOTE     PHYSICAL FLOWS
00012 NOTE
10020 L    PI.K=PI.J+(DT)(PAR.JK-PR.JK)
10021 N    PI=DDPI*CPR
10030 R    PAR.KL=DELAY3(POR.JK,PSDT)
```

```
10031 C      PSDT=60
10040 L      POO.K=POO.J+(DT)(POR.JK-PAR.JK)
10041 N      POO=PSDT*CPR
10042 NOTE
10043 NOTE        PARTS-ORDERING POLICY
10044 NOTE
10050 R      POR.KL=APR.K*POP.K
10060 A      APR.K=SMOOTH(PR.JK,TAPRPO)
10061 C      TAPRPO=5
10070 A      POP.K=TABLE(TPOP,PI.K/PIG.K,0,2,.5)
10071 T      TPOP=1.3/1.15/1/.85/.7
10080 A      PIG.K=DDPI*CPR
10081 C      DDPI=20
10082 NOTE
10083 NOTE        TEST INPUTS
10084 NOTE
10090 R      PR.KL=CPR*SPR.K*RPR.K
10091 C      CPR=400
10100 A      SPR.K=1+STEP(SH1,ST1)+STEP(SH2,ST2)
10101 C      SH1=0/ST1=0/SH2=0/ST2=0
10110 A      RPR.K=1+RAMP(RS1/240,RT1)
10111 C      RS1=0/RT1=0
10112 NOTE
10113 NOTE        SIMULATION RUN CONTROL CARDS
10114 NOTE
10115 N      TIME=-120
10116 C      DT=2
10117 C      LENGTH=480
10118 C      PLTPER=12
10119 C      PRTPER=0
10121 C      SAVPER=12
10122 SAVE       POR
10123 RUN COMPILE
READY


  ITID3R.DATA
10124 NOTE
10125 NOTE        RERUN CONTROL CARDS FOR ITID31.DYNAMO
10126 NOTE
10127 PLOT     PI=I,PIG=G(0,12E3)/PR=P,POR=O,PAR=A(350,550)/POO=X(18E3,30E3)
10128 RUN ITID311
10129 C      SH1=.1
10131 T      TPOP=1/1/1/1/1
10132 PLOT    PR=P(350,550)
10133 PLOT     PI=I,PIG=G(0,12E3)/PR=P,POR=O,PAR=A(350,550)/POO=X(18E3,30E3)
10134 RUN ITID312
10135 C      RS1=.15
10136 T      TPOP=1/1/1/1/1
10137 RUN ITID313
10138 CP     SH1=.1
10139 CP     TAPRPO=60
10141 T      TPOP=1/1/1/1/1
10142 PLOT     PI=I,PIG=G(0,12E3)/PR=P,POR=O,PAR=A(350,550)/POO=X(18E3,30E3)
10143 RUN ITID314
10144 RUN ITID315
10145 T      TPOP=1.45/1.225/1/.775/.55
10146 RUN ITID316
10147 T      TPOP=1.15/1.075/1/.925/.85
10148 CPLOT PR=P,POR.ITID315=1,POR.ITID316=2,POR.ITID317=3(350,550)
10149 PLOT     PI=I,PIG=G(0,12E3)/PR=P,POR=O,PAR=A(350,550)/POO=X(18E3,30E3)
10151 RUN ITID317
```

Appendix 3.2: Definition File for ITID31

```
NAME      NO    T  DEFINITION
   WHERE USED

APR        6    A  AVERAGE PRODUCTION RATE (UNITS/DAY)
   POR,R,5
CPR        9.1 C  CONSTANT PRODUCTION RATE (UNITS/DAY)
   PI,N,2.1/POO,N,4.1/PIG,A,8/PR,R,9
DDPI       8.1 C  DESIRED DAYS PARTS INVENTORY (DAYS)
   PI,N,2.1/PIG,A,8
DELAY3            DYNAMO MACRO FOR CALCULATING THIRD-ORDER
                     DELAY
   PAR,R,3
DT        11.6 C  DELTA TIME, SIMULATION SOLUTION INTERVAL
                     (DAYS)
   PI,L,2/POO,L,4
INVCOR            INVENTORY CORRECTIONS (UNITS/DAY)
ISWT              INVENTORY CORRECTION SWITCH (DIMENSIONLESS)
LENGTH    11.7 C
PAR        3    R  PARTS ARRIVAL RATE (UNITS/DAY)
   PI,L,2/POO,L,4
PI         2    L  PARTS INVENTORY (UNITS)
           2.1 N
   POP,A,7
PIC               PARTS INVENTORY CORRECTION (UNITS/DAY)
PIG        8    A  PARTS INVENTORY GOAL (UNITS)
   POP,A,7
PLTPER    11.8 C
POC               PARTS ON ORDER CORRECTION (UNITS/DAY)
POO        4    L  PARTS ON ORDER (UNITS)
           4.1 N
POOG              PARTS ON ORDER GOAL (UNITS)
POP        7    A  PRESSURE ON PARTS ORDERING (DIMENSIONLESS)
   POR,R,5
POR        5    R  PARTS ORDER RATE (UNITS/DAY)
   PAR,R,3/POO,L,4/SAVE,12.2
PR         9    R  PRODUCTION RATE (UNITS/DAY)
   PI,L,2/APR,A,6
PRTPER    11.9 C
PSDT       3.1 C  PARTS SUPPLIER DELIVERY TIME (DAYS)
   PAR,R,3/POO,N,4.1
PSWT              PARTS ON ORDER CORRECTION SWITCH
                     (DIMENSIONLESS)
RAMP              DYNAMO MACRO FOR RAMP FUNCTION
   RPR,A,11
RPR       11    A  RAMP CHANGE IN PRODUCTION RATE
                     (DIMENSIONLESS)
   PR,R,9
RS1       11.1 C  RAMP SLOPE ONE (DIMENSIONLESS)
   RPR,A,11
RT1               RAMP TIME ONE (DAYS)
   RPR,A,11/RS1,C,11.1
SAVPER    12.1 C
SH1       10.1 C  STEP HEIGHT ONE (DIMENSIONLESS)
   SPR,A,10
SH2               STEP HEIGHT TWO (DIMENSIONLESS)
   SPR,A,10/SH1,C,10.1


SMOOTH            DYNAMO MACRO FOR CALCULATING FIRST-ORDER
                     DELAY
```

```
      APR,A,6
SPR        10   A  STEP CHANGE IN PRODUCTION RATE
                      (DIMENSIONLESS)
      PR,R,9
STEP               DYNAMO MACRO FOR STEP FUNCTION
      SPR,A,10
ST1                STEP TIME ONE (DAYS)
      SPR,A,10/SH1,C,10.1
ST2                STEP TIME TWO (DAYS)
      SPR,A,10/SH1,C,10.1
TAPRPO    6.1 C  TIME TO AVERAGE PRODUCTION RATE FOR PARTS
                      ORDERING (DAYS)
      APR,A,6
TCPI               TIME TO CORRECT PARTS INVENTORY (DAYS)
TIME      11.5 N  TIME (DAYS)
TPOP       7.1 T  TABLE FOR PRESSURE ON PARTS ORDERING
                      (DIMENSIONLESS)
      POP,A,7


READY
```

Appendix 3.3: Equation Listing of Explicit Decision Rule Model ITID32

```
ITID32.DYNAMO
00001 *       PARTS-INVENTORY SYSTEM, EXPLICIT DECISION RULE
00002 NOTE
00003 NOTE     SIMPLE PARTS-INVENTORY SYSTEM MODEL -
00004 NOTE          EXPLICIT DECISION RULE ORDERING POLICY
00005 NOTE
00006 NOTE     MODEL USED IN CHAPTER 3 OF
00007 NOTE     'INTRODUCTION TO INDUSTRIAL DYNAMICS'
00008 NOTE      BY JAMES M. LYNEIS
00009 NOTE
00011 NOTE     PHYSICAL FLOWS
00012 NOTE
10020 L       PI.K=PI.J+(DT)(PAR.JK-PR.JK)
10021 N       PI=DDPI*CPR
10030 R       PAR.KL=DELAY3(POR.JK,PSDT)
10031 C       PSDT=60
10040 L       POO.K=POO.J+(DT)(POR.JK-PAR.JK)
10041 N       POO=PSDT*CPR
10042 NOTE
10043 NOTE     PARTS-ORDERING POLICY
10044 NOTE
10050 R       POR.KL=APR.K+ISWT*PIC.K+PSWT*POC.K
10051 C       ISWT=1
10052 C       PSWT=1
10060 A       APR.K=SMOOTH(PR.JK,TAPRPO)
10061 C       TAPRPO=60
10070 A       PIC.K=(PIG.K-PI.K)/TCPI
10071 C       TCPI=60
10080 A       PIG.K=DDPI*APR.K
10081 C       DDPI=20
10090 A       POC.K=(POOG.K-POO.K)/TCPI
10100 A       POOG.K=PSDT*APR.K
10101 NOTE
10102 NOTE     TEST INPUTS
10103 NOTE
10110 R       PR.KL=CPR*SPR.K*RPR.K
10111 C       CPR=400
```

```
10120 A       SPR.K=1+STEP(SH1,ST1)+STEP(SH2,ST2)
10121 C       SH1=0/ST1=0/SH2=0/ST2=0
10130 A       RPR.K=1+RAMP(RS1/240,RT1)
10131 C       RS1=0/RT1=0
10132 NOTE
10133 NOTE      SIMULATION RUN CONTROL CARDS
10134 NOTE
10135 N       TIME=-120
10136 C       DT=2
10137 C       LENGTH=480
10138 C       PLTPER=12
10139 C       PRTPER=0
10141 C       SAVPER=12
10142 SAVE      POR,PIC,POC
10150 A       INVCOR.K=PIC.K+POC.K
10151 RUN COMPILE
READY

11000 NOTE
11001 NOTE      RERUN CONTROL CARDS FOR ITID32.DYNAMO
11002 NOTE
11003 PLOT      PI=I,PIG=G(0,12E3)/PR=P,POR=0,PAR=A(350,550)/POO=X(18E3,30E3)
11004 CP       SH1=.1
11005 C        PSWT=0
11006 RUN ITID321
11007 PLOT      PR=P,APR=V(350,550)/INVCOR=I(0,60)
11008 PLOT      PI=I,PIG=G(0,12E3)/PR=P,POR=0,PAR=A(350,550)/POO=X(18E3,30E3)
11009 RUN   ITID322
11010 C        TAPRPO=30
11011 C        TCPI=30
11012 RUN ITID323
11013 C        TAPRPO=240
11014 C        TCPI=240
11015 PLOT      PI=I,PIG=G(0,12E3)/PR=P,POR=0,PAR=A(350,550)/POO=X(18E3,30E3)
11016 CPLOT     PR=P,POR.ITID322=1,POR.ITID323=2,POR.ITID324=3(350,550)
11018 CPLOT      PI.ITID322=1,PI.ITID323=2,PI.ITID324=3(0,12E3)
11035 RUN ITID324
11036 CP       SH2=-.1
11037 CP       ST2=150
11038 PLOT      PI=I,PIG=G(0,12E3)/PR=P,POR=0,PAR=A(350,550)/POO=X(18E3,30E3)
11039 RUN   ITID325
11040 C        TAPRPO=30
11041 C        TCPI=30
11042 RUN ITID326
11043 C        TAPRPO=240
11044 C        TCPI=240
11045 CPLOT     PR=P,POR.ITID325=1,POR.ITID326=2,POR.ITID327=3(350,550)
11046 CPLOT      PI.ITID325=1,PI.ITID326=2,PI.ITID327=3(0,12E3)
11047 PLOT      PI=I,PIG=G(0,12E3)/PR=P,POR=0,PAR=A(350,550)/POO=X(18E3,30E3)
11048 RUN ITID327
READY
```

Appendix 3.4: Definition File for ITID32

```
NAME     NO   T  DEFINITION
   WHERE USED

APR       6   A  AVERAGE PRODUCTION RATE (UNITS/DAY)
   POR,R,5/PIG,A,8/POOG,A,10
CPR      11.1 C  CONSTANT PRODUCTION RATE (UNITS/DAY)
   PI,N,2.1/POO,N,4.1/PR,R,11
DDPI      8.1 C  DESIRED DAYS PARTS INVENTORY (DAYS)
   PI,N,2.1/PIG,A,8
DELAY3           DYNAMO MACRO FOR CALCULATING THIRD-ORDER
                 DELAY
   PAR,R,3
DT       13.6 C  DELTA TIME, SIMULATION SOLUTION INTERVAL
                 (DAYS)
   PI,L,2/POO,L,4
INVCOR   15   A  INVENTORY CORRECTIONS (UNITS/DAY)
ISWT      5.1 C  INVENTORY CORRECTION SWITCH (DIMENSIONLESS)
   POR,R,5
LENGTH   13.7 C
PAR       3   R  PARTS ARRIVAL RATE (UNITS/DAY)
   PI,L,2/POO,L,4
PI        2   L  PARTS INVENTORY (UNITS)
          2.1 N
   PIC,A,7
PIC       7   A  PARTS INVENTORY CORRECTION (UNITS/DAY)
   POR,R,5/SAVE,14.2/INVCOR,A,15
PIG       8   A  PARTS INVENTORY GOAL (UNITS)
   PIC,A,7
PLTPER   13.8 C
POC       9   A  PARTS ON ORDER CORRECTION (UNITS/DAY)
   POR,R,5/SAVE,14.2/INVCOR,A,15
POO       4   L  PARTS ON ORDER (UNITS)
          4.1 N
   POC,A,9
POOG     10   A  PARTS ON ORDER GOAL (UNITS)
   POC,A,9
POP              PRESSURE ON PARTS ORDERING (DIMENSIONLESS)
POR       5   R  PARTS ORDER RATE (UNITS/DAY)
   PAR,R,3/POO,L,4/SAVE,14.2
PR       11   R  PRODUCTION RATE (UNITS/DAY)
   PI,L,2/APR,A,6
PRTPER   13.9 C
PSDT      3.1 C  PARTS SUPPLIER DELIVERY TIME (DAYS)
   PAR,R,3/POO,N,4.1/POOG,A,10
PSWT      5.2 C  PARTS ON ORDER CORRECTION SWITCH
                 (DIMENSIONLESS)
   POR,R,5
RAMP             DYNAMO MACRO FOR RAMP FUNCTION
   RPR,A,13
RPR      13   A  RAMP CHANGE IN PRODUCTION RATE
                 (DIMENSIONLESS)
   PR,R,11
RS1      13.1 C  RAMP SLOPE ONE (DIMENSIONLESS)
   RPR,A,13
RT1              RAMP TIME ONE (DAYS)
   RPR,A,13/RS1,C,13.1
SAVPER   14.1 C


SH1      12.1 C  STEP HEIGHT ONE (DIMENSIONLESS)
   SPR,A,12
```

```
SH2                STEP HEIGHT TWO (DIMENSIONLESS)
   SPR,A,12/SH1,C,12.1
SMOOTH             DYNAMO MACRO FOR CALCULATING FIRST-ORDER
                   DELAY
   APR,A,6
SPR     12  A  STEP CHANGE IN PRODUCTION RATE
                   (DIMENSIONLESS)
   PR,R,11
STEP               DYNAMO MACRO FOR STEP FUNCTION
   SPR,A,12
ST1                STEP TIME ONE (DAYS)
   SPR,A,12/SH1,C,12.1
ST2                STEP TIME TWO (DAYS)
   SPR,A,12/SH1,C,12.1
TAPRPO   6.1 C  TIME TO AVERAGE PRODUCTION RATE FOR PARTS
                   ORDERING (DAYS)
   APR,A,6
TCPI     7.1 C  TIME TO CORRECT PARTS INVENTORY (DAYS)
   PIC,A,7/POC,A,9
TIME    13.5 N  TIME (DAYS)
TPOP               TABLE FOR PRESSURE ON PARTS ORDERING
                   (DIMENSIONLESS)


READY
```

Part II
Dynamics of Production and Employment Instability

Dynamics of Inventory Systems

4.1 The Problem of Production and Inventory Stability

Many companies experience significant variations in production and inventory. In the business press one frequently reads of boom-and-bust, feast-or-famine cycles in the machine tool, airframe, and metals industries. Consumer goods manufacturers experience similar variations: factory production often fluctuates more widely than consumer purchase rate, sometimes by factors of two and three. Production and inventory instability is widespread in industry.

Production and inventory variations impose costs on the company, its employees, and the economy. During boom periods the company works large amounts of overtime, experiences production inefficiencies because of parts inventory shortages, new employees, and fatigue, and potentially loses business because of finished inventory shortages; employees are subject to the profitable but fatiguing overtime; the economy experiences inflationary cost and demand pressures, and growth is constrained by shortages. In bust periods the company has idle resources and excess inventory; employees are laid off; the economy bears the burden of high unemployment and growth below potential. Policies that reduce the severity of these variations offer the potential for numerous cost savings.

A major triggering force behind these variations is the random, seasonal, and cyclical changes in demand. A company can cope with demand changes in three ways:

1. use inventory and backlogs to absorb differences between production and demand,
2. change production to match changes in demand—short-run changes can be accomplished with overtime, long-term changes with changes in resources,

3. change demand to match production abilities—changes in product attractiveness affect market share and thereby company demand.

The policy set chosen will determine whether the company's production and employment vary more or less than demand. Part II explores the behavioral consequences of different policies for coping with demand changes.

The structure of inventory systems contributes significantly to these variations. In all manufacturing industries physical goods flow through a series of production-inventory stages, similar to those described in chapter 3. Consumer goods are produced and then shipped to distributors, wholesalers, and retailers. Each stage of the distribution system holds inventories, sends orders to the previous stage, and awaits delivery. For industrial products, or for the production stage of consumer products, the flow proceeds from raw materials to basic items such as sheet and rod steel, machined parts, subassemblies of parts, and finally complete assembly. Each stage of the production system holds inventories, sends orders to the previous stage, and awaits deliveries. While the length of delivery delays, the number of stages, the levels of inventory, and so on, varies from product to product, as well as within the stages for a given product, the basic system structure is identical and similar to that described in chapter 3. Thus a system of similar inventory stages should also exhibit greater variation in output (parts order rate) than in input (production rate).

Clearly an understanding of the basic dynamics of inventory systems is an important first step in understanding the behavior of individual companies. This chapter extends the material of chapter 3 by examining a two-stage inventory system, so that the concept of amplification can be more fully developed, and exploring the response of the system to a wider range of demand inputs.[1]

4.2 Structure Creating Instability

The structure of a two-stage inventory system is shown in figure 4.1. Shipment rate depletes finished inventory; production completions build finished inventory. Work in process accumulates the difference between production rate and production completions. Production rate

1. Forrester develops more elaborate production-distribution system models in several of his works, see Forrester (1958, 1959, and 1961, chapters 2, 15, and 16).

depletes parts inventory; parts arrival rate builds parts inventory. Parts on order accumulates the difference between parts order rate and parts arrival rate.

The two-stage system in figure 4.1 represents the assembly and machining operations of a much larger production-distribution system, or one that might feed another assembly operation before the distribution system. The parts supplier segment draws on the output of raw material and metals or other materials segments.

The two-stage system is large enough to produce the instability observed in larger systems, yet small enough for a modeler to understand the causes of such instability and design policies to lessen it. The conclusions drawn from an analysis of the simpler system apply equally well to other stages of the larger system.

The two-stage system also corresponds to the boundary of the normal company, or company profit center. As such it serves as the basic building block to which other interactions important to corporate policy design are added (for example, labor hiring, capacity expansion, and financing).

The inventory system in figure 4.1 contains two policies—production rate and parts order rate. The structure of both policies is identical in the figure and equivalent to the policy developed in chapter 3: average usage rate plus inventory and parts on order corrections.

In the remainder of this section, as well as throughout the rest of the book, each model equation is described in detail, starting with the physical flows and then proceeding to company policies.

Physical Flows

Equation 1 states that finished inventory FI accumulates the difference between production completions PC and shipment rate SR. Finished inventory is initialized to its equilibrium value: desired days finished inventory DDFI multiplied by constant customer order rate CCOR.

$$FI.K = FI.J + (DT)(PC.JK - SR.JK) \qquad\qquad 1, L$$
$$FI = DDFI * CCOR \qquad\qquad 1.1, N$$

where

FI	= finished product inventory (units)
DT	= delta time, simulation solution interval (days)
PC	= production completions (units/day)
SR	= shipment rate (units/day)

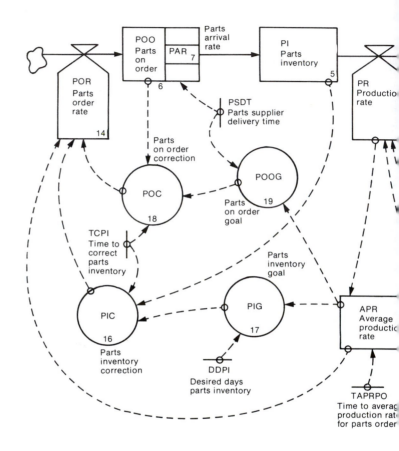

Figure 4.1   Structure of inventory system model

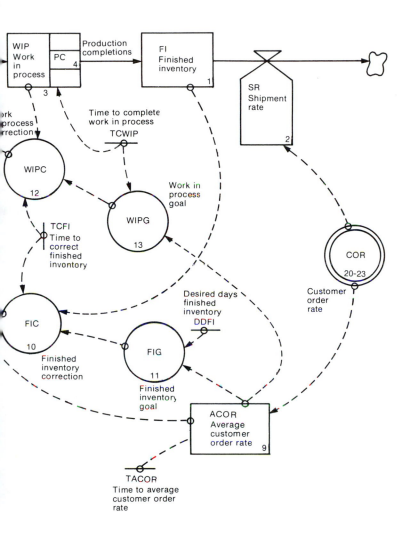

DDFI = desired days finished inventory (days)
CCOR = constant customer order rate (units/day).

In equation 2, shipment rate SR is set equal to customer order rate COR. Equation 2 implies that shipment rate is not constrained by the availability of finished inventory. This unrealistic assumption is relaxed in chapter 8.

$$\text{SR.KL} = \text{COR.K} \qquad\qquad\qquad\qquad\qquad 2, R$$

where
SR   = shipment rate (units/day)
COR = customer order rate (units/day).

Equation 3 states that work in process WIP accumulates the difference between production rate PR and production completions PC. Work in process is initialized to its equilibrium value: time to complete work in process TCWIP multiplied by constant customer order rate CCOR.

$$\text{WIP.K} = \text{WIP.J} + (\text{DT})(\text{PR.JK} - \text{PC.JK}) \qquad\qquad 3, L$$
$$\text{WIP} = \text{TCWIP} * \text{CCOR} \qquad\qquad\qquad\qquad\qquad 3.1, N$$

where
WIP   = work in process (units)
DT   = delta time, simulation solution interval (days)
PR   = production rate (units/day)
PC   = production completions (units/day)
TCWIP = time to complete work in process (days)
CCOR = constant customer order rate (units/day).

Production completions PC are represented in equation 4 as a third-order delay of production rate PR. Time to complete work in process TCWIP is set to 20 days, characteristic of the scheduling and production time inherent in an assembly operation. The days measured in this model are working days; therefore 20 days are equal to 1 month.

$$\text{PC.KL} = \text{DELAY3}(\text{PR.JK,TCWIP}) \qquad\qquad\qquad 4, R$$
$$\text{TCWIP} = 20 \qquad\qquad\qquad\qquad\qquad\qquad\qquad 4.1, C$$

where
PC   = production completions (units/day)
PR   = production rate (units/day)
TCWIP = time to complete work in process (days).

Equation 5 states that parts inventory accumulates the difference between parts arrival rate PAR and production rate PR. Parts inventory is initialized to its equilibrium value: desired days parts inventory DDPI multiplied by constant customer order rate CCOR.

PI.K = PI.J + (DT)(PAR.JK − PR.JK)   5, L
PI = DDPI * CCOR   5.1, N

where

PI   = parts inventory (units)
DT   = delta time, simulation solution interval (days)
PAR   = parts arrival rate (units/day)
PR   = production rate (units/day)
DDPI = desired days parts inventory (days)
CCOR = constant customer order rate (units/day).

Similarly parts on order POO accumulates the difference between parts order rate POR and parts arrival rate PAR (equation 6). Parts on order is also initialized to its equilibrium value: parts supplier delivery time PSDT multiplied by constant customer order rate CCOR.

POO.K = POO.J + (DT)(POR.JK − PAR.JK)   6, L
POO = PSDT * CCOR   6.1, N

where

POO   = parts on order (units)
DT   = delta time, simulation solution interval (days)
POR   = parts order rate (units/day)
PAR   = parts arrival rate (units/day)
PSDT   = parts supplier delivery time (days)
CCOR = constant customer order rate (units/day).

Parts arrival rate PAR is represented in equation 7 as a third-order delay of parts order rate POR. Parts supplier delivery time PSDT is set equal to 60 days, a delay representative of the time required for the scheduling and production of machined parts.

PAR.KL = DELAY3(POR.JK,PSDT)   7, R
PSDT = 60   7.1, C

where

PAR   = parts arrival rate (units/day)
POR   = parts order rate (units/day)
PSDT = parts supplier delivery time (days).

Policies

Equation 8 defines the company's production rate policy. Production rate is set equal to the sum of average customer order rate ACOR, finished inventory correction FIC, and work in process correction WIPC. The logic behind each of these components was developed in chapter 3.

$$PR.KL = ACOR.K + FIC.K + WIPC.K \qquad\qquad 8, R$$

where
PR   = production rate (units/day)
ACOR = average customer order rate (units/day)
FIC   = finished inventory correction (units/day)
WIPC = work in process correction (units/day).

Average customer order rate ACOR is represented in equation 9 as an exponential average of customer order rate COR. Time to average customer order rate TACOR is set equal to 60 days. The consequences of different values for TACOR on company behavior are examined in a later section.

$$ACOR.K = SMOOTH(COR.K, TACOR) \qquad\qquad 9, A$$
$$TACOR = 60 \qquad\qquad 9.1, C$$

where
ACOR = average customer order rate (units/day)
COR   = customer order rate (units/day)
TACOR = time to average customer order rate (days).

Equation 10 defines finished inventory correction FIC. FIC equals the difference between finished inventory goal FIG and finished inventory FI divided by time to correct finished inventory TCFI. Time to correct finished inventory is also set to 60 days.

$$FIC.K = (FIG.K - FI.K)/TCFI \qquad\qquad 10, A$$
$$TCFI = 60 \qquad\qquad 10.1, C$$

where
FIC = finished inventory correction (units/day)
FIG = finished inventory goal (units)
FI   = finished product inventory (units)
TCFI = time to correct finished inventory (days).

Finished inventory goal FIG is defined in equation 11 to equal desired days finished inventory DDFI multiplied by average customer order rate ACOR. In other words the company's finished inventory goal responds to the average volume of business as represented by average customer order rate. DDFI is here set to 30 days. Since time to complete work in process equals 20 days, the company carries sufficient inventory to fill shipments out of inventory plus a 10-day buffer.

$$\text{FIG.K} = \text{DDFI} * \text{ACOR.K} \qquad\qquad\qquad 11,\ A$$
$$\text{DDFI} = 30 \qquad\qquad\qquad 11.1,\ C$$

where
FIG   = finished inventory goal (units)
DDFI = desired days finished inventory (days)
ACOR = average customer order rate (units/day).

Work in process correction WIPC is defined in equation 12 to equal work in process goal WIPG minus work in process WIP divided by time to correct finished inventory TCFI. Equation 13 states that work in process goal WIPG equals time to complete work in process TCWIP multiplied by average customer order rate ACOR.

$$\text{WIPC.K} = (\text{WIPG.K} - \text{WIP.K})/\text{TCFI} \qquad\qquad 12,\ A$$

where
WIPC = work in process correction (units/day)
WIPG = work in process goal (units)
WIP   = work in process (units)
TCFI = time to correct finished inventory (days);

$$\text{WIPG.K} = \text{TCWIP} * \text{ACOR.K} \qquad\qquad\qquad 13,\ A$$

where
WIPG   = work in process goal (units)
TCWIP = time to complete work in process (days)
ACOR   = average customer order rate (units/day).

Equations 14 through 19 define parts order rate POR. The structure of the parts order rate policy is identical to the structure of the production rate policy. The primary difference between parts order rate policy and production rate policy is that average production rate APR replaces average customer order rate ACOR in the parts order rate equations. In other words the parts-ordering system perceives production rate rather than customer order rate as the average volume of business for the parts inventory system. In addition desired parts inventory equals 60 days. This gives the company enough inventory to meet production needs without recourse to supplier shipments.

$$POR.KL = APR.K + PIC.K + POC.K \qquad\qquad 14, R$$

where
POR = parts order rate (units/day)
APR = average production rate (units/day)
PIC = parts inventory correction (units/day)
POC = parts on order correction (units/day);

$$APR.K = SMOOTH(PR.JK,TAPRPO) \qquad\qquad 15, A$$
$$TAPRPO = 60 \qquad\qquad\qquad\qquad\qquad\qquad 15.1, C$$

where
APR   = average production rate (units/day)
PR   = production rate (units/day)
TAPRPO = time to average production rate for parts ordering
                (days);

$$PIC.K = (PIG.K - PI.K)/TCPI \qquad\qquad 16, A$$
$$TCPI = 60 \qquad\qquad\qquad\qquad\qquad\qquad 16.1, C$$

where
PIC   = parts inventory correction (units/day)
PIG   = parts inventory goal (units)
PI   = parts inventory (units)
TCPI = time to correct parts inventory (days);

$$PIG.K = DDPI * APR.K \qquad\qquad 17, A$$
$$DDPI = 60 \qquad\qquad\qquad\qquad\qquad 17.1, C$$

where
PIG   = parts inventory goal (units)
DDPI = desired days parts inventory (days)
APR   = average production rate (units/day);

$$POC.K = (POOG.K - POO.K)/TCPI \qquad\qquad 18, A$$

where
POC   = parts on order correction (units/day)
POOG = parts on order goal (units)
POO   = parts on order (units)
TCPI = time to correct parts inventory (days);

$$POOG.K = PSDT * APR.K \qquad\qquad 19, A$$

where
POOG = parts on order goal (units)
PSDT = parts supplier delivery time (days)
APR   = average production rate (units/day).

Test Inputs

Equation 20 defines customer order rate COR. COR equals constant
customer order rate CCOR multiplied by a series of exogenous disturbances. These exogenous disturbances are typical of the changes in
demand patterns experienced by companies: sudden permanent
changes in demand, seasonal variations, cyclical variations, growth,
and random noise. Each of these disturbances is described in more
detail in section 4.5.

COR.K = CCOR * (1 + STEP(COSH,COST) + ACOS	
$\quad$ * SIN(6.28 * TIME.K/PCOS) + ACOS2	
$\quad$ * SIN(6.28 * TIME.K/PCOS2) + COGF.K	
$\quad$ + PKNSE(MCON,SDVCON,TCCON))	20, A
CCOR = 400	20.2, C
COSH = 0	20.3, C
COST = 60	20.4, C
ACOS = 0	20.5, C
PCOS = 240	20.6, C
ACOS2 = 0	20.7, C
PCOS2 = 960	20.8, C
MCON = 0	20.9, C
SDVCON = 0	21.1, C
TCCON = 10	21.2, C

where
COR   = customer order rate (units/day)
CCOR   = constant customer order rate (units/day)
COSH   = customer orders step height (dimensionless)
COST   = customer orders step time (days)
ACOS   = amplitude of customer orders sine (dimensionless)
TIME   = time (days)
PCOS   = period of customer orders sine (days)
ACOS2   = amplitude of customer orders sine two (dimensionless)
PCOS2   = period of customer orders sine two (days)
COGF   = customer orders growth factor (dimensionless)

PKNSE   = pink (correlated) noise variation
MCON   = mean of customer orders noise (dimensionless)
SDVCON = standard deviation of customer orders noise
                (dimensionless)
TCCON   = time constant of customer orders noise (days);

COGF.K = COG.K − 1   22, A

where
COGF = customer orders growth factor (dimensionless)
COG   = customer orders growth (dimensionless);

COG.K = COG.J + (DT) (COGR * COG.J)   23, L
COG = 1   23.1, N
COGR = 0   23.2, C

where
COG   = customer orders growth (dimensionless)
DT   = delta time, simulation solution interval (days)
COGR = customer orders growth rate (percent/day).

4.3 Understanding Instability

The model described in the previous section captures the structure and
policies believed to be a cause of instability in inventory systems.
Simulation of the model will verify or refute this hypothesis.

To test the hypothesis, the model is driven from equilibrium by some
exogenous disturbance. The STEP input, a sudden one-shot change, is
a very simple and uncomplicated, yet informative, disturbance. Response of a system to a STEP input reveals

1. any tendency of a system toward instability—a system that exhibits
instability for a STEP input will generally do so for more realistic
inputs;
2. the response time, or the length of time the system takes to adjust to
new conditions—long response times may indicate trouble in adjusting
to growth or decline in business.

Because of its simplicity, the STEP is also useful for understanding the
causes of instability or slow response time. A system's response to more
complicated inputs is often difficult to analyze.

Figure 4.2 shows the response of the inventory system to a 10 percent (40-unit) STEP increase in customer order rate at day 60. The 10
percent increase in customer order rate results in a 14 percent peak

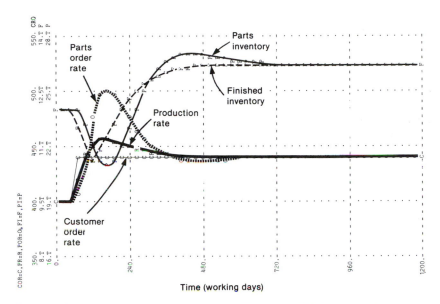

Figure 4.2 Inventory system response to a 10 percent STEP increase in customer order rate

increase in production rate, and a 25 percent peak increase in parts order rate. Each stage amplifies the disturbance transmitted from the prior stage.

In chapter 3 amplification was defined as a change in output greater than a change in input—for example, parts order rate increased more than production rate when production rate increased by 10 percent. The source of amplification was identified as the need to increase parts order rate above production rate to rebuild inventories; inventories decline because parts arrival rate lags parts order rate, which in turn lags production rate. Moreover parts order rate must rise above production rate for parts on order and parts inventory to achieve their higher desired levels.

The amount of amplification depends on two factors:

1. Length of the supply lead time—the longer the delay between parts order and arrival rates, the greater the inventory decline, and therefore the more parts order rate must increase above production rate to rebuild inventory.

2. Aggressiveness of management in responding to changes in production rate and in rebuilding inventory—the more quickly the company

tries to rebuild inventory, the more parts order rate must increase above production rate.

The affects of a long supply lead time are illustrated in figure 4.2. Notice that the peak in production rate is 3.6 percent greater than the peak in customer order rate (456 versus 440), while the peak in parts order rate is 9.6 percent greater than the peak in production rate (500 versus 456).

Greater relative amplification results from the longer delay in the physical flow channel of the second stage—parts supplier delivery time (60 days) as compared to time to complete work in process (20 days). Because parts arrival rate lags farther behind parts order rate than production completion behind production rate, parts inventory falls more than finished inventory. To rebuild parts inventory then, parts order rate must rise farther than the increase of production over customer order rate.

Before proceeding to management aggressiveness, which will be discussed in the next section on policy design, a characteristic of multi-stage inventory systems warrants discussion.

In figure 4.2 a 10 percent change in an input to the first stage produces a 14 percent change as input to the second stage. The second stage then amplifies not the 10 percent change but the 14 percent change and sets inventory goals on the basis of the amplified disturbance. When production rate falls back to 440 units per day, the parts-ordering stage recognizes it has built up too much parts inventory. Consequently parts order rate is reduced below production rate until the excess is corrected. By amplifying the input of the prior stage, each successive stage in a multistage system exhibits greater amplification relative to the initial disturbance and greater instability or tendency to overshoot the final equilibrium. Hence the boom-and-bust cycles in these systems.

4.4 Improving Behavior through Policy Design

Management has little leverage in changing the two structural features of inventory systems that contribute to amplification and instability:

1. delays in physical flow channels causing inventory to decline in response to an increase in usage rate so that reorder rate must rise above usage rate to rebuild inventory;

Table 4.1
Policy parameter sets

	TACOR	TCFI	TAPRPO	TCPI
Aggressive	60	60	60	60
Moderate	60	240	60	240
Slow	240	240	240	240

2. a spiraling usage rate, where the value at each stage is an amplification of the preceding stage usage rate.

Delays in flow channels are relatively fixed. The information required to separate the initial disturbance from each stage's inventory correction orders is very difficult to obtain. Consequently policy design must focus on the parameters associated with the reorder rate policies

Reorder rate policy parameters affect stability and amplification in two ways. First, the averaging time determines how quickly the company establishes inventory goals. The longer the averaging time, the less the company responds to the short-term inventory correction orders of the preceding stage. Second, the inventory correction time determines the magnitude of inventory correction orders. The longer the correction time, the lower the correction orders and the amplification. Policies with longer averaging and correction times should therefore improve stability.

Table 4.1 gives three alternative policy parameter sets.[2] The aggressive policy set represents the current set of model parameters. The moderate policy set increases the inventory correction times from 60 to 240 days. The slow policy set further increases the averaging times to 240 days.

Under the aggressive policy set management responds quickly to changes in the base volume of business (either customer order rate or production rate) and promptly tries to correct inventory discrepancies. Such an aggressive policy might be characteristic of a company where the costs of holding inventory are substantially higher than the costs of production or parts-ordering instability. Thus the company would hold minimum levels of inventory and change production or parts ordering quickly to correct inventory discrepancies.

Under the moderate policy set management does not respond im-

2. These policy parameter sets are meant to be representative of the range of management options. For a complete analysis of these and other parameter sets see Lyneis (1977).

mediately to changes in the base volume of business but permits a sixty-day average to smooth most short-term variations in customer orders. Management corrects inventory discrepancies even more slowly, however. A moderate policy might be characteristic of a company in which the costs of holding inventory are approximately the costs of instability. The company changes production relatively quickly in an effort to follow longer-term changes in demand (seasonal and business cycles, growth or decline), so as to keep inventory from getting too far out of line. But, by correcting inventory discrepancies only slowly, the company reduces the amplification inherent in the system.

Under the slow policy parameter set, management is reluctant to change production and parts order rates. Such a policy would be found in a company where the costs of changing production far outweigh the costs of holding inventory. Production is changed only gradually, with enough inventory held to decouple effectively production from customer orders without stockouts.

In the simulation runs of this chapter the desired levels of inventory remain the same under all three policy sets. In so doing, the relative variations of inventory can be compared. In actual practice the desired level of inventory would be set to a value consistent with the variations that result from the chosen policy set.

Figures 4.3 and 4.4 compare the behaviors of production rate and parts order rate, respectively, for the three policy parameter sets. For both rates the aggressive policy set causes substantially greater amplification, whereas the difference in amplification between the moderate and slow sets is hardly noticeable. Notice that past a certain point, further increases in averaging and correction times apparently have little marginal effect on the amount of amplification (for a STEP change in demand).

The nonlinearity in amplification reduction occurs as averaging and adjustment times are increased because of two different sources of inventory loss. When there is a sudden increase in demand, some decline in inventory is unavoidable because of physical flow delays. The quicker the unavoidable decline is corrected, the greater the amplification. But a further decline in inventory is caused by an intentionally slow response. For example, figure 4.5 compares the behavior of finished inventory for the three policy sets. The slower the response, the greater the inventory decline. Past a point, the benefits of slower responses are nearly offset by greater inventory losses.

Figure 4.6 points out the trade-off between amplification and inven-

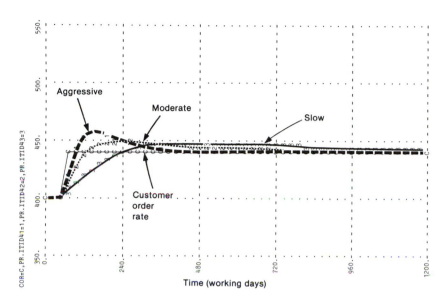

Figure 4.3   Comparison of production rate for three policy sets

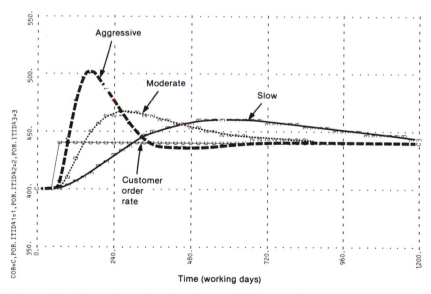

Figure 4.4   Comparison of parts order rate for three policy sets

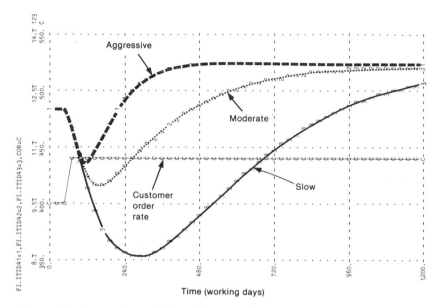

Figure 4.5 Comparison of finished inventory for three policy sets

tory stability more clearly. In the figure three performance indices are plotted:

1. Amplification—the increase in production rate above the 40-unit input change divided or normalized by the change for the 60/60 or aggressive policy set.
2. Inventory loss—the bottom inventory loss divided by the inventory loss for the aggressive policy set.
3. Composite index—an equal weighting of the amplification and inventory loss indices.

At the vertical axis performance is measured on a relative scale from 0 to 3.5, with zero being the best possible, although unattainable, performance. On the horizontal axis are different values for time to average customer order rate TACOR and time to correct finished inventory TCFI.

Figure 4.6 shows that amplification performance improves with increasing TACOR and TCFI values, but at a decreasing rate. Inventory loss, however, increases with TACOR and TCFI. A composite performance index would weight the two, based on relative costs of a unit of stability and a unit of inventory loss. Figure 4.6 gives one composite index which assumes equal weighting.

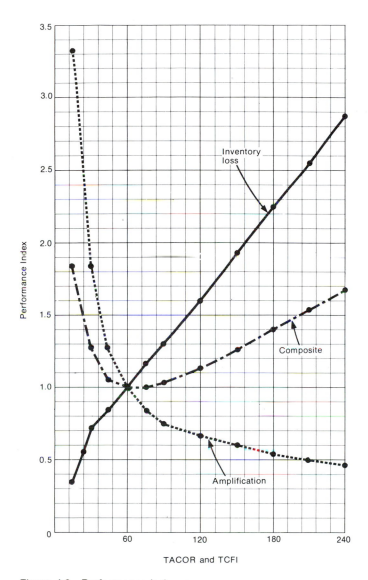

TACOR and TCFI

Figure 4.6   Performance indexes

The composite index has a relatively flat portion between policy parameters 45/45 and 120/120 (the 60/240 moderate policy set falls in this flat region). In the flat region variations in parameters produce offsetting changes in amplification and inventory loss. Outside the flat region changes in one of the performance indexes dominate.

Such a flat region on the performance curve is comforting to the policy designer. Any policy within the region is equally good. Given the uncertainties involved in estimating relative costs, a flat region gives the designer confidence that performance of the chosen policy is insensitive to some errors. The designer can then choose any policy in this region for other than cost factors (for example, production to bring about employment stability).

The following policy design guidelines summarize the results of this section:[3]

Policy design guideline 4.1 As the averaging and correction times in an inventory system increase, (1) order amplification decreases, but at a decreasing rate, and (2) inventory losses increase.

Policy design guideline 4.2 A composite performance index sometimes shows a relatively flat portion within which any policy choice is equally good.

4.5 Testing Scenarios in Policy Design

Companies experience many other types of demand changes in addition to a STEP. A good set of policies cannot be chosen until policy performance is evaluated under the range of demand conditions the company is likely to face.

Test Conditions

A model of a company is tested, or subjected to various input disturbances, for three primary reasons:

1. To gain an understanding of why problem corporate behavior results.

---

3. The guidelines presented in this book summarize the results of model experiments. Generally, they do not tell the policy designer what to do but point out trade-offs, behavioral tendencies, and procedures that are useful in policy design.

2. To develop policies that improve corporate behavior.

3. To develop confidence in the model as a representation of the real company.

Two fundamentally different types of input disturbances are used in the testing process: historical times series of actual inputs, for example orders and costs of labor, and pure disturbances such as the STEP input used in section 4.3. Each has a role in the testing process.

The historical time-series input is useful for developing confidence in the model. Model output should look like the past experience of the company. However, correspondence between past experience and model output is not sufficient for generating confidence. Because many models that have fit well to past data have proven to be poor predictors of the future, management must have confidence that the model pro duces a good fit for the right reasons. Moreover, for management to change policies that produce the undesirable corporate behavior, they must understand why current policies (which intuition says are the right ones) create problem behavior and why the proposed policies improve behavior. Finally, management must have confidence that the proposed policies will work in other than historical market conditions. Pure test inputs are useful for developing understanding and testing policy performance to other than historical conditions.

Historical time series consist of some combination of five pure inputs:

1. STEP—a sudden, permanent change.

2. NOISE—random, unpredictable variations such as strikes, the weather, or news events.

3. SEASONAL—a regular, yearly variation.

4. CYCLICAL—a less regular, but not random, variation associated with business cycles (three- to five-year period).

5. GROWTH or DECLINE—any underlying long-term growth or decline in the volume of business.

In the remainder of this section, the response of the inventory system to the NOISE, CYCLICAL, and GROWTH inputs is analyzed and interpreted. SEASONAL variations are best handled by policies based on forecasts of the seasonality. Such policies are beyond the scope of this book.

NOISE

Random disturbances impinge on every decision point in the system. For ease of analysis, however, it is common modeling practice to use only one NOISE input. In addition most random disturbances in corporate systems are correlated, the disturbance is statistically related to past disturbances. For example, if sales have been abnormally high for a couple of days, chances are they will be high the next day. Over time, however, the disturbances vary randomly about some constant value. Consequently system dynamics models use as a test input correlated noise called pink noise.

Figure 4.7 shows the response of the inventory system to a NOISE variation in customer order rate with the aggressive policy parameter set. Customer order rate exhibits a behavior pattern characteristic of correlated noise: short-term variations superimposed on a longer-term variation, where the long-term variation results from the correlation of the short term. Production rate varies nearly as much as customer order rate, while parts order rate varies more than customer order rate. Before analyzing this behavior, system response to NOISE with the slow policy set is reviewed.

Figure 4.8 shows the response of the inventory system to a NOISE

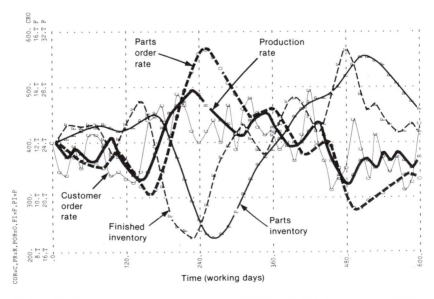

Figure 4.7 Inventory system response to a NOISE variation in customer order: aggressive policy set

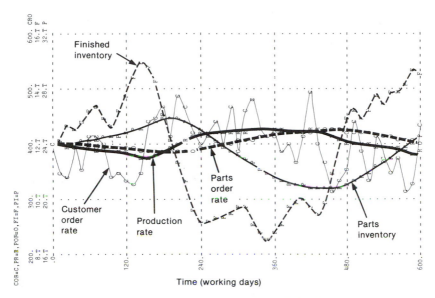

Figure 4.8 Inventory system response to a NOISE variation in customer order rate: slow policy set

variation in customer order rate with the slow policy set. Production and parts order rates vary little in response to the changes in customer order rate.

The difference in stability observed for the two policies is attributable to the different philosophies about the use of inventory implied by policy parameters. With the slow policy finished and parts inventories act as buffers, absorbing differences between customer order rate and production completions, and production and parts arrival rates, respectively. With the aggressive policy inventory no longer acts as a buffer. By using a short averaging time, the policy causes production rate to follow closely changes in customer order rate. In the extreme case where the averaging time is zero, production completions would equal customer order rate such that finished inventory would remain constant (and hence have a neutral effect on stability). In the production-inventory system inventory only buffers the difference between customer order rate and production completions caused by the unavoidable information collecting, scheduling, and production delays. But the aggressive policy also tries to build inventory to match the short-run changes in demand. Thus, rather than being neutral, inventory acts as a source of greater instability.

Instability, however, is not necessarily an undesirable behavior pattern. Presumably, if the wide fluctuations in production and parts order rates prevent fluctuations in inventory (and thereby allow the company to hold less inventory), and if inventory is more costly than production fluctuations, an aggressive policy makes sense. What happens to inventory under the two policy sets?

A comparison of figures 4.7 and 4.8 indicates that the range of finished inventory is about the same for the two policy parameter sets, while parts inventory fluctuates with a wider range with the aggressive policy. This behavior is in direct contrast to what might at first be expected—quick reactions should cause inventory to fluctuate less. What causes intuition to be so far wrong?

The reason lies in the structure and policy of the system coupled with the nature of the disturbance. The aggressive policy changes inventory levels to match changes in customer order and production rates—if the flow rates increase, inventory is increased, and vice versa. But the nature of random disturbances is that if rates increase in one time span, they will probably decrease in the next time span. The aggressive policy builds inventory to match the increase. But then the decrease causes inventory to rise farther because of the unavoidable delays in production and in receiving parts. In contrast, the slow policy set relies on offsetting changes in customer order rate, rather than changes in production or parts ordering, to keep inventory in line for a NOISE variation.

For example, compare system behavior with the two policy sets following the decline in customer order rate beginning around day 90 in figures 4.7 and 4.8. Initially finished inventory increases with both policy sets. The aggressive policy, however, quickly cuts back production rate so that finished inventory rises less quickly. But customer order rate reverses at approximately day 132. Given the unavoidable delays in increasing production and in receiving parts, finished inventory falls. Because with the aggressive policy finished inventory starts at a lower value at the onset of the increase in customer order rate, it also falls to a lower value. The slow policy reacts less quickly but has a larger buffer to absorb unanticipated changes. The following guideline summarizes these results:

Policy design guideline 4.3. For a permanent change such as a STEP, aggressive policies trade production and parts-ordering instabilities for inventory stability. For temporary changes, however, aggressive policies cause greater instability in production, parts ordering, and inventory.

CYCLICAL

Business cycles are the 3- to 5-year variations in aggregate business activity characteristic of western economies. A 20 percent, 960-day (4-year) variation is used to represent CYCLICAL variations in this book.

Figure 4.9 shows the response of the inventory system to a CYCLICAL variation with the aggressive policy parameter set. The amplification through the system stages is apparent: production rate varies more than customer order rate; parts order rate varies more than production rate. Moreover parts inventory and finished inventory fluctuate substantially—19,000 and 14,000 units, respectively.

The cause of such behavior is explained by examining the cycle from day 1200 to day 2160. At day 1200 customer order rate peaks and begins to decline. Production rate is initially above customer order rate but also peaks and begins to decline. As the company perceives the decline in customer order rate, finished inventory is recognized as

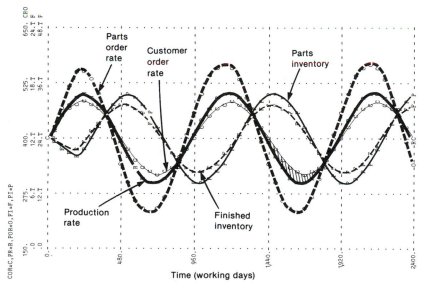

Figure 4.9   Inventory system response to CYCLICAL variation in customer order rate: aggressive policy set

above the declining goal. Consequently production rate is reduced below customer order rate in an effort to reduce finished inventory.

From day 1440 to day 1680 production rate leads customer order rate down as negative inventory correction orders cause production rate to fall faster than customer order rate. But at day 1,680 customer order rate bottoms and begins to increase. On detecting the change, production rate also reverses. Now finished inventory falls below goal, as production rate increases faster and leads customer order rate up. A similar set of relationships describes the behavior of parts order rate relative to production rate.

With the aggressive policy inventory is falling in downswings and rising in upswings. Inventory correction orders therefore contribute to instability and amplification.

Figure 4.10 shows the response of the inventory system to a CYCLICAL variation with the slow policy parameter set. While the amplification through the system has been reduced, fluctuations in parts inventory and finished inventory have increased. Business cycle changes are no longer short-term or temporary changes. Thus slow responses introduce a long lag between, for example, an increase in customer order rate and the corresponding increase in production rate.

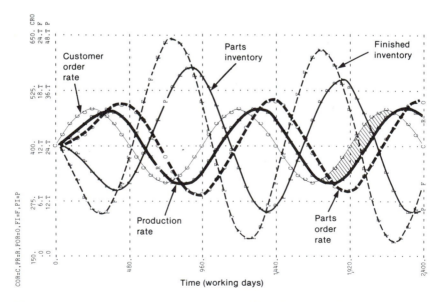

Figure 4.10 Inventory system response to CYCLICAL variation in customer order rate: slow policy set

A comparison of the hatched areas in figures 4.9 and 4.10 indicates that with the slower response customer order rate exceeds production rate by a greater amount and the phasing is different.

Again examining the cycle from day 1200 to day 2160, production rate is seen to lag rather than lead customer order rate. The long averaging time causes the average customer order rate component of production rate to lag and attenuate the variations in customer order rate; inventory goal therefore also lags. Moreover the long correction time reduces the magnitude of inventory correction orders. The net result is variations in production rate of the same magnitude as those of customer order rate but lagged by approximately 110 days.

With the slow policy inventory is falling in upturns and rising in downturns. Inventory correction orders therefore do not contribute to amplification.

Figure 4.11 plots three performance indexes for the CYCLICAL variation:

1. Amplification—the change in production rate from 400 units per day divided by the change for the 1,200/1,200 parameter set.
2. Inventory variation—the variation in finished inventory, about 12,000 units, divided by the variation for the 1,200/1,200 parameter set.
3. Composite index—an equal weighting of the amplification and inventory variation indexes.

A rather wide range of values is given for the policy parameters time to average customer order rate TACOR and time to correct finished inventory TCFI. The wide range is given to show the relatively small improvements or costs achieved after the 960/960 policy set.

Figure 4.11 indicates that the greatest deterioration in inventory performance occurs when the policy parameters are increased from 60/60 to 240/240. Past 240/240 relatively little increased variation occurs. The greatest improvement in amplification performance also occurs when policy parameters are increased from 60/60 to 240/240, but some improvement occurs past 1,200/1,200.

The composite index shows two relatively flat regions: from 60/60 to 240/240 and from 960/960 upward. In the first region improvements in amplification are offset by deterioration in inventory variation. Past 960/960 amplification improvements once more are offset by inventory deterioration. Again the policy designer has relatively flat regions from which to chose a policy. The exact weighting will determine which region dominates, but the policy designer can select a best policy.

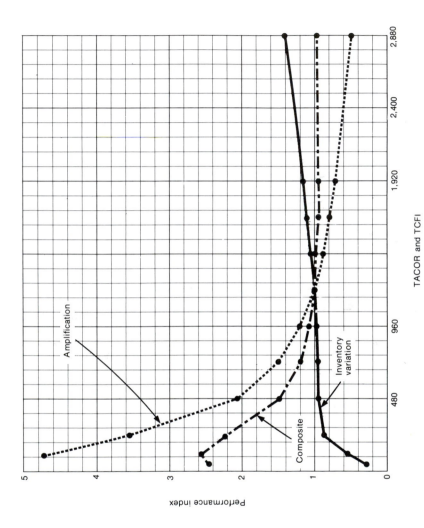

Figure 4.11   Performance indexes for CYCLICAL variation

Policy design guideline 4.4 A substantial trade-off between production stability and inventory fluctuations exists for CYCLICAL demand variations. Aggressive responses cause greater production instability but much lower inventory variations; slower responses yield more stable production but at the cost of substantial inventory variations. Nevertheless a good policy will surface when performance measures are developed, weighted, and plotted.

GROWTH

Companies experience underlying growth and decline trends on which the other variations are superimposed. In this book only growth trends are analyzed—decline trends are for the most part mirror images of the growth trends. A 10 percent per year compounded input is used to represent growth.

Figure 4.12 shows the response of the inventory system to a GROWTH trend on customer order rate with the moderate policy set. Initially production rate lags customer order rate, and parts order rate lags production rate so that finished inventory and parts inventory decline. When inventory falls low enough, inventory correction grows large enough to cause production rate to exceed customer order rate

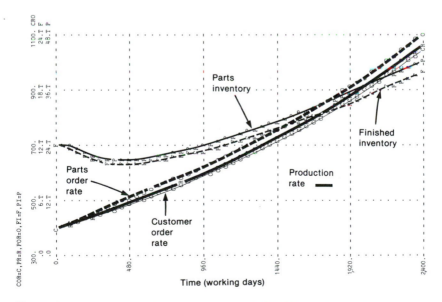

Figure 4.12 Inventory system response to a GROWTH trend in customer order rate: moderate policy set

(and parts order rate to exceed production rate). Thereafter inventory gradually rebuilds.

However, inventory never reaches its desired level. For example, at day 2400 finished inventory goal equals 30,000 units while finished inventory equals 20,000 units. A policy that responds to, rather than anticipates, changes guarantees such a steady-state inventory discrepancy: because average customer order rate always lags customer order rate, finished inventory correction must be positive; a positive inventory correction in turn requires a shortfall of inventory.

Only the degree of inventory shortage is affected by policy parameters. For example, figure 4.13 compares the behavior of finished inventory in response to growth under the three policy parameter sets. The slower the policy response, the greater the inventory discrepancy. Nevertheless, even the aggressive policy has some inventory discrepancy.

Policy design guideline 4.5 Policies that respond to, rather than anticipate, changing conditions will always result in a permanent inventory discrepancy in GROWTH or DECLINE—the slower the response, the greater the discrepancy.

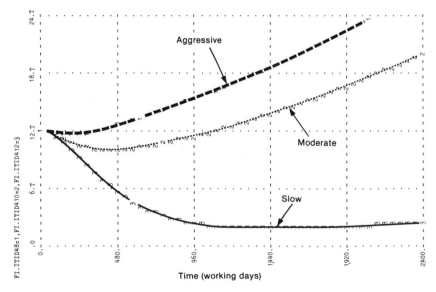

Figure 4.13 Comparison of finished inventory in response to GROWTH for the three policy sets

Summary

With the production rate and parts order rate policy structure developed thus far, a conflict between stability and response to growth exists. Aggressive responses, which give reasonable performance for GROWTH and avoid large inventory swings for CYCLICAL, also yield unacceptable variations in both production and inventory for NOISE. Slower-responding policies, while exhibiting good performance for short-term, temporary changes, fail to respond adequately to the long-term changes represented by CYCLICAL variations and GROWTH.

The policy designer faced with such a trade-off has two recourses: design a different policy that improves the trade-off (in chapter 5 a forecasting policy is developed that improves the trade-off), or develop a composite performance index that weights the relevant performance indexes for the range of disturbances experienced by the company. One useful procedure is to assemble one composite test input that captures the range of disturbances. The performance of different policy parameters is determined and plotted for the composite input. Such a plot should reveal the range of good policy choices.

As a final note the policy designer should consider more than just financial data in evaluating performance because in some cases quantitative measures do not capture everything important to the company. For example, employment stability may be valued for social reasons independent of cost savings. Moreover quantitative measures fail to give a complete picture of a variable. For example, the best policy in terms of profits may also produce periods of severe cash shortage. Given the uncertainty in any model and its inputs, the company may feel safer with a less profitable policy that yields no cash shortages. By providing a time history of system performance, a system dynamics model allows the company to consider qualitative as well as quantitative measures.

4.6 Summary

Multistage inventory systems, the building blocks of most industry and company structures, exhibit strong tendencies toward amplification and instability. Elements of structure and policies that cause the tendency are (1) the delay between changes in inventory outflow rate and inflow rate (for example, an increase in outflow rate depletes inventory because inflow rate lags the increase; then inflow rate must increase above outflow rate to rebuild inventory); (2) the policy of basing inventory goals on volume of business; and (3) increments at each successive stage in the system, where orders from a preceding stage become the base volume of business and amplify an order stream that contains inventory correction orders. Management policies influence system performance through aggressive responses to changes in business volume and to inventory discrepancies. Policy guidelines 4.1 and 4.2 summarize policy trade-offs and procedures.

The best policy depends on the exogenous disturbances the company might experience, as summarized by guidelines 4.3 through 4.5. These three policy guidelines point out trade-offs and changes in performance elements that depend on the disturbance. In selecting the best policy, the analyst must weigh trade-offs and either (1) design a policy to improve the trade-off or (2) develop a composite performance index for a representative composite disturbance.

References

Forrester, Jay W. 1958. Industrial Dynamics: A Major Breakthrough for Decision-Makers. *Harvard Business Review*. 36: 37–66. Reprinted in *Managerial Applications of System Dynamics*. Edited by Edward B. Roberts. Cambridge, Mass.: Wright-Allen Press, 1977.

Forrester, Jay W. 1959. Advertising: A Problem in Industrial Dynamics. *Harvard Business Review*. 37: 100–110. Reprinted in *Managerial Applications of System Dynamics*. Edited by Edward B. Roberts. Cambridge, Mass.: Wright-Allen Press, 1977.

Forrester, Jay W. 1961. *Industrial Dynamics*. Cambridge, Mass.: The MIT Press.

Lyneis, James M. 1977. Setting Aggregate Production and Parts-Ordering Rates: A Policy Design Framework. System dynamics group memorandum D-2696. Massachusetts Institute of Technology, Cambridge, Mass.

5.1 Types of Forecasts

Chapter 4 identified two behavior problems of a policy based on averages concerning trade-offs between permanent and temporary changes and lags in production's response to changes. How might forecasting resolve these two problems?

A forecast is an assumption about the future, based on current and past information. In an average-based policy the forecast is the current average of past conditions. But more information is available from past conditions than the current average. For example, if customer order rate has been growing over the past several years, the forecast might incorporate this information. Although average customer order rate lags growth in customer order rate, forecast customer order rate need not once growth is recognized. Therefore the policy designed should respond slowly to short-term changes but also anticipate long-term changes once recognized.

Information about regular cyclical patterns is also contained in historical data. Many products are subject to strong seasonal variations in sales. By anticipating or forecasting these variations, and increasing production in advance of them, production will more nearly match shipments so that inventory will fluctuate little.

A forecast then is one type of information input to decision making. It should be evaluated like any other possible information input:

1. How does the use of the forecast affect corporate behavior?
2. Can the benefits of the forecast be obtained by other means at less cost?
3. What type of forecast should be used?
4. What are the consequences of using inaccurate forecasts?

The first three points stress that the value of a forecast (or any other information source) rests not so much on its accuracy but on the quality of decisions made. Simulation provides a means of investigating the consequences of alternative information sources. The fourth point emphasizes that policy design should consider the consequences of other than the most likely forecast. The system dynamics approach is one of designing robust policies rather than making optimal decisions based on an assumed forecast.

A wide range of forecasting techniques exist—from management intuition and gut feeling to sophisticated econometric and time-series models. For the purpose of understanding the effect of forecasts on corporate behavior, the techniques can be classified into two categories:

1. Extrapolative forecasts—forecasts that rely on corporate time-series data (some subjective forecasts of managers, exponential growth trends, moving averages, exponential smoothing and extrapolation, and time-series analysis fall into this category).
2. Exogenous forecasts—forecasts that rely on variables external to the company (other subjective forecasts of managers, market research, and forecasts from econometric models fall into this category).

Extrapolative forecasts exist within the feedback loops of the company: company data are used to generate a forecast which in turn is used to make decisions that affect future company data. The extrapolative forecasting process is built into the model. The model can be used to determine the effect of different forecasting techniques or parameters on company behavior. Moreover, because extrapolative techniques are generally much cheaper than exogenous forecasts, the model might be used to design a policy based on some extrapolative forecasting technique that performs as well as an exogenous forecast.

For exogenous forecasts, all or part of the forecast is based on data external to the company (for example, Gross National Product estimates). The external data can be treated as outside the boundary of the model. The forecast is input to the model, and the model is used to answer such questions as, What is the value of a perfect forecast? How should the company use the forecast? How should the company handle forecast inaccuracies? But to the extent that company data is also used to generate the forecast, that data should be a part of the feedback structure of the model.

Extrapolative forecasts are probably the most common type in use today. As Forrester (1961, p. 33) states:

Most attempts at forecasting turn out to be heavily dependent on extrapolation into the future of the course of events in the rather recent past. Many other factors presumably go into forecasts, but usually these other factors do not carry enough weight to override extrapolation as the major forecasting component. Sales departments see orders increasing and estimate still greater rises to encourage the production department to meet any possible future demands. Delivery delays are increasing so that we accelerate ordering in anticipation of still tighter delivery. Prices are falling so that orders are cut back in the hope of still lower future prices.

Extrapolative forecasts are the easiest and cheapest to generate. Consequently, if company performance can be improved by using the most common, easiest, and cheapest forecast, the greater the ease in implementing policy change.

Nevertheless, the search for better forecasts of the external factors affecting a company has led to the development of many sophisticated forecasting techniques. Little research has been devoted, however, to evaluating the benefits of using the forecasts produced by these techniques. Section 5.4 presents a framework for such an evaluation.

5.2 Policy Design for Improving Response to Growth

One of the problems of the average-based policy identified in chapter 4 was that inventory levels remain well below their goals when customer order rate grows continuously, as illustrated in figure 5.1.

Figure 5.1 gives the response of the inventory system with the moderate policy parameter set to GROWTH in customer order rate. Initially both finished and parts inventories equal their respective goals, and customer order, production, parts arrival, and parts order rates all equal 400 units per day.

At day zero customer order rate begins to grow at 10 percent per year compounded growth rate. Because of the delays introduced by averaging information, completing production, and receiving parts, production completions (not shown) lag customer order rate, and parts arrival rate (not shown) lags production rate; thus finished and parts inventories fall. The inventories fall until day 480 and then grow only slowly, never reaching their respective goals. At day 2400 finished inventory equals 20,000 units while finished inventory goal equals

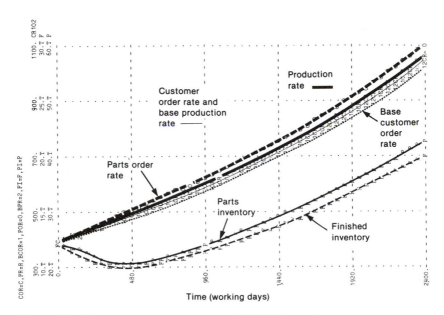

Figure 5.1 Inventory system response to GROWTH trend in customer order rate: moderate policy set

30,000 units, and parts inventory equals 43,000 units while parts inventory goal equals 63,000 units.

Inventories behave in such a manner because base customer order and base production rate equal average customer order and average production rate. As shown in figure 5.1, averages always lag the unaveraged value when that value grows. As a result, when customer order rate grows, finished inventory falls below its goal until the finished inventory correction term exceeds the difference between customer order and production rates. Figure 5.2 helps explain the behavior.

Ignoring work in process, figure 5.2a shows customer order rate COR depletes finished inventory FI while production rate PR builds it. Equations for an average-based policy are given in figure 5.2b: production rate PR equals average customer order rate ACOR plus finished inventory correction FIC. Figure 5.2c shows the base customer order rate, here average customer order rate, lags customer order rate COR when COR grows. Thus finished inventory falls until FIC equals the difference between COR and ACOR. Thereafter, because finished inventory goal increases with ACOR, FI also increases. But a finished inventory discrepancy must persist. A better policy would allow

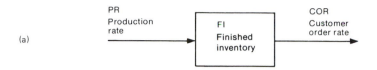

(a)

$$PR.K = ACOR.K + FIC.K$$

PR   -Production rate (units/day)
ACOR-Average customer order
          rate (units/day)
FIC   -Finished inventory
          correction (units/day)

(b)

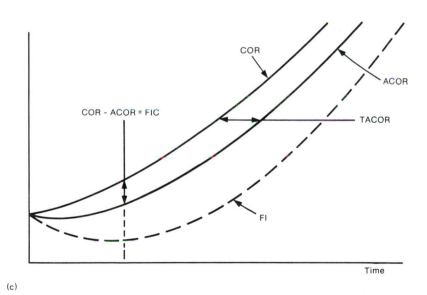

(c)

Figure 5.2   Structure causing inventory discrepancy

production rate to equal customer order rate without an inventory discrepancy.

Structure of Extrapolative Forecasts

As illustrated in figure 5.3, the average value of a variable (here average customer order rate ACOR) lags the trend growth in that variable by the averaging time (here time to average customer order rate TACOR). A long averaging time, which might be necessary to smooth short-term variations, causes the average value to lag well behind the true trend growth in the value. But if the true trend is recovered and used in place of average customer order rate in the production rate policy, production rate will equal the trend growth without inventory discrepancy.

Figure 5.4 demonstrates how this recovery is accomplished. At time t_1, average customer order rate equals $ACOR(t_1)$, while the trend growth in customer order rate is denoted $TGCOR(t_1)$. At time t_2 average customer order rate $ACOR(t_2)$ will equal $TGCOR(t_1)$. Consequently trend growth can be recovered by adding to $ACOR(t_1)$ time to average customer order rate TACOR multiplied by the slope of average customer order rate. The slope of average customer order rate

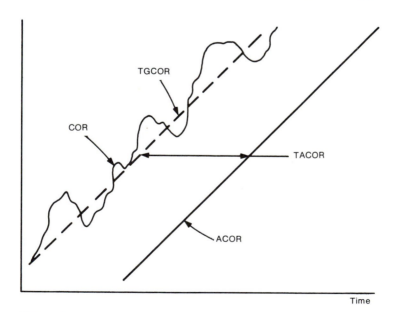

Figure 5.3 Lag created by averaging

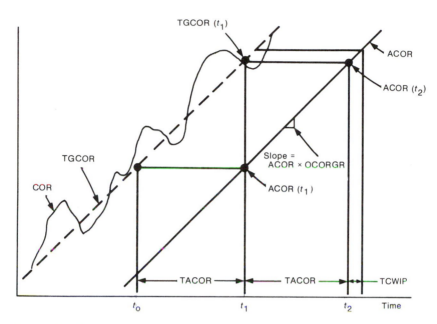

Figure 5.4 Trend extrapolation process

equals average customer order rate multiplied by observed customer order rate growth rate OCORGR.

A second objective of trend extrapolation might be to anticipate the trend growth in customer order far enough in advance for production to adapt to it. Here the company might anticipate customer orders 20 days ahead (the time to complete work in process). To accomplish this, the forecasting time is extended to equal TACOR plus TCWIP.

Figure 5.5 gives a flow diagram of an inventory system that incorporates trend forecasting in determining production and parts order rates. The revised equation 8 states that production rate PR equals the sum of base customer order rate BCOR, finished inventory correction FIC, and work in process correction WIPC.

$$PR.KL = BCOR.K + FIC.K + WIPC.K \qquad 8, R$$

where

PR   = production rate (units/day)
BCOR = base customer order rate (units/day)
FIC   = finished inventory correction (units/day)
WIPC = work in process correction (units/day).

Base customer order rate BCOR calculated in equation 9 incorpo-

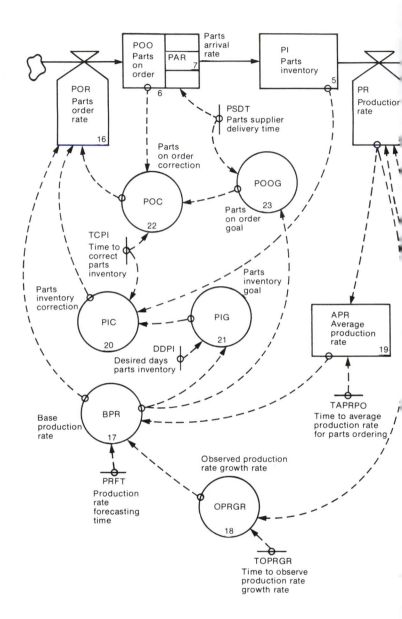

Figure 5.5 Structure of inventory system with trend forecasting

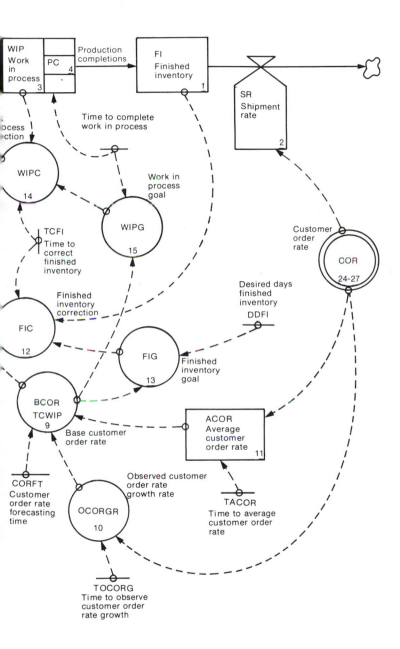

rates trend extrapolation. BCOR equals 1.0 plus customer order rate forecasting time CORFT multiplied by observed customer order rate growth rate OCORGR, all multiplied by average customer order rate ACOR. Customer order rate forecasting time CORFT is set to the sum of time to average customer order rate TACOR and time to complete work in process TCWIP.

$$\text{BCOR.K} = (1 + \text{CORFT} * \text{OCORGR.K}) * \text{ACOR.K} \qquad 9, \text{A}$$
$$\text{CORFT} = \text{TACOR} + \text{TCWIP} \qquad\qquad\qquad 9.1, \text{N}$$

where
BCOR   = base customer order rate (units/day)
CORFT   = customer order rate forecasting time (days)
OCORGR = observed customer order rate growth rate (percent/day)
ACOR   = average customer order rate (units/day)
TACOR   = time to average customer order rate (days)
TCWIP   = time to complete work in process (days).

Observed customer order rate growth rate is calculated by a user-defined function, or macro, called TRND (equation 10). The inputs to this macro are customer order rate COR, time to observe customer order rate growth TOCORG, and initial customer order rate growth rate ICORGR. The macro outputs the percent per day growth rate in customer order rate observed over TOCORG. Equations for the TRND macro are given in appendix 5.1.

$$\text{OCORGR.K} = \text{TRND(COR.K,TOCORG, ICORGR)} \qquad 10, \text{A}$$
$$\text{TOCORG} = 50000 \qquad\qquad\qquad\qquad\qquad\qquad 10.1, \text{C}$$
$$\text{ICORGR} = 0 \qquad\qquad\qquad\qquad\qquad\qquad\qquad 10.2, \text{C}$$

where
OCORGR = observed customer order rate growth rate (percent/day)
TRND   = macro for detecting trends in input time series
                  (percent/day)
COR   = customer order rate (units/day)
TOCORG = time to observe customer order rate growth (days)
ICORGR = initial customer order rate growth rate (percent/day).

Equations 11 and 12 for average customer order rate and finished inventory correction are identical to those developed in chapter 4.

$$\text{ACOR.K} = \text{SMOOTH(COR.K,TACOR)} \qquad 11, \text{A}$$
$$\text{TACOR} = 60 \qquad\qquad\qquad\qquad\qquad\qquad 11.1, \text{C}$$

where
ACOR   = average customer order rate (units/day)
COR   = customer order rate (units/day)
TACOR = time to average customer order rate (days);

FIC.K = (FIG.K − FI.K)/TCFI   12, A
TCFI = 240   12.1, C

where
FIC = finished inventory correction (units/day)
FIG = finished inventory goal (units)
FI   = finished product inventory (units)
TCFI = time to correct finished inventory (days).

In equation 13 finished inventory goal FIG is now calculated as de-sired days finished inventory DDFI multiplied by base customer order rate BCOR. The company desires inventory for the base volume of business, as given by the recovered trend BCOR.

FIG.K = DDFI * BCOR.K   13, A
DDFI = 30   13.1, C

where
FIG   = finished inventory goal (units)
DDFI = desired days finished inventory (days)
BCOR = base customer order rate (units/day).

Similarly, while equation 14 for work in process correction remains unchanged, equation 15 for work in process goal incorporates base customer order rate.

WIPC.K = (WIPG.K − WIP.K)/TCFI   14, A

where
WIPC = work in process correction (units/day)
WIPG = work in process goal (units)
WIP = work in process (units)
TCFI = time to correct finished inventory (days);

WIPG.K = TCWIP * BCOR.K   15, A

where
WIPG = work in process goal (units)
TCWIP = time to complete work in process (days)
BCOR = base customer order rate (units/day).

The parts order rate policy is also changed to incorporate trend extrapolation, as given in equations 16 through 23.

POR.KL = BPR.K + PIC.K + POC.K   16, R

where
POR = parts order rate (units/day)
BPR = base production rate (units/day)
PIC = parts inventory correction (units/day)
POC = parts on order correction (units/day);

BPR.K = (1 + PRFT * OPRGR.K) * APR.K   17, A
PRFT = TAPRPO + PSDT   17.1, N

where
BPR   = base production rate (units/day)
PRFT   = production rate forecasting time (days)
OPRGR   = observed production rate growth rate (percent/day)
APR   = average production rate (units/day)
TAPRPO = time to average production rate for parts ordering (days)
PSDT   = parts supplier delivery time (days);

OPRGR.K = TRND(PR.JK,TOPRGR,IPRGR)   18, A
TOPRGR = 50000   18.1, C
IPRGR = 0   18.2, C

where
OPRGR   = observed production rate growth rate (percent/day)
TRND   = macro for detecting trends in input time series
                 (percent/day)
PR   = production rate (units/day)
TOPRGR = time to observe production rate growth rate (days)
IPRGR   = initial production rate growth rate (percent/day);

APR.K = SMOOTH(PR.JK,TAPRPO)   19, A
TAPRPO = 60   19.1, C

where
APR   = average production rate (units/day)
PR   = production rate (units/day)
TAPRPO = time to average production rate for parts ordering
                 (days);

PIC.K = (PIG.K − PI.K)/TCPI   20, A
TCPI = 240   20.1, C

where
PIC = parts inventory correction (units/day)
PIG = parts inventory goal (units)
PI   = parts inventory (units)
TCPI = time to correct parts inventory (days);

$$PIG.K = DDPI * BPR.K \qquad\qquad 21, A$$
$$DDPI = 60 \qquad\qquad 21.1, C$$

where
PIG = parts inventory goal (units)
DDPI = desired days parts inventory (days)
BPR = base production rate (units/day);

$$POC.K = (POOG.K - POO.K)/TCPI \qquad\qquad 22, A$$

where
POC = parts on order correction (units/day)
POOG = parts on order goal (units)
POO = parts on order (units)
TCPI = time to correct parts inventory (days);

$$POOG.K = PSDT * BPR.K \qquad\qquad 23, A$$

where
POOG = parts on order goal (units)
PSDT = parts supplier delivery time (days)
BPR = base production rate (units/day).

Performance of New Policy

Figure 5.6 shows that a policy based on trend extrapolation is capable of adequately responding to growth in customer order rate. In the figure time to observe both customer order rate and production growth rate equals 240 days. Thus base production rate does not exceed production rate until approximately one year later, and base customer order rate does not exceed customer order rate for one year. As a result both finished and parts inventories initially decline. After one year, however, base production rate leads production rate as the trend-forecasting procedure anticipates future values of production rate. The situation is similar for customer order rate. Finished and parts inventories increase and nearly equal their desired value by day 2400.

Figure 5.7 compares parts inventory from several simulations with different values for time to observe production rate growth rate

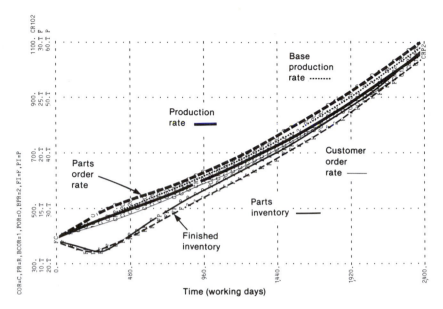

Figure 5.6 Inventory system response to GROWTH trend in customer rate with trend extrapolation, time to observe growth rates equal to 240 days

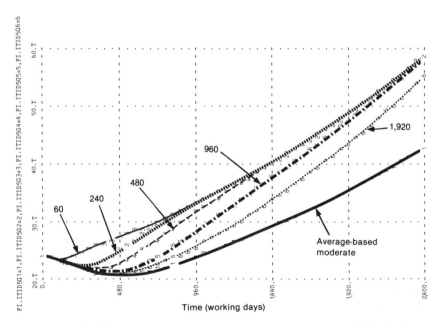

Figure 5.7 Comparison of parts inventory behavior in response to GROWTH trend in customer order

TOPRGR (and time to observe customer order rate growth). The longer the TOPRGR, the greater the initial drop in parts inventory and the longer the span before parts inventory increases to its desired value (as indicated by the TOPRGR = 60 curve). Similar behavior is observed for finished inventory. Depending on the cost of such inventory shortages, the company might select a value of 60, 240, 480, or 960 as an adequate response to growth.

5.3 Testing Response of Policy to Other Inputs

While trend extrapolation improves system performance for GROWTH in customer order rate, the policy designer must check that the policy does not worsen performance for other customer order rate patterns. Policy response to STEP, NOISE, and CYCLICAL patterns is examined.

Response to STEP

Figure 5.8 serves as a basis for comparing STEP changes. Given in the figure is the response of the inventory system to a STEP change in

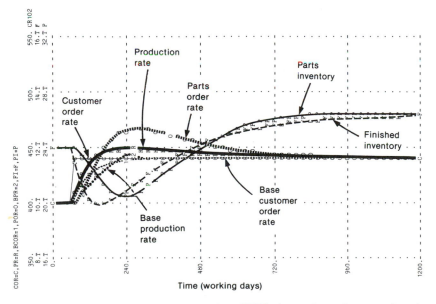

Figure 5.8 Inventory system response to a STEP change in customer order rate: moderate policy set and no forecasting

customer order rate with the moderate policy set and no forecasting. Note that (1) a 10 percent increase in customer order rate causes a 12.5 percent increase in production rate and an 18 percent increase in parts order rate (amplification) and (2) finished and parts inventories do not rise to their desired values until day 720. These elements of behavior were discussed in chapter 4.

Figure 5.9 gives the response of the inventory system to a STEP change in customer order rate using the moderate policy set and trend extrapolation, with time to observe trends equal to 240 days. The behavior is similar to that of the average-based policy in that production completions and parts arrivals lag sudden, unanticipated changes. Thus inventories decline. But the behavior differs from that of the average-based policy in three respects:

1. Amplification is increased.
2. Inventory does not fall as far and rises to goal sooner.
3. Inventory overshoots.

The cause of the greater amplification and inventory overshoot lies in the behaviors of base customer order rate and base production rate. In

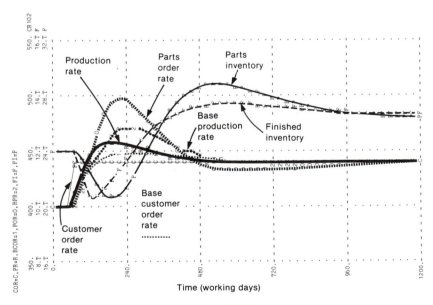

Figure 5.9 Inventory system response to STEP change in customer order rate: moderate policy and trend extrapolation, time to observe trends equal to 240

contrast to the average-based policy, these bases overshoot customer order rate.

The cause of overshoot in base customer order rate, for example, is that the trend extrapolation policy perceives a growth in customer order rate and extrapolates average customer order rate by the growth rate to arrive at an anticipated future customer order rate. Since the growth in customer order rate is temporary, it is not detected by the trend extrapolation process for nearly a year after the STEP change. After that year the trend forecast anticipates further increases in customer order rate, although at a declining rate.

Because base customer order rate overshoots its final value, the company orders finished inventory for a higher volume of business. When base customer order rate decreases, the excess inventory must be eliminated by ordering less than that produced.

Figure 5.10 compares the performances of the production segment of the inventory system for average-based and extrapolation policies. Extrapolation appears to improve performance: the increase in amplification is small, while finished inventory does not fall as low and is rebuilt more quickly.

Figure 5.11 compares the performance of the parts segment of the

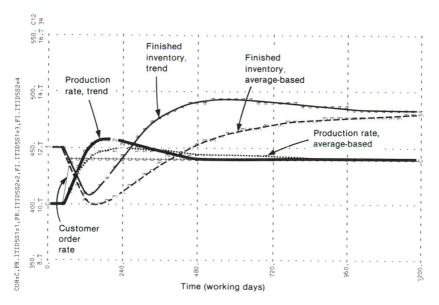

Figure 5.10   Comparison of relative performance of production part of inventory system

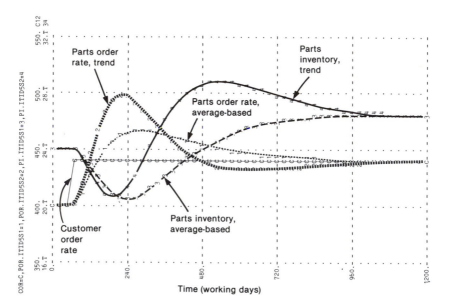

Figure 5.11   Comparison of relative performance of parts portion of inventory system

inventory system. The overall behavior is similar to that of production, but the amplification and inventory overshoot are greater. The reasons for the greater amplification and overshoot are twofold:

1. The extrapolation is for 60 days (the parts supplier delivery time) rather than 20 days (the time to complete work in process). The observed growth rate is therefore multiplied by 60 rather than 20 to give the base.

2. The input amplified has already been amplified by the forecasting of the production segment.

Therefore, while the first stage of the system benefits from forecasting, performance is worse for latter stages. Moreover the longer the physical delay, the worse the performance.

The decline in performance for temporary changes in growth rate can be avoided by choosing a long time to observe trends. Figure 5.12 shows that, as the observation time increases, amplification is reduced. The longer the time to observe growth rate, the less the impact of such temporary changes as a STEP input. When viewed over, say, a 960-day period, a sudden increase is given little weight.

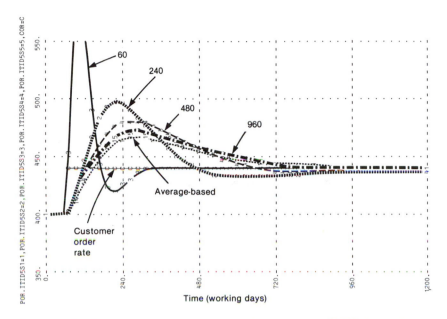

Figure 5.12 Comparison of parts order rate in response to STEP change in customer order rate with different time to observe trends

In summary trend extrapolation introduces an additional source of amplification to the inventory system. The amplification increases with

1. shorter trend observation times,
2. longer extrapolation times,
3. the latter stages in the system.

The benefits of trend extrapolation for a GROWTH input can still be achieved, however, without substantial deterioration in performance for temporary changes in growth rate if the trend observation times are greater than 480 days.

Response to NOISE

The amplifying characteristics of the STEP response generally foretell the amplifying characteristics of the NOISE response, since NOISE is similar to a STEP series of differing magnitude and duration. Such is the case here.

Figures 5.13 and 5.14 compare the behaviors of production and parts order rates, respectively, in response to a NOISE variation in customer order rate for different time to observe growth trends. As for STEP,

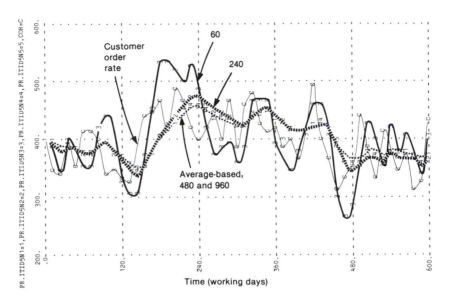

Figure 5.13   Comparison of production rate in response to NOISE variation in customer order rate for different time to observe trend values

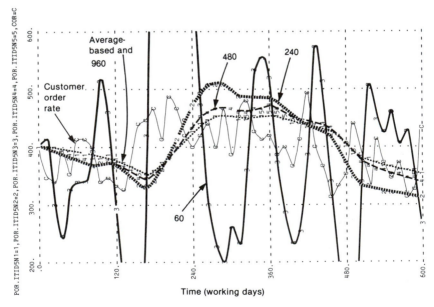

Figure 5.14   Comparison of parts order rate in response to NOISE variation in customer order rate for different time to observe trend values

amplification increases the shorter the observation time. Amplification is also greater for the parts stage because it has a longer forecasting time and is amplifying an already amplified disturbance. Computer runs not given here show that inventory also varies more with shorter observation times, which was the case for the STEP response.

The same policy guidelines emerging from the STEP response apply for the NOISE response: time to observe growth trends greater than 480 days are sufficiently long that temporary changes in growth rate are not acted on.

Response to CYCLICAL

A four-year cyclical variation in production rate produces two-year growth and decline trends. In responding to such trends, average-based policies result in significant inventory variations: in the upswing delays introduced by averaging and delays in physical flow channels cause inventory to fall; in the downswing the delays cause inventory to rise. Figure 5.15 illustrates these variations in the inventory system response to a CYCLICAL variation in customer order rate for the moderate policy parameter set. Since forecasting reduced the magnitude

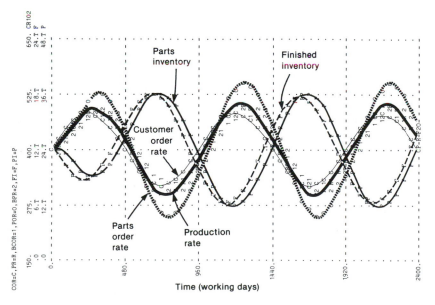

Figure 5.15 Inventory system response to a CYCLICAL variation in customer order rate: moderate policy set

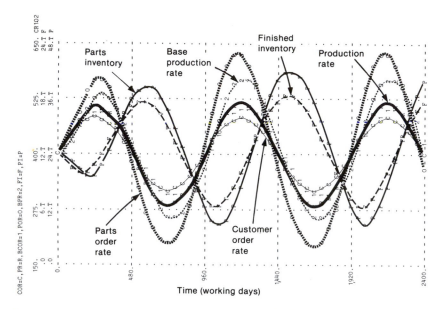

Figure 5.16 Response of inventory system to CYCLICAL variation in customer order rate: trend extrapolation, time to observe trends equal to 240

and duration of inventory shortfall for the GROWTH input, it might also reduce the inventory variation for the CYCLICAL input.

Figure 5.16 shows the response of the trend extrapolation policy to a CYCLICAL variation in customer order rate, with trend observation times equal to 240 days. Contrary to initial expectations, production rate, parts order rate, finished inventory, and parts inventory exhibit greater variations. The cause of this unexpected behavior lies in the length of time to observe growth rate relative to the length of the growth and decline trends.

Each growth and decline trend lasts 480 days. It takes 240 days to fully perceive these trends. Thus the full growth rate is not perceived until half way up (or down) the cycle. Note in figure 5.16 base production rate does not lead production rate until more than half way up (or down) the cycle. But just as the growth or decline trend is fully perceived, production rate begins to grow (or decline) more slowly. Because base production rate is following a faster trend, it overshoots (or undershoots). Parts order rate, which responds directly to base production rate, also overshoots and undershoots so that inventory exhibits greater variation.

Figures 5.17 and 5.18 demonstrate the effect of trend observation

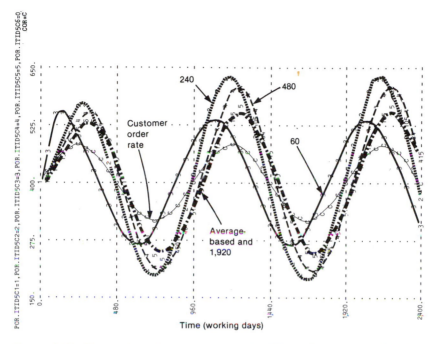

Figure 5.17 Comparison of parts order rate for different trend observation times

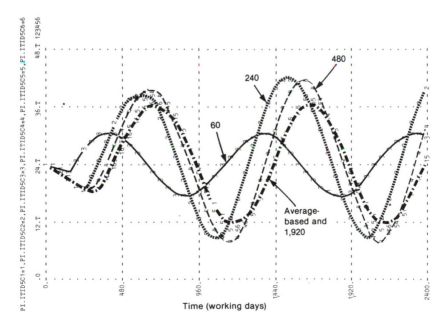

Figure 5.18 Comparison of parts inventory for different trend observation times

time on stability. Figure 5.17 compares parts order rate for different observation times, while figure 5.18 compares parts inventory. A short, 60-day observation time quickly detects growth and decline trends. Consequently parts order rate leads customer order rate through most of the upswing and downswing. Parts inventory therefore varies relatively little. Trend observation times 960 days or greater effectively filter the 480-day growth and decline trends so that the extrapolation policy produces a response nearly identical to the average-based policy. Trend observation times between 60 and 960 days cause greater instability in both parts order rate and parts inventory, for reasons already described. As a result only very short observation times improve performance for the CYCLICAL input.

Policy Guideline

With a proper selection of parameters, trend extrapolation forecasts can improve the trade-off between responses to growth and shorter-term changes. Nevertheless, some trade-off remains:

1. Response to GROWTH is improved with any trend observation time, but times between 240 and 960 days cause inventory to bottom and grow within 480 days after the change in growth rate.
2. Response to STEP and NOISE is worsened because trend forecasting is an additional source of amplification, but the increased amplification is minimal for observation times greater than 480 days.
3. Response to CYCLICAL is improved only for short (60-day) observation times, worsened for observation times between 240 and 480 days (or one-quarter to one-half the period of the cyclical variation), and unchanged for 960-day or greater observation times.

Therefore the following policy guideline emerges:

Policy design guideline 5.1 Given that a company experiences STEP, NOISE, CYCLICAL, and GROWTH variations in demand, response to GROWTH is improved without worsening performance for the shorter variations only if the trend observation time is greater than 480 days.

If a company does not experience the full range of demand variations, or if, for example, the costs of instability are far less than the costs of running short of inventory, then a company may choose a trend observation time other than that greater than 480 days.

The policy parameter sets used in this text are expanded to include

Table 5.1
Policy parameter sets including trend-forecasting parameter

	TACOR	TCFI	TOCORG	TAPRPO	TCPI	TOPRGR
Aggressive	60	60	240	60	60	240
Moderate	60	240	480	60	240	480
Slow	240	240	960	240	240	960

trend forecasting, as given in table 5.1. The aggressive set, representative of a company where instability is less costly than inventory, incorporates a 240-day trend observation time. The moderate set, representative of a company where stability and inventory are equally costly, incorporates a 480-day observation time. The slow policy set, representative of a company where inventory is less costly than instability, incorporates a 960-day trend observation time.

5.4 Using Exogenous Forecasts in Policy Design

Many managers assume that an accurate forecast will automatically improve decision making. The potential use of exogenous forecasts raises at least three issues that must be resolved by the company: Given an accurate forecast, how should it be used? How should forecasting inaccuracies be handled, for example, with inventory or adaptive policies? Might the same results be obtained with other forecasting methods at lower cost? To answer these questions, the company must evaluate the dynamic consequences of using a forecast and compare them with the consequences of policies using other types of forecasts. These questions should be considered before money is spent developing a forecast.

The first step in evaluating an exogenous forecast is to determine the best way to use the information, assuming it is accurate. For example, the company might have an accurate forecast of seasonal variations in business. Given the forecast, should the company change production to match the changes in business, or keep production constant and let inventory absorb differences between shipments and production? Moreover how quickly should inventory discrepancies be corrected? Once the best use of an accurate forecast is determined, the company has a performance measure against which the costs of obtaining the forecast can be compared.

Unfortunately an accurate forecast is valid only over a very short time span, if at all. To believe in the existence of an accurate forecast is to believe that a company has no control over its customer order rate. This is true only in the immediate, short time frame where past actions completely determine the future. In a longer time frame customer order rate can be changed by company and competitor actions. An accurate forecast is achievable only if the company can completely specify its own and competitor actions, as well as their consequences—not to mention external factors such as business and seasonal cycles, population trends, and so on. Any actions the company or competitor take will alter a forecast.

As a result successful companies will be those that design policies to maintain superior competitive positions, which take into account future uncertain events. The logical next step in evaluating the use of exogenous forecasts is to determine the most effective means of handling inaccuracy. Does the company hold sufficient inventories to absorb possible errors, or does it adapt in some way to discrepancies between forecast and actual performance? The answer of course depends on the severity and nature of forecasting errors, the costs of inventory, and the dynamic consequences of different adaptive policies. But performing this evaluation not only prepares the company for the consequences of forecast inaccuracies but also gives an estimate of the likely corporate performance using the forecast.

Except for perhaps the seasonal forecast most other exogenous forecasts are difficult and costly to develop. Consequently, in designing policies, a company should always assess whether results equivalent to those obtainable with an accurate forecast might not be achieved with some other policy. The policy might use, for example, a cheaper forecast coupled with a different inventory policy.

The final step in evaluating the use of exogenous forecasts is to determine corporate performance using other forecasting methods, such as trend extrapolation, and other policies, such as holding more inventory. Any performance improvement from using the accurate or inaccurate exogenous forecast tells the company the value of having the forecast. If the cost of generating the exogenous forecast is greater than its value, clearly the company is better off with a cheaper policy.

Reference

Forrester, Jay W. 1961. *Industrial Dynamics*. Cambridge, Mass.: The MIT Press.

Appendix 5.1: Equations for TRND Macro

The calculation of a trend is determined within the TRND macro given by equations .1, 1, 2, and 3. The trend TRND is computed as the difference between two averages of the input variables, $AIN1 and $AIN2, divided by the second average, and multiplied by the time to average the second input $TASI. $AIN1 removes short-term variations from the input time series. Variations shorter than 40 percent of time to observe trend are effectively filtered. $AIN2 establishes a reference condition against which $AIN1 is compared to calculate the trend.

MACRO TRND(INPUT,TOTRND,ITRND)   .1

where

TRND   = macro for detecting trends in input time series
                 (percent/day)
INPUT   = input to trend detection macro (units)
TOTRND = time to observe trend in trend detection macro (days)
ITRND   = initial trend in input data to trend detection macro
                 (percent/day);

TRND.K = ($AIN1.K − $AIN2.K)/($AIN2.K * $TASI)   1, A

where

TRND = macro for detecting trends in input time series
               (percent/day)
$AIN1 = average input one in trend macro (units)
$AIN2 = average input two in trend macro (units)
$TASI = time to average second input in trend macro (days);

$AIN1.K = $AIN1.J + (DT/$TSI)(INPUT.J − $AIN1.J)   2, L
$AIN1 = INPUT/(1 + $TSI * ITRND)   2.1, N
$TSI = .4 * TOTRND   2.2, N

where

$AIN1   = average input one in trend macro (units)
DT   = delta time, simulation solution interval (days)
$TSI   = time to smooth input in trend macro (days)
INPUT   = input to trend detection macro (units)
ITRND   = initial trend in input data to trend detection macro
                 (percent/day)
TOTRND = time to observe trend in trend detection macro (days);

$AIN2.K = $AIN2.J + (DT/$TASI)($AIN1.J − $AIN2.J)   3, L

$AIN2 = $AIN1/(1 + $TASI * ITRND)   3.1, N

$TASI = TOTRND − $TSI   3.2, N

where

$AIN2	= average input two in trend macro (units)
DT	= delta time, simulation solution interval (days)
$TASI	= time to average second input in trend macro (days)
$AIN1	= average input one in trend macro (units)
ITRND	= initial trend in input data to trend detection macro (percent/day)
TOTRND	= time to observe trend in trend detection macro (days)
$TSI	= time to smooth input in trend macro (days).

MEND

Dynamics Created by Interactions with Company Suppliers

6

6.1 Product Shortages and Increased Instability

In conjunction with boom-and-bust cycles companies in multistage, production-distribution systems experience alternating periods of product shortages and excesses. As demonstrated in chapter 4, the boom-and-bust cycles themselves cause, and are in part caused by, variations in product inventory which create the shortages and excesses. Two additional factors, however, intensify the shortages and excesses and in the process increase the amplification inherent in the multistage system.

The first of these factors is internal to the company: decreases in parts inventory on the upswing of a cycle constrain production rate so that finished inventory falls lower than it otherwise would; thus the company experiences greater shortages of finished product. Then, because inventory falls lower, production rate must rise higher than customer order rate, increasing system amplification.

Both product shortages and increased amplification are costly to the company. Shortages of parts inventory can cause manufacturing inefficiencies, resulting in higher production costs. Shortages of finished inventory limit sales in the short run and can cause loss of market share in the long run if customers switch to more reliable suppliers. Greater amplification increases costs by lowering manufacturing efficiency (through use of overtime or training people for new jobs) and increasing labor turnover.

A second factor intensifying product shortages and system amplification is in part external to the company: an increase in parts order rate of the company exceeds supplier capacity, thereby increasing parts supplier delivery time. The increase in delivery time causes parts inventory to fall lower than it otherwise would. The larger drop in parts inventory has two effects: it constrains production rate, lowering finished inventory more than it otherwise would, and it necessitates an even larger increase in parts order rate. Both act to increase system amplification, product shortages, and costs.

The following sections highlight the importance of examining possible feedback interactions between the company and its environment. Such feedback can have an important effect on company behavior and on policies to improve that behavior.

Companies also often experience exogenous disturbances or shocks imposed by elements of the environment. The variations in customer order rate examined in chapters 4 and 5 represent one such external disturbance. Another example, exogenous changes in supplier delivery time, is examined in section 6.8. How should the company cope with these changes? They cause a company's parts inventory to fluctuate more than with a fixed supplier delivery time. Should the company act quickly or slowly in correcting inventory fluctuations? Should the company develop an information system that rapidly tracks variations in supplier lead times and then act on these variations?

A system dynamics model allows the company to design policies capable of coping with, or even exploiting, a wide range of exogenous shocks and disturbances. Such an analysis should be an important component of company-planning studies.

6.2 Company Structure Creating Product Shortages

Figure 6.1 shows the company structure creating product shortages. The structure is identical to that examined in chapter 5, except that production rate is now influenced by effect of parts inventory level on production rate. As production rate depletes parts inventory, days supply of parts inventory falls. The decline in days supply causes production rate to fall below desired production rate. The equations for the variables follow.

Equation 7 states that production rate PR equals desired production rate DPR multiplied by effect of parts inventory level on production rate EPILPR.

$$PR.KL = DPR.K * EPILPR.K \qquad\qquad 7, R$$

where
PR   = production rate (units/day)
DPR   = desired production rate (units/day)

EPILPR = effect of parts inventory level on production rate
(dimensionless).

Equation 8 defines effect of parts inventory level on production rate
EPILPR as a function of days supply of parts inventory DSPI. Figure
6.2 illustrates the function assumed in the model. For DSPI values 60
days or greater, EPILPR equals 1.0 so that production rate equals
desired production rate. As DSPI falls below 60 days, EPILPR falls
below 1.0, slowly at first but more rapidly as DSPI falls below 40 days.
When DSPI falls to 0, EPILPR equals 0, and thus production rate is
also 0.

EPILPR.K = TABHL(TEPIPR,DSPI.K,0,90,10)   8, A
TEPIPR = 0/.25/.5/.7/.85/.95/1/1/1/1   8.1, T

where

EPILPR = effect of parts inventory level on production rate
(dimensionless)

TEPIPR = table for effect of parts inventory level on production
rate (dimensionless)

DSPI   = days supply of parts inventory (days).

The function shown in figure 6.2 embodies three assumptions: if
parts inventory is zero, production is impossible; increasing parts inventory increases production but with diminishing returns, because
each additional unit of inventory increases production less than the
increase caused by the last unit; and at some inventory level, here 60
days, further increases in parts inventory elicit no increase in production rate.

The exact shape of the relationship between parts inventory and
production rate depends on the nature of the inventory being modeled.
If the inventory consists of only one item, then production is possible,
providing there is one unit in inventory—the EPILPR curve would rise
sharply to 1.0 as DSPI increases from 0. The greater the number of
items in inventory, the less sharply EPILPR rises as DSPI increases;
the greater the number of items, the more likely one or more items will
be in short supply, and thereby constrain production. Mix is therefore
an important factor. To the extent production is of constant mix, the
curve is sharper because planning is easier. All of these factors enter
into the derivation of the EPILPR–DSPI curve.

The curve shown in figure 6.2 also assumes something about the
policy of the company. In system dynamics, modeling convention

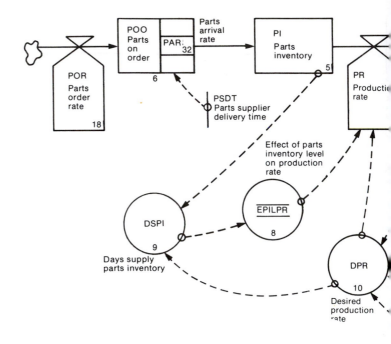

Figure 6.1 Structure of a company creating product shortages

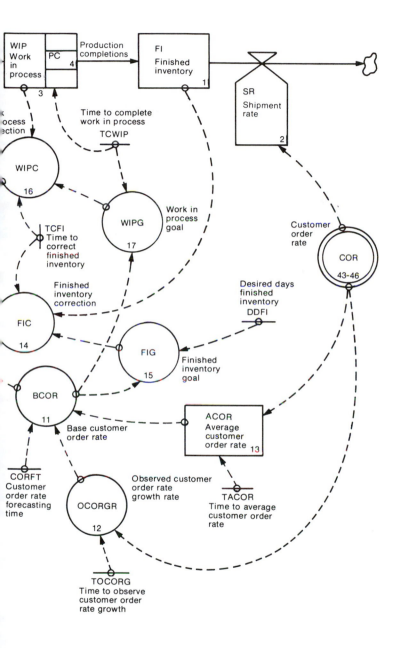

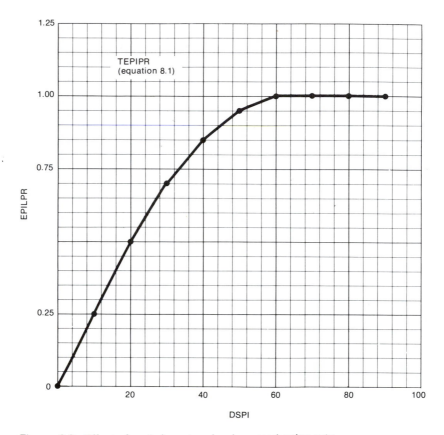

Figure 6.2   Effect of parts inventory level on production rate

places the 1.0 point of table functions at the normal operating point of the company; in figure 6.2 this is at the 60-day supply of parts inventory (the company goal). The 1.0 point does not always happen to fall in the flat portion of the curve. A different company with, say, a 30-day supply would operate in the steeper portion of the curve, which indicates the strong affect of swings in parts inventory on production rate. The company with the 30-day supply must also use extra labor and capital because the lower inventory means a less efficient operation—smaller lot sizes, more setup time, and greater shortages. But the use of extra labor and capital may or may not be more costly than holding greater parts inventory. The curve shown in figure 6.2 is one of many possible shapes and operating points.

Days supply of parts inventory DSPI is defined in equation 9 to equal parts inventory PI divided by desired production rate DPR.

$$DSPI.K = PI.K/DPR.K \qquad\qquad 9, A$$

where
DSPI = days supply of parts inventory (days)
PI = parts inventory (units)
DPR = desired production rate (units/day).

Equation 10 defines desired production rate DPR. DPR equals the sum of base customer order rate BCOR, finished inventory correction FIC, and work in process correction WIPC. The DPR equation is identical to that for production rate in chapter 5.

$$DPR.K = BCOR.K + FIC.K + WIPC.K \qquad\qquad 10, A$$

where
DPR = desired production rate (units/day)
BCOR = base customer order rate (units/day)
FIC = finished inventory correction (units/day)
WIPC = work in process correction (units/day).

6.3 Understanding Causes of Product Shortages

Figure 6.3 serves as a basis for comparing the response of the inventory system to a 15 percent STEP increase in customer order rate without and with a parts inventory constraint on production rate. In the simulation that produced figure 6.3 the company followed the aggressive policy set.

The causes of the behavior shown in figure 6.3 were described in chapters 4 and 5; several features are worth repeating. First is the system amplification: a 15 percent change in customer order rate (400 to 460) elicits a 24 percent increase in production rate (400 to 495) and a 60 percent change in parts order rate (400 to 640). Second is the unavoidable drops in both finished inventory and parts inventory. And third is the overshoot in the parts portion of the system: excess parts inventory is built and must be reduced by lowering parts order rate below production rate.

How does feedback from parts inventory to production rate change this behavior? Figure 6.4 shows the response of the inventory system to the STEP change with the parts inventory constraint. As expected, the constraint causes a deeper and longer drop in finished inventory.

Following the STEP increase in customer order rate, finished inventory falls because of the delayed production rate response. When pro-

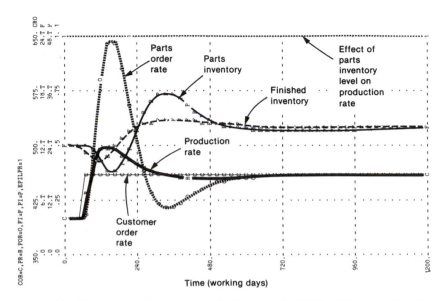

Figure 6.3 Inventory system response to 15 percent STEP increase in customer order rate without parts inventory constraint: aggressive policy set

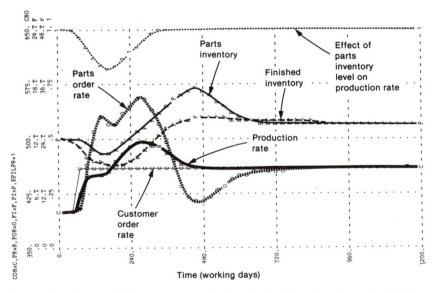

Figure 6.4 Inventory system response to STEP with parts inventory constraint: aggressive policy set

duction rate does increase, parts inventory falls because of the delayed parts order rate (and parts arrival rate) response. In contrast to figure 6.3, the decline in parts inventory causes production rate to fall below desired production rate (not shown) as indicated by effect of parts inventory level on production rate. As a result production rate levels off around day 120 such that finished inventory continues to fall.

As production rate approaches a steady level, parts order rate peaks and declines to meet it shortly after day 120. Production rate, or usage of parts, is the basis for parts ordering. When production rate levels off, the parts order rate policy responds, even though a shortage of parts inventory caused the leveling off. Parts order rate seeks the production rate level because just enough parts are ordered to build parts inventory to attain the production goal.

When around day 168 parts inventory begins to increase, days supply of parts inventory (not shown) improves. As a result effect of parts inventory level on production rate bottoms and then begins to increase. Production rate increases in an effort to build finished inventory. But as it rises, parts order rate does as well, eventually increasing parts inventory which allows further increases in production rate.

From day 168 to 288 the company is in a self-reinforcing mode: an increase in parts inventory allows production rate to increase; the production rate increase stimulates parts order rate which in turn is responsible for an additional increase in parts inventory; again the production rate advances even higher, and onward continues a spiral where ordering based on usage feeds on itself.

Around day 120 ordering based on usage had intensified the parts inventory shortage: the drop in parts inventory constrained production rate; as production rate (usage) leveled off, parts order rate peaked and declined. Production rate could not increase until parts inventory was rebuilt, but parts order rate did not increase until production rate increased. Only because parts inventory goal rose did the company order sufficient parts to break the deadlock and move to the self-reinforcing mode.

After production rate rises to equal desired production rate, as indicated by effect of parts inventory level on production rate returning to 1.0, system behavior is similar to behavior without the inventory constraint. Finished inventory rebuilds, and production rate falls to equal customer order rate. When production rate falls, the parts order rate policy recognizes it has ordered too much parts inventory and reduces parts order rate below production rate until parts inventory falls to goal.

Ordering based on usage creates problems for a company because it prolongs the period of inventory shortfall. This is particularly true the slower the company rebuilds inventory, as shown in figure 6.5.

The company represented in the figure follows the moderate policy set: inventory corrections are made over 240 rather than 60 days. Slower inventory corrections reduce the strength of the self-reinforcing feedback by lowering the parts inventory correction term. A slower rise in parts inventory level has a smaller affect on production rate which in turn influences parts order rate. Consequently production remains below its desired rate much longer, and finished inventory falls lower and remains below its goal longer. Ordering based on usage prolongs and deepens the inventory shortage.

6.4 Improving Behavior through Policy Design

Ordering Based on Desired Production Rate

Desired production rate is the amount of production, as specified by policy parameters, necessary to meet customer order rate and correct inventory discrepancies. Thus, if desired rather than actual production rate is used in the parts order rate policy, the company no longer orders based on actual usage but on desired usage.

Figure 6.6 shows inventory system response to a STEP increase when desired replaces actual production rate in the parts order rate policy. In the simulation that produced figure 6.6 the company followed the aggressive policy set.

A comparison of figures 6.4 and 6.6 indicates that, while the policy based on desired production rate does not prevent a parts inventory shortage, it does reduce the period of parts inventory shortage. Some drop in parts inventory is unavoidable because of the parts supplier delivery time. Consequently around day 120 in figure 6.6 production rate levels off, as effect of parts inventory level on production rate falls below 1.0. A similar leveling off occurs in figure 6.4.

But because parts order rate in figure 6.6 is based on desired and not actual production rate, parts order rate does not level off and decline as it does in figure 6.4. Consequently parts inventory rises, and effect of parts inventory level on production rate returns to 1.0 sooner. Thereby

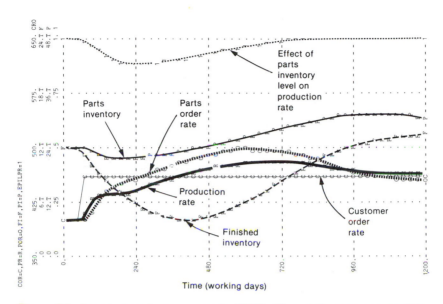

Figure 6.5   Inventory system response to STEP with parts inventory constraint: moderate policy set

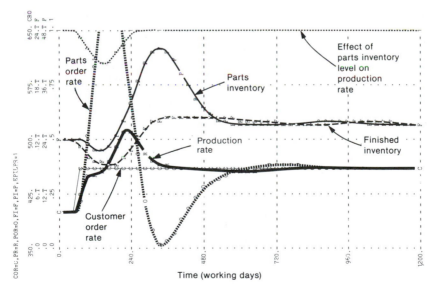

Figure 6.6   Inventory system response to STEP with parts order rate based on desired production rate: aggressive policy set

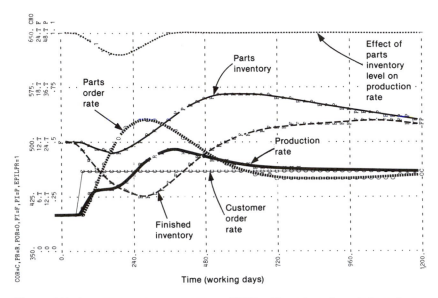

Figure 6.7   Inventory system response to STEP with parts order rate based on desired production rate: moderate policy set

production rate increases as does finished inventory which returns to its goal sooner.

Figure 6.7 shows the inventory system response to a STEP increase with parts order rate based on desired production rate for the moderate policy set. A comparison of figures 6.5 and 6.7 indicates that the change in policy information source substantially reduces the period when production is below the desired level: in figure 6.7 the effect of parts inventory level on production rate returns to 1.0 at day 360, versus day 720 in figure 6.5. Nevertheless, the drop in effect of parts inventory on production rate is not eliminated by the information source change.

The introduction of the parts constraint on production rate does, however, increase amplification. This can be seen by comparing figures 6.3 and 6.6. With the parts constraint production is held below the desired rate so that finished inventory falls lower. To rebuild inventory, production rate must rise even higher.

Carry Extra Parts Inventory

The only way to prevent the shortage of parts inventory, and the subsequent greater shortage and amplification of finished inventory, is to carry extra parts inventory. Such a policy exploits the flat portion of the effect of parts inventory on production rate curve. If sufficient extra parts inventory is carried, the unavoidable drop in parts inventory following the STEP increase in production rate will not cause effect of parts inventory level on production rate to fall below 1.0.

For example, figure 6.8 shows the inventory system response to a STEP increase with desired days parts inventory increased from 60 to 80 days. In the simulation that produced figure 6.8 the company follows the aggressive policy set with parts order rate based on production rate. The revised policy of carrying extra parts inventory is successful in preventing effect of parts inventory level on production rate from falling much below 1.0. As a result, except for the larger parts inventory, the behavior in figure 6.8 is nearly identical to that without a parts constraint on production shown in figure 6.3.

Plan Production in Advance

The decline in parts inventory, with the resulting drop in factory efficiency when extra inventory is not carried, can be avoided if production is planned, parts ordered, and then production changed only after parts arrive. Ideally production should be planned 60 days in advance of actual production changes.

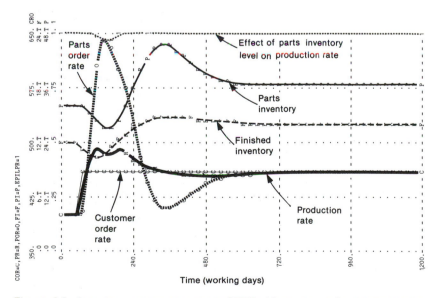

Figure 6.8   Inventory system response to STEP with extra parts inventory: aggressive policy set

The advantage of such a policy is that fluctuations in parts inventory caused by unanticipated production rate changes are eliminated. Consequently less parts inventory can be carried efficiently. The company saves on carrying costs and factory idleness due to parts shortage.

The disadvantage of such a policy is that it takes a long time for production rate to satisfy customer order rate changes. Thus finished inventory varies more. A higher level of finished inventory must be carried or the company will experience stockouts and lost sales.

Policy Design Guidelines

Before selecting a good policy, the analyst should examine each policy's performance under other test inputs such as NOISE, CYCLICAL, and GROWTH. Such an examination is not warranted here. Because NOISE, CYCLICAL, and GROWTH are similar to a series of STEP's, general policy guidelines can be inferred from the STEP response.

Policy design guideline 6.1 Ordering based on usage causes product shortages when demand is increasing because required inventory is not ordered. By creating large drops in inventory that must be rebuilt, ordering based on usage also increases amplification.

A company has two primary solutions to this problem: (1) order inventory based on desired production rate (this avoids the longer-term shortage caused by ordering based on usage but does not prevent short-term drop in inventory and the subsequent greater shortage of finished inventory and system amplification) and (2) carry extra parts inventory.

Ordering based on usage with inventory corrections is characteristic of inventory reorder rules based on economic order quantity and reorder point. Such rules, generally derived to minimize static inventory costs, are common in industry. But the rules contribute to problems of product shortage and greater amplification when viewed from a broader perspective. Effective policy design must evaluate policies from a perspective that examines dynamic behavior over a long time span under different test inputs and interactions beyond the inventory system to include production and the supplier. When viewed from this perspective, supposedly optimal decision rules are seen to create additional costs.

Ordering based on desired production rate is characteristic of computerized materials requirement planning systems. While these ordering rules were seen to eliminate the long-run shortages caused by ordering based on usage, they do so at the cost of greater amplification.

A full treatment of materials-planning systems is beyond the scope of this book. Nevertheless, it appears that such systems employ averaging and correction times even shorter than the aggressive parameters used in this book. One wonders if the benefits of such systems are again calculated from too isolated a perspective. A detailed examination of these systems can be found in Morecroft (1979).

6.5 Product Shortages and Instability Due to Interactions with Suppliers

Up to this point the parts supplier was modeled as a simple third-order delay of parts order rate. Parts arrival rate lagged parts order rate by a constant delay time equal to the parts supplier delivery time. In this chapter a more detailed representation of a parts supplier is developed. In particular the dynamics created by a limited supplier production capacity are examined. Limited capacity is a fact of life in most industries.

Figure 6.9 illustrates the structure of the more detailed parts supplier sector. Parts order rate accumulates in parts supplier order backlog. Parts supplier production starts depend on parts supplier production capacity and capacity utilization rate, which in turn is a function of parts supplier desired production rate. After a parts supplier production delay parts arrival rate follows parts supplier production starts.

The parts supplier is assumed to carry no finished parts inventory. Everything is built to a specific customer order. The production delay represents machine-type operations. These assumptions are representative of suppliers who turn raw materials into piece-parts and semi-finished assemblies. Specific equations for the supplier sector follow.

With a variable parts supplier delivery time the company no longer has up-to-date information on the current value of parts supplier delivery time. Consequently perceived parts supplier delivery time PPSDT is represented in equation 28 as an exponential average of parts supplier delivery time PSDT. Time to perceive parts supplier delivery time TPPSDT reflects the delay involved in updating information on supplier delivery times. The length of the delay depends on how quickly the company perceives and acts on new information. A management information system might allow the company to perceive changes in parts supplier delivery time very quickly, say, in 60 days. To achieve the minimum, the company must use information on the

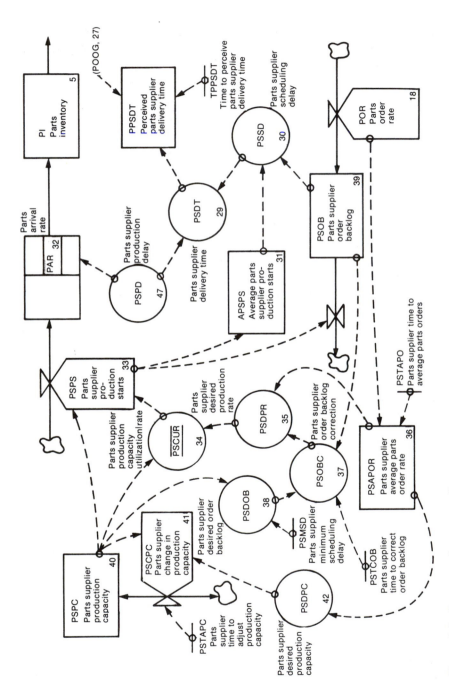

Figure 6.9   Structure of parts supplier sector

last orders. The consequences of longer perception delays are evaluated in later sections.

PPSDT.K = SMOOTH(PSDT.K,TPPSDT)   28, A
TPPSDT = 60   28.1, C

where
PPSDT = perceived parts supplier deliver time (days)
PSDT   = parts supplier delivery time (days)
TPPSDT = time to perceive parts supplier delivery time (days).

Total supplier delivery time consists of scheduling delay and production delay components; therefore in equation 29 parts supplier delivery time PSDT equals the sum of parts supplier production delay PSPD and parts supplier scheduling delay PSSD.

PSDT.K = PSPD.K + PSSD.K   29, A

where
PSDT = parts supplier delivery time (days)
PSPD = parts supplier production delay (days)
PSSD = parts supplier scheduling delay (days).

Parts supplier scheduling delay PSSD is modeled in equation 30 as parts supplier order backlog PSOB divided by average parts supplier production starts APSPS. Because production starts may be constrained by parts supplier production capacity, the scheduling delay reflects any increase in lead time caused by parts orders in excess of supplier capacity. When parts order rate exceeds parts supplier production starts (constrained by parts supplier production capacity), parts supplier order backlog builds so that parts supplier scheduling delay increases.

PSSD.K = PSOB.K/APSPS.K   30, A

where
PSSD = parts supplier scheduling delay (days)
PSOB = parts supplier order backlog (units)
APSPS = average parts supplier production starts (units/day);

APSPS.K = SMOOTH(PSPS.JK,20)   31, A

where
APSPS = average parts supplier production starts (units/day)
PSPS = parts supplier production starts (units/day).

Parts arrival rate PAR is represented in equation 32 as a third-order delay of parts supplier production starts PSPS. Parts supplier production delay PSPD is modeled as an exogenous variable that can vary over time. The equation for PSPD is defined in equation 47.

$$PAR.KL = DELAY3(PSPS.JK,PSPD.K) \qquad\qquad 32, R$$

where

PAR   = parts arrival rate (units/day)
PSPS = parts supplier production starts (units/day)
PSPD = parts supplier production delay (days).

Equation 33 states that parts supplier production starts PSPS equals parts supplier production capacity PSPC multiplied by parts supplier production capacity utilization rate PSPCUR. Thus production starts are constrained by supplier production capacity.

$$PSPS.KL = PSPC.K * PSPCUR.K \qquad\qquad 33, R$$
$$PSPS = CCOR \qquad\qquad\qquad\qquad\qquad 33.1, N$$

where

PSPS   = parts supplier production starts (units/day)
PSPC   = parts supplier production capacity (units/day)
PSPCUR = parts supplier capacity utilization rate (percent)
CCOR   = constant customer order rate (units/day).

Parts supplier production capacity utilization rate PSPCUR is a nonlinear function of parts supplier desired production rate PSDPR divided by parts supplier production capacity PSPC. Equation 34 defines the relationship; figure 6.10 illustrates it. When desired production rate falls below production capacity, the supplier cuts back utilization rate proportionately. When desired production rate exceeds production capacity, the supplier increases utilization rate less than proportionately. An increase in utilization rate above capacity represents the use of overtime. The supplier is assumed to go to a six-day week (1.2 utilization rate) when desired production rate exceeds capacity by more than 25 percent. The supplier, however, does not increase his work week to six and one-half days (1.3 utilization rate) until desired production rate is 1.75 of production capacity. Effective seven-day utilization is costly and difficult to achieve.

$$PSPCUR.K = TABLE(TPSCUR,PSDPR.K/PSPC.K,0,2,.25) \quad 34, A$$
$$TPSCUR = 0/.25/.5/.75/1/1.15/1.25/1.3/1.3 \qquad\qquad 34.1, T$$

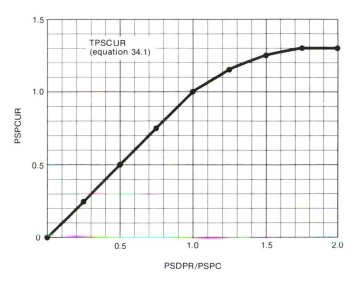

Figure 6.10   Parts supplier production capacity utilization rate as a function of parts supplier desired production rate relative to parts supplier production capacity

where

PSPCUR = parts supplier capacity utilization rate (percent)
TPSCUR = table for parts supplier capacity utilization rate (percent)
PSDPR   = parts supplier desired production rate (units/day)
PSPC   = parts supplier production capacity (units/day).

Parts supplier desired production rate PSDPR equals the sum of parts supplier average parts order rate PSAPOR and parts supplier order backlog correction PSOBC, equation 35. The parts supplier desired production rate equation is very similar to the production and parts order rate equations developed in previous chapters. Because the parts supplier carries no finished inventory, the desired production rate equation contains no inventory correction. The parts supplier order backlog correction, which is in some sense a negative inventory, gives the supplier feedback control over order backlog. When order backlog rises above desired order backlog, desired production rate increases above average parts order rate; the reverse occurs when order backlog falls below desired order backlog.

PSDPR.K = PSAPOR.K + PSOBC.K   35, A

where

PSDPR   = parts supplier desired production rate (units/day)
PSAPOR = parts supplier average parts order rate (units/day)
PSOBC   = parts supplier order backlog correction (units/day).

Parts supplier average parts order rate PSAPOR is represented in equation 36 as an exponential average of parts order rate POR. Parts supplier time to average parts orders PSTAPO is set to a small 30 days, thus reflecting quick adjustments by the parts supplier in response to changes in parts order rate. Such quick responses are necessitated by the lack of finished parts inventory.

$$PSAPOR.K = SMOOTH(POR.JK,PSTAPO) \qquad\qquad 36, A$$
$$PSTAPO = 30 \qquad\qquad 36.1, C$$

where

PSAPOR = parts supplier average parts order rate (units/day)
POR   = parts order rate (units/day)
PSTAPO = parts supplier time to average parts orders (days).

Parts supplier order backlog correction PSOBC equals the difference between parts supplier order backlog PSOB and parts supplier desired order backlog PSDOB divided by parts supplier time to correct order backlog PSTCOB (equation 37). A correction time of 60 days again reflects an aggressive response to backlog discrepancies because of the lack of finished product inventory.

$$PSOBC.K = (PSOB.K - PSDOB.K)/PSTCOB \qquad\qquad 37, A$$
$$PSTCOB = 60 \qquad\qquad 37.1, C$$

where

PSOBC   = parts supplier order backlog correction (units/day)
PSOB   = parts supplier order backlog (units)
PSDOB   = parts supplier desired order backlog (units)
PSTCOB = parts supplier time to correct order backlog (days).

Equation 38 states that parts supplier desired order backlog PSDOB equals parts supplier minimum scheduling delay PSMSD multiplied by parts supplier production capacity PSPC. Equation 33 assumes that the parts supplier would like to maintain a minimum order backlog consistent with production capacity.

$$PSDOB.K = PSMSD * PSPC.K \qquad\qquad 38, A$$
$$PSMSD = 10 \qquad\qquad 38.1, C$$

where

PSDOB = parts supplier desired order backlog (units)
PSMSD = parts supplier minimum scheduling delay (days)
PSPC   = parts supplier production capacity (units/day).

Equation 39 states that parts supplier order backlog PSOB is a level variable increased by parts order rate POR and decreased by parts supplier production starts PSPS. Parts supplier order backlog is initialized to its equilibrium value.

$$PSOB.K = PSOB.J + (DT)(POR.JK - PSPS.JK) \qquad 39, L$$
$$PSOB = PSMSD * CCOR \qquad 39.1, N$$

where

PSOB   = parts supplier order backlog (units)
DT   = delta time, simulation solution interval (days)
POR   = parts order rate (units/day)
PSPS   = parts supplier production starts (units/day)
PSMSD = parts supplier minimum scheduling delay (days)
CCOR   = constant customer order rate (units/day).

Parts supplier production capacity PSPC is a level variable changed by parts supplier change in production capacity PSCPC (equation 40). Parts supplier production capacity is initialized to the average volume of business in the system, here constant customer order rate CCOR.

$$PSPC.K = PSPC.J + (DT)(PSCPC.JK) \qquad 40, L$$
$$PSPC = CCOR \qquad 40.1, N$$

where

PSPC   = parts supplier production capacity (units/day)
DT   = delta time, simulation solution interval (days)
PSCPC = parts supplier change in production capacity
               (units/day/day)
CCOR   = constant customer order rate (units/day).

In equation 41 parts supplier change in production capacity PSCPC is defined as the difference between parts supplier desired production capacity PSDPC and parts supplier production capacity PSPC divided by parts supplier time to adjust production capacity PSTAPC. Equation 41 assumes that the parts supplier adjusts capacity up or down in response to changes in desired production capacity. In this model production capacity represents the capacity of the supplier allocated to producing parts for the company. This capacity may differ from the

parts supplier total production capacity in that some of the supplier
capacity may be allocated to other companies. Changes in capacity
therefore reflect both physical increases in the total size of the supplier
capacity and changes in the allocation of supplier capacity among competing companies. The supplier corrects capacity discrepancies over a
480-day (2-year) period.

$$PSCPC.KL = (PSDPC.K - PSPC.K)/PSTAPC \qquad 41, R$$
$$PSTAPC = 480 \qquad 41.1, C$$

where
PSCPC   = parts supplier change in production capacity
           (units/day/day)
PSDPC   = parts supplier desired production capacity (units/day)
PSPC   = parts supplier production capacity (units/day)
PSTAPC = parts supplier time to adjust production capacity (days).

Equation 42 states that parts supplier desired production capacity
PSDPC equals parts supplier average parts order rate PSAPOR. Desired capacity allocated to the company therefore equals the average
volume of orders from the company.

$$PSDPC.K = PSAPOR.K \qquad 42, A$$

where
PSDPC   = parts supplier desired production capacity (units/day)
PSAPOR = parts supplier average parts order rate (units/day).

Parts supplier production delay is an exogenous input that allows the
modeler to explore random, permanent, and temporary changes in
parts supplier lead times. Equation 47 defines PSPD.

$$PSPD.K = PSPDN * (1 + STEP(PSPDSH,PSPDST)$$
$$+ STEP(PSSH2, PSST2)$$
$$+ PKNSE(MPSPDN,SDVPSN,TCPSN)) \qquad 47, A$$

PSPDN = 50	47.2, C
PSPDSH = 0	47.3, C
PSPDST = 60	47.4, C
PSSH2 = 0	47.5, C
PSST2 = 180	47.6, C
MPSPDN = 0	47.7, C
SDVPSN = 0	47.8, C
TCPSN = 10	47.9, C

where

PSPD	=	parts supplier production delay (days)
PSPDN	=	parts supplier production delay normal (days)
PSPDSH	=	parts supplier production delay STEP height (dimensionless)
PSPDST	=	part supplier production delay STEP time (days)
PSSH2	=	parts supplier STEP height two (dimensionless)
PSST2	=	parts supplier STEP time two (days)
PKNSE	=	pink (correlated) noise variation
MPSPDN	=	mean of parts supplier production delay noise (dimensionless)
SDVPSN	=	standard deviation of parts supplier noise (dimensionless)
TCPSN	=	time constant of parts supplier noise (days).

6.6 Understanding Causes of Shortages and Instability

When suppliers have limited production capacity, aggressive policies worsen boom-and-bust cycles. Figure 6.11 illustrates one set of causal forces producing greater variability. If during business upturns parts order rate exceeds parts supplier production capacity, parts supplier order backlog increases. An increase in order backlog lengthens parts

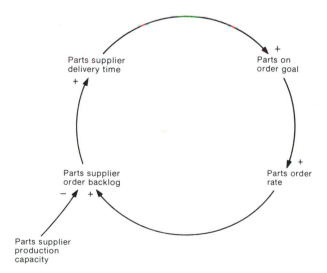

Figure 6.11 Positive feedback loop causing increased variability when parts supplier production is limited

supplier delivery time so that parts on order goal increases. An increase in parts on order goal increases parts order rate, thus completing the feedback loop.

The feedback loop shown in figure 6.11 is positive because, other things being equal, the changes are self-reinforcing: an increase in parts order rate increases order backlog, delivery time, and parts on order goal, which in turn increases parts order rate, and so on. The positive feedback loop acts to raise parts order rate farther up than it would be without a supplier capacity constraint. Should parts order rate then fall, the positive feedback loop causes parts order rate to plunge lower than without the constraint.

To illustrate the increased amplification of boom-and-bust cycles, a 15 percent STEP increase in customer order rate is input to the inventory system with limited supplier capacity. Figure 6.12 shows the response of that system, with aggressive policies and time to perceive parts supplier delivery time of 60 days. For comparison purposes figure 6.13 shows system response under the same conditions but without a supplier capacity limit (figure 6.13 is identical to figure 6.6 except for a change in scales).[1] As expected, with limited supplier capacity product shortages are more severe, and system amplification increases.

Following the STEP increases in customer order rate at day 60, finished inventory falls because of the delay in increasing production rate. Similarly parts inventory falls because of the delay in increasing and receiving parts order rate. With the increase in production rate and decline in parts inventory parts order rate rises sharply around day 84.

In contrast to earlier simulations, however, the increase in parts order rate exceeds parts supplier production capacity (not shown) so that parts supplier delivery time increases. From day 96 to day 240 the self-reinforcing feedback loop acts to intensify the amplification in parts order rate: an increase in parts order rate increases parts supplier delivery time, which in turn increases parts on order goal (not shown); then the increase in parts on order goal further increases parts order rate. Amplification is also increased because parts inventory falls lower: with the supplier capacity constraint parts arrival rate cannot keep pace with parts order rate.

The self-reinforcing cycle breaks and reverses direction shortly after

1. Computer runs in the remainder of this chapter derive from a parts order rate policy of ordering based on desired production rate.

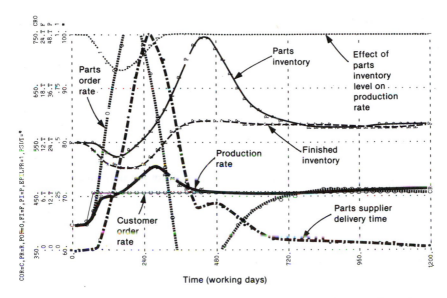

Figure 6.12 Response of inventory system with limited supplier capacity to STEP increase: aggressive policy set

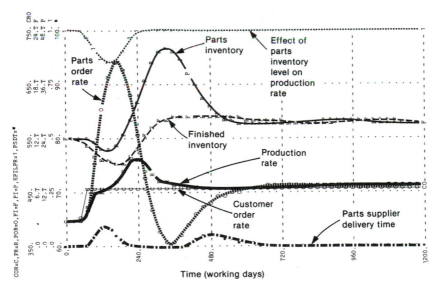

Figure 6.13 Response of inventory system with unlimited supplier capacity to STEP increase: aggressive policy set

day 240 when parts inventory increases enough to cause parts order rate to fall. As parts order rate decreases, the supplier works off the accumulated backlog with increased capacity, reducing parts supplier delivery time. But as delivery time falls so does the parts on order goal (not shown), and parts order rate falls even farther. The parts ordered to fill the supplier pipeline because of the increased delivery time now appear in parts inventory. Parts inventory therefore rises well above its goal. As a result parts order rate drops below production rate so that the excess inventory is depleted.

In reacting to changes in parts supplier delivery time that result from a limited parts supplier production capacity, the company intensifies boom-and-bust cycles: parts order rate overshoots and undershoots by greater amounts; parts inventory overshoots by an even greater amount. These swings may in fact be greater in practice because of two other self-reinforcing loops not represented in the model. The first of these loops works as follows: when parts supplier delivery time increases, companies place multiple orders with the same supplier (to get a higher priority allocation) and with different suppliers (to get the best possible delivery); these multiple orders further overload capacity and stretch lead times; the companies then cancel the extra orders when one is finally received. The second loop involves the parts inventory goal: as delivery times vary, companies tend to alter inventory goals to agree with the fluctuations, increasing goals when supply lead times are long (and when profits are good because of the business upturn) and decreasing goals when supply lead times are short (and profits are low because of the business downturn). Thus company reactions to supplier lead time changes intensify boom-and-bust cycles. On the other hand, these swings may be lessened if the supplier has excess capacity normally allocated to other customers that can be used to satisfy the company's demand.

6.7 Improving Behavior through Policy Design

The self-reinforcing cycle can be broken, or reduced in strength, in three ways:

1. if suppliers carry sufficient excess capacity,
2. if the company does not respond to changes in supplier delivery time,

3. if the company does not overload supplier lead time and cause delivery time to increase.

The first method requires a commitment from suppliers that a company is unlikely to get, or want to rely on. The other two methods will be evaluated in this section.

Slower Response to Changes in Supplier Delivery Time

The company's response to changes in parts supplier delivery time is governed by time to perceive parts supplier delivery time TPPSDT (equation 28.1). The 60-day value used in previous simulation runs represents quick responses that might be attained with a computerized management information system. A slower response is implemented by increasing TPPSDT to 240 days. Figure 6.14 shows the results.

The slower response to changes in parts supplier delivery time does reduce amplification in parts order rate and overshoot of parts inventory. While the self-reinforcing feedback loop still operates, its strength is reduced by the slower reaction. Consequently amplification is approximately the same as amplification without a supplier constraint,

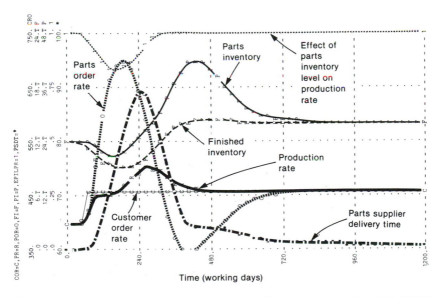

Figure 6.14 Response of inventory system with limited supplier capacity to STEP increase: aggressive policy set and TPPSDT of 20 days

although the duration of the overshoot is longer (compare figure 6.14 with 6.13).

Slower reactions to supplier delivery times therefore improve system performance only up to the point where system response is dominated by the strength of inventory corrections. When TPPSDT equaled 60 days, the contributions of the self-reinforcing loop were noticeable. When TPPSDT equaled 240 days, the contributions were small enough for the basic inventory corrections to dominate system response.

Reduce Magnitude of Parts Order Rate

The self-reinforcing loop comes into play only when supplier capacity is overloaded. Consequently the greater boom-and-bust cycles can be prevented by a company policy that does not overload the supplier. As shown in figure 6.15, if parts order rate (and production rate) is governed by the moderate policy parameters, very little overloading occurs. Parts supplier delivery time increases relatively little (8 percent) above its normal value. Consequently even with TPPSDT of 60 days the self-reinforcing loop is not activated. And, as discussed in previous chapters, the problem of product shortages can be solved by carrying extra inventory.

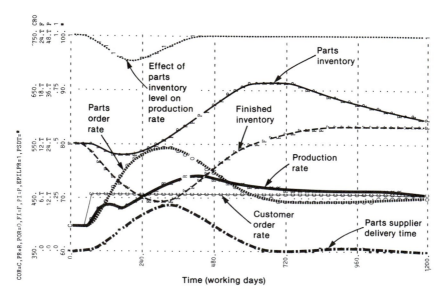

Figure 6.15 Response of inventory system with limited supplier capacity to STEP increase: moderate policy set and TPPSDT of 60 days

Policy Design Guidelines

The results of this chapter illustrate the importance of two policy guidelines. Guideline 6.2 applies specifically to inventory systems; guideline 6.3 reiterates a message of this entire book.

Policy design guideline 6.2 Aggressive responses increase system amplification and inventory variations in two ways: (1) by correcting inventory discrepancies quickly, supplier capacity is exceeded so that parts arrivals fall short of orders and parts inventory falls lower, thus necessitating even more orders; and (2) by responding quickly to changes in supplier delivery times, a self-reinforcing behavior mode of increased orders, lead time, parts on order goal, and orders results. The increased amplification can be reduced by eliminating either or both methods: by slower corrections of inventory discrepancies so that supplier capacity is not overloaded, or by slower responses to delivery time changes so that the strength of the self-reinforcing loop is reduced.

Policy design guideline 6.3 Effective policy design requires a broader perspective than is normally taken in management research and practice. Such a perspective includes (1) interactions of the policy with other parts of the company—a seemingly optimal policy for inventory control can cause production performance to decline, resulting in lower overall company performance; and (2) interactions of the policy with elements of the environment that might affect the performance—an aggressive policy that overloads supplier capacity can intensify boom-and-bust cycles without making inventory any more available in the short run.

6.8 Testing Exogenous Supplier Delivery Problems in Policy Design

Parts supplier delivery time rarely remains at a constant value. Three types of variations in parts supplier delivery times might occur:

1. Random variations—for example, machine breakdowns, weather, or shipping delays.
2. Permanent changes—for example, a move to a new location or a shift in production process.
3. Temporary shortages—for example, a strike or boycott.

Random Variations in Delivery Times

Random variations in delivery times are represented by a 10 percent variation in parts supplier production delay. Figure 6.16 shows the

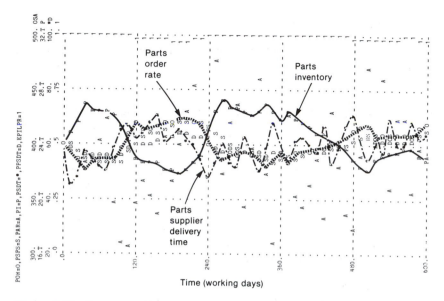

Figure 6.16 Response of inventory system to random variation in supplier delivery time: aggressive policy set and TPPSDT of 60 days

response of the inventory system to such a random variation with the aggressive policy set and with a 60-day TPPSDT.

Variations in parts supplier production delay cause parts arrival rate (plotted as A) to differ from the constant production rate (not shown). Consequently parts inventory absorbs differences between production and parts arrival rates. The aggressive policy set responds quickly to any discrepancies between parts inventory and its goal. For example, initially parts supplier delivery time falls so that parts arrival rate exceeds production rate, thus causing parts inventory to increase. In response the company reduces parts order rate to eliminate the parts inventory excess. After approximately 60 days (average parts supplier delivery time) parts inventory begins to decrease.

At approximately the same time, however, parts supplier delivery time increases, and parts arrival rate falls below its expected rate. Consequently parts inventory drops farther than anticipated below its goal. The company then increases parts order rate to rebuild parts inventory. By responding quickly to inventory discrepancies, the company contributes to inventory fluctuations because, just as the company is correcting the discrepancy, changes in parts supplier delivery time also correct the discrepancy.

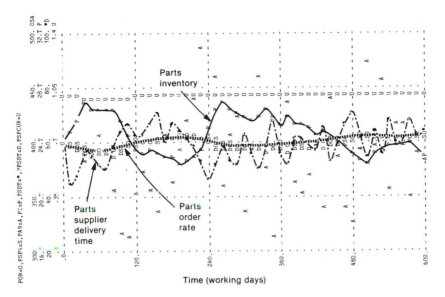

Figure 6.17 Response of inventory system to random variation in supplier delivery time: moderate policy set and TPPSDT of 60 days

Figure 6.17 shows the response of the production-inventory system with the moderate policy set to the same random variation in delivery time. Parts order rate is nearly constant; yet parts inventory fluctuations are slightly less than those with the aggressive policy set. As previously noted, random variations in parts supplier delivery time are in a sense self-correcting. If arrivals are below normal during one time frame, they are likely to be above normal during the next. Thus, while parts inventory increases one period, it declines the next. By reacting quickly to inventory discrepancies, the company is correcting a discrepancy that is also being corrected by the system. Overcorrection and increased instability result.

The short time to perceive parts supplier delivery time TPPSDT also contributes to the instability of parts order and production rates. In fact the discussion of the inventory shortages and excesses is only partly correct: the real shortages and excesses appear in parts on order not parts inventory. For example, initially in figure 6.16 parts supplier delivery time falls so that inventory increases above desired parts inventory (here a constant 24,000 units), but parts on order decreases below its goal (because parts arrival rate exceeds parts order rate). In fact parts on order corrections would exactly compensate parts inventory corrections, were it not for the change in parts on order goal as the company quickly responds to changes in parts supplier delivery time. As perceived parts supplier delivery time falls, parts on order goal decreases. Consequently an excess of inventory develops within the system of parts inventory and parts on order. The same excess occurred in figure 6.17, but the long time to correct parts inventory (TCPI of 240 days) prevented parts order rate from reacting to the excess.

Stability might also be achieved therefore by smoothing variations in parts supplier delivery time with a longer time to perceive parts supplier delivery time TPPSDT. For example, if TPPSDT equals 240 days, parts on order goal will remain nearly constant in the face of random parts supplier delivery time variations. Consequently total system shortages and excesses of inventory will not develop.

Figure 6.18 compares the behavior of parts order rate and inventory in response to a random variation in parts supplier delivery time for different values of TPPSDT. Even with the aggressive policy set, parts order rate is relatively stable and variations in parts inventory are reduced. Because parts on order goal does not change much in response to the changes in parts supplier delivery time, total system shortages and excesses of inventory do not develop.

In contrast, figure 6.19 shows that changes in TPPSDT have little

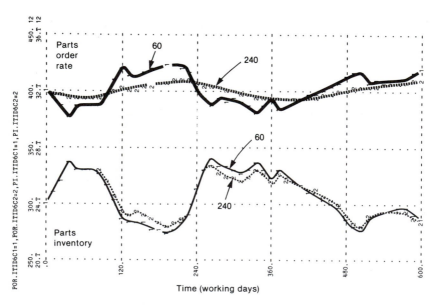

Figure 6.18 Comparison of parts order rate and parts inventory for different values of TPPSDT: aggressive policy set

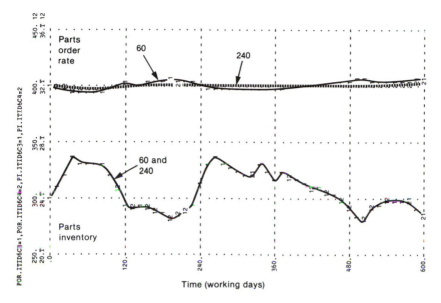

Figure 6.19 Comparison of parts order rate and parts inventory for different values of TPPSDT: moderate policy set

effect on system stability for the moderate policy set. With time to correct parts inventory equal to 240 days, inventory corrections contribute little to parts order rate. Consequently the increase in TPPSDT yields little additional benefit.

The results thus far question the need for quick information about supplier delivery times: quick information with aggressive responses yields instability in the face of random variation; quick information is of no value if the responses are slow. Quick information had a similar effect in the case of limited supplier capacity (see sections 6.6 and 6.7).

Permanent Changes in Delivery Times

A permanent change in delivery time causes a permanent change in the equilibrium value of parts on order. Thus parts order rate must be adjusted to reequilibrate the total system inventory. In figure 6.20 the inventory system is subjected to a permanent 10 percent increase in parts supplier delivery time. In response to such a change, parts arrival rate initially falls below production rate (not shown but a constant 400 units per day). Thus parts inventory declines while parts on order increases.

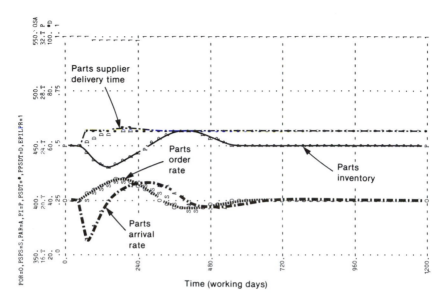

Figure 6.20   Response of inventory system to permanent change in supplier delivery time: aggressive policy set and TPPSDT of 60 days

As the company recognizes the increase in parts supplier delivery
time (determined by TPPSDT), parts on order goal (not shown)
increases. The company recognizes that the total system is short of
ventory and consequently increases parts order rate to rebuild inventory. The longer the time to perceive parts supplier delivery time
TPPSDT, the longer the company takes to rebuild inventory.

Temporary Shortages

A temporary shortage is something like a random increase in delivery
time, except more severe and perhaps longer lasting. Figure 6.21 shows
the response of the production-inventory system with limited supplier
capacity to a 50 percent increase in delivery time, lasting 120 days
(one-half year). In the figure the company uses the aggressive policy set
with TPPSDT of 60 days.

Notice the increase in parts supplier delivery time causes parts arrival rate to fall well below production rate (not shown but equal to a
constant 400 units per day). Consequently parts inventory falls dramatically to 18,000 units (goal of 24,000 units). Parts on order (not shown)
increases by a corresponding amount. Because perceived parts
supplier delivery time responds to the increase in delivery time, parts

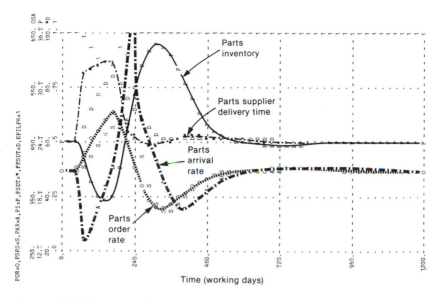

Figure 6.21   Response of inventory system to temporary shortage: aggressive policy set and TPPSDT of 60 days

on order goal increases. In response the company increases parts order rate to rebuild inventory. After the parts supplier delivery time, parts inventory begins to increase. At approximately the same time, however, parts supplier delivery time falls as the problem creating the temporary shortage is corrected. Parts arrival rate rises well above production rate so that parts inventory increases substantially. Then, reacting quickly to the temporary shortage, the company cuts back parts order rate to reduce the inventory buildup.

As for the random variation, when TPPSDT is increased to 240 days, stability of both parts order rate and parts inventory are improved (see figure 6.22). Because the company does not react as quickly to the increase in delivery time, parts order rate is not increased as much to build inventory. Consequently, when the temporary shortage is corrected, inventory does not overshoot as much.

But the greatest improvements in stability result when the company adopts the moderate policy set, as shown in figure 6.23. Because inventory corrections are made slowly, parts order rate increases slowly. Moreover, because the shortage turns out to be temporary, parts inventory corrects itself with little overshoot. For temporary changes slower responses improve both stability of parts order rate and parts inventory.

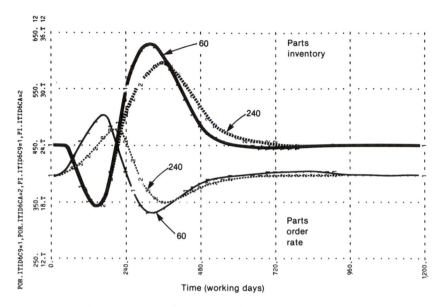

Figure 6.22 Comparison of parts order rate and parts inventory for different values of TPPSDT: aggressive policy set

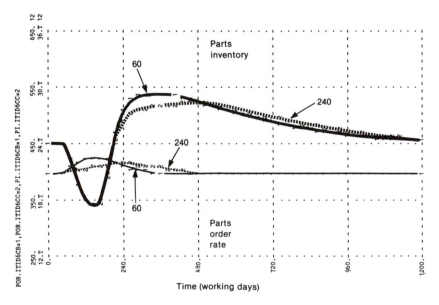

Figure 6.23 Comparison of parts order rate and parts inventory for different values of TPPSDT: moderate policy set

Policy Design Guidelines

The simulation experiments in this section illustrate the process a company can use to design policies to cope with exogenous changes in the environment. The simulations allow the company to estimate the variations in such inputs as parts order rate and parts inventory for different types (and magnitude) of changes. A policy can then be selected to balance the trade-off between the cost of stability and the cost of inventory. In preparing for such shocks, the company has already calculated their consequences and deemed them acceptable.

The experiments in this section also give a procedure for determining the type of information system required by a company. Many companies install computerized management information systems without first evaluating all of the costs and benefits. As Forrester (1961, appendix J) states,

The manager is interested in more useful information on which to base decisions. Greater utility can be obtained both by improving existing information sources and by basing decisions on new and different sources that have not been used in the past. The cost of obtaining improved information can usually be estimated with fair accuracy. But what is better information worth? This is not so easily answered. Better information is worth the value that we attach to the improved industrial performance which results when the better information is available. Unless we can determine the change in system performance that will result from a changed information flow, we cannot determine its value.

The value of information has usually been determined by highly subjective means that necessarily include an estimate of what the information will do to the dynamic behavior of the system. Our ability to estimate the characteristics of information-feedback systems is poor. It is to be expected that one of the weakest areas of managerial judgment is in placing a dollar value on an information source.

The United States has a tremendous data-processing industry that caters to the managerial conviction that better information means better management. Machine processing of business data is usually justified on the basis of machine-processing costs relative to costs in the previously existing system. For lack of any real measure of the value of information, this justification is almost never made on the basis of the relationships between information cost and information value.

It is my belief, based on experiences with industrial organizations, that some of the most important and useful information is going unused and untouched. At the same time, great efforts are devoted to attempting to acquire information that even were it available would do little for the success of the organization. As an example, some organizations have succeeded in speeding up the flow of sales information and production scheduling to the point where the random-noise variations in the market can now be directly imposed on the production process. This tends to ignore the proper use of inventories for absorbing such variations. Carried to an extreme, the result of more timely information can be harmful. The effect can be to cause the manager to put more and more stress on short-range decisions.

Morecroft (1977) makes similar points.

The results of this chapter further highlight the costs of quicker information. But quick information need not always increase costs. Thus, as stated in the guideline 6.4, the value of quicker information can only be judged in relation to its effect on the dynamic behavior and profits of the company.

Policy design guideline 6.4 A management information system generally provides more recent information to decision-makers. The value of that information can only be judged in relation to its effect on the dynamic behavior of the company. Relevant questions include, (1) What is the impact of the information on company profits and other measures of performance? (2) Is the cost of the system worth the impact? (3) Might not the same benefits be achieved with a different policy that relies on slower, less costly information?

6.9 Summary

This chapter examined two factors that intensify boom-and-bust cycles in multistage inventory systems. The first of these factors is internal to the company: because of parts inventory feedbacks to production rate, decreases in parts inventory on the upswing of a cycle constrain production rate so that finished inventory falls lower than it otherwise would; as a result production rate must rise higher than customer order rate, and system amplification intensifies. Moreover ordering based on usage prolongs the period of inventory shortage because usage, the base order rate for ordering items for inventory, is reduced to coincide with inventory shortage. Solutions to these problems include determining ordering by desired production rate and carrying extra parts inventory.

The second factor intensifying boom-and-bust cycles was in part external to the company: an increase in parts order rate exceeds supplier capacity, thus increasing supplier delivery time; the rise in delivery time causes parts inventory to fall lower than it otherwise would, resulting in more system amplification; the increase in delivery time can set in motion a self-reinforcing feedback loop of increasing delivery time raising parts on order goal, parts order rate, and in turn itself in a continuous cycle. The second factor can be overcome through slower responses to changes in delivery time and slower corrections of inventory discrepancies.

This chapter also examined system response to several exogenous changes in supplier delivery time. Illustrated were the general process of scenario analysis and the process of evaluating the type of information system needed by a company.

References

Forrester, Jay W. 1961. *Industrial Dynamics*. Cambridge, Mass.: The MIT Press.

Morecroft, John D. W. 1977. A Framework for the Evaluation of Planning and Control Information in a Production Distribution System. System dynamics group working paper D-2728. Massachusetts Institute of Technology, Cambridge, Mass.

Morecroft, John D. W. 1979. Influences From Information Technology on Industry Cycles: A Case Study in Manufacturing Industry. Ph.D. dissertation. Massachusetts Institute of Technology, Cambridge, Mass.

7.1 The Problem of Labor Instability

Because labor is a human input to production, companies are usually more concerned with variations in labor than in other production resources such as parts inventory and capital equipment. Tradition, laws, and union contracts protect labor from the hardships of unemployment, leaving to the company some of the burden of instability: unemployment benefits paid to laid-off workers are charged to the company in proportion to the total unemployment attributable to that company; union contracts protect senior workers, with layoffs often entailing costly changes in job assignments; and in some industries workers are paid supplemental unemployment benefits from a fund supported by company contributions. Besides the financial costs of these labor protections, companies experience delays in reducing the labor force because advance notification of workers and additional time to reschedule production are required.

The costs of labor instability cause companies to adjust labor more slowly than other production resources. When orders increase, labor is increased only after the increase in orders persists long enough to warrant a more or less permanent increase in the size of the labor force; similarly for a decrease in business. A portion of the labor adjustment time is caused by delays inherent in advance notification of workers and time to reschedule production. The remainder of the labor adjustment time represents management's reluctance to change the size of the labor force given the costs of firing (and to a lesser extent hiring).

In view of the slow adjustment of labor, How does the company handle any differences between the production rate achievable with a given labor force and the production rate indicated by orders and inventory discrepancies? Obviously when production is maintained at the rate attainable with the given labor force, it will fall below the desired level in business upturns and rise above it in business downturns. As a result inventory will fluctuate more than if labor and production were adjusted. However, as inventory fluctuates more, so does the desired production rate. Consequently even with slow adjustments labor can fluctuate significantly because of greater swings in desired production rate. In fact, as demonstrated in section 7.3, labor fluctuations can be greater with slow adjustments than with quick adjustments. A seemingly stabilizing policy of slow labor adjustments produces an unexpected result.

Inventory fluctuations will be reduced to the extent a company uses over- and undertime to absorb differences between desired and attainable production rate with the given labor force. But over- and undertime entail significant costs. Moreover overtime is limited to at most 40 percent of normal production time. Some swings in business require greater overtime than that available.

While labor stability is an important goal, policies to achieve stability are not always obvious. A careful analysis of structure and behavior and a testing of policy performance under different scenarios are required for effective policy design. Chapter 7 addresses these issues.

7.2 Structure Creating Labor Instability

Figure 7.1 gives a flow diagram of how a labor and overtime sector connects to the production sector of a company. While production rate depends on labor and overtime (through potential output from labor) and on parts inventory (through effect of parts inventory level on production rate), scheduled production rate controls the acquisition of labor and the use of overtime.

Labor is increased by labor-hiring rate and depleted by labor-firing rate and labor attrition rate. Labor-hiring rate is a delayed value of labor-hiring starts, the delay representing the time to recruit labor. A complete description of the new model equations follows.

Production Rate

To effect a change in production rate, a company must alter either the level of production resources or the utilization of those resources. Three types of production resources are examined:

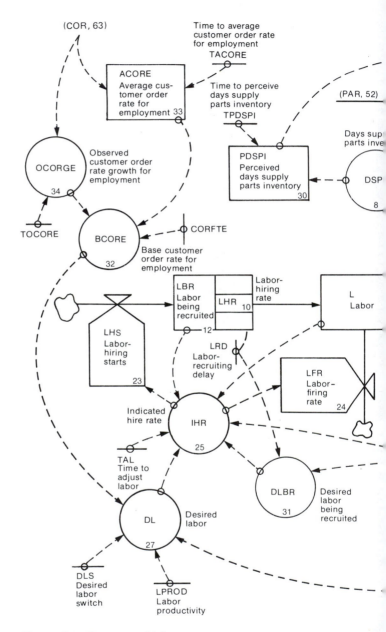

Figure 7.1   Structure of labor sector

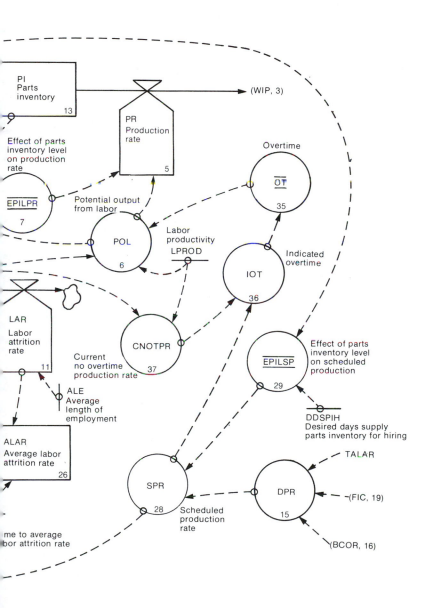

1. parts and raw materials inventory,
2. labor and over- or undertime,
3. capital equipment and its associated utilization rate.

These resources differ in the length of time required to acquire or dispose of them, in cost, and in use in the production process. Policy design naturally reflects such differences.

In chapter 6 the effect of parts inventory level on production rate was introduced. As long as days supply parts inventory exceeded a 60-day supply, the effect was 1.0, and production rate equaled desired production rate. But as parts inventory fell below 60 days, the effect fell below 1.0 so that production fell short of the desired rate. The affect on production rate was more severe the lower the level of parts inventory.

Parts and raw materials inventory are spent in the production process. The time to acquire these resources, as well as their cost, varies widely. However, for the hypothetical company modeled here the assumption is made that the cost of parts inventory is low enough that sufficient inventory is held to operate on the relatively flat portion of the effect of parts inventory level on production rate curve. Changes in parts inventory level therefore cause less than proportional changes in production rate until days supply falls to 30 days.

Capital equipment is generally a long lead time, expensive production resource; once acquired, the resource has a long, useful life. Consequently companies are conservative in capacity expansion. Production rate is therefore directly proportional to the level and utilization rate of capital equipment. In chapter 11 the effect of different expansion policies on ability to produce is examined. Until then the assumption is made that capital equipment does not constrain production.

Labor is a production resource whose lead time and cost also vary widely. Lead time is influenced by the tightness of labor markets and by the length of any training delays; costs, by skill level and the labor intensity of the product. Variations in labor and over- or undertime change the utilization of the company's capital equipment.

In this chapter the affect of labor availability on production rate is introduced. Production rate is assumed to be directly proportional to the level of labor. In other words a given percentage change in labor causes a corresponding change in production rate. Direct proportionality implies

1. The level of other resources is sufficient to allow the increased labor to perform at full productivity (here capital equipment is the primary

other resource because the effects of parts inventory level are modeled explicitly).

2. No scale factors in the operating range cause productivity to jump incrementally (for example, if it falls below a certain level of labor, the plant cannot be operated efficiently).

Equation 5 states that production rate PR equals the product of potential output from labor POL and effect of parts inventory level on production rate EPILPR.

$$PR.KL = POL.K * EPILPR.K \qquad\qquad 5, R$$

where

PR   = production rate (units/day)
POL   = potential output from labor (units/day)
EPILPR = effect of parts inventory level on production rate
         (dimensionless).

In equation 6 potential output from labor POL is set to the product of labor L, labor productivity LPROD, and overtime OT. Labor productivity is here arbitrarily set to 1.0 units per day per person. Overtime ranges between 0 and 1.4: an overtime value of 1.0 represents 5-day production; an overtime value of 1.4, 7-day production; and overtime values below 1.0, undertime. Undertime results when labor is not fired but assigned to tasks not directly related to production.

$$POL.K = L.K * LPROD * OT.K \qquad\qquad 6, A$$
$$LPROD = 1 \qquad\qquad\qquad\qquad\qquad 6.1, C$$

where

POL   = potential output from labor (units/day)
L   = labor (persons)
LPROD = labor productivity (units/day/person)
OT   = overtime (dimensionless).

Physical Flows

Labor L is a level variable increased by labor-hiring rate LHR and depleted by labor attrition rate LAR and labor-firing rate LFR (labor-firing rate is normally negative and thus is entered with a positive sign in the equation for labor, equation 9). Labor is initialized to its equilibrium value: constant customer order rate CCOR divided by labor productivity LPROD.

$$L.K = L.J + (DT)(LHR.JK + LFR.JK - LAR.JK) \qquad 9, L$$
$$L = CCOR/LPROD \qquad 9.1, N$$

where

L	= labor (persons)
DT	= delta time, simulation solution interval (days)
LHR	= labor-hiring rate (persons/day)
LFR	= labor-firing rate (persons/day)
LAR	= labor attrition rate (persons/day)
CCOR	= constant customer order rate (units/day)
LPROD	= labor productivity (units/day/person).

In equation 10 labor-hiring rate LHR is represented as a delayed value of labor-hiring starts LHS. The delay represents the time to recruit and train labor. Labor-recruiting delay LRD is here set to 20 days. Such a delay reflects the time required to recruit the relatively unskilled assembly labor for the particular company modeled here.

$$LHR.KL = DELAY3(LHS.JK,LRD) \qquad 10, R$$
$$LRD = 20 \qquad 10.1, C$$

where

LHR = labor-hiring rate (persons/day)
LHS = labor-hiring starts (persons/day)
LRD = labor-recruiting delay (days).

Equation 11 states that labor attrition rate LAR equals labor L divided by average length of employment ALE. ALE is here taken as 480 days (2 years), about the average duration of employment in manufacturing.

$$LAR.KL = L.K/ALE \qquad 11, R$$
$$ALE = 480 \qquad 11.1, C$$

where

LAR = labor attrition rate (persons/day)
L = labor (persons)
ALE = average length of employment (days).

Labor being recruited LBR is a level variable increased by labor-hiring starts LHS and depleted by labor-hiring rate LHR (equation 12). Labor being recruited is set initially to equal desired labor being recruited DLBR.

$$LBR.K = LBR.J + (DT)(LHS.JK - LHR.JK) \qquad 12, L$$
$$LBR = DLBR \qquad 12.1, N$$

where
LBR   = labor being recruited (persons)
DT   = delta time, simulation solution interval (days)
LHS   = labor-hiring starts (persons/day)
LHR   = labor-hiring rate (persons/day)
DLBR = desired labor being recruited (persons).

Policies

Equation 23 states that labor-hiring starts LHS is taken as the maximum of 0 or indicated hiring rate IHR. In equation 24 labor-firing rate LFR is taken as the minimum of 0 or indicated hiring rate IHR.

$$LHS.KL = MAX(0,IHR.K) \hspace{4cm} 23, R$$

where
LHS = labor-hiring starts (persons/day)
IHR = indicated hiring rate (persons/day);

$$LFR.KL = MIN(0,IHR.K) \hspace{4cm} 24, R$$

where
LFR = labor-firing rate (persons/day)
IHR = indicated hiring rate (persons/day).

This formulation assumes that labor firing can occur relatively more quickly than labor hiring. Consequently firing is separated from hiring. Hiring starts flow through the labor-recruiting delay before entering the labor pool. Firing, however, directly reduces the labor pool. Advance notification of layoff and work-rescheduling delays are built into the time to adjust labor, equation 25.1.

Equation 25 defines indicated hiring rate IHR. IHR consists of two components: average labor attrition rate ALAR and adjustments to the desired size of the labor force. In changing the labor force, this company adjusts discrepancies between desired labor DL and labor L, and between desired labor being recruited DLBR and labor being recruited LBR, over the time to adjust labor TAL. TAL is here set to 20 days, although different values for TAL will be explored in section 7.3. A value of 20 days is probably the minimum that could be achieved. Note that the indicated hire rate equation, which controls the level of labor, is structurally similar to the desired production rate and parts order rate equations, which control the levels of finished and parts inventory, respectively.

IHR.K = ALAR.K + (DL.K − L.K + DLBR.K

              − LBR.K)/TAL   25, A

TAL = 20   25.1, C

where

IHR   = indicated hiring rate (persons/day)

ALAR = average labor attrition rate (persons/day)

DL   = desired labor (persons)

L   = labor (persons)

DLBR = desired labor being recruited (persons)

LBR   = labor being recruited (persons)

TAL   = time to adjust labor (days).

Average labor attrition rate ALAR is represented in equation 26 as an exponential average of labor attrition rate LAR. Time to average labor attrition rate TALAR is set to 40 days. Because labor is not spent in the production process, and has a relatively long life, ALAR is a small component of indicated hire rate. Consequently TALAR is an unimportant parameter in terms of its effect on system stability.

ALAR.K = SMOOTH(LAR.JK,TALAR)   26, A

TALAR = 40   26.1, C

where

ALAR   = average labor attrition rate (persons/day)

LAR   = labor attrition rate (persons/day)

TALAR = time to average labor attrition rate (days).

Equation 27 defines desired labor DL. Desired labor depends on either scheduled production rate SPR or base customer order rate for employment BCORE, as well as on the value of desired labor switch DLS. When DLS equals 1.0, desired labor is based on scheduled production rate SPR. Because scheduled production rate contains production to build inventories, desired labor responds not only to the base volume of business (as represented by average customer order rate) but also to inventory discrepancies. In contrast, when desired labor switch is set to 0, desired labor responds to base customer order rate for employment. Base customer order rate for employment responds to the average volume of business as represented by average customer order rate for employment (defined in equation 33). In equation 27 scheduled production rate or base customer order rate for employment is divided by labor productivity to yield desired labor.

$$DL.K = (DLS * SPR.K + (1 - DLS) * BCORE.K)/LPROD \quad 27, A$$
$$DLS = 1 \quad\quad\quad 27.1, C$$

where

DL $\quad$ = desired labor (persons)
DLS $\quad$ = desired labor switch (dimensionless)
SPR $\quad$ = scheduled production rate (units/day)
BCORE = base customer order rate for employment (units/day)
LPROD = labor productivity (units/day/person).

Equation 28 states that scheduled production rate SPR equals desired production rate DPR multiplied by effect of parts inventory level on scheduled production EPILSP. DPR is the production rate indicated by customer order rate and inventory discrepancies. Sufficient parts inventory, however, may not be available to produce efficiently at that production rate. Consequently the company may decide to schedule less production than desired in order to operate efficiently. On the other hand, to offset the parts shortage, the company may continue to hire workers to expedite and finish incomplete assemblies. EPILSP represents company policy.

$$SPR.K = DPR.K * EPILSP.K \quad\quad 28, A$$
$$SPR = CCOR \quad\quad\quad 28.1, N$$

where

SPR $\quad$ = scheduled production rate (units/day)
DPR $\quad$ = desired production rate (units/day)
EPILSP = effect of parts inventory level on scheduled production
$\quad\quad\quad$ (dimensionless)
CCOR $\quad$ = constant customer order rate (units/day).

Equation 29 defines effect of parts inventory level on scheduled production EPILSP. EPILSP is a nonlinear function of perceived days supply parts inventory PDSPI divided by desired days supply parts inventory for hiring DDSPIH. Figure 7.2 illustrates several curves for EPILSP. The top curve (all 1.0 values) represents a company that schedules production and hires labor independent of the level of parts inventory—getting out the product is more important than operating efficiently. The bottom curve represents a company that produces only at a rate that allows it to operate efficiently at a 60-day supply of parts inventory. The bottom curve is calculated assuming the company knows the effect of parts inventory level on production rate and re-

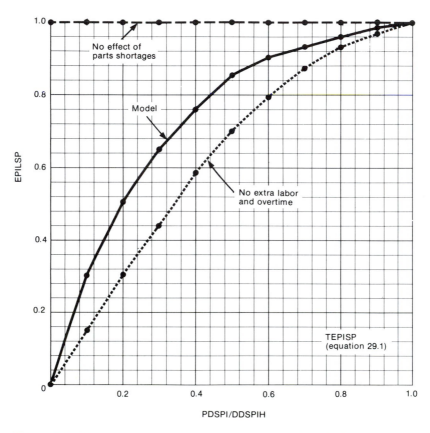

Figure 7.2   Effect of parts inventory level on scheduled production

duces production rate accordingly. The middle curve, presently used in the model, represents a compromise between the two extremes.

EPILSP.K = TABHL(TEPISP,PDSPI.K/DDSPIH,0,1,.1)   29, A
TEPISP = 0/.3/.5/.65/.75/.85/.9/.93/.96/.985/1   29.1, T
DDSPIH = 60   29.2, C

where

EPILSP = effect of parts inventory level on scheduled production
          (dimensionless)
TEPISP = table for effect of parts inventory level on scheduled
          production (units/day)
PDSPI   = perceived days supply parts inventory (days)
DDSPIH = desired days supply parts inventory for hiring (days).

Perceived days supply parts inventory PDSPI is represented in equation 30 as an exponential average of days supply parts inventory DSPI. Time to perceive days supply parts inventory TPDSPI is set to 20 days. Few companies have instantaneous information on the status of parts inventory. Consequently production decisions are based on perceptions of inventory levels. Computerized information systems would reduce TPDSPI.

$$\text{PDSPI.K} = \text{SMOOTH(DSPI.K,TPDSPI)} \qquad\qquad 30, A$$
$$\text{TPDSPI} = 20 \qquad\qquad 30.1, C$$

where
PDSPI = perceived days supply parts inventory (days)
DSPI   = days supply of parts inventory (days)
TPDSPI = time to perceive days supply parts inventory (days).

Equation 31 defines desired labor being recruited DLBR to equal average labor attrition rate ALAR multiplied by labor-recruiting delay LRD. DLBR is the equilibrium value of labor being recruited.

$$\text{DLBR.K} = \text{ALAR.K} * \text{LRD} \qquad\qquad 31, A$$

where
DLBR = desired labor being recruited (persons)
ALAR = average labor attrition rate (persons/day)
LRD   = labor-recruiting delay (days).

Base customer order rate for employment BCORE is identical conceptually to base customer order rate BCOR used in setting desired production rate. Equation 32 defines BCORE. BCORE is a trend forecast of customer order rate. The forecast responds to average customer order rate for employment ACORE. Observed customer order rate growth for employment OCORGE is extrapolated over customer order rate forecasting time for employment CORFTE. BCORE is used rather than BCOR so that labor can be made to respond to longer averages of customer order rate.

$$\text{BCORE.K} = (1 + \text{CORFTE} * \text{OCORGE.K}) * \text{ACORE.K} \qquad 32, A$$
$$\text{CORFTE} = \text{TACORE} + \text{TCWIP} + \text{LRD} \qquad 32.1, N$$

where
BCORE   = base customer order rate for employment (units/day)
CORFTE = customer order rate forecasting time for employment (days)
OCORGE = observed customer order rate growth for employment (percent/day)

ACORE   = average customer order rate for employment (units/day)
TACORE = time to average customer order rate for employment
              (days)
TCWIP   = time to complete work in process (days)
LRD   = labor-recruiting delay (days).

In equation 33 average customer order rate for employment ACORE
is represented as an exponential average of customer order rate COR.
Time to average customer order rate for employment TACORE is set
to 60 days. Different values for TACORE are examined in section 7.5.

ACORE.K = SMOOTH(COR.K,TACORE)   33, A
TACORE = 60   33.1, C

where
ACORE   = average customer order rate for employment (units/day)
COR   = customer order rate (units/day)
TACORE = time to average customer order rate for employment
              (days).

Equation 34 calculates observed customer order rate growth for employment OCORGE, using the trend extrapolation forecasting macro.

OCORGE.K = TRND(COR.K,TOCORE,ICORGR)   34, A
TOCORE = 240   34.1, C

where
OCORGE = observed customer order rate growth for employment
              (percent/day)
TRND   = macro for detecting trends in input time series
              (percent/day)
COR   = customer order rate (units/day)
TOCORE = time to observe customer order rate growth for
              employment (days)
ICORGR   = initial customer order rate growth rate (percent/day).

Equation 35 defines overtime OT. Overtime is set either to a nonlinear function of indicated overtime IOT, as shown in figure 7.3, or to
1.0, depending on the value of desired labor switch DLS. When DLS
equals 1.0, desired labor equals scheduled production rate. Consequently, when DLS equals 1.0, overtime is not used. In contrast,
when DLS equals 0, desired labor equals base customer order rate for
employment, and overtime is used. In other words, when desired labor
includes corrections for inventory, overtime is not used; when desired

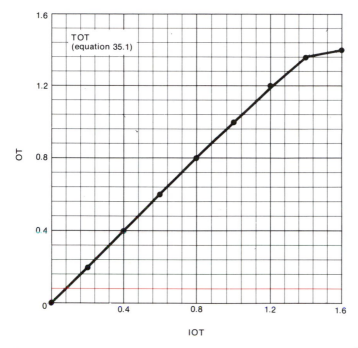

Figure 7.3   Overtime as a function of indicated overtime

labor does not include corrections for inventory, overtime is used. Clearly in practice DLS can take values other than zero or one. If so, some labor and some overtime are used for building inventory.

$$\text{OT.K} = \text{TABLE(TOT,IOT.K,0,1.6,.2)} * (1 - \text{DLS}) + \text{DLS} \quad 35, \text{A}$$
$$\text{TOT} = 0/.2/.4/.6/.8/1/1.2/1.35/1.4 \qquad\qquad\qquad 35.1, \text{T}$$

where
OT   = overtime (dimensionless)
TOT = table for overtime (dimensionless)
IOT = indicated overtime (dimensionless)
DLS = desired labor switch (dimensionless).

Figure 7.3 shows how overtime OT is related to indicated overtime IOT. An IOT value of 1.0 occurs when scheduled production rate equals the production attainable with the current labor force. Consequently overtime is also set to 1.0. As IOT increases above 1.0, scheduled production rate rises above the production attainable with the current labor force. Consequently, overtime also increases. Figure 7.3 shows, however, that overtime increases less than indicated overtime. When IOT equals 1.2, indicating 6-day-per-week production, overtime is also 1.2. However, when IOT equals 1.4, indicating 7-day-per-week production, overtime is only 1.35. IOT must rise to 1.6 to yield an overtime value of 1.4. The policy represented in figure 7.3 indicates that the company is reluctant to use 7-day-per-week overtime. Such reluctance might be based on the high cost, the effect on productivity, or the unwillingness of labor to work such overtime. Consequently the company is unable, or unwilling, to go to 7-day-per-week overtime until desired production rate exceeds available production from the current labor force by 60 percent. Figure 7.3 also shows that undertime is directly proportional to indicated overtime. In practice, however, companies may not cut back production proportionately until IOT falls significantly.

Equation 36 states that indicated overtime IOT equals scheduled production rate SPR divided by current no-overtime production rate CNOTPR.

$$IOT.K = SPR.K/CNOTPR.K \qquad\qquad 36, A$$

where
IOT   = indicated overtime (dimensionless)
SPR   = scheduled production rate (units/day)
CNOTPR = current no-overtime production rate (units/day).

Current no-overtime production rate CNOTPR equals the product of labor L and labor productivity LPROD (Equation 37).

$$CNOTPR.K = L.K * LPROD \qquad\qquad 37, A$$

where
CNOTPR = current no-overtime production rate (units/day)
L   = labor (persons)
LPROD = labor productivity (units/day/person).

7.3 Understanding Causes of Labor Instability

Recall from figure 7.1 the three different types of delays in corporate systems:

1. delays in physical flow channels (for example, time to complete work in process TCWIP and labor-recruiting delay LRD),
2. delays or adjustment times in correcting discrepancies in buffer levels (for example, time to correct finished inventory TCFI),

3. delays or adjustment times in correcting discrepancies in resource levels (for example, time to adjust labor TAL).

Previous chapters examined the impact of delays in physical flow channels and adjustment times in buffer levels on system stability. Such examination indicated

1. Increasing delays in physical flow channels make a system less stable in response to temporary changes, all other things being equal (for example, the longer the TCWIP, the lower finished inventory falls in response to a STEP change in customer order rate; consequently production rate must increase more than customer order rate to rebuild finished inventory).

2. Decreasing adjustment times in buffer levels make a system less stable in response to temporary changes, all other things being equal (for example, decreasing TCFI causes inventory corrections to be greater in response to a STEP change in customer order rate, thereby increasing production rate more than customer order rate; for a NOISE input inventory corrections tend to be self-correcting so that, if a temporary increase in customer order rate depletes inventory, the following temporary decrease in customer order rate will rebuild inventory; short adjustment times prevent inventory from acting as a buffer and thereby contribute to instability).

In this section the effect of changing resource level adjustment times is examined. The examination indicates that increasing adjustment times in resource levels make a system less stable in response to temporary changes, all other things being equal (just the opposite of the conclusion for buffer level adjustment times).

Figure 7.4 shows the response of the inventory-workforce system to a STEP change in customer order rate. In the simulation that produced figure 7.4, the company followed the aggressive policy set, with time to adjust labor set to 120 days. A value of 120 days represents the actions of a company attempting to achieve labor stability through long adjustment times. This simulation further assumed the company did not use over- or undertime. A 120-day desired days parts inventory is used in all of the simulation runs of this chapter in order to isolate the effects of labor interactions on production rate and system stability.

In figure 7.4 production rate fluctuates around customer order rate in response to a STEP change, before reaching an equilibrium after day 1200. No such fluctuations were observed in the system without labor. The STEP change in customer order rate above production rate causes

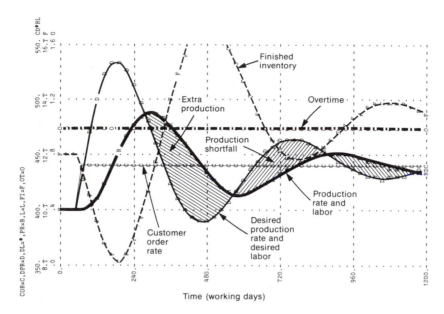

Figure 7.4 Inventory-workforce system response to STEP in customer order rate: aggressive policy set and TAL = 120

finished inventory to decline. In response to this decline, and to the increase in average customer order rate (not shown), desired production rate rises sharply. Because of the 120-day time to adjust labor TAL and the 20-day labor-recruiting delay LRD, however, production rate lags desired production rate (production rate and labor are identical because labor productivity LPROD equals 1.0). Finally, approximately 120 days after the STEP change, production rate crosses customer order rate, and finished inventory bottoms (actually FI bottoms slightly later because of the time to complete work in process).

Production rate increases above customer order rate in order to rebuild finished inventory to a higher equilibrium level. As finished inventory increases, desired production rate falls. When desired production falls below the actual rate, the company realizes it has enough workers and cuts back on hiring and begins firing (not shown). Labor and production rate do not respond immediately, however, because of TAL and LRD. Consequently production lags the desired rate on the downswing. It lags the desired rate by enough to cause extra production so that finished inventory overshoots its goal. As a result desired production rate is reduced below customer order rate to eliminate the excess finished inventory.

When production rate falls below customer order rate at day 480, finished inventory peaks and begins to fall. In response, desired production rate increases until it crosses production rate at day 576. The company then realizes production is below desired and begins hiring. But the delays again cause labor and production rate to lag the increasing desired labor and production rates. As a result finished inventory falls below goal, and the cycle repeats but with successively less amplitude.

The shaded areas in figure 7.4 indicate production excesses and shortfalls. Desired production rate accurately reflects the production necessary to correct finished inventory discrepancies. Consequently any production above the desired rate causes inventory to overshoot, and conversely for production that falls below it. The longer the time to adjust labor, the greater the fluctuations of production above and below the desired rate and therefore the less stable the system.

7.4 Improving Behavior through Policy Design

Decrease Time to Adjust Labor

The closer production follows the desired rate, the less it overshoots or undershoots and therefore the more stable the system. Desired production rate can be approached more closely by reducing time to adjust labor.

Figure 7.5 shows the response of the inventory-workforce system to a STEP change in customer order rate with the aggressive policy set and TAL set to 20 days (versus 120 days in figure 7.4). Because of the smaller TAL, production rate follows desired production rate more closely. Consequently, after the STEP increase, finished inventory does not fall as low as in figure 7.4. Because of this desired production rate and desired labor do not rise as high. Labor and production rate therefore rise no higher than in figure 7.4. A similar behavior occurs when desired production rate falls.

The resource adjustment delay acts like a delay in a physical flow channel. Both delays affect the speed with which a company adjusts to desired conditions. Neither directly affects the strength of the company's response. Strength of response is governed by the production rate policy. The shorter the time to correct finished inventory, the greater the production rate. Time to adjust labor and labor-recruiting delays (and time to complete work in process) do not directly affect

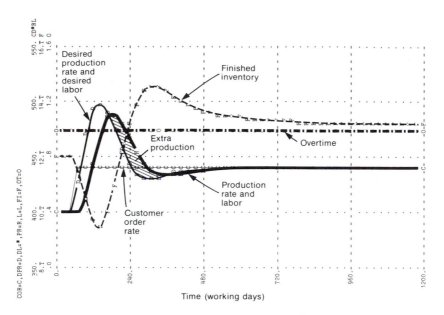

Figure 7.5 Inventory-workforce system response to STEP in customer order rate: aggressive policy set and TAL = 20

desired production rate. Rather they determine the speed with which production completions follow the desired rate. For a given production rate policy, the longer these delays, the more production completions lag the desired rate. As a result finished inventory falls (or rises) farther. Making these delays shorter improves inventory stability.

Policy design guideline 7.1 summarizes these results:

Policy design guideline 7.1 The type of delay determines its effect on system stability: (1) increasing delays in physical flow channels reduce stability, (2) decreasing adjustment times in buffer levels reduce stability, and (3) increasing adjustment times in resource levels reduce stability.

A difficulty in implementing guideline 7.1 is determining the proper classification of a delay. For example, because parts inventory is a production resource, does that mean that time to correct parts inventory is a resource adjustment delay? In the system developed thus far in this book, the answer is no. Parts inventory acts like a buffer rather than a resource because of the way it affects production. The company operates on the relatively flat portion of the effect of parts inventory level on production rate curve. Consequently shortages or excesses of parts inventory do not effect a significant change in production rate. Production remains close to the desired rate. In contrast, shortages or excesses of labor have a strong affect on production. A different company might operate in the steeper region of the effect of parts inventory level on production rate curve, in which case parts inventory would act more like a resource level.

The analyst must carefully examine the structure surrounding a delay before classifying it and always check the results of using policy design guidelines with simulation.

Policy design guideline 7.2 A resource level is a production resource that influences production rate proportionately, or nearly so. A production resource that acts through other company policies effecting a weak change in production rate is a buffer level.

Reduce Aggressiveness of Basic Policy

No matter how short the time to adjust labor, production will always lag the desired rate. There are limits to how quickly companies can adjust labor; as a result some instability is unavoidable.

The degree of instability can be minimized, however, by reducing the aggressiveness of the basic production rate policy. The less quickly desired production rate changes, the less production lags the desired rate. Figure 7.6 demonstrates the improved stability.

Figure 7.6 shows the response of the inventory-workforce system to a STEP change in customer order rate with the moderate policy set and TAL equal to 20 days. The moderate policy set by itself improves stability; it also reduces the strength of the destabilizing effects of labor adjustments, as evidenced by the slight overshoot of finished inventory. While production lags the desired rate, the change in desired production rate is so gradual that the amount of extra production is minimal. In contrast, when desired production rate changes quickly as in figure 7.5, even with a time to adjust labor of 20 days the lag is significant enough to cause inventory to overshoot by 1,500 units (approximately 10 percent).

Use Over- and Undertime

By bypassing the proportional link between the level of labor and production rate, labor can be made to act more like a buffer level. Over- and undertime are commonly used to bypass the link. With undertime

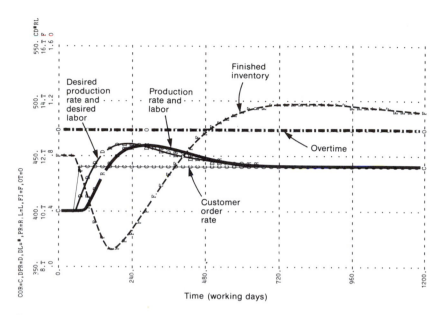

Figure 7.6 Inventory-workforce system response to STEP in customer order rate: moderate policy set and TAL = 20

production need not exceed the desired rate; with overtime production can be increased to the desired rate.

Figure 7.7 shows inventory-workforce system response to a STEP change in customer order rate, with the aggressive policy set, over-time, and time to adjust labor equal to 120 days. System stability is much improved over the stability without overtime (figure 7.4). The use of overtime allows production rate to increase with desired production rate even though labor increases only slowly. Consequently finished inventory does not fall as low as in the no-overtime simulation. Be-cause finished inventory does not fall as low, the desired and actual production rates do not rise as high. Moreover finished inventory does not overshoot because of a lag between these production rates (the overshoot in finished inventory is caused by trend forecasting). Be-cause labor is lower than the desired level when desired production rate falls, actual and desired production rates can be made to fall simultaneously by reducing overtime. The use of proportional under-time would produce a similar effect even if labor were above that desired. As a result finished inventory does not overshoot more than the amount caused by trend forecasting.

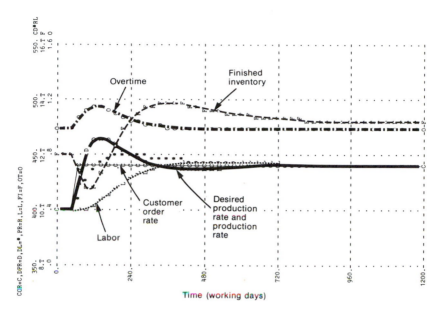

Figure 7.7 Inventory-workforce system response to a STEP change in customer order rate: aggressive policy set, overtime, and TAL = 120

In contrast, figure 7.8 shows inventory-workforce system response to a STEP increase in customer order rate, with the aggressive policy set, overtime, and time to adjust labor of 20 days (rather than 120 as in figure 7.7). While the stability of production rate is no longer affected by the change in time to adjust labor, the stability of the labor sector is. With the shorter time to adjust labor, labor rises more quickly to the desired level. However, because of trend forecasting desired labor overshoots, and because desired labor is reached more quickly, labor overshoots its equilibrium value. Although not plotted in figure 7.8, hiring rate rises significantly for a short period of time, and then an increase in the firing rate eliminates the excess labor (as evidenced by the increase and decrease in the labor curve). In contrast, hiring rate in figure 7.7 rises more gradually, and not as high, so little firing occurs.

Hiring rate corresponds to parts order rate. When labor acts like a buffer level, the stability of hiring rate and labor are improved by increasing time to adjust labor. Policy design guideline 7.3 summarizes these results.

Policy design guideline 7.3 Labor can be converted from a resource to buffer level through the use of over- and undertime. System stability is improved because production follows more closely the desired rate.

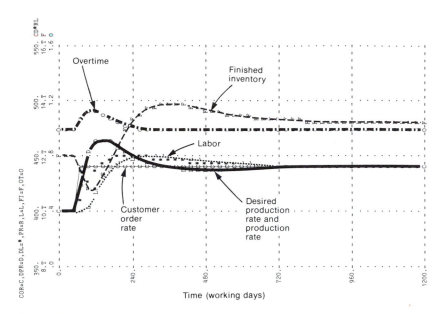

Figure 7.8 Inventory-workforce system response to a STEP change in customer order rate: aggressive policy set, overtime, and TAL = 20

Then, because labor is decoupled from production, the stability of hiring rate and labor can be improved by increasing time to adjust labor.

The decoupling process is effective only if desired production rate varies within the limits achievable by overtime and if undertime is used in direct proportion to indicated undertime. Should desired production rate exceed these limits, labor reverts to its resource level role; should full undertime not be used, inventory will overshoot. In selecting an appropriate time to adjust labor, the analyst must be cognizant of scenarios that might cause these factors.

Although effective in improving stability, the use of over- and undertime may not be the most profitable policy option. Financial performance is examined in chapter 9.

Summary

Policy design guideline 7.4 summarizes the results of this section:

Policy design guideline 7.4 The stability of a resource level such as labor is improved not by increasing time to adjust labor but rather by either (1) improving the stability of policy controlling desired production rate, or (2) using over- and undertime to convert the resource level to a buffer level, in which case increasing time to adjust labor improves stability.

7.5 Testing Scenarios in Policy Design

CYCLICAL

In any changing environment desired production rate consists not only of production for the base volume of business but also for inventory corrections. Consequently, if desired labor responds to desired production rate, labor is hired to build inventory and then fired as inventory approaches its goal. The use of labor for inventory corrections is one factor contributing to labor instability. This factor is particularly strong for CYCLICAL variations in customer order rate.

Figure 7.9 shows the response of the inventory-workforce system to a cyclical variation in customer order rate. The following policy options produced the simulation shown in figure 7.9:

1. moderate desired production rate policy parameter set,
2. desired labor responding to desired production rate,

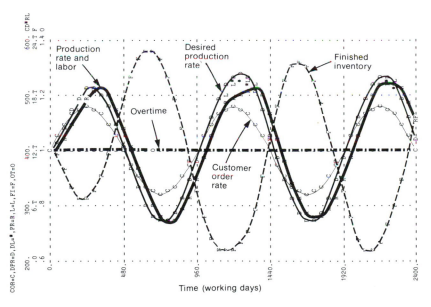

Figure 7.9 Inventory-workforce system response to CYCLICAL variation in customer order rate without overtime

3. time to adjust labor of 20 days,

4. no over- or undertime.

Consequently, although time to adjust labor is short, production rate lags the desired rate because it is directly proportional to labor.

In figure 7.9 the amplitude of production rate fluctuations is greater than the amplitude of customer order rate fluctuations because production rate contains inventory corrections. Inventory deviates from desired for three reasons: (1) production completions lag shipment rate because of the physical delay between production rate and completions, (2) desired production rate lags shipment rate because of delays introduced by the averaging of information, and (3) production lags the desired rate because of the delays in adjusting and recruiting labor.

When desired labor responds to desired production rate, labor is hired and fired for changes in average customer order rate and inventory corrections. As a result labor fluctuates between 280 and 520, even though the labor needed to match changes in customer order rate fluctuates between 320 and 480.

As shown in figure 7.10, if desired labor responds to base customer order rate rather than to desired production rate (by setting DLS = 0 in

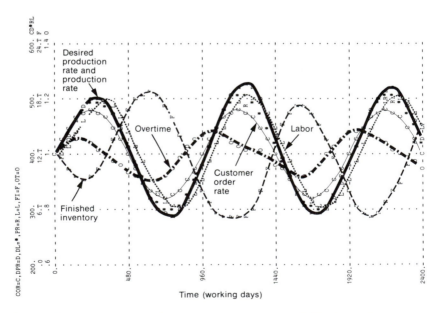

Figure 7.10 Inventory-workforce system response to a CYCLICAL variation in customer order rate with overtime

equation 27), labor fluctuations are reduced to between 300 and 500. Over- and undertime are used to build and reduce inventory. As a result overtime fluctuates between 0.92 and 1.08. Moreover with the use of overtime production rate stability is improved because the third source of inventory discrepancy is eliminated—with over- and undertime production rate no longer lags desired production rate. Labor stability is improved because over- and undertime are used to build and reduce inventory.

Nevertheless, labor fluctuations are still substantial because desired labor responds to a 60-day average of customer order rate (with trend forecasting). Further improvements in labor stability can be achieved by using over- and undertime for some of the changes in base customer order rate, as shown in figure 7.11.

In the simulation that produced figure 7.11, time to average customer order rate for employment TACORE was increased from 60 to 480 days and time to observe customer order rate for employment TOCORE (trend observation time) from 480 to 960 days. As a result labor fluctuations (between 350 and 450) are less than customer order rate fluctuations (between 320 and 480). To absorb the discrepancy between desired production rate and that attainable with the labor force, overtime

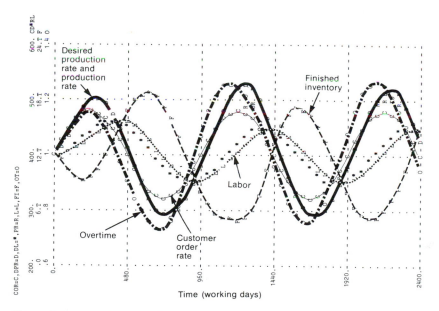

Figure 7.11 Inventory-workforce system response to CYCLICAL variation in customer order rate with overtime and greater employment stability

fluctuates between 0.76 (less than a 4-day week) and 1.26 (more than a 6-day week).

The use of overtime offers performance advantages in that it allows the company to change production rate quickly and substantially without corresponding employment swings. Over- and undertime, however, may not be as profitable a means of achieving labor stability as a slower-reacting production policy with greater inventory. Policy design involves evaluating many trade-offs and alternatives.

The use of overtime is an alternative policy action. Like other policy changes (information source and adjustment delay), this policy action must be evaluated for its affect on system performance.

GROWTH

The use of overtime also offers performance advantages in a growing market. Figure 7.12 shows the response of the inventory-workforce system to GROWTH in customer order rate. The primary feature of the system's response is that production lags the desired rate because of the delay in adjusting labor. Consequently finished inventory is lower than it would be were labor not a constraint to production.

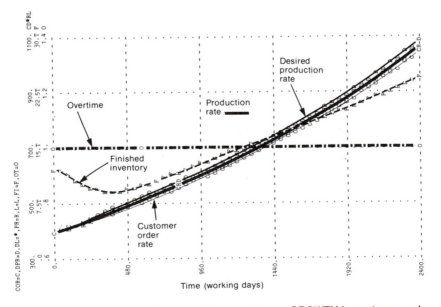

Figure 7.12 Inventory-workforce system response to GROWTH in customer order rate without overtime

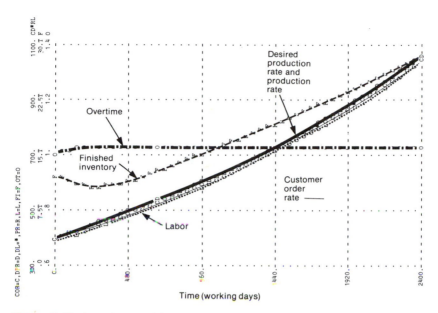

Figure 7.13 Inventory-workforce system response to GROWTH in customer order rate with overtime

Figure 7.13 shows the response of the inventory-workforce system to GROWTH in customer order rate with overtime. Overtime is now used to offset the delay in adjusting labor so that finished inventory does not fall as low as in the policy without overtime. But because of the time to adjust labor, labor always lags desired labor. As a result overtime becomes a permanent input to production.

7.6 Summary

Production rate depends on several types of resources: parts inventory, labor, and capital equipment. Company policy determines how a particular resource affects production. If production rate is directly proportional to the resource, the resource is classified as a resource level (for example, labor without the use of over- and undertime). If production rate is weakly proportional to the resource, the resource is classified as a buffer level (for example, parts inventory when the company holds enough inventory).

Because resource levels exert a strong effect on production rate, long resource level adjustment delays worsen system stability. If the resource is not available, or in excess, production rate falls short of, or exceeds, desired production rate. As a result inventory falls lower or rises higher than it otherwise would, thereby necessitating greater changes in desired production rate. The longer the resource adjustment delay, the greater the shortage, or excess, and the required changes in desired production rate. Adjustment times for resource levels are therefore similar to delays in physical flow channels.

Because buffer levels have only a minor effect on production rate, production follows closely the desired rate. Then the stability of the resource level and order rate becomes the dominant concern. Stability is improved with increasing adjustment times (unless the adjustment time is long enough, in combination with changes in desired production rate, to cause the buffer level to fall so low as to exert a strong effect on production rate and thereby act like a resource level). Policy design guidelines 7.1 and 7.2 summarize these results.

Sometimes a resource level can be effectively converted to a buffer level through a change in company policy: over- and undertime for labor and utilization rate for capital equipment. As stated in policy design guideline 7.3, the policy conclusion for time to adjust resource level therefore changes.

In contrast to initial expectations, increasing time to adjust labor improves stability of labor only under certain circumstances. Policy design guideline 7.4 summarizes the methods of improving labor stability.

Finally, overtime can be used to improve labor stability in CYCLICAL markets and production response in GROWTH markets. But before adopting any policy, the analyst must check that (1) possible variations in customer order rate and desired production rate do not convert buffer levels to resource levels and (2) the use of over- and undertime is feasible and profitable for the possible variations.

Dynamics Created by Interactions with Customers and Competitors

8

8.1 Introduction

One of the most important interactions between a company and its environment is with the customers and competitors comprising the market. As identified in chapter 1, the market orders goods from a company as a function of market demand and market share. Market share in turn is a function of company product attractiveness relative to competitor product attractiveness. Changes in product attractiveness result from changes in company competitive variables such as availability, price, quality, marketing effort, and product newness. These competitive variables are a function of company resources. Company resources are acquired and allocated by company policies in response to discrepancies between performance (for example, customer orders) and goals. The additional feedback loops introduced by company-market interactions affect the stability of orders, production, and inventory as well as market share.

Company-market interactions can be classified into one of two types: those that affect the long-run competitive position of the company (product newness, overall quality, average price) and those that affect short-run competitive position (availability, price, sales effort). The long-run competitive position depends on resource allocations to product development and design and to engineering cost-reducing production facilities. These long-run shifts (here five to ten years) are the subject of chapter 13.

Short-run changes in the company's competitive position result from attempts to correct imbalances between the supply of and demand for its products. Supply and demand are balanced, or markets cleared, when supply is changed to match demand, or demand to match supply, or a combination of both. The balancing can be accomplished in three distinct ways:

1. The company can change production rates to match changes in customer order rate.

2. Because of availability customers can change order rate to match the company's production rate.[1]

3. The company can change some other competitive variable, for example, price or advertising, to induce changes in customer order rate.

Each balancing method has distinct implications for stability, market share, and profits. The implications depend on the speed with which the balancing is achieved and the equilibrium conditions achieved. These implications are the subject of chapter 8.

8.2 Structure of Market-Clearing Interactions

Figure 8.1 shows the structure of market-clearing interactions. Supply is synonymous with production rate, demand with customer order rate. Three negative feedback loops attempt to balance supply and demand:

1. Desired and actual production rates respond to customer order rate, finished inventory, and unfilled orders, so that changes in demand elicit changes in supply.

2. Customer order rate and market share respond to delivery delay, so that discrepancies between supply and demand induce compensating changes in demand because of changes in delivery delay.

3. Customer order rate and market share respond to price which in turn responds to inventory discrepancies, so that an imbalance be-

1. In this and subsequent chapters a decrease in availability increases delivery time and causes a decrease in customer order rate. In contrast, in chapter 6 an increase in delivery time caused the company to increase order rate. The effect of delivery time on orders depends on the situation being modeled. If the company is the only supplier, or if the costs of shifting to a different supplier are large, then at least in the short run an increase in delivery time increases order rate. On the other hand, with multiple suppliers, and easy conversion among them, an increase in delivery time of the company decreases order rate (unless total industry capacity is exceeded). In this book the supplier represents aggregate industry capacity available to the company with a long lead time in obtaining more capacity. Hence an increase in supplier delivery time increases order rate. For the purpose of illustrating other dynamics, the company here represents one of several suppliers with easy shift among them. Hence an increase in delivery time decreases orders.

tween supply and demand causes the company to change price and thereby induce a correcting shift in demand.

Two of the loops are controlled by company policy; one, by the customer. Each loop contains delays between the time an imbalance occurs, corrective actions are taken, and results occur.

In figure 8.1 customer order rate is a function of market demand (an exogenous input) and market share. Market share here depends only on delivery delay and price, delivery delay and price being the only dynamic components of product attractiveness in the model developed thus far. Delivery delay is an index of product availability: quick deliveries imply an available product; slow deliveries, an unavailable one.

Customer order rate increases the level of unfilled orders. Unfilled orders, as well as finished inventory, are depleted by shipment rate. Shipment rate depends on the availability of both unfilled orders and finished inventory—without either, shipments cannot be made. As a result, in contrast to earlier chapters, as finished inventory falls, shipment rate also falls so that unfilled orders and delivery delay increase. Eventually the increase in delivery delay feeds back to reduce customer order rate.

Equations that govern these market-clearing interactions in the model follow.

Market Share

Equation 87 states that customer order COR equals the product of market demand MD and market share MS.

$$COR.K = MD.K * MS.K \qquad\qquad 87, A$$

where
COR = customer order rate (units/day)
MD = market demand (units/day)
MS   = market share (percent).

In equation 88 market share MS is modeled as the product of traditional market share TMS, effect of delivery delay on market share EDDMS, and effect of price on market share EPMS. Traditional market share represents the company's loyal customer base. Changes in market share are in direct proportion to this loyal customer base. Such changes in market share occur because of changes in product attractiveness, here as a consequence of changes in delivery delay or price.

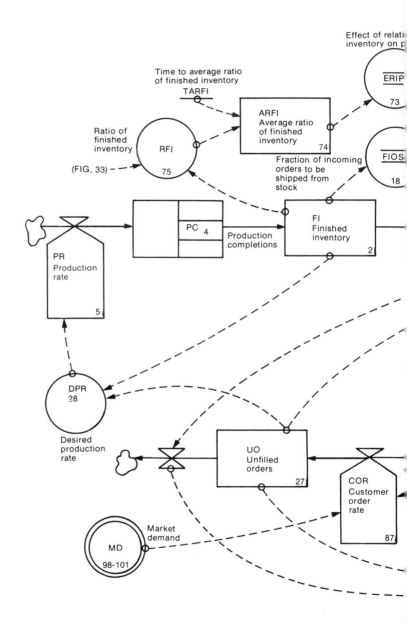

Figure 8.1   Structure of market-clearing interactions

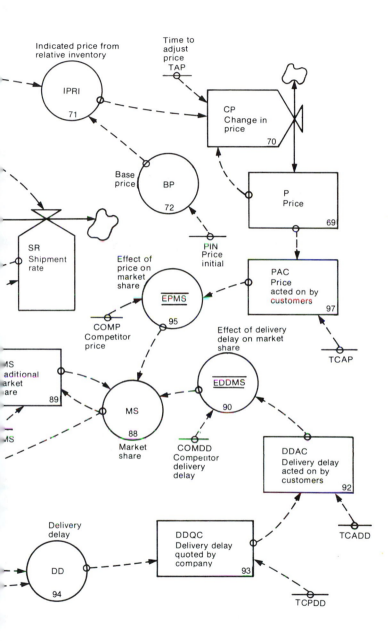

MS.K = TMS.K * EDDMS.K * EPMS.K   88, A

where

MS   = market share (percent)
TMS   = traditional market share (percent)
EDDMS = effect of delivery delay on market share (dimensionless)
EPMS   = effect of price on market share (dimensionless).

Traditional market share TMS is represented as an exponential average of market share MS (equation 89). Time to develop traditional market share TDTMS reflects the loyalty of customers to suppliers. A short TDTMS implies that customers have no brand loyalty. A long TDTMS implies that customers have high brand loyalty. For example, suppose that the company's delivery delay should suddenly increase. Customers will shift to competitors, and the company will lose market share in the short run. TDTMS governs what happens in the long term. If company delivery delay returns to normal after, say, several months, a long TDTMS implies that the company regains most of its lost customers. On the other hand, a short TDTMS implies that the company does not regain its lost customers. In summary TDTMS is the time required for customers to develop confidence in alternative suppliers and forget past relationships with the company. In this model TDTMS is set to a relatively long 960 days (4 years). TDTMS probably depends on the length of time that a customer uses the product. If the customer uses the product for, say, 10 years, it will take a long time to develop traditional market share. If, however, the product lasts only 10 weeks, time to develop traditional market share will be much shorter.

TMS.K = SMOOTH(MS.K,TDTMS)   89, A
TMS = TMSI   89.1, N
TMSI = .1   89.2, C
TDTMS = 960   89.3, C

where

TMS   = traditional market share (percent)
MS   = market share (percent)
TDTMS = time to develop traditional market share (days)
TMSI   = traditional market share, initial (percent).

Equation 90 states that effect of delivery delay on market share EDDMS is a nonlinear function of delivery delay acted on by customers DDAC relative to competitor delivery delay COMDD (see also figure 8.2). When DDAC is equal to or less than COMDD, effect of

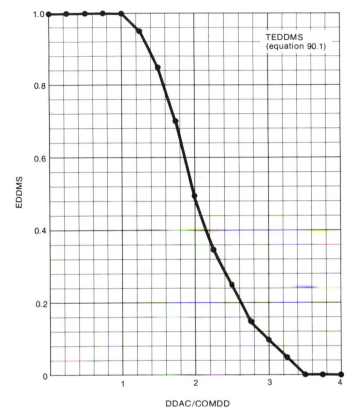

Figure 8.2 Effect of delivery delay on market share

delivery delay on market share equals 1.0. As DDAC rises above
COMDD, EDDMS begins to fall below 1.0. The decrease is gradual at
first, but the slope increases as DDAC increases. Then, as DDAC
approaches four times COMDD, the slope levels off, and EDDMS
approaches 0.

EDDMS.K = TABLE(TEDDMS,DDAC.K/COMDD.K,

              0,4,.25)   90, A

TEDDMS = 1/1/1/1/1/.95/.85/.7/.5/.35/.25/.15/.1/.05/0/0/0   90.1, T

where

EDDMS   = effect of delivery delay on market share (dimensionless)
TEDDMS = table for effect of delivery delay on market share
             (dimensionless)
DDAC   = delivery delay acted on by customers (days)
COMDD   = competitor delivery delay (days).

Competitors are modeled implicitly in this chapter (and in the remainder of the text). It is assumed that the aggregate competition maintains a constant delivery delay equal to the time to ship from stock TSS
(equation 91). In practice the importance of this assumption varies
from industry to industry. In cases where changes in competitor
availability are important, the causes of such changes would be included in the model. The purpose of this chapter, however, is to
explore the dynamics created when the company's product is less
available than the competitor's. Consequently a constant competitor
delivery delay is assumed for simplicity.

COMDD.K = TSS   91, A

where
COMDD = competitor delivery delay (days)
TSS   = time to ship from stock (days).

Delivery delay acted on by customers DDAC is represented in equation 92 as an exponential average of delivery delay quoted by company
DDQC. Time for customers to act on delivery delay TCADD represents time required by customers to perceive and change buying habits.
The length of TCADD depends primarily on how much customers are
locked into the company's product design. If competing products are
very similar to company products, TCADD will be relatively short. If
products are dissimilar, it may take longer for customers to redesign
their product to adapt to competing goods. Consequently TCADD will
be longer.

DDAC.K = SMOOTH(DDQC.K,TCADD)   92, A
TCADD = 60   92.1, C

where
DDAC   = delivery delay acted on by customers (days)
DDQC   = delivery delay quoted by company (days)
TCADD = time for customers to act on delivery delay (days).

Delivery delay quoted by company DDQC is represented by an exponential average of delivery delay DD (equation 93). Time for company to perceive delivery delay is set to 20 days.

DDQC.K = SMOOTH(DD.K,TCPDD)   93, A
TCPDD = 20   93.1, C

where
DDQC = delivery delay quoted by company (days)
DD   = delivery delay (days)
TCPDD = time for company to perceive delivery delay (days).

Equation 94 defines delivery delay DD as unfilled orders UO divided by the sum of shipment rate from stock SRS and shipment rate from production SRP. Therefore delivery delay represents the average time required for customers to receive the product.

$$DD.K = UO.K/(SRS.JK + SRP.JK) \qquad\qquad 94, A$$

where
DD = delivery delay (days)
UO = unfilled orders (units)
SRS = shipment rate from stock (units/day)
SRP = shipment rate from production (units/day).

Effect of price on market share EPMS is a nonlinear function of price acted on by customers PAC divided by competitor price COMP (equation 95 and figure 8.3). Small price differences are seen to produce

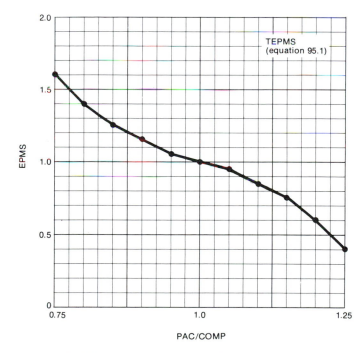

Figure 8.3   Effect of price on market share

relatively less change in market share than large price differences, on the assumption the customers will stay with a known supplier as long as the company is not too out of line in its price.

EPMS.K = TABLE (TEPMS,PAC.K/COMP.K,.75,1.25,
                      .05)   95, A
TEPMS = 1.6/1.4/1.25/1.15/1.05/1/.95/.85/.75/.6/.4   95.1, T

where
EPMS = effect of price on market share (dimensionless)
TEPMS = table for effect of price on market share (dimensionless)
PAC   = price acted on by customers ($/unit)
COMP = competitor price ($/unit).

Competitor price COMP is set in equation 96 to initial price PIN. As in delivery delay the competitor is assumed to maintain a constant price. In practice, where competitor prices change in response to company price changes, such interactions would be included in the model.

COMP.K = PIN   96, A

where
COMP = competitor price ($/unit)
PIN   = price, initial ($/unit).

Price acted on by customers PAC is represented in equation 97 by an exponential average of price P. Time for customers to act on price TCAP is here set to 60 days, equivalent to time for customers to act on delivery delay TCADD.

PAC.K = SMOOTH(P.K,TCAP)   97, A
TCAP = 60   97.1, C

where
PAC   = price acted on by customers ($/unit)
P   = price ($/unit)
TCAP = time for customers to act on price (days).

Shipping Equations

The equations governing shipment rate and unfilled orders are somewhat detailed and thus are described in appendix 8.1. Only the constraint placed on shipment rate due to finished inventory availability is of primary concern here.

In the shipping equations customer order rate is split into two flows: those customer orders to be shipped from stock and those to be shipped from production. The split depends on the fraction of incoming orders to be shipped from stock, which in turn depends on available finished inventory. If inventory is available, customer orders build the pool consisting of unfilled orders to be shipped from stock. These orders can be shipped in the relatively short time it takes to ship from stock. As finished inventory falls, however, ever fewer orders can be shipped from stock and must be shipped from production. The longer lead time on production causes average delivery time on orders to increase.

The fraction of incoming orders to be shipped from stock FIOSS is a nonlinear function of uncommitted finished inventory UFI divided by average customer order rate for shipping ACORS (figure 8.4). UFI divided by ACORS equals the number of days of inventory, not committed to current customer orders, remaining in finished inventory. If there are greater than 25 days uncommitted inventory in stock, FIOSS

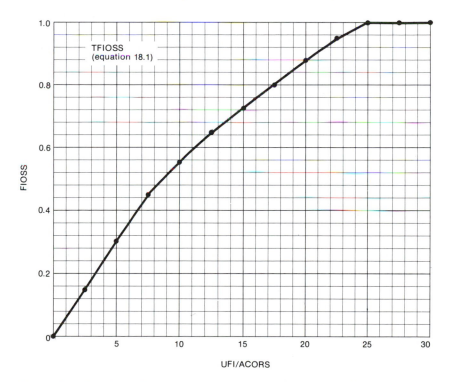

Figure 8.4   Fraction of incoming orders to be shipped from stock

equals 1.0 (100 percent of orders shipped from stock). As days supply of inventory falls below 25 days, FIOSS decreases rapidly. Finally, if days supply equals 0, FIOSS equals 0 because shipment from stock is impossible.

The shape of the relationship between FIOSS and uncommitted finished inventory depends on the number of different items the company holds in stock and the variability around a normal sales mix. If the company sells only one product, or the sales mix is completely constant, then FIOSS would be 1.0 for all values except 0 finished inventory. As the number of products, or the variability of sales mix, increases, the larger the inventory a company must hold to avoid stockouts. The relationship depicted in figure 8.4 represents a company with a large number of product options and a variable sales mix.

Desired Production Rate Policy

The policy governing desired production rate DPR has been revised in two ways. First, as given in equation 28, desired production rate DPR equals the sum of the original three components, base customer order rate BCOR, finished inventory correction FIC, and work in process correction WIPC, plus now an additional term unfilled orders correction UOC. UOC adjusts production up or down depending on whether or not unfilled orders exceed or drop below the company's goal for unfilled orders.

$$\text{DPR.K} = \text{BCOR.K} + \text{FIC.K} + \text{WIPC.K} + \text{UOC.K} \qquad \text{28, A}$$

where
DPR   = desired production rate (units/day)
BCOR = base customer order rate (units/day)
FIC   = finished inventory correction (units/day)
WIPC = work in process correction (units/day)
UOC   = unfilled order correction (units/day).

Equation 37 defines unfilled order correction to equal the difference between unfilled UO and desired unfilled orders DUO divided by time to correct finished inventory TCFI.

$$\text{UOC.K} = (\text{UO.K} - \text{DUO.K})/\text{TCFI} \qquad \text{37, A}$$

where
UOC = unfilled order correction (units/day)
UO   = unfilled orders (units)

DUO = desired unfilled orders (units)

TCFI = time to correct finished inventory (days).

The second change to the desired production rate policy comes in the definition of company goals. Equation 38 states that desired unfilled orders DUO equals desired days unfilled orders DDUO multiplied by base customer order rate BCOR. In contrast to the fixed company goals assumed previously, DDUO is now made a variable.

$$\text{DUO.K} = \text{DDUO.K} * \text{BCOR.K} \qquad\qquad\qquad 38, A$$

where

DUO   = desired unfilled orders (units)

DDUO = desired days unfilled orders (days)

BCOR = base customer order rate (units/day)

In equation 39 desired days unfilled orders DDUO is represented as an exponential average of delivery delay DD. DDUO is the company's goal for delivery delay. Delivery delay DD is the company's performance. Equation 39 states that the company's goal responds to company performance. Time to develop company traditions TDCT determines how quickly goals adjust to performance. Acceptance of traditional performance as a goal reflects the human tendency to assume that, if conditions have persisted for a long time, they must be acceptable, or at least inevitable. Furthermore, most new employees have no experience to recognize that things can be done better than they have been; so they endorse the traditional performance as a standard against which to measure their own performance.

$$\text{DDUO.K} = \text{SMOOTH(DD.K,TDCT)} \qquad\qquad 39, A$$
$$\text{DDUO} = \text{TSS} \qquad\qquad\qquad\qquad\qquad 39.1, N$$

where

DDUO = desired days unfilled orders (days)

DD   = delivery delay (days)

TDCT = time to develop company traditions (days)

TSS   = time to ship from stock (days).

The company's goal for desired days finished inventory DDFI is similarly modeled as responding to actual company performance for days finished inventory (as determined by dividing FI by COR). Equation 34 is the alternative way of modeling an exponential average. In equation 34.3 time to develop company traditions TDCT is set to an arbitrarily large value, thereby reflecting that company traditions are a constant. TDCT is reduced in a later section.

DDFI.K = DDFI.J + (DT/TDCT)((FI.J/COR.J) − DDFI.J)   34, L
DDFI = DDFIN   34.1, N
DDFIN = 30   34.2, C
TDCT = 50000   34.3, C

where
DDFI   = desired days finished inventory (days)
DT   = delta time, simulation solution interval (days)
TDCT   = time to develop company traditions (days)
FI   = finished product inventory (units)
COR   = customer order rate (units/day)
DDFIN = desired days finished inventory normal (days).

Pricing Policy

Equation 69 states that price P is a level variable increased by change in price CP. P is arbitrarily initialized to a price, initial value of $100 per unit. In chapter 9 all costs are referenced to this value.

P.K = P.J + (DT)(CP.JK)   69, L
P = PIN   69.1, N
PIN = 100   69.2, C

where
P   = price ($/unit)
DT   = delta time, simulation solution interval (days)
CP   = change in price ($/unit/day)
PIN   = price, initial ($/unit).

In equation 70 the change in price CP equals the difference between indicated price from relative inventory IPRI and price P, corrected over time to adjust price TAP. Price changes are switched in or out by setting price switch PSWT to 1.0 or 0, respectively. TAP is here set to 60 days. Different values are examined in a later section.

CP.KL = PSWT * (IPRI.K − P.K)/TAP   70, R
PSWT = 0   70.1, C
TAP = 60   70.2, C

where
CP   = change in price ($/unit/day)
PSWT = price switch (dimensionless)
IPRI   = indicated price from relative inventory ($/unit)
P   = price ($/unit)
TAP   = time to adjust price (days).

Equation 71 states that indicated price from relative inventory IPRI equals base price BP multiplied by effect of relative inventory on price ERIP.

$$IPRI.K = BP.K * ERIP.K \qquad\qquad 71, A$$

IPRI = indicated price from relative inventory ($/unit)
BP   = base price ($/unit)
ERIP = effect of relative inventory on price (dimensionless).

Base price BP is a reference price that might be based on costs plus a normal markup (equation 72). Here BP is set to price initial PIN.

$$BP.K = PIN \qquad\qquad 72, A$$

where
BP   = base price ($/unit)
PIN = price, initial ($/unit).

Equation 73 states that effect of relative inventory on price ERIP is a nonlinear function of average relative inventory ARFI (see also figure 8.5). ERIP is a linear function of average relative inventory ARFI. If

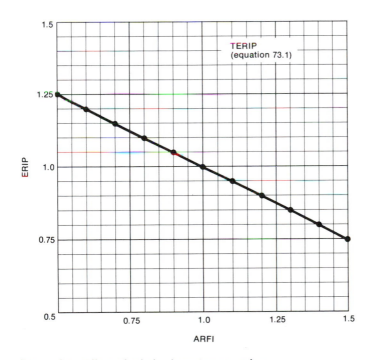

Figure 8.5 Effect of relative inventory on price

average relative inventory ARFI equals 1.0 (finished inventory equals finished-inventory goal), ERIP equals 1.0. Deviations of ARFI from 1.0 here cause the company to change price in proportion.

ERIP.K = TABLE(TERIP,ARFI.K,.5,1.5,.1)   73, A
TERIP = 1.25/1.2/1.15/1.1/1.05/1/.95/.9/.85/.8/.75   73.1, T

where

ERIP   = effect of relative inventory on price (dimensionless)
TERIP = table for effect of relative inventory on price
           (dimensionless)
ARFI   = average ratio of finished inventory (dimensionless).

Average relative finished inventory ARFI is represented in equation 74 as an exponential average of relative finished inventory RFI. Time to average relative inventory TARFI reflects the length of time an inventory discrepancy must persist before the company responds with a price change. Values of TARFI are examined in the simulation runs in a later section.

ARFI.K = SMOOTH(RFI.K,TARFI)   74, A
TARFI = 60   74.1, C

where

ARFI   = average ratio of finished inventory (dimensionless)
RFI   = ratio of finished inventory (dimensionless)
TARFI = time to average ratio of finished inventory (days).

Relative finished inventory RFI is defined in equation 75 to equal finished inventory FI divided by finished inventory goal FIG.

RFI.K = FI.K/FIG.K   75, A

RFI = ratio of finished inventory (dimensionless)
FI   = finished product inventory (units)
FIG = finished inventory goal (units).

8.3 Understanding Causes of Instability and Lost Market Share

Production, availability, and price are all market-clearing mechanisms. This section analyzes production and availability performances in terms of stability and market share. Section 8.5 analyzes price performance.

The approach taken is first to analyze production and availability performances separately as market-clearing mechanisms and then production and availability together. Finally, production, availability, and price are analyzed. In this way the contribution of each mechanism can be determined.

Production Alone

In chapters 4 through 7 the market-clearing mechanism was production rate. A change in demand (customer order rate) elicited a change in supply (production rate). In fact the change in production rate was greater than the change in customer order rate because of inventory corrections.

Figures 8.6 and 8.7 show the response of the production system to a STEP change in customer order rate with the aggressive and moderate policy sets, respectively. In the simulation runs that produced these figures, the effect of delivery delay on market share was neutralized. As discussed in earlier chapters, the aggressive policy set yields greater amplification of production rate, but finished inventory does not fall as far, or take as long to reach its goal, as with the moderate policy set. The consequence of the inventory shortfall is a longer delivery delay.

Recall from earlier chapters that a long delivery delay had no effect

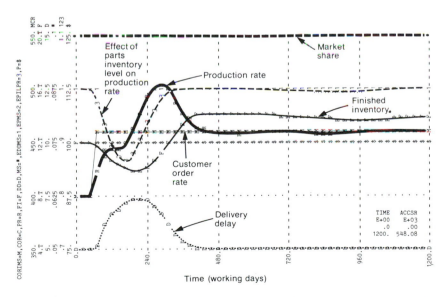

Figure 8.6   System response to a STEP change in market demand: production as market-cleaning mechanism with aggressive policy set

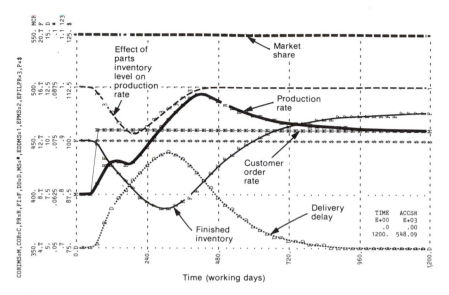

Figure 8.7   System response to a STEP change in market demand: production as
market-cleaning mechanism with moderate policy set

on customer order rate. As indicated in the bottom right-hand corner of
the figures, accumulated shipment rate over the length of the simulation (ACCSR) is the same under both policies. Consequently the only
real policy question to consider is the degree of production stability the
company wants to achieve for efficiency reasons. Without delivery
delay feedback to order rate, the costs of a slow-reacting policy cannot
be adequately identified.

Availability Alone

Under certain circumstances availability alone can be the market-
clearing mechanism. For example, if a company has limited production
capacity, in the short run an increase in customer order rate above
capacity causes availability to act as the balancing mechanism. The
long lead times on increasing capacity, the reluctance to change price,
and the follow-the-leader-pricing policies of many companies often
force availability into the market-clearing role. Chapter 11 addresses
the issue of capacity expansion; the remainder of this subsection
analyzes the dynamics of availability as a market-clearing mechanism.
   Availability clears the market by reducing market share until cus-

tomer order rate equals production rate. For example, assuming a constant production rate, an increase in market demand will initially cause customer order rate to exceed production rate. Consequently unfilled orders increase so that delivery delay lengthens (availability falls). As the longer delivery delay is perceived and acted upon by first the company and then customers, market share falls, thereby reducing customer order rate. Delivery delay will continue to rise, and market share fall, until customer order rate is reduced to production rate.

Availability does not necessarily balance supply and demand in a smooth adjustment, as figure 8.8 illustrates. Figure 8.8 gives the response of the production system with constant production rate to a STEP change in market demand. Following the STEP change, customer order rate is eventually reduced to equal production rate. However, the adjustment process follows a series of ups and downs: customer order rate undershoots and overshoots its equilibrium value. The cause of this behavior is described next.

At day 60 customer order rate increases in a steplike fashion because of the exogenously imposed STEP increase in market demand (not shown). A customer order rate above production rate causes finished inventory to fall and unfilled orders to rise (not shown). As a result delivery delay increases. The market perceives and acts on the increas-

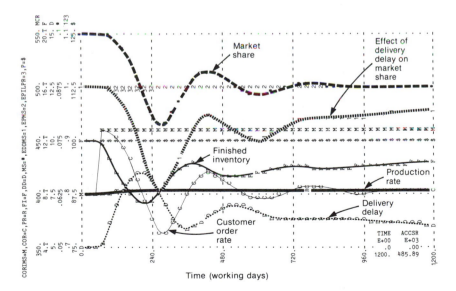

Figure 8.8   System response to a STEP change in market demand: availability as a market-clearing mechanism

ing delivery delay so that market share falls. As market share falls, so does customer order rate. At approximately day 200 customer order rate has fallen to equal production rate—a possible equilibrium point. However, market share continues to fall, causing customer order rate to undershoot production rate. Why does market share continue to fall? Because customer order rate responds not to delivery delay but to a delayed value of delivery delay. Consequently, even though delivery delay peaks when customer order rate crosses production rate, delivery delay acted on by customers (not shown) continues to increase.

The decrease in customer order rate below production rate, as caused by customers acting on a delayed value of delivery delay, is like an exogenously imposed STEP decrease in market demand. As a result customer order rate overshoots as it rises toward production rate. Eventually, the oscillations damp out, as each successive self-induced step change is of lower magnitude.

This analysis suggests that (1), if the delay between delivery delay and its effect on market share could be eliminated, customer order rate would fall quickly and smoothly to equal production rate and (2) the longer the delay, the greater the amplitude and period of oscillations. Further the more sensitive customers are to delivery delay, the greater the amplitude and the shorter the period of oscillations. Figures 8.9, 8.10, and 8.11 illustrate these points.

In the simulation run that produced figure 8.9, the delay between delivery delay and market share has been essentially eliminated (time for company to perceive delivery delay TCPDD and time for customers to act on delivery delay TCADD were reduced to 8 days from 20 and 60 days, respectively). Such a change makes the availability feedback loop effectively first order—customer order rate adjusts almost instantaneously to production rate. With instantaneous adjustment customers reduce order rate to equal production rate without overshoot.

Figure 8.10 shows that the longer TCADD (here 240 days), the greater the amplitude and period of oscillations: the slower customers react, the longer customer order rate remains above production rate, and thus the lower inventory falls and the higher delivery delay rises. When customers finally react to the higher delivery delay, market share falls even lower—the system is in effect hit by a larger STEP decrease and consequently overshoots more in the opposite direction.

The stronger the effect of delivery delay on market share, the greater the amplitude of fluctuations (compare figure 8.11 with 8.8). Moreover

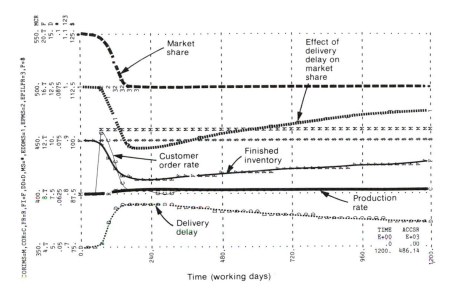

Figure 8.9   System response to a STEP change in market demand: availability as a market-clearing mechanism with short response time

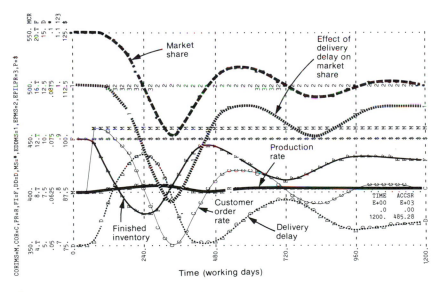

Figure 8.10   System response to a STEP change in market demand: availability as a market-clearing mechanism with a long response time

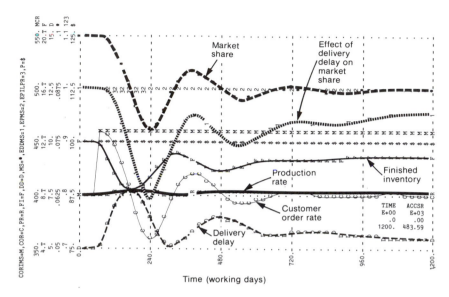

Time (working days)

Figure 8.11 System response to a STEP change in market demand: availability as a market-clearing mechanism with a stronger market response

a stronger response causes the system to adjust more quickly. A detailed explanation of this behavior is beyond the scope of this book.

In summary availability clears the market by changing market share until customer order rate equals production rate. But because the market responds to a delayed value of delivery delay, the market overcorrects and then must adjust in the opposite direction.

Production and Availability

When both production and availability act to clear the market, the two negative feedback loops shown in figure 8.12 operate. In previous chapters only the loop at the left was active: a decrease in inventory causes an increase in production starts, which after a delay increases production completions and inventory. The goal of the negative loop is to keep the inventory equal to the company's goal for inventory.

But the market also tries to control a company's inventory through the feedback loop shown at the right in figure 8.12. A decrease in inventory now decreases the availability of the company's product. As availability decreases, delivery delay increases. In response customers seek suppliers offering shorter delivery times. Order rates fall lowering the rate at which inventory declines.

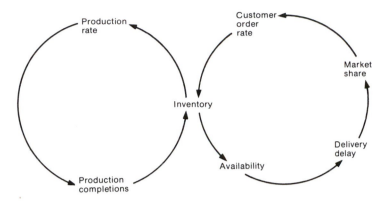

Figure 8.12   Negative feedback loops controlling inventory

The goal of the negative market loop is to equate customer order rate with production completions: should customer order rate rise above production completions, and thereby deplete inventory, product availability decreases and eventually causes customer order rate to fall. Availability continues to decrease until customer order rate equals production completions. The negative market loop works in the opposite manner should customer order rate fall below production completions.

Instability is a possible result of interaction between the two negative feedback loops. For example, suppose customer order rate should suddenly rise above production completions, thereby depleting inventory. The decline in inventory initiates two corrective actions: the company increases production starts to rebuild inventory (and to match the higher customer order rate), and customers perceive the decrease in availability and thus reduce ordering to match the lower production rate. Potentially production completions can be increasing just as customer order rate is decreasing. As a result inventory increases, and the company initiates correction action in the opposite direction.

Figure 8.13 shows the response of the inventory system to a STEP increase in market demand with production and availability as market-clearing mechanisms. The company in this figure has adopted the moderate policy parameter set. The sudden increase in customer order rate above production rate causes finished inventory to decrease. In response production rate increases as the company attempts to match the higher volume of business and to rebuild inventory to a

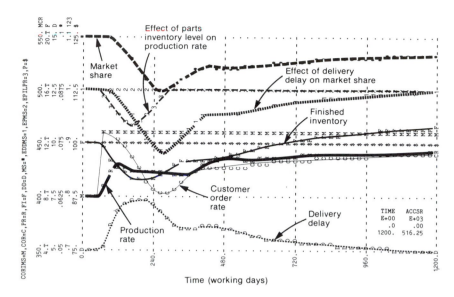

Figure 8.13 System response to a STEP increase in market demand: production and availability as market-clearing mechanisms with moderate policy set

higher level. But around day 120 production rate peaks and declines because effect of parts inventory level on production rate drops below 1.0. When production alone clears the market, similar parts shortages only delay eventual production and rebuilding of inventory. But when production and availability clear the market, parts shortages cause loss of market share.

Because production rate cannot increase to match the rise in customer order rate, finished inventory declines. As a result delivery delay increases. The increase in delivery delay causes customer order rate to fall. Again, because of the delayed market response to delivery delay, customer order rate falls below production rate. The parts shortage prevents production from clearing the market.

But at day 264, when sufficient parts inventory is available for production (effect of parts inventory level on production rate equal to 1.0), customer order rate is below production rate. Consequently the company sees no need to increase production rate. Nevertheless, production rate is maintained above customer order rate in order to build finished inventory. As finished inventory increases, delivery delay falls so that customer order rate increases. As customer order rate increases, production rate increases to build more finished inventory, and so on. When effect of delivery delay on market share finally returns to 1.0 around day 1200, market share stabilizes at approximately 9.6 percent (initial share of 10 percent).

In summary the loss of market share comes in two phases. In the first phase (from approximately day 120 to day 300), customer order rate rises well above production rate so that delivery delay increases sharply, causing a sharp drop in market share. In this phase a shortage of parts inventory which constrains production rate contributes to the loss of market share.

The second phase occurs from day 300 onward when the company gradually loses loyal customers (decline in traditional market share). The cause of this second loss is that the company is planning production around a customer order rate suppressed by a long delivery delay. Customer order rate does not necessarily reflect the true demand for a company's product. Note that, as production is increased, inventory increases, delivery delay falls, and customer order rate rises so that production increases further. But by producing below demand, the company eventually pulls the loyal customer base down to production. These dynamics are similar to those described in chapter 6 when parts order rate was based on production rate, but production rate was constrained by a shortage of parts inventory. In chapter 6 the problem was resolved by basing parts order rate on desired production rate. Here a similar solution would require basing production rate on market demand, in most cases an unknowable quantity. An alternative solution is proposed in section 8.4.

8.4 Improving Behavior through Policy Design

Carry Extra Parts Inventory

One of the constraints to increasing production rate can be overcome by carrying extra parts inventory. Figure 8.14 shows system response when days supply parts inventory is increased from 60 to 90 days. Market share performance is much improved.

Because parts inventory is in adequate supply, production rate rises higher than in figure 8.13. However, because of the delay in increasing production and time to complete work in process, production rate lags customer order rate so that finished inventory falls. As a result delivery delay increases so that, just as production rate increases, customer order rate falls. In response the company reduces production rate.

From day 240 to day 600 the company again bases production rate on

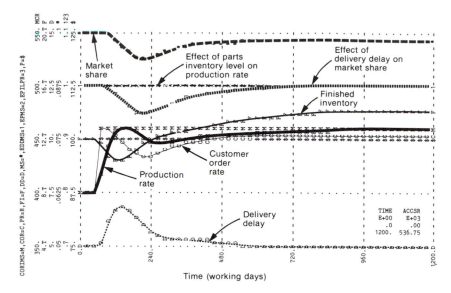

Figure 8.14 System response to a STEP increase in market demand: production and availability as market-clearing mechanisms with moderate policy set and extra parts inventory

a customer order rate suppressed by a long delivery delay. Because the company loses some loyal customers, market share never returns to 10 percent.

Thus, while carrying extra parts inventory reduces the loss of market share, it does not eliminate it.

Carry Extra Parts Inventory and Adopt More Aggressive Production Rate Policy

Because the aggressive policy reacts more quickly to market fluctuations, it might be used to reduce the loss of market share that follows a sudden change in market demand. As inventory corrections are made over 60 rather than 240 days, in the period following the initial market share loss production rate increases more rapidly and along with it customer order rate. Therefore the company loses fewer loyal customers.

In figure 8.15 the aggressive policy set with extra parts inventory eliminates most of the loss of market share as expected. However, the cost is greater amplification in production rate. Under a more realistic NOISE variation in market demand such greater amplification causes greater instability in both production rate and finished inventory. Thus,

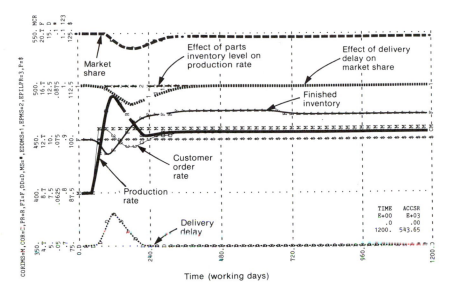

Time (working days)

Figure 8.15 System response to a STEP increase in market demand: production and availability as market-clearing mechanisms with aggressive policy set and extra parts inventory

while the policy is beneficial in terms of market share, it is not in terms of stability.

Carry Extra Finished and Parts Inventory

The only way to prevent a loss of market share and still achieve production stability is to carry extra finished inventory. By carrying sufficient extra inventory, the company can ship from stock even with unanticipated increases in customer order rate. Moreover extra finished inventory is an effective means of taking business from competitors during periods of business growth.

Figure 8.16 illustrates the market share and stability benefits of carrying extra finished product inventory. In the figure days supply parts inventory is increased by 50 percent and days supply finished inventory by 33 percent. The company is therefore able to absorb the unanticipated increase in customer order rate with inventory. With extra inventory a slower-reacting policy can provide stability without loss of market share. Even much slower-reacting policies are possible.

Determining the most profitable means of handling unanticipated increases in business requires much more analysis, however. First,

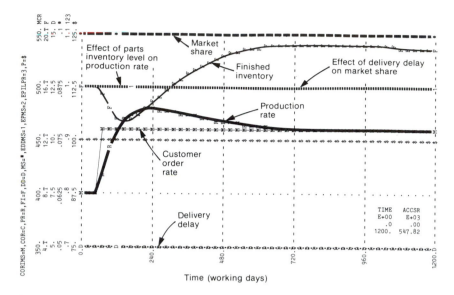

Time (working days)

Figure 8.16 System response to a STEP increase in market demand: production and availability as market-clearing mechanisms with moderate policy set and extra finished and parts inventory

financial equations necessary to calculate profits need to be added. Second, a wider range of inventory levels and policy parameters must be analyzed. And third, response to different magnitude and types of variations in customer demand must be evaluated. These issues are discussed in chapter 9.

Policy Design Guideline

The following policy design guideline summarizes the results of these sections:

Policy design guideline 8.1 Availability clears the market by reducing a company's market share until customer order rate equals production rate. By doing so, market clearing via availability can (1) increase instability because, just as production rate is increasing supply to meet the new demand, availability can be decreasing demand to match the old supply, and (2) cause lost market share in the short run and loss of loyal customers in the long run.

Because availability is a market-clearing mechanism in all markets, the only way to neutralize its effects without increasing production and inventory instability is to carry sufficient extra finished product inventory, so that changes in customer order rate can be absorbed without increases in delivery delay.

8.5 Understanding Causes of Instability When Price Is a Market-Clearing Mechanism

Availability is but one of several competitive variables that might change to balance supply and demand. Others include price and advertising. For example, should customer order rate exceed production rate so that finished inventory falls, the company might increase prices or reduce advertising to bring customer order rate down. This section explores the use of pricing policy as a market-clearing mechanism, but the conclusions should generally apply to advertising and other, similar competitive variables.

Figure 8.17 shows system response to a STEP change in market demand with production, availability, and price as market-clearing mechanisms. The company in the figure follows the moderate policy set with the normal levels of parts and finished inventory. Figure 8.17 should be compared to figure 8.13.

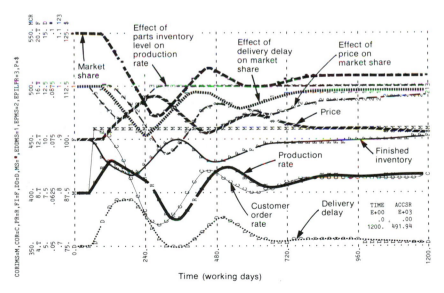

Figure 8.17 System response to a STEP change in market demand: production, availability, and price as market-clearing mechanisms with moderate policy set and extra finished and parts inventory

The addition of pricing policy as a market-clearing mechanism here substantially worsens system stability. One cause of the deterioration in performance is that the effect of price on market share comes into force after other mechanisms have already cleared the market. For example, around day 192 customer order rate falls below production rate largely because delivery delay has increased (note effect of delivery delay on market share). But even though the market has already been cleared, in the sense that excess demand has been eliminated, the effect of price on market share is inevitable and causes demand (customer order rate) to fall well below supply (production rate). In response corrective actions are taken in the opposite direction.

The response time of the availability-clearing mechanism is governed by market perception and action delays, here totaling around 80 days. The response time of the price-clearing mechanism includes company as well as market perception and action delays, totaling 180 days (120 days for the company and 60 for the market). Consequently price increases take effect well after availability clears the market and therefore contribute to further instability.

Might not then shorter company perception and action delays for price help clear the market? Figure 8.18 shows system response when

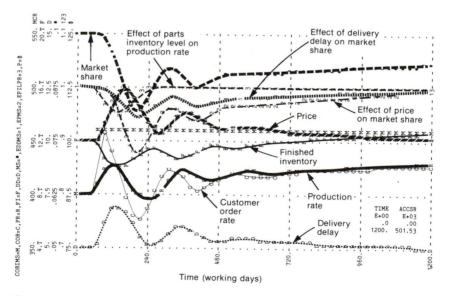

Figure 8.18 System response to a STEP change in market demand: production, availability, and price as market-clearing mechanisms with quick price changes

company delay is cut to 20 days. In fact price again worsens stability. Now both price and availability clear the market at the same time, but together they overreact. Not only is the customer hit with slow deliveries but also with high prices. Consequently market share falls farther down than when production and availability alone clear the market. Because customer order rate falls well below production rate, compensating actions in the other direction must be taken.[2]

When the response time of price is equal to or longer than that of other, nonoptional market-clearing mechanisms, pricing policy leads to instability and so is not an effective means of clearing markets. However, pricing policy is a more profitable means of clearing the market. Note how this is accomplished in figure 8.18, as compared to figure 8.13: most of the market share is lost as a result of higher prices; thus order rate is lower, and availability improves somewhat. As a result total revenues may actually be greater because the net market share loss is not as great as if price and availability acted alone.

If a company has to lose market share (for example, because production cannot be increased), it is better off losing it through high prices than product unavailability. Such is the situation described in chapter 12.

Nevertheless, losing market share is a dangerous practice. Past a point it becomes difficult for a company to compete effectively with larger competitors. Competitive research and development, marketing, and sales and service networks become more difficult to support as market share declines. Consequently a company is better advised to design policies to prevent a loss of market share.

The following guideline summarizes the results of this section:

Policy design guideline 8.2 Pricing policy is an effective market-clearing mechanism only if price aggregate response time (company plus market action time) is shorter than the response time of other, nonoptional mechanisms such as availability. If price response time is equal to other response times, overcorrection and increased instability are likely to occur, although total revenues may increase. If price response time is longer than other response times, price takes effect only after markets have been cleared and therefore contributes to instability and lost market share.

---

2. These conclusions apply only to heterogeneous products for which price and availability are distinct competitive variables. For homogeneous, commodity products price and availability are effectively the same.

8.6 Testing Scenarios in Policy Design

CYCLICAL

Figure 8.19 shows the response of the inventory system with market feedback to a more realistic CYCLICAL variation in market demand. The company in the figure follows the moderate policy set with no extra finished or parts inventory. The response looks similar to that which might be expected from a series of STEP inputs: periods of sharp declines in market share followed by a partial recovery to a lower market share level than before the increase in business. Moreover each growth phase exhibits the fluctuations in production rate and customer order rate characteristic of the STEP response. Because the CYCLICAL response is similar to the STEP response, policies that improved performance for the STEP should also improve performance for business cycles.

Figure 8.20 shows system response when the company carries extra finished and parts inventory. The performance of market share is improved, although even 33 percent extra finished inventory is insufficient to prevent some loss of share given the magnitude of the cyclical variation.

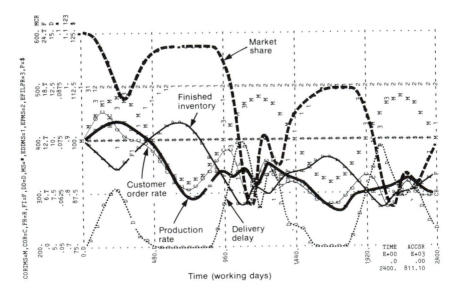

Figure 8.19 Inventory system response to CYCLICAL variation in market demand: production and availability as market-clearing mechanisms with moderate policy set

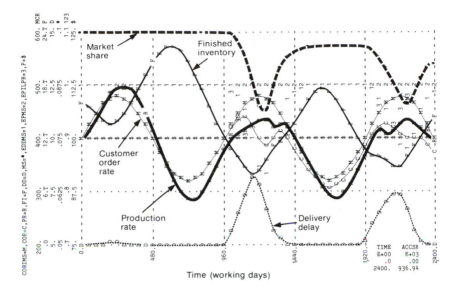

Figure 8.20   Inventory system response to CYCLICAL variation in market demand: production and availability as market-clearing mechanisms with moderate policy set and extra inventory

The final noteworthy characteristic of system response to a CYCLICAL variation is that market share gradually declines over time. This decline is caused by two interacting elements of the system: the company's production policy which responds to a customer order rate suppressed below demand by a long delivery delay, and the tendency of formerly loyal customers to switch permanently to competitors offering continued better performance (decline in traditional market share).

Handling Growth in Business

Any unanticipated growth in business will result in production rate falling below customer order rate. Consequently finished inventory will fall, resulting in delivery delay increases. The increase in delivery delay in turn causes customer order rate to decline below true demand. If the company now plans production on the basis of customer order rate, it is locking itself into a permanently lower market share.

Figure 8.21 illustrates the problem. In the figure market demand is growing at a compounded rate of about 10 percent per year; the company adopts the moderate policy set with no extra finished or parts

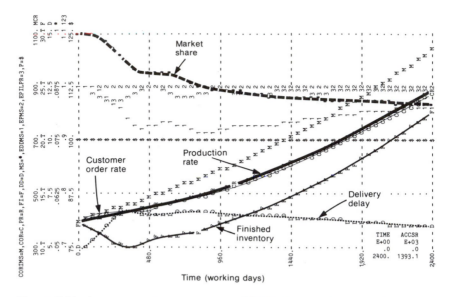

Figure 8.21   Inventory system response to GROWTH in market demand: production and availability as market-clearing mechanisms with moderate policy set

inventory. Initially growth in customer order rate is unanticipated. Production rate falls below customer order rate; inventory declines; and delivery delay increases. The increase in delivery delay causes a loss of market share, and therefore customer order rate falls below demand (customer order rate at initial market share is plotted as an *M* but not highlighted).

In planning production, the company extrapolates a customer order rate which is growing below and at a rate less than market demand because of increasing delivery delay. Desired inventory levels (which determine future delivery delay) are based on this suppressed customer order rate. Consequently the company does not increase production rate sufficiently to bring delivery delay down to the value that would allow the company to achieve demand.

In this scenario company production rate, not market demand, is controlling customer order rate. As production rate increases, delivery delay falls, and customer order rate rises to follow the change in production rate. Should production rate fall, delivery delay would rise to bring customer order rate down. In contrast to normal expectations that customer order rate controls production rate, production rate can control customer order rate with availability effects on market share.

Customer order rate is not necessarily market demand for the company's product. The only way a company can be sure that a long delivery delay is not suppressing customer order rate is by carrying extra inventory. Extra inventory is necessary because inventory goals are usually based on customer order rate. If the company only strives for inventory based on a suppressed customer order rate, then traditional market share will probably fall (reducing demand) before the company realizes the true potential. Extra inventory prevents loss of market share in a growing market, as shown in figure 8.22. With extra inventory customer order rate is not suppressed below demand because delivery delay remains at its minimum value.

Policy guideline 8.3 summarizes these results:

Policy design guideline 8.3 In a growing market planning desired production rate on customer order rate can lead to growth slower than the market rate of growth and to lost market share because customer order rate does not necessarily equal market demand. The only way of assuring demand will be satisfied is by carrying extra finished inventory. Carrying extra inventory may be an effective means of taking market share from less aggressive competitors.

Importance of Adhering to Goals

Corporate operating goals are generally not fixed. In many cases traditional performance becomes the benchmark against which current accomplishments are measured. But as current performance changes, the benchmark also changes. Potentially the company can experience a downward spiral of declining performance, lowering of standards, and then even lower performance until a crisis is reached.

Figure 8.23 illustrates the problem. In the figure market demand grows at a 10 percent compounded annual rate; the company adopts the moderate policy set, but with corporate goals for desired days finished inventory and desired days unfilled orders based on 2-year averages of actual performance. Figure 8.23 should be compared to figure 8.21.

The downward spiral caused by variable goals is clearly evident. As before, the unanticipated growth in customer order rate causes finished inventory to fall and delivery delay to rise. But now, as delivery delay increases, the delivery delay goal increases. Consequently production rate does not increase as much as in figure 8.21. Delivery delay must then rise further to keep customer order rate in line with production rate and so on.

The downward spiral is prevented by either maintaining fixed goals

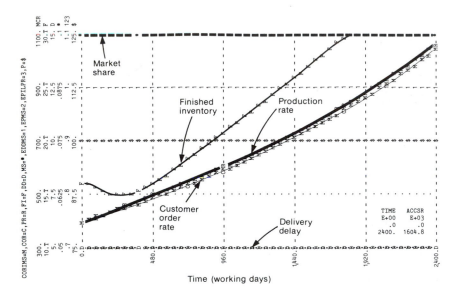

Figure 8.22 Inventory system response to GROWTH in market demand: production and availability as market-clearing mechanisms with moderate policy set
and extra inventory

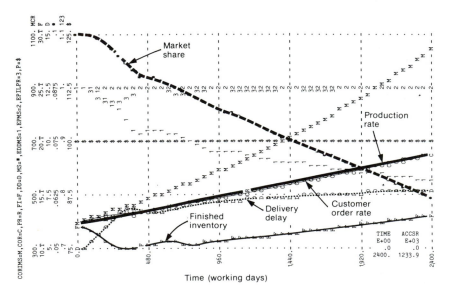

Figure 8.23 Inventory system response to GROWTH in market demand: production and availability as market-clearing mechanisms with moderate policy set
and variable goals

or taking actions (for example, extra finished inventory) that prevent performance from deteriorating.

Policy design guideline 8.4 Variable performance goals potentially create a downward spiral of declining performance, lowering of standards, and further declining performance. The downward spiral is prevented by either (1) maintaining fixed goals or (2) preventing performance from deteriorating.

8.7 Summary and Generalizations

An important set of interactions between the company and the market are those that balance the supply of and demand for the company's product. These market-clearing interactions include (1) company changes in production rate, (2) customer changes in order rate as a consequence of availability, and (3) customer changes in order rate as a consequence of company changes in, for example, price or advertising. The combination of interactions influences stability and market share.

Corporate policy design must reflect three generalizations regarding market-clearing mechanisms:

1. Market-clearing mechanism(s) with the shortest aggregate response time (company action time plus market reaction time) will clear the market first.
2. Mechanisms that respond with the same aggregate time can cause overcorrection and thereby lead to instability.
3. Mechanisms that respond after the market has been cleared lead to needlessly lost orders and instability.

Company policies must be consistent for good corporate performance. For example, while the company can rely on changes in production rate to clear the market, such changes must be effectively and efficiently accomplished before availability comes into play. Otherwise, as summarized in policy design guideline 8.1, availability and production, or just availability alone, clear the market with undesirable consequences. Carrying extra inventory prevents the adverse consequences of availability if production cannot be changed quickly.

Likewise, while price changes are effective market-clearing mechanisms, price response time must be shorter than availability and/or production response times. Otherwise, as stated in guideline 8.2, price changes can increase instability and loss of market share. Higher prices can be advantageous from a revenue standpoint when production cannot be increased to clear the market, and price response time is approximately the same as availability response time. Higher prices then function as a substitute for availability in reducing customer order rate, thereby potentially increasing total revenue.

Nevertheless, losing market share is not a recommended option. Past a point, as large competitors take over the company's market share, it becomes difficult for a company to regain it. Competitive research and development, marketing, and sales and service networks are reduced or phased out, as market share declines. Many quantitative analyses of the costs of holding extra inventory versus the benefits of the sales achieved consider only the short run. As a result they may lead to a long-run disaster. Clearly both quantitative and qualitative factors must be considered in selecting a policy.

To avoid loss of market share in growing markets, sufficient extra inventory must be carried to prevent (1) basing production rate on a customer order rate suppressed by long delivery delays and (2) declining goals. Policy design guidelines 8.3 and 8.4 summarize the reasons.

Consistency among corporate policies requires careful examination of the aggregate response times of the different market-clearing mechanisms and the interactions among them. As a result, for company policies to be consistent, they must be the responsibility of a manager high enough in the organization to balance the potential trade-offs. If marketing is responsible for prices, and manufacturing for production rate and inventory levels, someone higher up must give policy guidelines that assure the policies work together rather than against each other.

Appendix 8.1: Shipping Equations

Figure 8.24 gives a flow diagram of the structure governing the receipt of orders from customers and the subsequent shipping of goods. Customer order rate is split into two flows—those orders to be shipped from stock and those to be shipped directly from production. The two flows increase corresponding levels of unfilled orders. The split depends on the fraction of incoming orders to be shipped from stock, which in turn depends on available finished inventory. Shipments are then made from either inventory or production. The shipping equations follow.

Equation 15 defines shipment rate from stock SRS as unfilled orders

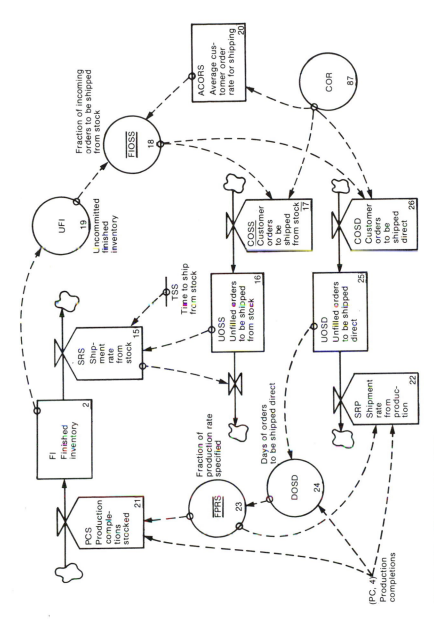

Figure 8.24 Shipping equations

to be shipped from stock UOSS divided by time to ship from stock TSS. TSS represents the minimum order processing and filling time.

SRS.KL = UOSS.K/TSS   15, R
TSS = 5   15.1, C

where
SRS   = shipment rate from stock (units/day)
UOSS = unfilled orders to be shipped from stock (units)
TSS   = time to ship from stock (days).

Unfilled orders to be shipped from stock UOSS is a level variable increased by customer orders to be shipped from stock COSS and decreased by shipment rate from stock SRS (equation 16). UOSS is initialized at its equilibrium value.

UOSS.K = UOSS.J + (DT)(COSS.JK − SRS.JK)   16, L
UOSS = TSS * CCOR   16.1, N

where
UOSS = unfilled orders to be shipped from stock (units)
DT   = delta time, simulation solution interval (days)
COSS = customer orders to be shipped from stock (units/day)
SRS   = shipment rate from stock (units/day)
TSS   = time to ship from stock (days)
CCOR = constant customer order rate (units/day).

Equation 17 states that customer orders to be shipped from stock COSS equals the product of customer order rate COR and fraction of incoming orders to be shipped from stock FIOSS.

COSS.KL = COR.K * FIOSS.K   17, R

where
COSS = customer orders to be shipped from stock (units/day)
COR   = customer order rate (units/day)
FIOSS = fraction of incoming orders to be shipped from stock
            (dimensionless).

Fraction of incoming orders to be shipped from stock FIOSS is a nonlinear function of uncommitted finished inventory UFI divided by average customer order rate for shipping ACORS (equation 18 and figure 8.25). UFI divided by ACORS equals the number of days of inventory, not committed to current customer orders, remaining in finished inventory. If there are greater than 25 days uncommitted inventory in stock, FIOSS equals 1.0 (100 percent of orders shipped from

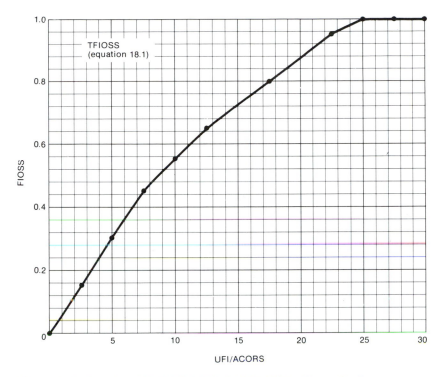

Figure 8.25   Fraction of incoming orders to be shipped from stock

stock). As days supply of inventory falls below 25 days, FIOSS decreases at an increasing rate. Finally, if days supply equals 0, FIOSS
equals 0. The shape of the relationship between FIOSS and uncommitted finished inventory depends on the number of different items the
company holds in stock and the variability around a normal sales mix.
If the company sells only one product, or the sales mix is completely
constant, then FIOSS would be 1.0 for all values except 0 finished
inventory. As the number of products increases, or the variability of
sales mix increases, the more inventory the company must hold to
avoid stockouts. The relationship depicted in figure 8.25 represents a
company with a large number of product options and a variable sales
mix.

FIOSS.K = TABHL(TFIOSS,(UFI.K/ACORS.K),0,30,2.5)   18, A
TFIOSS = 0/.15/.3/.45/.55/.65/.725/.8/.875/.95/1/1/1   18.1, T

where
FIOSS   = fraction of incoming orders to be shipped from stock
          (dimensionless)
TFIOSS = table for fraction of incoming orders to be shipped from
          stock (dimensionless)
UFI   = uncommitted finished inventory (units)
ACORS = average customer order rate for shipping (units/day).

Equation 19 defines uncommitted finished inventory UFI to equal the difference between finished product inventory FI and unfilled orders to be shipped from stock UOSS.

$$UFI.K = FI.K - UOSS.K \qquad\qquad 19, A$$

where
UFI   = uncommitted finished inventory (units)
FI   = finished product inventory (units)
UOSS = unfilled orders to be shipped from stock (units).

Average customer order rate for shipping ACORS is represented as an exponential average of customer order rate. ACORS is simply a reference against which the amount of finished inventory available for shipping is measured.

$$ACORS.K = SMOOTH(COR.K,20) \qquad\qquad 20, A$$

where
ACORS = average customer order rate for shipping (units/day)
COR   = customer order rate (units/day).

Equation 21 defines production completions stocked PCS as the product of 1.0 minus fraction production rate specified FPRS and production completions PC. Similarly equation 22 defines shipment rate from production SRP as the product of fraction production rate specified FPRS and production completions PC. In other words production completions are split into two flows, the size of each depends on FPRS.

$$PCS.KL = (1 - FPRS.K) * PC.K \qquad\qquad 21, R$$

where
PCS   = production completions stocked (units/day)
FPRS = fraction of production rate specified (dimensionless)
PC   = production completions (units/day);

$$SRP.KL = FPRS.K * PC.K \qquad\qquad 22, R$$

where

SRP   = shipment rate from production (units/day)

FPRS = fraction of production rate specified (dimensionless)

PC   = production completions (units/day).

Fraction of production rate specified FPRS is a nonlinear function of days orders to be shipped direct DOSD divided by the sum of time to complete work in process TCWIP and time to ship from stock TSS (equation 23 and figure 8.26). FPRS states how many customer orders can be matched directly to a unit coming off the production line. If days orders to be shipped direct is greater than time to complete work in process and time to process orders, then 100 percent of the orders coming off the production line can be specified for a customer order. If days orders to be shipped direct equals 0, then 0 orders coming off the production line are specified for an actual customer order (because there are no customer orders).

The slope of FPRS between zero and one again depends on the nature and mix of the product sold by the company. If the company sells only one product, or has a constant mix, then FPRS is 1.0 as long as DOSD is positive. On the other hand, if every customer order has to

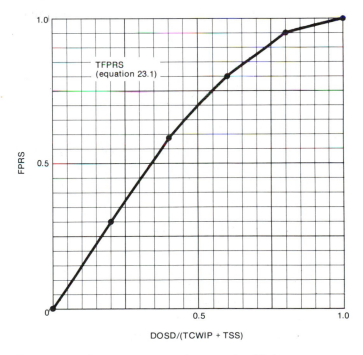

Figure 8.26   Fraction of production rate specified

be built to customer specification, then the FPRS curve is a straight line between zero and one. In other words, if DOSD were half the time to complete work in process, then only 50 percent of product coming off the line could be specified by a customer order. The relationship shown in figure 8.26 for FPRS assumes that not every customer order needs to be directly specified, because the company sells a finite type and number of products.

$$\text{FPRS.K} = \text{TABLE(TFPRS,DOSD.K/(TCWIP + TSS),}$$
$$\qquad\qquad 0,1,.2) \qquad\qquad\qquad\qquad\qquad\qquad 23, \text{A}$$
$$\text{TFPRS} = 0/.3/.58/.8/.95/1 \qquad\qquad\qquad\qquad 23.1, \text{T}$$

where

FPRS   = fraction of production rate specified (dimensionless)
TFPRS = table for fraction of production rate specified
            (dimensionless)
DOSD = days of orders to be shipped direct (days)
TCWIP = time to complete work in process (days)
TSS   = time to ship from stock (days).

Equation 24 defines days orders to be shipped direct DOSD as unfilled orders to be shipped direct UOSD divided by production completions PC.

$$\text{DOSD.K} = \text{UOSD.K/PC.K} \qquad\qquad\qquad\qquad 24, \text{A}$$

where

DOSD = days of orders to be shipped direct (days)
UOSD = unfilled orders to be shipped direct (units)
PC   = production completions (units/day).

Unfilled orders to be shipped direct UOSD is defined in equation 25 as a level variable increased by customer orders to be shipped direct COSD and decreased by shipment rate from production SRP. UOSD is initialized to its equilibrium value.

$$\text{UOSD.K} = \text{UOSD.J} + (\text{DT})(\text{COSD.JK} - \text{SRP.JK}) \qquad 25, \text{L}$$
$$\text{UOSD} = 0 \qquad\qquad\qquad\qquad\qquad\qquad\qquad\qquad 25.1, \text{N}$$

where

UOSD = unfilled orders to be shipped direct (units)
DT   = delta time, simulation solution interval (days)
COSD = customer orders to be shipped direct (units/day)
SRP   = shipment rate from production (units/day).

Customer orders to be shipped direct COSD equals customer order rate COR multiplied by 1.0 minus the fraction of incoming orders to be shipped from stock FIOSS (equation 26).

$$COSD.KL = COR.K * (1 - FIOSS.K) \hspace{3cm} 26, R$$

where

COSD = customer orders to be shipped direct (units/day)
COR   = customer order rate (units/day)
FIOSS = fraction of incoming orders to be shipped from stock
        (dimensionless).

Unfilled orders UO, defined in equation 27, equals the sum of unfilled orders to be shipped from stock UOSS and unfilled orders to be shipped direct UOSD.

$$UO.K = UOSS.K + UOSD.K \hspace{3cm} 27, A$$

where

UO   = unfilled orders (units)
UOSS = unfilled orders to be shipped from stock (units)
UOSD = unfilled orders to be shipped direct (units).

Using a Model to Evaluate Financial Performance

9.1 Introduction

In preceding chapters policy performance was evaluated through a qualitative comparison of the time paths of important system variables. In some situations such a qualitative comparison yields a clear-cut answer as to which is the better policy, for example, a policy that improves both market share and stability without additional costs, perhaps by changing the sources of information used. In many situations, however, improvement in one system variable comes at the expense of some other system variable(s), such as was the case in the delivery delays problem where extra inventory costs were incurred to avoid loss of market share. For the most part a qualitative comparison gives no definite strategy for selecting the best policy.

Fortunately in corporate models qualitative comparisons can be supplemented by a numerical index that captures the costs and benefits of alternative policies—profits. In a real business setting the effect of every policy eventually shows up in the behavior of profits. And since profits are the dominant performance measure applied to corporations, they provide a measure by which alternative policies can be evaluated. In theory then model profits provide a relevant method of ranking alternative policies.

But model profits should not be the sole method of ranking policies for a number of reasons. First, the model may not accurately capture all of the important effects of the different policies on profits. For example, to capture adequately the costs of instability of labor and production, a model might need to represent

1. the costs of machine setup and down time,
2. the costs of shifting jobs on an assembly line and any learning curve effects,

3. unemployment benefits and the costs of recruiting and training,
4. the costs of attracting labor when a company has a reputation of instability.

Many of these costs are difficult to determine. Second, profits may not capture everything of importance to the company. For example, employment stability may be valued for social reasons independent of cost savings. Third, quantitative measures such as accumulated profits do not give a complete picture of financial performance. For example, the best policy in terms of profits may also produce periods of severe cash shortage. And fourth, the best policy may improve profits in the short run at the expense of profits beyond the period simulated in the model. Consequently, while profit is an important performance measure, it is not the only one. Profit comparisons should be supplemented by qualitative comparisons of the time paths of system variables.

By providing a time history of system performance in addition to such summary statistics as accumulated profits, a system dynamics model allows the company to consider qualitative as well as quantitative measures of performance. This chapter demonstrates the use of a model to produce financial performance indicators.

9.2 Accounting and Financing Equations

The financial performance of a company is monitored by the company's balance sheet, income statement, and financial ratios. Financial performance is affected by the way the company finances its operations (debt levels, dividend policy) as well as by the operations themselves. Equations representing accounting procedures (balance sheet and income statement), financial ratios, and financing policies of a typical company follow. Cost figures are based on those for an average manufacturing company (Robert Morris Associates 1973).

Balance Sheet

Figure 9.1 shows the structure of the accounting sector. The levels shown in the figure are the items on the balance sheet of a company's books. The levels at the left are the company's assets (dollar value of inventory, accounts receivable, cash, book value of fixed assets), the levels at the right the company's liabilities and equity (accounts payable, short-term debt, long-term debt, equity). The sum of the assets must equal the sum of the liabilities and equity. Consequently any

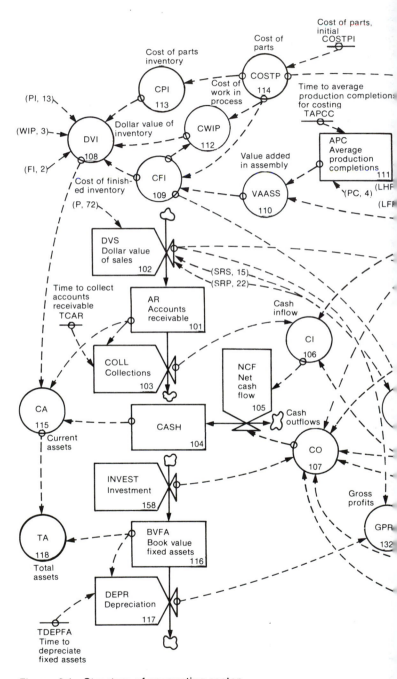

Figure 9.1   Structure of accounting sector

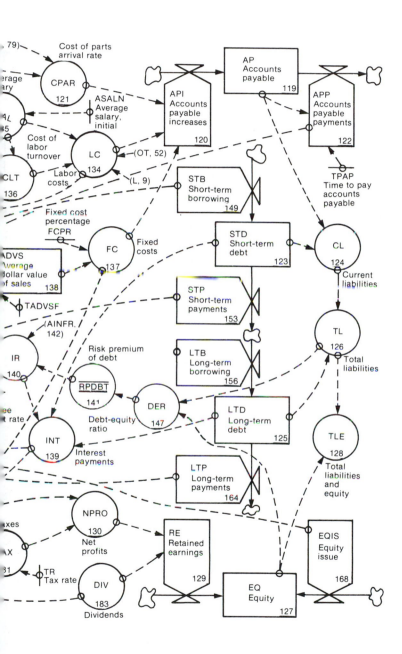

increase in an asset level must produce a corresponding decrease in another asset level or increase in a liability or equity level.

The rates and auxiliaries of figure 9.1 determine either the company's cash flow or profits, or both. The difference between cash flow and profits are important. First, cash outflows increase (and thereby cash decreases) in order to pay for increases in book value of fixed assets, whereas profits decrease only with the depreciation of those fixed assets. Second, cash is increased by the collection of accounts receivable, whereas profits are increased by dollar value of sales. And third, cash is decreased for parts arrivals as accounts payable payments are made, whereas profits are decreased only as shipments are made. The effect of these differences on financial performance is analyzed in section 9.3.

Accounts receivable AR is a level variable increased by dollar value of sales DVS and decreased by collections COLL (equation 101). AR is initialized to its equilibrium value, time to collect accounts receivable TCAR multiplied by DVS.

$$AR.K = AR.J + (DT)(DVS.J - COLL.J) \qquad\qquad 101, L$$
$$AR = TCAR * DVS \qquad\qquad 101.1, N$$

where
AR   = accounts receivable ($)
DT   = delta time, simulation solution interval (days)
DVS   = dollar value of sales ($/day)
COLL = collections ($/day)
TCAR = time to collect accounts receivable (days).

Equation 102 defines dollar value of sales DVS to equal price P multiplied by the sum of shipment rate from stock SRS and shipment rate from production SRP.

$$DVS.K = P.K * (SRS.JK + SRP.JK) \qquad\qquad 102, A$$

where
DVS = dollar value of sales ($/day)
P   = price ($/unit)
SRS = shipment rate from stock (units/day)
SRP = shipment rate from production (units/day).

Collections COLL are defined in equation 103 to equal accounts receivable AR divided by time to collect accounts receivable TCAR. Collections are therefore a first-order delay of dollar value of sales.

TCAR is set to forty days, an average value for manufacturing companies.

COLL.K = AR.K/TCAR   103, A
TCAR = 40   103.1, C

where
COLL = collections ($/day)
AR   = accounts receivable ($)
TCAR = time to collect accounts receivable (days).

Equation 104 defines cash as a level variable altered by net cash flow NCF. Cash is initialized to equal desired cash DCASH.

CASH.K = CASH.J + (DT)(NCF.J)   104, L
CASH = DCASH   104.1, N

where
CASH   = cash ($)
DT   = delta time, simulation solution interval (days)
NCF   = net cash flow ($/day)
DCASH = desired cash ($).

Net cash flow NCF equals the difference between cash inflows CI and cash outflows CO (equation 105). Cash inflows equal the sum of collections COLL, short-term borrowing STB, long-term borrowing LTB, and equity issue EQIS (equation 106). Collections are the cash generated by operations; short-term borrowing, long-term borrowing, and equity issue are the cash generated by external financing. Cash outflows CO equal the sum of accounts payable APP, short-term payments STP, long-term payments LTP, interest INT, dividends DIV, taxes TAX, and investment INVEST (equation 107). Accounts payable payments are the cash outflow from operations; short-term and long-term payments are repayments of external financing; interest and dividends are the costs of such external financing; taxes are income taxes; and investment is payments for capacity expansion.

NCF.K = CI.K − CO.K   105, A

where
NCF = net cash flow ($/day)
CI = cash inflows ($/day)
CO = cash outflows ($/day);

CI.K = COLL.K + STB.K + LTB.K + EQIS.K   106, A

where
CI   = cash inflows ($/day)
COLL = collections ($/day)
STB   = short-term borrowing ($/day)
LTB   = long-term borrowing ($/day)
EQIS = equity issue ($/day);

$$\text{CO.K} = \text{APP.K} + \text{STP.K} + \text{LTP.K} + \text{INT.K} + \text{DIV.K} + \text{TAX.K} + \text{INVEST.K} \qquad \text{107, A}$$

where
CO   = cash outflows ($/day)
APP   = accounts payable payments ($/day)
STP   = short-term payments ($/day)
LTP   = long-term payments ($/day)
INT   = interest payments ($/day)
DIV   = dividends ($/day)
TAX   = taxes ($/day)
INVEST = investment ($/day).

Equation 108 defines dollar value of inventory DVI to equal the sum of three terms: cost of finished inventory CFI multiplied by finished product inventory FI (the dollar value of finished inventory), cost of work in process CWIP multiplied by work in process WIP (the dollar value of work in process), and cost of parts inventory CPI multiplied by parts inventory (the dollar value of parts inventory).

$$\text{DVI.K} = \text{CFI.K} * \text{FI.K} + \text{CWIP.K} * \text{WIP.K} + \text{CPI.K} * \text{PI.K} \qquad \text{108, A}$$

where
DVI   = dollar value of inventory ($)
CFI   = cost of finished inventory ($/unit)
FI   = finished product inventory (units)
CWIP = cost of work in process ($/unit)
WIP   = work in process (units)
CPI   = cost of parts inventory ($/unit)
PI   = parts inventory (units)

Cost of finished inventory CFI is defined in equation 109 to equal the sum of cost of parts COSTP plus value added in assembly VAASS. COSTP represents the average cost of purchase parts contained in a unit. VAASS represents the average labor content in a unit, as determined in equation 110 by dividing labor costs LC by average production completions APC (equation 111).

$$CFI.K = COSTP.K + VAASS.K \qquad 109, A$$

where
CFI $\quad$ = cost of finished inventory (\$/unit)
COSTP = cost of parts (\$/unit)
VAASS = value added in assembly (\$/unit);

$$VAASS.K = LC.K/APC.K \qquad 110, A$$

where
VAASS = value added in assembly (\$/unit)
LC $\quad$ = labor costs (\$/day)
APC $\quad$ = average production completions (units/day);

$$APC.K = SMOOTH(PC.K,TAPCC) \qquad 111, A$$
$$TAPCC = 20 \qquad 111.1, C$$

where
APC $\quad$ = average production completions (units/day)
PC $\quad$ = production completions (units/day)
TAPCC = time to average production completions for costing (days).

Equation 112 defines cost of work in process CWIP as a weighted average of cost of parts COSTP and cost of finished inventory CFI, on the assumption the average unit in process contains 50 percent of the value added in assembly. (The equation for CWIP can be rewritten to equal COSTP + .5 * VAASS.)

$$CWIP.K = .5 * COSTP.K + .5 * CFI.K \qquad 112, A$$

where
CWIP $\quad$ = cost of work in process (\$/unit)
COSTP = cost of parts (\$/unit)
CFI $\quad$ = cost of finished inventory (\$/unit).

Equation 113 states that cost of parts inventory CPI equals cost of parts COSTP. In equation 114 COSTP is defined to equal cost of parts, initial COSTPI. COSTP can be made to vary from COSTPI by incorporating an inflation multiplier.

$$CPI.K = COSTP.K \qquad 113, A$$

where
CPI   = cost of parts inventory ($/unit)
COSTP = cost of parts ($/unit);

$$COSTP.K \quad = COSTPI \qquad\qquad\qquad 114, A$$
$$COSTPI = 30 \qquad\qquad\qquad\qquad\qquad 114.1, C$$

where
COSTP   = cost of parts ($/unit)
COSTPI = cost of parts, initial ($/unit).

Current assets CA equals the sum of accounts receivable AR, cash CASH, and dollar value of inventory DVI (equation 115).

$$CA.K = AR.K + CASH.K + DVI.K \qquad\qquad 115, A$$

where
CA   = current assets ($)
AR   = accounts receivable ($)
CASH = cash ($)
DVI   = dollar value of inventory ($).

Equation 116 states that book value of fixed assets BVFA is a level variable increased by investment INVEST and decreased by depreciation DEPR. BVFA is initialized to equal capital equipment CE multiplied by cost per unit of capital equipment CPUCE.

$$BVFA.K = BVFA.J + (DT)(INVEST.J - DEPR.J) \qquad 116, L$$
$$BVFA = CE * CPUCE \qquad\qquad\qquad\qquad\qquad 116.1, N$$

where
BVFA   = book value of fixed assets ($)
DT   = delta time, simulation solution interval (days)
INVEST = investment ($/day)
DEPR   = depreciation ($/day)
CE   = capital equipment (units/day)
CPUCE = cost per unit of capital equipment ($/unit/day).

Depreciation DEPR is modeled in equation 117 as book value of fixed assets BVFA divided by time to depreciate fixed assets TDEPFA. TDEPFA is here set to 2,400 days, or 10 years. Ten years is approximately the average lifetime of such diverse fixed assets as tools, machines, and floor space. A more detailed model might contain individual asset levels for each different age category of fixed assets. Equation 117 approximates straight-line depreciation for the company that replaces assets as they depreciate.

DEPR.K = BVFA.K/TDEPFA   117, A
TDEPFA = 2400   117.1, C

where
DEPR   = depreciation ($/day)
BVFA   = book value of fixed assets ($)
TDEPFA = time to depreciate fixed assets (days).

Equation 118 defines total assets TA as the sum of current assets CA and book value of fixed assets BVFA.

TA.K = CA.K + BVFA.K   118, A

where
TA   = total assets ($)
CA   = current assets ($)
BVFA = book value of fixed assets ($).

Accounts payable AP is modeled as a level variable increased by accounts payable increases API and decreased by accounts payable payments APP (equation 119). AP is initialized to its equilibrium value, time to pay accounts payable TPAP multiplied by accounts payable increases API.

AP.K = AP.J + (DT)(API.J − APP.J)   119, L
AP = TPAP * API   119.1, N

where
AP   = accounts payable ($)
DT   = delta time, simulation solution interval (days)
API   = accounts payable increases ($/day)
APP   = accounts payable payments ($/day)
TPAP = time to pay accounts payable (days).

Equation 120 defines accounts payable increases API to equal the sum of cost of parts arrival rate CPAR, fixed costs FC, and labor costs LC. API therefore is the cash outflow from operations.

API.K = CPAR.K + FC.K + LC.K   120, A

where
API   = accounts payable increases ($/day)
CPAR = cost of parts arrival rate ($/day)
FC   = fixed costs ($/day)
LC   = labor costs ($/day).

Costs of parts arrival rate CPAR equals parts arrival rate PAR multiplied by cost of parts COSTP (equation 121).

$$CPAR.K = PAR.JK * COSTP.K \qquad\qquad 121, A$$

where
CPAR = cost of parts arrival rate ($/day)
PAR   = parts arrival rate (units/day)
COSTP = cost of parts ($/unit).

Equation 122 defines accounts payable payments APP to equal accounts payable AP divided by time to pay accounts payable TPAP. TPAP is here set to 30 days.

$$APP.K = AP.K/TPAP \qquad\qquad 122, A$$
$$TPAP = 30 \qquad\qquad 122.1, C$$

where
APP   = accounts payable payments ($/day)
AP   = accounts payable ($)
TPAP = time to pay accounts payable (days).

Short-term debt STD is modeled in equation 123 as a level variable increased by short-term borrowing STB and decreased by short-term payments STP. Short-term debt is initialized to achieve a constant current ratio initial CRI.

$$STD.K = STD.J + (DT)(STB.J - STP.J) \qquad\qquad 123, L$$
$$STD = (CA/CRI) - AP \qquad\qquad 123.1, N$$
$$CRI = 2.5 \qquad\qquad 123.2, C$$

where
STD = short-term debt ($)
DT   = delta time, simulation solution interval (days)
STB = short-term borrowing ($/day)
STP = short-term payments ($/day)
CA   = current assets ($)
CRI = current ratio, initial (dimensionless)
AP   = accounts payable ($).

Equation 124 defines current liabilities CL to equal the sum of accounts payable AP and short-term debt STD.

$$CL.K = AP.K + STD.K \qquad\qquad 124, A$$

where
CL = current liabilities ($)
AP = accounts payable ($)
STD = short-term debt ($).

Long-term debt LTD is modeled in equation 125 as a level variable increased by long-term borrowing LTB and decreased by long-term payment LTP. Long-term debt is initialized to achieve a constant debt-equity ratio initial DERI.

$$\text{LTD.K} = \text{LTD.J} + (\text{DT})(\text{LTB.J} - \text{LTP.J}) \qquad \text{125, L}$$
$$\text{LTD} = \text{DERI} * \text{EQ} - \text{CL} \qquad \text{125.1, N}$$
$$\text{DERI} = .5 \qquad \text{125.2, C}$$

where
LTD = long-term debt ($)
DT   = delta time, simulation solution interval (days)
LTB = long-term borrowing ($/day)
LTP = long-term payments ($/day)
DERI = debt-equity ratio, initial (dimensionless)
EQ   = equity ($)
CL   = current liabilities ($).

Equation 126 defines total liabilities TL to equal current liabilities CL plus long-term debt LTD.

$$\text{TL.K} = \text{CL.K} + \text{LTD.K} \qquad \text{126, A}$$

where
TL   = total liabilities ($)
CL   = current liabilities ($)
LTD = long-term debt ($).

Equity EQ is modeled in equation 127 as a level variable increased by retained earnings RE and equity issue EQIS. Retained earnings are the profits not returned to stockholders as dividends. Equity issue represents the cash inflows from new equity offerings. Equity is initialized to achieve a constant debt-equity ratio initial DERI.

$$\text{EQ.K} = \text{EQ.J} + (\text{DT})(\text{RE.J} + \text{EQIS.J}) \qquad \text{127, L}$$
$$\text{EQ} = \text{TA}/(1 + \text{DERI}) \qquad \text{127.1, N}$$

where
EQ   = equity ($)
DT   = delta time, simulation solution interval (days)
RE   = retained earnings ($/day)

EQIS = equity issue ($/day)
TA   = total assets ($)
DERI = debt-equity ratio, initial (dimensionless).

Equation 128 defines total liabilities and equity TLE as the sum of total liabilities TL and equity EQ.

$$TLE.K = TL.K + EQ.K \hspace{4cm} 128, A$$

where
TLE = total liabilities and equity ($)
TL = total liabilities ($)
EQ = equity ($).

Income Statement

In equation 129 retained earnings equal net profits NPRO minus dividends DIV.

$$RE.K = NPRO.K - DIV.K \hspace{4cm} 129, A$$

where
RE   = retained earnings ($/day)
NPRO = net profits ($/day)
DIV   = dividends ($/day).

Net profits NPRO equal gross profits GPRO minus taxes TAX (equation 130). Taxes TAX equal gross profits GPRO multiplied by tax rate TR. TR is here set to 50 percent (equation 131). Fifty percent is the approximate tax rate on corporate taxable income. In a more complete model tax write-offs and investment tax credit might be included.

$$NPRO.K = GPRO.K - TAX.K \hspace{3cm} 130, A$$

where
NPRO = net profits ($/day)
GPRO = gross profits ($/day)
TAX   = taxes ($/day);

$$TAX.K = GPRO.K * TR \hspace{4cm} 131, A$$
$$TR = .5 \hspace{6cm} 131.1, C$$

where
TAX   = taxes ($/day)
GPRO = gross profits ($/day)
TR   = tax rate (dimensionless).

Equation 132 defines gross profits GPRO as the difference between dollar value of sales DVS and cost of material shipped CMS, fixed costs FC, depreciation DEPR, and interest INT. Equation 132 features some of the differences between profits and cash flow. Profits are increased when the sale is made (DVS), not when the cash is received. Profits are decreased when the shipment is made (CMS), not when materials and labor are paid for. Profits are decreased by depreciation DEPR, not by cash outflows for capital expenditures (INVEST).

$$GPRO.K = DVS.K - CMS.K - FC.K - DEPR.K - INT.K \quad \text{132, A}$$

where
GPRO = gross profits ($/day)
DVS = dollar value of sales ($/day)
CMS = cost of material shipped ($/day)
FC   = fixed costs ($/day)
DEPR = depreciation ($/day)
INT = interest payments ($/day).

In equation 133 cost of materials shipped CMS equals shipment rate from stock SRS and shipment rate from production SRP multiplied by the cost of finished inventory CFI.

$$CMS.K = CFI.K * (SRS.JK + SRP.JK) \quad \text{133, A}$$

where
CMS = cost of material shipped ($/day)
CFI = cost of finished inventory ($/unit)
SRS = shipment rate from stock (units/day)
SRP = shipment rate from production (units/day).

Equation 134 defines labor costs LC. Labor costs are added to the cost of parts to determine cost of finished inventory. Labor costs LC equal the sum of three terms: standard labor costs (labor L multiplied by average salary ASAL), overtime costs (charged only when overtime exceeds 1.0 and is equal to 150 percent of average salary), and costs of labor turnover CLT.

$$LC.K = L.K * ASAL.K + MAX(OT.K - 1,0) * L.K * 1.5$$
$$* ASAL.K + CLT.K \quad \text{134, A}$$

where
LC   = labor costs ($/day)
L   = labor (persons)
ASAL = average salary ($/day/person)

OT   = overtime (dimensionless)
CLT   = cost of labor turnover ($/day).

Equation 135 defines average salary ASAL to equal average salary, initial ASALN. ASALN is set to $40 per day per person. The costs assigned in this chapter are representative of the average manufacturing firm, given a price of $100 per unit. Like cost of parts, ASAL could be made to vary from ASALN by an inflation multiplier.

$$\text{ASAL.K} = \text{ASALN} \hspace{8em} \text{135, A}$$
$$\text{ASALN} = 40 \hspace{10em} \text{135.1, C}$$

where
ASAL   = average salary ($/day/person)
ASALN = average salary, initial ($/day/person).

Cost of labor turnover CLT is defined in equation 136 to equal 6.0 times average salary ASAL multiplied by the sum of labor-hiring rate LHR and labor-firing rate LFR. The cost of labor turnover is the only cost of instability included in this model. Cost of machine setup and training for new jobs might need to be included in a more complete model.

$$\text{CLT.K} = 6 * \text{ASAL.K} * (\text{LHR.JK} + \text{LFR.JK}) \hspace{4em} \text{136, A}$$

where
CLT   = cost of labor turnover ($/day)
ASAL = average salary ($/day/person)
LHR   = labor-hiring rate (persons/day)
LFR   = labor-firing rate (persons/day).

Equation 137 defines fixed costs FC as fixed cost percentage FCPR multiplied by average dollar values of sales ADVS. Fixed costs here include administration, marketing, and research. Companies often budget these costs on the basis of past sales. Average dollar value of sales ADVS is represented in equation 138 as an exponential average of dollar value of sales DVS.

$$\text{FC.K} = \text{FCPR} * \text{ADVS.K} \hspace{7em} \text{137, A}$$
$$\text{FCPR} = .17 \hspace{10em} \text{137.1, C}$$

where
FC   = fixed costs ($/day)
FCPR = fixed cost percentage (dimensionless)
ADVS = average dollar value of sales ($/day);

$$ADVS.K = SMOOTH(DVS.K,TADVSF) \qquad \text{138, A}$$
$$TADVSF = 480 \qquad \text{138.1, C}$$

where
ADVS = average dollar value of sales ($/day)
DVS = dollar value of sales ($/day)
TADVSF = time to average dollar value of sales for fixed costs
    (days).

Equation 139 defines interest payments INT to equal interest rate IR multiplied by the sum of long-term debt LTD and short-term debt STD and divided by 240 days per year because interest rate is expressed in percent per year. For simplicity the interest rate on long- and short-term debt is assumed equal.

$$INT.K = IR.K * (LTD.K + STD.K)/240 \qquad \text{139, A}$$

where
INT = interest payments ($/day)
IR   = interest rate (percent/year)
LTD = long-term debt ($)
STD = short-term debt ($).

Interest rate IR is defined in equation 140 as the sum of risk free interest rate RFIR, risk premium of debt RPDBT, and average inflation rate AINFR. RFIR is commonly assumed to equal 2 percent per year. Actual interest rates vary from the risk free rate as a consequence of debt levels and inflation rates.

$$IR.K = RFIR + RPDBT.K + AINFR.K \qquad \text{140, A}$$
$$RFIR = .02 \qquad \text{140.1, C}$$

where
IR = interest rate (percent/year)
RFIR = risk free interest rate (percent/year)
RPDBT = risk premium of debt (percent/year)
AINFR = average inflation rate (percent/year).

Risk premium of debt RPDBT is represented as a nonlinear function of debt-equity ratio DER (equation 141 and figure 9.2). RPDBT increases at an increasing rate as debt-equity ratio increases. The higher the debt-equity ratio, the greater the probability a company will default on debt payments, and consequently the higher the risk premium of debt. The risk premium should probably fall to zero, rather than 1.5 percent per year, as given in equation 141.1.

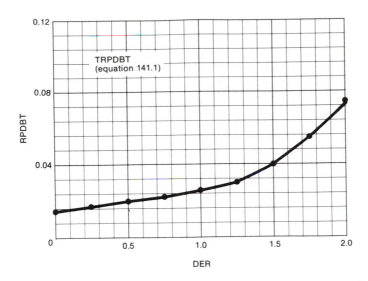

Figure 9.2   Risk premium of debt as a function of debt-equity ratio

RPDBT.K = TABLE(TRPDBT,DER.K,0,2,.25)   141, A
TRPDBT = .015/.0175/.02/.0225/.025/.03/.04/.055/.075   141.1, T

where
RPDBT   = risk premium of debt (percent/year)
TRPDBT = table for risk premium of debt (percent/year)
DER   = debt-equity ratio (dimensionless).

Average inflation rate AINFR is represented in equation 142 as an exponential average of inflation rate INFLR. Investors are assumed to respond to inflation rates after the time to perceive inflation for interest rates TPINFI. TPINFI is here set to 240 days. INFLR is set to a constant zero in this model (equation 143).

AINFR.K = SMOOTH(INFLR.K,TPINFI)   142, A
TPINFI = 240   142.1, C

where
AINFR   = average inflation rate (percent/year)
INFLR   = inflation rate (percent/year)
TPINFI = time to perceive inflation for interest rates (days);

INFLR.K = INFLRI   143, A
INFLRI = 0   143.1, C

where

INFLR = inflation rate (percent/year)
INFLRI = inflation rate, initial (percent/year).

Financial Ratios

Financial ratios are used by investors to monitor corporate financial performance. Financial ratios influence the company's ability to raise external financing and the cost of that external financing. Financial ratios are also used by the company to monitor performance and take corrective actions.

Equation 144 defines return on sales ROS to equal net profits NPRO divided by dollar value of sales DVS.

$$ROS.K = NPRO.K/DVS.K \qquad \qquad 144, A$$

where

ROS = return on sales (dimensionless)
NPRO = net profits ($/day)
DVS = dollar value of sales ($/day).

Return on equity ROE equals 240 (days per year) multiplied by net profits NPRO and divided by equity EQ (equation 145).

$$ROE.K = 240 * NPRO.K/EQ.K \qquad \qquad 145, A$$

where

ROE = return on equity (percent/year)
NPRO = net profits ($/day)
EQ   = equity ($).

Equation 146 defines current ratio to equal current assets CA divided by current liabilities CL.

$$CR.K = CA.K/CL.K \qquad \qquad 146, A$$

where

CR = current ratio (dimensionless)
CA = current assets ($)
CL = current liabilities ($).

Debt equity ratio DER is defined in equation 147 as total liabilities TL divided by equity EQ.

$$DER.K = TL.K/EQ.K \qquad \qquad 147, A$$

where
DER = debt-equity ratio (dimensionless)
TL   = total liabilities ($)
EQ   = equity ($).

Equation 148 defines annual inventory returns AIT to equal 240 (days per year) multiplied by dollar value of sales DVS and divided by dollar value of inventory DVI.

$$AIT.K = 240 * DVS.K/DVI.K \hspace{3cm} 148, A$$

where
AIT = annual inventory turns (1/year)
DVS = dollar value of sales ($/day)
DVI = dollar value of inventory ($).

Financing Policies

Financing policies govern the manner in which a company raises external financing through short- and long-term debt and equity. Equity financing consists of earnings retention, as governed by dividend policy and new stock issue. Stock price determines the dilution in earnings per share that results from a new stock issue. Therefore stock price influences the willingness of a company to issue new shares.

As shown in figure 9.3, short-term borrowing responds to discrepancies between a company's desired and actual cash balance. Short-term borrowing is used to correct temporary, or short-term, discrepancies. Permanent cash shortages are corrected by either long-term financing or equity financing. (In practice short-term debt is also used to tide the company over between the relatively lumpy long-term financing issues. The lumpiness of long-term financing is not considered here.)

Equation 149 defines short-term borrowing STB. STB equals indicated change in cash ICC when ICC is positive, multiplied by effect of current ratio on short-term borrowing ECRSTB. As described next, ECRSTB places financial constraints on borrowing.

$$STB.K = MAX(0,ICC.K) * ECRSTB.K \hspace{2cm} 149, A$$

where
STB   = short-term borrowing ($/day)
ICC   = indicated change in cash ($/day)
ECRSTB = effect of current ratio on short-term borrowing
              (dimensionless).

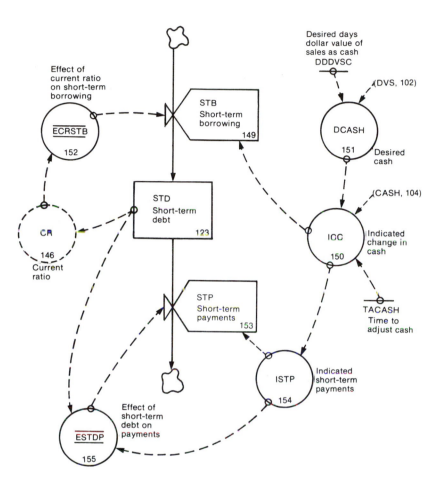

Figure 9.3   Short-term borrowing policy

Indicated change in cash ICC is defined in equation 150 to equal the difference between desired cash DCASH and cash CASH, divided by time to adjust cash TACASH. TACASH is here set to 10 days. Equation 151 defines desired cash DCASH to equal desired days dollar value of sales as cash DDDVSC multiplied by dollar value of sales DVS. Desired cash in this equation reflects a transaction demand for cash. A DDDVSC value of 15 days is representative of the cash and marketable securities held by the average manufacturing firm.

ICC.K = (DCASH.K − CASH.K)/TACASH   150, A
TACASH = 10   150.1, C

where
ICC   = indicated change in cash ($/day)
DCASH   = desired cash ($)
CASH   = cash ($)
TACASH = time to adjust cash (days);

DCASH.K = DDDVSC * DVS.K   151, A
DDDVSC = 15   151.1, C

where
DCASH   = desired cash ($)
DDDVSC = desired days dollar value of sales as cash (days)
DVS   = dollar value of sales ($/day).

Effect of current ratio on short-term borrowing ECRSTB represents the constraints placed on companies by financial institutions (equation 152). As shown in figure 9.4, as current ratio CR falls below 2.0, companies have an increasingly difficult time obtaining short-term financ-

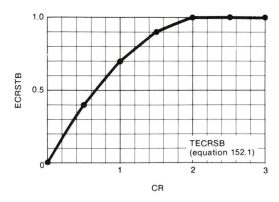

Figure 9.4   Effect of current ratio on short-term borrowing

ing. A current ratio near zero implies current liabilities much greater than current assets, so that short-term financing becomes difficult.

$$ECRSTB.K = TABHL(TECRSB,CR.K,0,3,.5) \qquad 152, A$$
$$TECRSB = 0/.4/.7/.9/1/1/1 \qquad 152.1, T$$

where

ECRSTB = effect of current ratio on short-term borrowing (dimensionless)

TECRSB = table for effect of current ratio on short-term borrowing (dimensionless)

CR = current ratio (dimensionless).

Equation 153 states that short-term payments STP equals indicated short-term payments ISTP multiplied by effect of short-term debt on payments ESTDP. As given by equation 154, indicated short-term payments are positive when indicated change in cash is negative (cash greater than desired cash).

$$STP.K = ISTP.K * ESTDP.K \qquad 153, A$$

where

STP = short-term payments ($/day)

ISTP = indicated short-term payments ($/day)

ESTDP = effect of short-term debt on payments (dimensionless);

$$ISTP.K = (-1) * MIN(0,ICC.K) \qquad 154, A$$

where

ISTP = indicated short-term payments ($/day)

ICC = indicated change in cash ($/day).

Effect of short-term debt on payments ESTDP represents the difficulty of repaying short-term debt as it falls (equation 155). Figure 9.5 illustrates this relationship. The independent variable is short-term debt STD divided by indicated short-term payments ISTP (a maximum function is used to avoid division by zero when indicated change in cash is positive). The independent variable measures the number of days of short-term debt outstanding at the indicated short-term payments rate. Division by ISTP essentially gives a scaling to the level of short-term debts. At low levels of short-term debt repayment of loans becomes increasingly difficult until, for a value of zero short-term debt, no debt payments can be made.

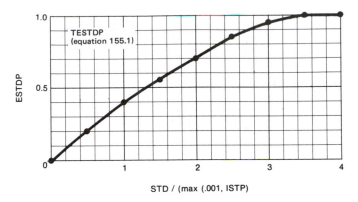

Figure 9.5   Effect of short-term debt on payments

ESTDP.K = TABHL(TESTDP,STD.K/(MAX(.001,
                ISTP.K)),0,4,.5)   155, A

TESTDP = 0/.2/.4/.55/.7/.85/.95/1/1   155.1, T

where

ESTDP   = effect of short-term debt on payments (dimensionless)

TESTDP = table for effect of short-term debt on payments
           (dimensionless)

STD   = short-term debt ($)

ISTP   = indicated short-term payments ($/day).

As shown in figure 9.6, long-term financing responds to differences between investment and cash flow from operations. A company uses long-term financing to invest in capital equipment. Positive cash flow from operations reduces the amount of long-term financing needed for such investment.

Equation 156 states that long-term borrowing LTB equals indicated long-term financing ILTF multiplied by the percent debt financing PDF.

LTB.K = ILTF.K * PDF.K   156, A

where

LTB   = long-term borrowing ($/day)

ILTF = indicated long-term financing ($/day)

PDF   = percent debt financing (percent).

Indicated long-term financing ILTF is defined in equation 157 as investment INVEST minus average cash flow from operations ACFO, whenever that difference is greater than zero.

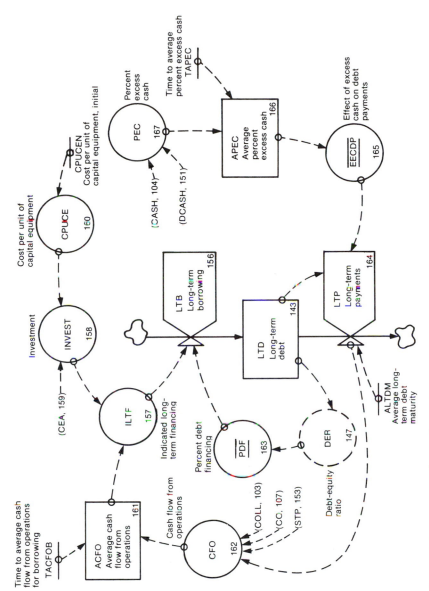

Figure 9.6 Long-term borrowing policy

$$\text{ILTF.K} = \text{MAX}(0, \text{INVEST.K} - \text{ACFO.K}) \qquad \text{157, A}$$

where
ILTF   = indicated long-term financing ($/day)
INVEST = investment ($/day)
ACFO   = average cash flow from operations ($/day).

Investment INVEST represents payments for capital equipment arrivals. In the present model capacity expansion is not explicitly represented. Consequently, to represent some cash outflows for capital expenditures, the company is assumed to replace depreciation and add capacity to match current customer order rate. Equations 158 and 159 represent this expansion policy. Capacity expansion is modeled in chapter 11.

$$\text{INVEST.K} = \text{CEA.JK} * \text{CPUCE.K} + \text{DEPR.K} \qquad \text{158, A}$$

where
INVEST = investment ($/day)
CEA   = capital equipment arrivals (units/day/day)
CPUCE = cost per unit of capital equipment ($/unit/day)
DEPR   = depreciation ($/day);

$$\text{CEA.KL} = (\text{COR.K} - \text{SMOOTH}(\text{COR.K}, 240))/240 \qquad \text{159, R}$$
$$\text{CE} = \text{CCOR} \qquad \text{159.1, N}$$

where
CEA   = capital equipment arrivals (units/day/day)
COR   = customer order rate (units/day)
CE   = capital equipment (units/day)
CCOR = constant customer order rate (units/day).

Cost per unit of capital equipment CPUCE is defined in equation 160 to equal cost per unit of capital equipment, initial CPUCEN.

$$\text{CPUCE.K} = \text{CPUCEN} \qquad \text{160, A}$$
$$\text{CPUCEN} = 6000 \qquad \text{161.1, C}$$

where
CPUCE   = cost per unit of capital equipment ($/unit/day)
CPUCEN = cost per unit of capital equipment, initial ($/unit/day).

Average cash flow from operations ACFO is represented in equation 161 as an exponential average of cash flow from operations CFO. Time to average cash flow from operations for borrowing TACFOB is set to

240 days. The company therefore responds to cash flow averaged over the past year in determining how much long-term financing is necessary to finance investment.

ACFO.K = SMOOTH(CFO.K,TACFOB)   161, A
TACFOB = 240   161.1,C

where
ACFO   = average cash flow from operations ($/day)
CFO   = cash flow from operation ($/day)
TACFOB = time to average cash flow from operations for
         borrowing (days).

Equation 162 defines cash flow from operations CFO. CFO equals collections COLL minus those cash outflows used to support operations. Cash outflows to support operations equals cash outflows CO minus investment INVEST, short-term payments STP, and long-term payments LTP, hence INVEST, STP, and LTP enter with a positive sign.

CFO.K = COLL.K − CO.K + INVEST.K + STP.K
        + LTP.K   162, A

where
CFO   = cash flow from operation ($/day)
COLL   = collections ($/day)
CO   = cash outflows ($/day)
INVEST = investment ($/day)
STP   = short-term payments ($/day)
LTP   = long-term payments ($/day).

Percent debt financing PDF is a nonlinear function of debt-equity ratio DER (equation 163 and figure 9.7). Most firms have a debt-equity ratio beyond which they are unable or unwilling to issue additional debt. Such a maximum debt-equity ratio, generally imposed by the financial markets, is based on company and industry traditional debt-equity ratios. Figure 9.7 shows that, as debt-equity ratio approaches a maximum debt-equity ratio (here assumed to equal 1.25), the company issues less and less debt.

PDF.K = TABLE(TPDF,DER.K,0,2,.25)   163, A
TPDF = 1/1/.9/.5/.1/0/0/0/0   163.1, T

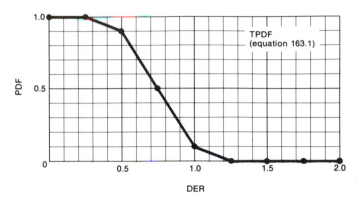

Figure 9.7   Percent debt financing as a function of debt-equity ratio

where
PDF   = percent debt financing (percent)
TPDF = table for percent debt financing (percent)
DER   = debt-equity ratio (dimensionless).

Equation 164 defines long-term payments LTP as long-term debt LTD divided by average long-term debt maturity ALTDM and multiplied by effect of excess cash on debt payments EECDP. Equation 164 states that the company repays debt as it matures but might alter payments when excess cash exists.

$$\text{LTP.K} = (\text{LTD.K/ALTDM}) * \text{EECDP.K} \qquad\qquad 164, \text{ A}$$
$$\text{ALTDM} = 2400 \qquad\qquad 164.1, \text{ C}$$

where
LTP   = long-term payments ($/day)
LTD   = long-term debt ($)
ALTDM = average long-term debt maturity (days)
EECDP = effect of excess cash on debt payments (dimensionless).

Effect of excess cash on debt payments EECDP is modeled as a nonlinear function of average percent excess cash APEC (equation 165 and figure 9.8). As APEC rises above zero, the company repays debt at a faster rate than that indicated by normal debt maturity. EECDP levels off at 1.5, on the assumption that the company will be unable or unwilling to repay all of its debt even with large excesses of cash.

$$\text{EECDP.K} = \text{TABHL(TEECDP,APEC.K,0,3,.5)} \qquad\qquad 165, \text{ A}$$
$$\text{TEECDP} = 1/1.05/1.15/1.25/1.35/1.45/1.5 \qquad\qquad 165.1, \text{ T}$$

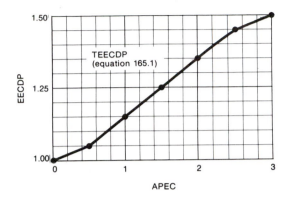

Figure 9.8 Effect of excess cash on debt payments

where

EECDP   = effect of excess cash on debt payments (dimensionless)
TEECDP = table for effect of excess cash on debt payments
             (dimensionless)
APEC   = average percent excess cash (percent).

Average percent excess cash APEC is represented in equation 166 as an exponential average of percent excess cash PEC. Time to average percent excess cash TAPEC is here taken as 240 days. The company therefore responds to excess cash which persists for 240 days (1 year).

$$\text{APEC.K} = \text{SMOOTH(PEC.K,TAPEC)} \qquad\qquad 166, \text{A}$$
$$\text{TAPEC} = 240 \qquad\qquad 166.1, \text{C}$$

where

APEC   = average percent excess cash (percent)
PEC   = percent excess cash (percent)
TAPEC = time to average percent excess cash (days).

Equation 167 defines percent excess cash PEC as the difference between cash CASH and desired cash DCASH, divided by desired cash DCASH.

$$\text{PEC.K} = (\text{CASH.K} - \text{DCASH.K})/\text{DCASH.K} \qquad\qquad 167, \text{A}$$

where

PEC   = percent excess cash (percent)
CASH   = cash ($)
DCASH = desired cash ($).

Figure 9.9 shows the structure governing changes in equity. New

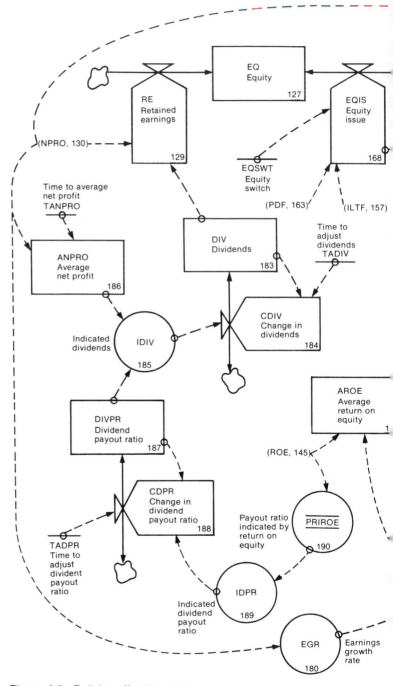

Figure 9.9 Policies affecting equity

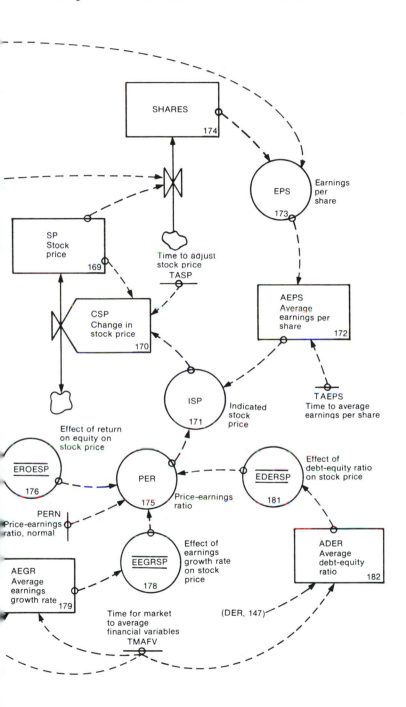

equity is issued for the portion of indicated long-term financing not filled by long-term debt. Stock price determines the number of new shares that must be issued to obtain a given dollar value of equity issue. Stock price is seen to respond to return on equity, earnings growth rate, and debt-equity ratio. Retained earnings are reduced by dividend payments. Dividend payments here respond only to return on equity.

Equation 168 states that equity issue EQIS equals indicated long-term financing ILTF multiplied first by 1.0 minus percent debt financing PDF, and then by equity switch EQSWT. Under some circumstances a company may be unable or unwilling to issue new equity. Such circumstances can be modeled by setting equity switch to zero. A more complete model might represent the desirability of issuing equity as a function of stock price.

$$EQIS.K = ILTF.K * (1 - PDF.K) * EQSWT \qquad\qquad 168, A$$
$$EQSWT = 1 \qquad\qquad 168.1, C$$

where
EQIS   = equity issue ($/day)
ILTF   = indicated long-term financing ($/day)
PDF   = percent debt financing (percent)
EQSWT = equity switch (dimensionless).

The stock valuation model presented in equations 169 through 182 attempts to capture the causal determinants of stock price related to corporate financial policies. The existence of noneconomic and other psychological impacts on stock value makes it next to impossible to predict accurately the behavior of a company's stock price. However, a model that relates corporate financial performance to stock price can be developed. In this way the effect of corporate financial performance on stock price can be estimated.

Stock price SP is modeled in equation 169 as a level variable altered by change in stock price CSP.

$$SP.K = SP.J + (DT)(CSP.JK) \qquad\qquad 169, L$$
$$SP = ISP \qquad\qquad 169.1, N$$

where
SP   = stock price ($/share)
DT   = delta time, simulation solution interval (days)
CSP = change in stock price ($/share/day)
ISP = indicated stock price ($/share).

Equation 170 states that change in stock price CSP equals indicated stock price ISP minus stock price SP divided by time to adjust stock price TASP. The model assumes that the stock market adjusts stock price to indicated stock price relatively quickly.

$$\text{CSP.KL} = (\text{ISP.K} - \text{SP.K})/\text{TASP} \qquad\qquad 170, R$$
$$\text{TASP} = 20 \qquad\qquad 170.1, C$$

where
CSP = change in stock price ($/share/day)
ISP = indicated stock price ($/share)
SP   = stock price ($/share)
TASP = time to adjust stock price (days).

Indicated stock price ISP is determined by average earnings per share AEPS multiplied by price earnings ratio PER (equation 171). The market is assumed to average earnings per share over a year in determining stock price (equation 172).

$$\text{ISP.K} = \text{AEPS.K} * \text{PER.K} \qquad\qquad 171, A$$

where
ISP = indicated stock price ($/share)
AEPS = average earnings per share ($/year/share)
PER = price-earnings ratio ($/$/year);

$$\text{AEPS.K} = \text{SMOOTH}(\text{EPS.K},\text{TAEPS}) \qquad\qquad 172, A$$
$$\text{TAEPS} = 240 \qquad\qquad 172.1, C$$

where
AEPS = average earnings per share ($/year/share)
EPS   = earnings per share ($/year/share)
TAEPS = time to average earnings per share (days).

Equation 173 calculates earnings per share EPS as 240 (days per year) multiplied by net profits NPRO and divided by SHARES.

$$\text{EPS.K} = 240 * \text{NPRO.K}/\text{SHARES.K} \qquad\qquad 173, A$$

where
EPS   = earnings per share ($/year/share)
NPRO   = net profits ($/day)
SHARES = shares (shares).

SHARES is modeled in equation 174 as a level variable increased by equity issue EQIS divided by stock price SP. The initial level of shares is arbitrarily set to 100,000.

SHARES.K = SHARES.J +(DT)(EQIS.J/SP.J)   174, L

SHARES = 100000   174.1, N

where

SHARES = shares (shares)

DT   = delta time, simulation solution interval (days)

EQIS   = equity issue ($/day)

SP   = stock price ($/share).

Equation 175 defines price earnings ratio PER. PER equals price earnings ratio normal PERN multiplied by effect of return on equity on stock price EROESP, effect of earnings growth rate on stock price EEGRSP, and effect of debt-equity ratio on stock price EDERSP. Only the effect of dividend payout on stock price is not included in this model. A price earnings ratio normal of 10 represents a 10 percent return to shareholders.

PER.K = PERN * EROESP.K * EEGRSP.K   175, A
        * EDERSP.K

PERN = 10   175.1, C

where

PER   = price-earnings ratio ($/$/year)

PERN   = price earnings ratio, normal ($/$/year)

EROESP = effect of return on equity on stock price (dimensionless)

EEGRSP = effect of earnings growth rate on stock price
         (dimensionless)

EDERSP = effect of debt-equity ratio on stock price
         (dimensionless).

Effect of return on equity on stock price EROESP is modeled as a nonlinear function of average return on equity AROE (equation 176 and figure 9.10). Other things being equal, an AROE of 0.05 yields a price earnings ratio of 10.0. As AROE falls below 0.05, the price earnings ratio increases, rapidly at first but then more slowly as AROE approaches 0.45.

EROESP.K = TABLE(TEROES,AROE.K,0,.45,.05)   176, A

TEROES = .1/1/1.85/2.6/3.25/3.75/3.85/3.95/4/4   176.1, T

where

EROESP = effect of return on equity on stock price (dimensionless)

TEROES = table for effect of return on equity on stock price
         (dimensionless)

AROE   = average return on equity (percent/year).

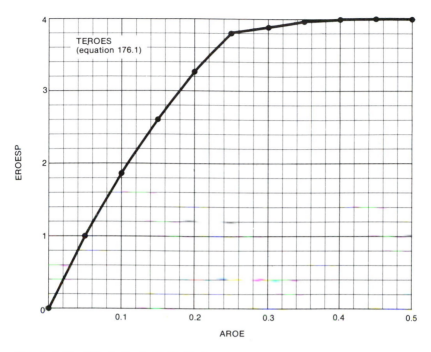

Figure 9.10   Effect of return on equity on stock price

Average return on equity AROE is modeled as an exponential average of return on equity ROE (equation 177). Time for market to average financial variables TMAFV is here taken as 480 days.

AROE.K = SMOOTH(ROE.K,TMAFV)   177, A
TMAFV = 480   177.1, C

where
AROE   = average return on equity (percent/year)
ROE   = return on equity (percent/year)
TMAFV = time for market to average financial variables (days).

Effect of earnings growth rate on stock price EEGRSP is modeled as a nonlinear function of average earnings growth rate AEGR (equation 178 and figure 9.11). AEGR values below zero cause the price earnings ratio to fall below 10.0; AEGR values above zero cause it to rise above 10.0. Investors are assumed to attach less significance to progressively higher growth rates. Consequently the effect of earnings growth rate on stock price levels off.

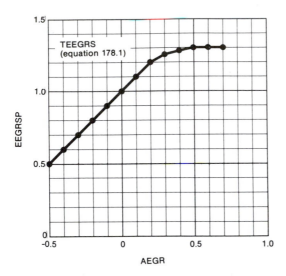

Figure 9.11   Effect on earnings growth rate on stock price

EEGRSP.K = TABHL(TEEGRS,AEGR.K, − .5,.7,.1)   178, A
TEEGRS = .5/.6/.7/.8/.9/1/1.1/1.2/1.25/1.275/1.3/1.3/1.3   178.1, T

where

EEGRSP = effect of earnings growth rate on stock price
               (dimensionless)
TEEGRS = table for effect of earnings growth rate on stock price
               (dimensionless)
AEGR   = average earnings growth rate (percent/year).

Average earnings growth rate is represented in equation 179 as an exponential average of earnings growth rate EGR.

AEGR.K = SMOOTH(EGR.K,TMAFV)   179, A

where

AEGR   = average earnings growth rate (percent/year)
EGR   = earnings growth rate (percent/year)
TMAFV = time for market to average financial variables (days).

Earnings growth rate EGR is calculated by using the trend detection MACRO. Equation 180 specifies the calculation.

EGR.K = 240 * TRND(NPRO.K,240,0)   180, A

where

EGR   = earnings growth rate (percent/year)
TRND = macro for detecting trends in input time series
          (percent/day)
NPRO = net profits ($/day).

Effect of debt-equity ratio on the stock price is modeled as a non-linear function of average debt-equity ratio ADER (equation 181 and figure 9.12). A debt-equity ratio value of 0.5 is assumed to be normal for companies in this industry. At a value of 0.5 effect of debt-equity ratio on stock price equals 1.0. Changes in ADER from 0.5 cause the price earnings ratio to fall below normal: values below 0.5 cause PER to fall because investors feel the company is not taking full advantage of leverage; values above 0.5 cause PER to fall because the risk of bankruptcy increases as debt levels increase.

EDERSP.K = TABLE(TEDERS,ADER.K,0,2,.25)   181, A
TEDERS = .9/.95/1/.95/.9/.85/.8/.75/.7   181.1, T

where
EDERSP = effect of debt-equity ratio on stock price (dimensionless)
TEDERS = table for effect of debt-equity ratio on stock price
          (dimensionless)
ADER   = average debt-equity ratio (dimensionless).

Average debt-equity ratio ADER is represented in equation 182 as an exponential average of debt-equity ratio DER.

ADER.K = SMOOTH(DER.K,TMAFV)   182, A

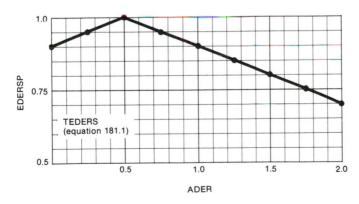

Figure 9.12 Effect of debt-equity ratio on stock price

where
ADER   = average debt-equity ratio (dimensionless)
DER   = debt-equity ratio (dimensionless)
TMAFV = time for market to average financial variables (days).

Dividends DIV is modeled in equation 183 as a level variable increased by change in dividends CDIV.

DIV.K = DIV.J + (DT)(CDIV.JK)   183, L
DIV = DIVPR * NPRO   183.1, N

where
DIV   = dividends ($/day)
DT   = delta time, simulation solution interval (days)
CDIV   = change in dividends ($/day/day)
DIVPR = dividend payout ratio (percent)
NPRO   = net profits ($/day).

Equation 184 states that change in dividends CDIV equals indicated dividends IDIV minus dividends DIV divided by time to adjust dividends TADIV. TADIV is set to 120 days because dividends are changed only at board meetings, which occur several times a year.

CDIV.KL = (IDIV.K − DIV.K)/TADIV   184, R
TADIV = 120   184.1, C

where
CDIV   = change in dividends ($/day/day)
IDIV   = indicated dividends ($/day)
DIV   = dividends ($/day)
TADIV = time to adjust dividends (days).

Indicated dividends IDIV equal dividend payout ratio DIVPR multiplied by average net profits ANPRO (equation 185).

IDIV.K = DIVPR.K * ANPRO.K   185, A

where
IDIV   = indicated dividends ($/day)
DIVPR   = dividend payout ratio (percent)
ANPRO = average net profits ($/day).

Average net profits ANPRO are represented in equation 186 as an exponential average of net profits over the last year.

ANPRO.K = SMOOTH(NPRO.K,240)   186, A

where
ANPRO = average net profits ($/day)
NPRO   = net profits ($/day).

Dividend payout ratio DIVPR is modeled in equation 187 as a level variable increased or decreased by change in dividend payout ratio CDPR.

$$DIVPR.K = DIVPR.J + (DT)(CDPR.JK) \qquad 187, L$$
$$DIVPR = IDPR \qquad 187.1, N$$

where
DIVPR = dividend payout ratio (percent)
DT   = delta time, simulation solution interval (days)
CDPR   = change in dividend payout ratio (percent/day)
IDPR   = indicated dividend payout ratio (percent).

Equation 188 states that change in dividend payout ratio CDPR equals indicated dividend payout ratio IDPR minus dividend payout ratio DIVPR divided by time to adjust dividend payout ratio TADPR. TADPR is set to 120 days because companies change the information on which dividends are based at most quarterly.

$$CDPR.KL = (IDPR.K - DIVPR.K)/TADPR \qquad 188, R$$
$$TADPR = 120 \qquad 188.1, C$$

where
CDPR   = change in dividend payout ratio (percent/day)
IDPR   = indicated dividend payout ratio (percent)
DIVPR = dividend payout ratio (percent)
TADPR = time to adjust dividend payout ratio (days).

Equation 189 defines indicated dividend payout ratio IDPR to equal payout ratio indicated by return on equity PRIROE.

$$IDPR.K = PRIROE.K \qquad 189, A$$

where
IDPR   = indicated dividend payout ratio (percent)
PRIROE = payout ratio indicated by return on equity (percent).

Payout ratio indicated by return on equity PRIROE is a function of return on equity ROE (equation 190 and figure 9.13). Historically companies with low return on equity pay out higher percentages of earnings than companies with high return on equity. The logic behind such a relationship is that for a low-return company investors would rather

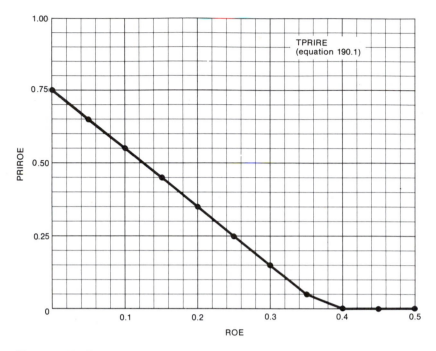

Figure 9.13 Payout ratio indicated by return on equity

have the earnings paid as dividends so that they can be invested in a higher-return company, whereas for a high-return company investors prefer that the company reinvest the dividends.

PRIROE.K = TABHL(TPRIRE,ROE.K,0,45,.05)   190, A
TPRIRE = .75/.65/.55/.45/.35/.25/.15/.05/0/0   190.1, T

where

PRIROE = payout ratio indicated by return on equity (percent)

TPRIRE = table for payout ratio indicated by return on equity (percent)

ROE   = return on equity (percent/year).

Equation 198 defines accumulated profit ACCPRO to equal a level variable increased by net profit NPRO. ACCPRO accumulates total profits over the length of the simulation and is used as a measure of financial performance. NPRO could be discounted to determine ACCPRO.

ACCPRO.K = ACCPRO.J + (DT)(NPRO.J)   198, L
ACCPRO = 0   198.1, N

where
ACCPRO = accumulated profits ($)
DT   = delta time, simulation solution interval (days)
NPRO   = net profits ($/day).

9.3 Using the Model to Produce Time Paths of Financial Variables

A system dynamics model provides a vehicle for determining the time paths of important financial variables. By tracing the magnitude and timing of cash flows, time paths indicate borrowing requirements and possible cash shortages and variations in important financial ratios. If the patterns the time paths project are undesirable, policies can be designed to improve them. If no improvement is possible, at least through the use of time paths company management and investors can be made aware of potential problems and their causes, so that panic reactions are avoided.

In this section the behavior of company financial variables for STEP, CYCLICAL, and GROWTH market demand patterns is examined. In the simulation runs the effect of delivery delay on market share was switched out. The purpose of these runs is narrowed to the basic behavior of financial variables in three common, market demand patterns.

STEP

Figure 9.14a through c gives the response of the model to a 15 percent STEP increase in market demand. Figure 9.14a shows the behavior of several operating variables as described in earlier chapters, 9.14b the behavior of important financial variables, and 9.14c the behavior of stock price and its determinants.

In part b net profits and return on sales fall immediately after the STEP increase. Net profits fall in spite of the fact that shipment rate increases. Profits and return fall because of several additional costs: (1) the cost of overtime (not shown) used in the short run in lieu of additional labor (not shown), (2) the cost of hiring additional labor, and (3) the costs of additional labor and overtime to offset the decline in effect of parts inventory level on production rate. As these additional costs are reduced, net profits increase to a higher equilibrium value, and return on sales returns to normal around day 480.

Also in part b cash flow from operations exhibits a markedly differ-

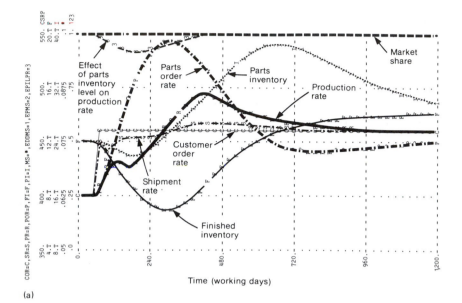

(a)

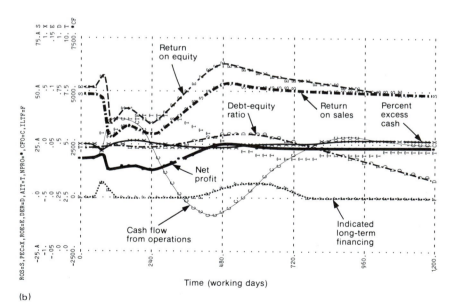

(b)

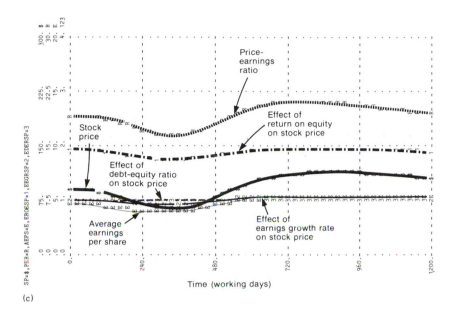

Time (working days)

(c)

Figure 9.14   Model response to a STEP increase in market demand

ent behavior from that of net profits (both are plotted on the same scale and are initially equal). Immediately after the STEP increase cash flow from operations increases and remains at an elevated level until approximately day 192. Cash flow increases because shipment rate depletes inventory—the company is receiving a cash return on the prior cash investment in inventory. From day 192 until day 432, when the company is building inventory rapidly, cash flow from operations declines—the company is investing in inventory. As the inventory buildup slows after day 432, cash flow gradually increases to a higher equilibrium level.

In the situation modeled here the decrease in cash flow does not cause any cash problems. From day 360 until day 552, during which time cash flow from operations is negative, the company is able to borrow sufficient cash to keep percent excess cash at 0. Debt-equity ratio rises during this time and then is reduced when cash flow increases.

Part c shows the performance of stock price. Until day 480 stock price declines as a consequence of the decrease in average earnings per share, the drop in effect of return on equity on stock price in response to the drop in return on equity, and the decline in effect of debt-equity ratio on stock price in response to the increase in debt-equity ratio. Then after day 480, as net profits and return on sales improve, stock price also increases to a higher level.

CYCLICAL

Figure 9.15 shows the model's behavior for a CYCLICAL variation in market demand. For reference, figure 9.15a gives the behavior of operating variables, as described in earlier chapters. Figure 9.15b gives the behavior of financial variables. The most noteworthy characteristic of financial behavior is that cash flow from operations varies much more than net profits, and with different phasing. The reason for the greater variation in cash flow lies in the behavior of inventory. Cash flow begins to decline before the peak in customer order rate because the company is building inventory. Cash flow declines sharply after the peak in customer order rate because the company is building inventory while shipment rate, and hence collections, is falling. The opposite behavior occurs in the cash flow upswing.

The magnitude of cash flow variations is determined by the amount of inventory building and depleting. Cash outflows, and inventory inflows, depend on parts order rate and production rate; cash inflows, and inventory outflows, depend on shipment rate. The greater the inventory variations, the greater by which parts orders and production differ from shipments, and therefore the greater the variation in cash flow.

Variations in net profits, on the other hand, are governed by the variation in shipment rate and the proportion of fixed costs in the company's cost structure. The costs of building inventory are not charged against profits until that inventory is shipped. Consequently profits do not decline when inventory is built, nor do they rise when inventory is depleted (except insofar as shipment rate varies).

The phasing of profit and cash flow variations is also different. Because of shipping delays and shortages, shipment rate slightly lags customer order rate. But net profits generally increase and decrease with customer order rate, except for the period when overtime and shortages of parts cause costs of meeting customer order rate to rise above normal, as explained for the STEP input (for example, the drop in net profit from day 1008 to day 1296).

The phasing of cash flow variations is governed, however, by the company's production and parts-ordering policies. To the extent inven-

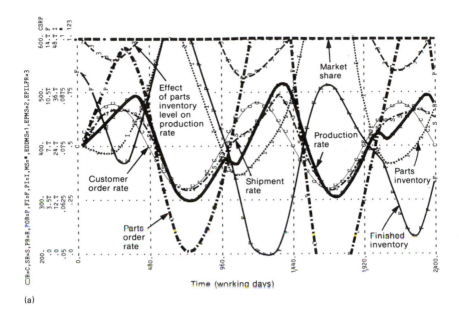

(a)

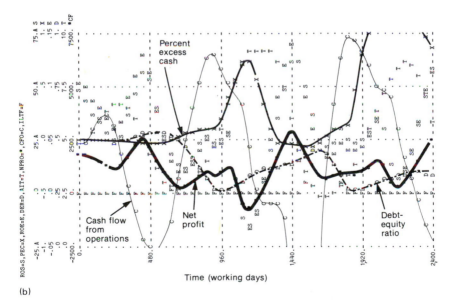

(b)

Figure 9.15   Model behavior in response to CYCLICAL variation in market demand

tories are being built as shipments are still increasing, figure 9.15, cash flow peaks prior to net profits. The phasing (and magnitude) of cash flow variations can be controlled by changing the timing of inventory building and depleting relative to variations in shipment rate.

In figure 9.15 the periods of negative cash flow do not cause any cash shortages—percent excess cash does not fall much below 0 (a value lower than −1.0 would indicate negative cash balance). Short- and long-term borrowing are able to compensate for the cash outflows, as evidenced by the increases in debt-equity ratio. Periods of cash excess do occur, however, because of limitations in the amount of long-term debt that can be repaid in any one year.

In summary because of accounting procedures cash flow from operations varies substantially more than net profits in response to CYCLICAL fluctuations in market demand. Inventory building and depleting cause the variations in cash flow; but because the costs of building are not charged against profits until a shipment is made, net profits do not experience these large variations.

GROWTH

Figure 9.16 shows the model's response to GROWTH in market demand. As in the case of the STEP change, the sudden increase in

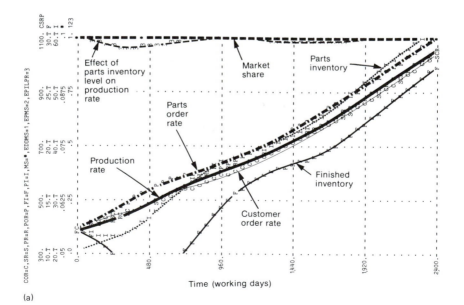

Time (working days)

(a)

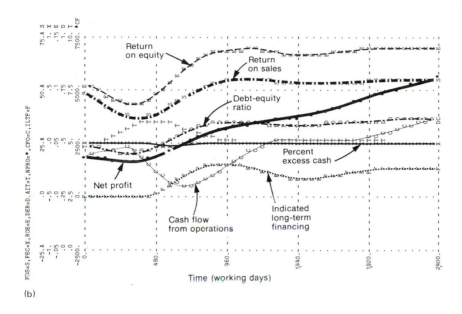

(b)

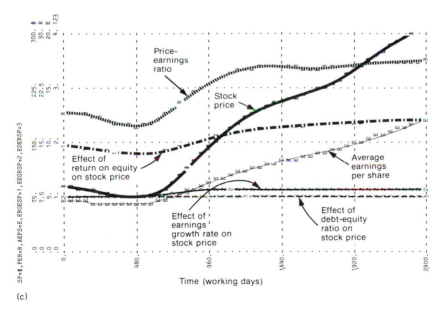

(c)

Figure 9.16 Model behavior in response to GROWTH in market demand

customer order rate over production rate causes finished inventory to fall. The effect is similar for parts inventory. Because shipment rate depletes inventory, cash flow from operations initially increases. In contrast net profits fall because of cost increases that result from parts shortages and the use of overtime.

Net profits increase as these additional costs are eliminated. But cash flow peaks and declines with the buildup of parts and finished inventory. After the major building phase from day 240 until day 720, cash flow increases, but never enough to equal net profits (as it did for the STEP change).

Cash flow lags net profits for two reasons:

1. To build parts and finished inventory, more parts must be received and labor hired than can be charged against profits (parts arrival rate and production rate exceed shipment rate).

2. Accounts receivables increase more than accounts payable because time to collect accounts receivable exceeds time to collect accounts payable.

Companies experience reduced cash flow just at the time they need money to finance expansion of capital equipment. For one year debt-equity ratio rises as indicated long-term financing exceeds cash flow from operations.

Figure 9.16c shows the behavior of stock price and its determinants in response to GROWTH in market demand. Stock price initially falls, as it did for the STEP changes, because net profits (average earnings per share) and return on equity fall. But then stock price rises, rapidly at first and then gradually with the growth in average earnings per share.

The rapid rise in stock price is caused by an increase in price earnings ratio, which in turn results from increases in return on equity and earnings growth rate. The increase in earnings growth rate is a direct consequence of the growth in market demand. The increase in return on equity is caused by fixed costs growing more slowly than other costs because fixed costs only increase with a 480-day average of dollar value of sales. Once the higher price earnings ratio is reached around day 1200, stock price grows more slowly than earnings per share.

In summary the growing company experiences reduced cash flows because it needs to build inventory and accounts receivable at a time when demand for cash investment expenditures is high. The severity of any potential problem this causes will depend on (1) the amount and cost of capital expenditures, (2) the availability of debt financing, and (3) the availability and cost of equity financing. These issues are the subject of chapter 12.

9.4 Using the Model to Rank Policy Options

Chapter 4 introduced the concept of an aggregate performance index that weights important variables and can be used to rank policy alternatives. In chapter 4 the performance index was an equal weighting of amplification and inventory loss. A plotting of the index against policy parameters showed a relatively flat portion from which a policy could be chosen, with confidence that the policy performance would be insensitive to some errors in parameter estimates.

Accumulated profits is a performance index that weights all variables that affect financial performance according to their contribution to costs or revenue. This section plots accumulated profits as a function of different production and parts order rate policy parameters for several test variations in market demand. The simulations are made with a model that incorporates the effect of delivery delay on market share but not price as a market-clearing mechanism.

Table 9.1 gives the simulated policy parameters. In addition each policy parameter was simulated with three different goals for finished and parts inventory: 30/60, 40/80, and 50/100.

CYCLICAL

Figure 9.17 plots accumulated profits as a function of policy parameter set for a CYCLICAL variation in market demand. For each inventory level profits are high with the 30-policy set, drop off sharply with the 60- and 120-policy sets, and then rise sharply with the 240-policy set and gradually with the slower sets.

The 30-policy set follows customer order rate very quickly. Consequently inventories do not fall much so that market share is maintained and parts shortages do not occur. The cost is a fair amount of fluctuation in production rate and parts order rate.

As the policy set is increased to 60 and then to 120, not only does the

Table 9.1
Policy parameter sets

Policy index	Policy parameter							
	TACOR	TCFI	TOCORG	TACORE	TOCORE	TAPRPO	TCPI	TOPRGR
30	30	30	120	30	120	30	30	120
60	60	60	240	60	240	60	60	240
120	120	120	360	120	360	120	120	360
240	240	240	960	240	960	240	240	960
480	480	480	1,200	480	1,200	480	480	1,200
960	960	960	1,800	960	1,800	960	960	1,800

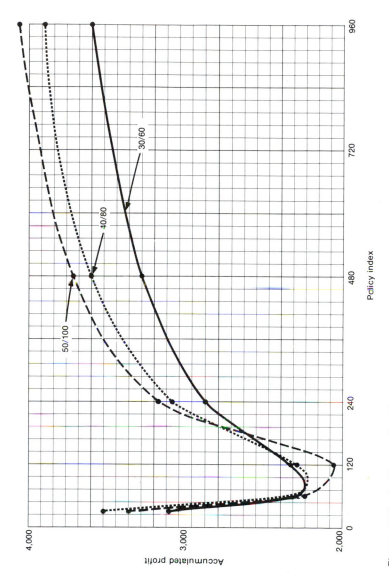

Policy index

Accumulated profit

Figure 9.17 Profits as a function of policy parameter set for CYCLICAL variation

company lose market share but also encounters greater fluctuations in production and parts order rates. The loss of market share occurs because the company responds more slowly to changes in customer order rate, allowing shortages in finished and parts inventory. Then the trend-forecasting process causes greater fluctuations in production rate, finished inventory, parts order rate, and parts inventory. As described in chapter 5, the trend detection times with the 60- and 120-policy sets are such that the company is perceiving maximum growth rates just as growth is slowing down. In extrapolating at maximum rates, while growth is slowing, the company causes greater overshoots in production and parts order rates and thus greater fluctuations in inventory. Because the inventory peaks come at the wrong time, they do not help market share. The 60- and 120-policy sets therefore cause both a loss of market share and greater instability, and profits decline sharply.

As the policy set increases from 120 to 240, market share falls some but not much more. Because inventory can only fall so much for a given size of variation in customer order rate, the loss of market share must level off. The 240 policy vastly improves stability so that the loss of revenue is offset by cost savings, and profits improve.

As the policy set is raised past 240, profits gradually increase. In fact the profits with the 480 set are greater than those with the 30 set. The profit improvement over the 240 set comes from two sources: (1) improved stability and (2) improved market share. Market share improves with the slower policy sets, for the CYCLICAL variation, because the phasing of inventory is improved. Inventory peaks later so that more is available for the next upturn in customer order rate. The profit improvement over the 30-policy set occurs because, under the assumptions of this model, the savings from stability must more than balance the loss of market share.

Figure 9.17 further indicates that for any given policy set the higher the level of inventory, the higher the profits. This statement is true only for policy sets 240 and slower. For these sets the profit gains from greater market share (not losing market share in upturns), offset the losses from carrying extra inventory. For policy sets below 240 some extra inventory is beneficial; however, past a point the losses of market share cannot be circumvented any further, and the additional inventory-holding costs cause profits to fall. (This must also be true for high enough inventory levels when slow policy sets are used.)

GROWTH

Figure 9.18 gives a plot of accumulated profits as a function of policy set for GROWTH in market demand. The slower the policy set, the lower the profits because of loss of market share. Stability is not a factor with the growth input.

For the slower policy sets the more inventory, the greater the profits because the loss of market share is not as large. For the quicker policies more inventory is beneficial up to a point.

Combination Input

Figure 9.19 gives a plot of accumulated profits as a function of policy set for a combination input: (1) a 10 percent NOISE variation, (2) a CYCLICAL variation, and (3) GROWTH. Because the 30-policy set is too unstable for a NOISE variation, it was not simulated.

Figure 9.19 shows that with a realistic combination input both very quick and very slow policies reduce profits: quick policies because of increased instability, slow policies because of loss of market share. The figure further shows for each inventory level a relatively flat portion where profits change little with relation to changes in policy parameters.

In this model increasing inventory levels improve profits. Past a point, however, further increases in inventory will cause profits to fall since no more gains in market share accrue. Additional experiments would need to be performed to calculate the appropriate inventory level and range of policy parameters from which to choose a policy.

The relatively flat portion of the performance curve is encouraging to the policy designer. Any policy within the region is equally good. Given the uncertainties involved in estimating relative costs, a flat region gives the designer confidence that the performance of the chosen policy is insensitive to some errors. Moreover the designer can then choose any policy in this region for other than cost factors (for example, labor stability).

9.5 Summary

A system dynamics model provides the policy designer with both quantitative and qualitative performance measures. Quantitative measures such as accumulated profits over the length of the simulation provide an index for ranking alternative policies. Such a ranking often indicates

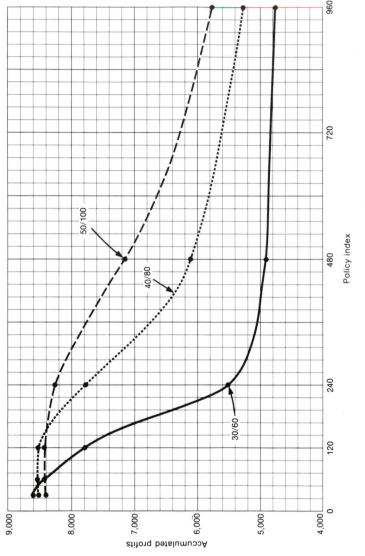

Figure 9.18   Profits as a function of policy parameter set for GROWTH

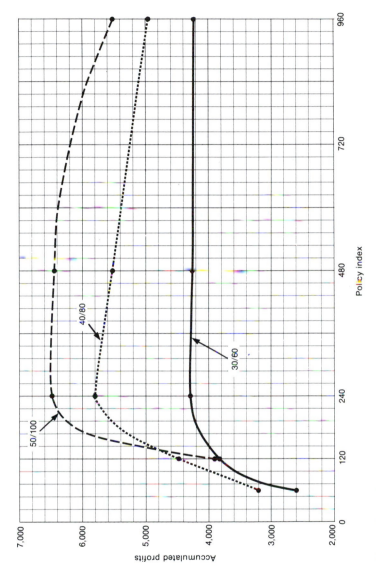

Figure 9.19 Profits as a function of policy parameter set for COMBINATION

a number of policies for which the quantitative measure is nearly the same. The designer can then choose a policy based on qualitative consideration.

The ability to choose a policy based on qualitative measures is important. Given the uncertainties in parameter estimates, the difficulty in modeling every factor that affects profits, and the fact that one index cannot capture everything of importance to the company, a range of nearly equal policy options gives the company an opportunity to incorporate qualitative factors in the selection. Such qualitative factors might include labor stability, magnitude of variations in production and inventory, and magnitude of variations in cash flow and profits.

A system dynamics model also provides a measure of these qualitative factors. Time plots of important system variables allow visual comparison of the performance of important system variables. By comparing these plots for the nearly equal policies, the policy designer has a qualitative input to the selection process.

Reference

Robert Morris Associates. 1973. *Annual Statement Studies*. Philadelphia: Robert Morris Associates.

Dynamics Created by Financial Control

10

10.1 Introduction

Most companies do not passively monitor financial performance measures because of their importance to investors. Rather, as performance deviates from corporate goals, corrective actions are taken. For example, should profit margins fall below goal, actions to reduce costs and/or increase prices are taken. In time the corrective actions work to alleviate the problem.

This financial control sequence, however, has one serious shortcoming—it fails to consider the multiple feedback consequences of the corrective actions. A price increase does improve profit margins, other factors remaining equal. But the increase also reduces unit sales and, depending on the elasticity, may reduce revenue. Moreover the reduction in unit sales means that fixed costs must be spread over fewer units, resulting in cost per unit increases. The net effect of the price increase on margins and revenue depends on multiple feedback consequences. Similar feedback consequences follow actions to reduce costs. In the short run a reduction in costs improves margins. But as the cost reductions restrict the allocation of resources to research, development, marketing, and so on, the longer-run competitive position of the company is hurt. Effective financial control therefore requires that the company evaluate these multiple feedback interactions.

Because of its ability to calculate the consequence of multiple feedback interactions, a system dynamics model is a useful tool for the design of financial control policies. This chapter examines the use of the model to design policies for the control of annual inventory turnover. Chapter 12 discusses the use of the model to design policies for the control of debt-equity ratio in the growing company. These examples demonstrate that the failure to consider multiple feedback interactions in the design of control policies can lead to poor, overall company performance.

10.2 Structure of Financial Control of Inventory

Manufacturing companies carry significant parts and finished goods inventory. The holding costs on this inventory is such that, if inventory can be reduced without causing a loss of sales, profits improve. Higher inventory turns (dollar value of sales divided by dollar value of inventory) mean higher profits, and conversely.

As a result many companies use inventory turns as a measure of financial performance and actively attempt to control it. In observing actual company practices, one can hear stories such as "Trucks lined up for a mile because the receiving door was closed, on orders from management, to avoid further increases in end-of-month inventory (even though the assembly line was short of parts)," or "Three people suffered nervous breakdowns in the round-the-clock effort to reduce inventory during the last business downturn." While these are undoubtedly extreme cases, many companies exert financial pressures on production operations in an effort to reduce perceived excesses of inventory.

To illustrate the possible consequences of these pressures, financial pressures from discrepancies between inventory turnover and its goal now affect desired production rate and parts order rate. Equations 28 and 55 for desired production rate DPR and parts order rate POR have been modified to incorporate a multiplicative effect of financial pressures. These effects act to reduce DPR and POR below the values indicated by the volume of business and inventory corrections.

$$DPR.K = (BCOR.K + FIC.K + WIPC.K + UOC.K)$$
$$* EFPDPR.K \qquad\qquad 28, A$$

where

DPR   = desired production rate (units/day)
BCOR   = base customer order rate (units/day)
FIC   = finished inventory correction (units/day)
WIPC   = work-in-process correction (units/day)
UOC   = unfilled order correction (units/day)
EFPDPR = effect of financial pressures on desired production rate
                 (dimensionless);

$$POR.KL = (BPR.K + PIC.K + POC.K) * EFPPOR.K \qquad 55, R$$

where

POR = parts order rate (units/day)
BPR = base production rate (units/day)
PIC = parts inventory correction (units/day)
POC = parts on order correction (units/day)
EFPPOR = effect of financial pressure on parts order rate
(dimensionless).

Effect of financial pressure on desired production rate EFPDPR (equation 69) and effect of financial pressure on parts order rate EFPPOR (equation 70) respond to perceived annual inventory turns PAIT relative to annual inventory turns goal AITG, as shown in figure 10.1. When PAIT exceeds AITG, the effects are 1.0—no financial pressure is exerted to reduce inventory. However, as PAIT falls below AITG, increasingly greater pressure causes effect of financial pressure to reduce desired production rate and parts order rate. EFPPOR is assumed to be stronger than EFPDPR because a company will find it easier to cut back orders to a supplier than to cut its own production.

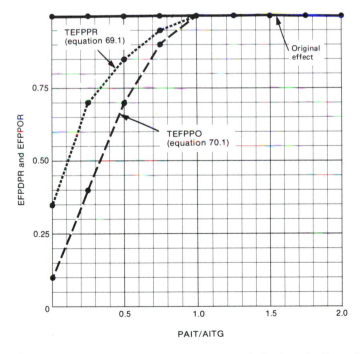

Figure 10.1 Effect of financial pressure on desired production rate and parts order rate

EFPDPR.K = TABHL(TEFPPR,PAIT.K/AITG,0,2,.25)   69, A
TEFPPR = 1/1/1/1/1/1/1/1/1   69.1, T
AITG = AIT   69.2, N

where

EFPDPR = effect of financial pressures on desired production rate
                 (dimensionless)
TEFPPR = table for effect of financial pressures on desired
                 production rate (dimensionless)
PAIT   = perceived annual inventory turns (1/year)
AITG   = annual inventory turns goal (1/year)
AIT   = annual inventory turns (1/year);

EFPPOR.K = TABHL(TEFPPO,PAIT.K/AITG,0,2,.25)   70, A
TEFPPO = 1/1/1/1/1/1/1/1/1   70.1, T

where

EFPPOR = effect of financial pressure on parts order rate
                 (dimensionless)
TEFPPO = table for effect of financial pressure on parts order rate
                 (dimensionless)
PAIT   = perceived annual inventory turns (1/year)
AITG   = annual inventory turns goal (1/year).

Perceived annual inventory turns PAIT is represented as an exponential average of annual inventory turns AIT (equation 71).

PAIT.K = SMOOTH(AIT.K,TPAIT)   71, A
TPAIT = 20   71.1, C

where

PAIT   = perceived annual inventory turns (1/year)
AIT   = annual inventory turns (1/year)
TPAIT = time to perceive annual inventory turns (days).

10.3 Understanding the Adverse Consequences of Financial Control

Figure 10.2 provides a basis for comparing the effects of financial pressure on model behavior for a CYCLICAL variation in market demand with the moderate policy parameter set. The behavior mode exhibited in figure 10.2a was described in chapter 8. Because production rate lags customer order rate, inventories are falling as customer order rate is rising, and rising as customer order rate is falling. This behavior of

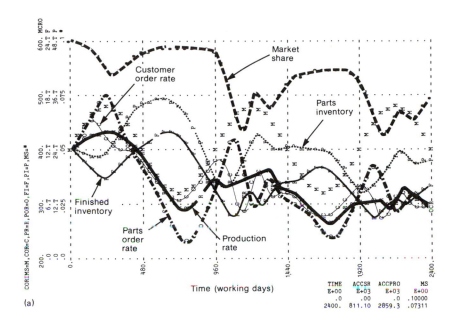

(a)

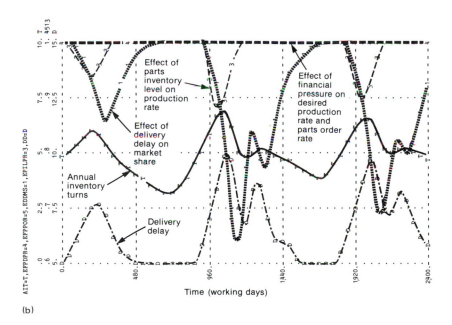

(b)

Figure 10.2   Model behavior for CYCLICAL variation on market demand

finished inventory causes delivery delay (figure 10.2b) to rise in business upturns so that market share falls. In addition the behavior of parts inventory causes effect of parts inventory level on production rate to suppress production rate further below customer order rate in business upturns. As a result finished inventory falls lower, delivery delay rises higher, and market share declines. In summary the behavior of both parts and finished inventories, as caused by the company's production and parts-ordering policies, causes the loss of market share.

Figure 10.2b also shows the behavior of annual inventory turns during the business cycle swings. Inventory turns fall during business downturns because inventory is increasing while sales are falling; inventory turns rise during business upturns because inventory is falling while sales are rising. Annual inventory turns goal is a constant equal to the initial value of annual inventory turns. Consequently during business downturns inventory turns fall below inventory turns goal.

The company that attempts to control annual inventory turns through financial pressures on production and parts ordering would exert such pressures during business downturns. Figure 10.3 shows that these pressures are only marginally successful in improving annual inventory turns (figure 10.3 compares the behavior of annual inventory turns, on an expanded scale, for the simulation runs of figures 10.2 and

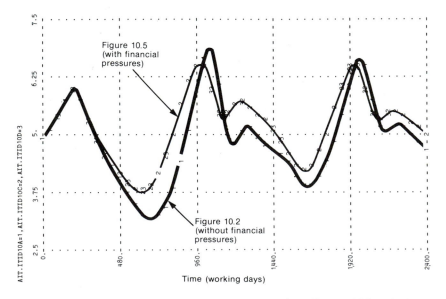

Figure 10.3 Comparison of annual inventory turns from figures 10.2 and 10.5

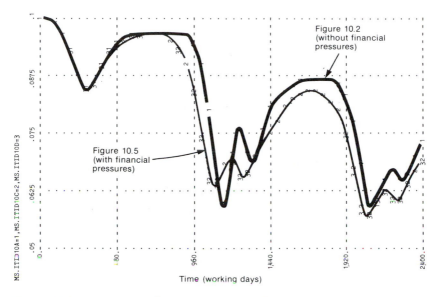

Figure 10.4 Comparison of market share from figures 10.2 and 10.5

10.5). Moreover, as shown in figure 10.4, the improvement in inventory turns comes at the expense of profits. At the end of the simulation market share is down by 5.8 percent, and accumulated profits are down by 7.5 percent. Financial controls only marginally accomplish their objective and in the process cause a loss of market share and profits.

The failure of financial controls to improve performance can be explained by examining the more detailed simulation output given in figure 10.5. As shown in figure 10.5b, financial pressures begin to take effect as annual inventory turns fall below goal at approximately day 336. Financial pressures cause production and parts order rates to fall faster and lower than in the simulation without financial pressures (figure 10.2). As a result parts and finished inventories peak sooner and at a lower level. But because financial pressures respond after the fact to a change in annual inventory turns, and because of the delays in completing work in process and receiving goods from suppliers, the pressures act slowly in improving inventory turns.

At day 720 the downturn ends as customer order rate increases. Inventory turns improve at day 720, even without financial pressure. While financial pressures do reduce the amount by which annual inventory turns fall, by the time the pressures are effective, changes in customer order rate are improving annual inventory turns so that the

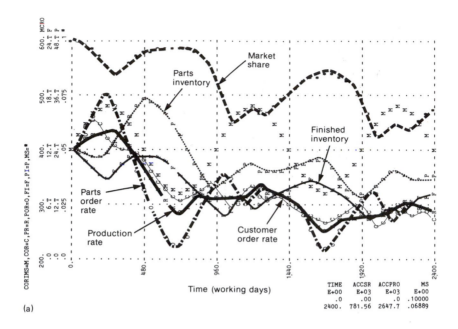

(a)

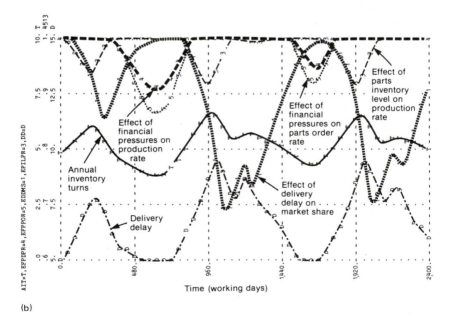

(b)

Figure 10.5   Model behavior for CYCLICAL variation in market demand: financial pressures

net improvement is small. Should customer order rate not recover, then financial pressures would improve performance. In the case of business cycle demand, however, the increase in customer order rate corrects the inventory turns problem only after the financial controls begin to take effect.

As business recovers beginning at day 720, the company has less parts and finished inventory as a buffer. As a result shortages of finished and parts inventory cause effect of parts inventory level on production rate and effect of delivery delay on market share to deter business recovery much sooner. Even though market share falls no lower with financial pressures, it falls sooner, causing the company to lose sales and profits in the aggregate. Performance in the recovery is worsened because financial pressures reduce the amount of excess inventory the company can use to absorb the increase in customer order rate.

A similar pattern repeats in each cycle. During the downturn, annual inventory turns decrease, but corrective actions are too slow to have much impact. What little impact they do have causes performance to deteriorate in the business recovery. In fact the more successful the financial controls, the lower the inventories are just before the recovery, and the greater the eventual loss of market share. Financial controls on day-to-day inventory management are not an effective means of improving total company performance.

10.4 Improving Behavior through Policy Design

The behavior of annual inventory turns is governed by the behavior of inventory relative to customer order rate. This relationship is controlled by the company's production rate and parts order rate policies. The most effective means of improving performance of annual inventory turns is to design production and parts-ordering policies that give the desired performance.

For example, figure 10.6 shows model behavior with production rate and parts order rate policies that correct inventory discrepancies in 60 days (versus 240 days in prior figures) and perceive growth trends in 60 days (versus 480 days in prior figures). Such a policy causes inventories to peak and bottom along with the peaks and bottoms of customer order rate. As a result annual inventory turns remain nearly flat. Recall, however, that such a policy would result in a very unstable be-

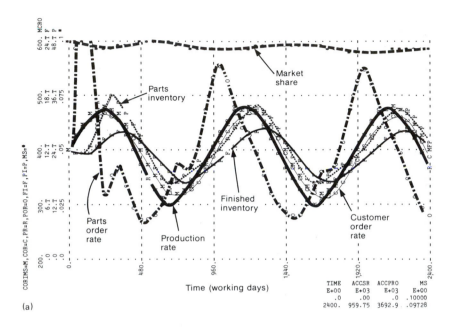

(a)

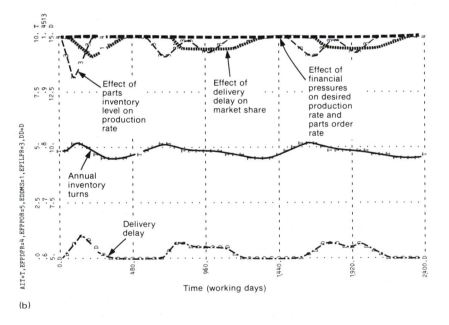

(b)

Figure 10.6   Model behavior for CYCLICAL variation in market demand: very aggressive policy set

havior under shorter-term market demand variations. The policy may therefore be deemed unacceptable.

Nevertheless, the policy serves to illustrate a basic point: the most effective means of exerting financial control is in the design of operating policies. Operating policies are designed and selected on the basis of their financial performance. The design process uses a model that incorporates the multiple feedback interactions operating in the system and further tests policy response under a wide range of business conditions. While the best policy may include some financial controls, once it is selected, no additional financial pressures are placed on operating decisions.

Part III
Dynamics of Corporate Growth

Dynamics Created by
Capacity Expansion

11

11.1 Introduction

While corporate growth is the overriding objective of many companies, the factors that distinguish the successful growth company from the unsuccessful one are not clearly understood. One set of factors that stands out, however, is managerial policies for the acquisition and allocation of resources. That managerial policies play an important role in the dynamics of corporate growth is evidenced by the widely varying growth patterns experienced by companies in the same general line of business, with the same market.

Part III discusses two important aspects of managerial policies that distinguish the successful from the unsuccessful growth company: (1) the ability to acquire sufficient resources to maintain an attractive product in the face of growth in market demand and (2) the ability to select an appropriate method for limiting sales when the potential market exceeds company resources.

In the following chapters policy guidelines that decrease the probability of a company being resource constrained are presented as well as a method for determining the best way to limit sales when a company cannot acquire sufficient resources: what aspect of product attractiveness—availability, quality, product newness, or price—should be used to balance supply and demand.

One of the most important and fundamental decisions facing a growing company is how much to invest in production capacity. Insufficient capacity can result in loss of market share, growth below potential, and reduced profits. Excess capacity can lead to low profitability and price cutting.

The business press contains numerous examples of the problems caused by incorrect expansion plans: the electronics components manufacturer that continually introduces new products only to lose a substantial share of the market within two years, the capital goods manufacturer that sees a ten-year erosion of market share even though volume increases, the leisure goods producer that experiences a loss of share from 100 percent to 30 percent in three years, even while volume quadruples. On the other side of the coin are the numerous examples of the companies whose expansion decisions come to fruition after market growth has slowed and competitors have also expanded, for example, in calculators and CB radios. Many of these companies fail to gain market share and end up suffering substantial losses.

This chapter examines the causes of these behavior patterns and the role played by capacity expansion policies. The objective of any resource-ordering policy is to provide sufficient resources to match demand, balancing the costs of shortfall against the costs of excess. The primary difficulties in designing a resource-ordering policy are caused by the lead time on the resource and the impossibility of knowing future demand. The difficulties are greatest for long lead time resources such as capital equipment. If a company waits for demand to develop before ordering capital equipment, then customer orders may exceed capacity before the company can acquire more, and as a result the company loses market share. On the other hand, for the company to order capital equipment in anticipation of demand requires an estimate of future demand. The company infers future demand from current customer order rate, market demand, and past growth rates. The inference can easily be above or below the demand that actually develops. How the inference or forecast is generated, and how the company prepares for the consequences of an inaccurate forecast, have significant effects on market share and profits.

This chapter evaluates ordering rules for a production resource with a long lead time—capital equipment. Shorter lead time resources pose less severe problems. Nevertheless, the general conclusions developed herein apply equally well to these other resources.

The policies developed in this chapter draw on and extend the work of several authors: Nord (1963), Swanson (1969), and Forrester (1968).

11.2 Structure Creating Problem Behavior

Figure 11.1 shows the policy structure governing the ordering and the physical flows of capital equipment from orders to arrivals and finally to scrappage. Capital equipment orders are seen to depend on average capital equipment scrappage and corrections to bring the actual capacity in line with that desired. Equations determining the physical flows, the ordering policy, and the effect of capital equipment on production rate are detailed.

Flows of Orders and Equipment

Equation 17 states that capital equipment scrappage CES equals a third-order delay of capital equipment arrivals CEA.[1] Time to scrap capital equipment TSCE is here set to 2400 days (10 years). TSCE represents the average lifetime of capital equipment in a manufacturing firm. The sum of the three levels in the third-order delay is defined as capital equipment CE.

CES.KL = DELAY3I(CEA.JK,TSCE,CE.K,CEI)	17, R
TSCE = 2400	17.1, C
CEI = CCOR * (1 + CEGM)	17.2, N

where

CES	= capital equipment scrappage (units/day/day)
DELAY3I	= third-order delay with user-specified initial value
CEA	= capital equipment arrivals (units/day/day)
TSCE	= time to scrap capital equipment (days)
CE	= capital equipment (units/day)
CEI	= capital equipment, initial (units/day)
CCOR	= constant customer order rate (units/day)
CEGM	= capital equipment growth margin (dimensionless).

In equation 18 capital equipment arrivals CEA is represented as a third-order delay of capital equipment orders CEO. Time to acquire capital equipment is here set to 360 days. The sum of the three levels in the third-order delay is defined as capital equipment on order CEOO.

CEA.KL = DELAY3I(CEO.JK,TAQCE,CEOO.K,CEOOI)	18, R
TAQCE = 360	18.1, C
CEOOI = (CEI/TSCE) * TAQCE	18.2, N

where

CEA	= capital equipment arrivals (units/day/day)
DELAY3I	= third-order delay with user-specified initial value

1. DELAY3I is a third-order delay that allows the user to specify the initial values of the sum of the three levels. DELAY3I equations are given in appendix C.

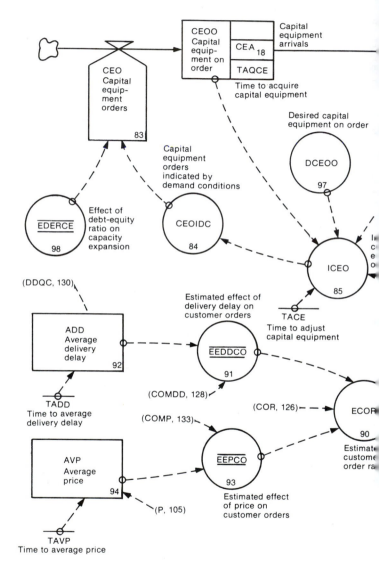

Figure 11.1   Structure of capital equipment-ordering policy

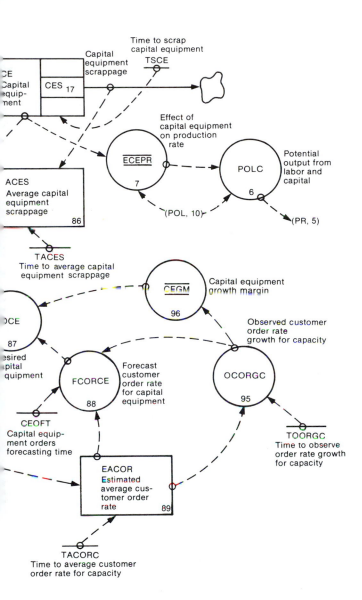

CEO   = capital equipment orders (units/day/day)
TAQCE   = time to acquire capital equipment (days)
CEOO   = capital equipment on order (units/day)
CEOOI   = capital equipment on order, initial (units/day)
CEI   = capital equipment, initial (units/day)
TSCE   = time to scrap capital equipment (days).

Capital Equipment-Ordering Policy

Equation 83 sets capital equipment orders CEO equal to capital equipment orders indicated by demand conditions CEOIDC multiplied by effect of debt-equity ratio on capacity expansion EDERCE. EDERCE is set to 1.0 until chapter 12.

$$CEO.KL = CEOIDC.K * EDERCE.K \qquad\qquad 83, R$$

where
CEO   = capital equipment orders (units/day/day)
CEOIDC   = capital equipment orders indicated by demand
             conditions (units/day/day)
EDERCE   = effect of debt-equity ratio on capacity expansion
             (dimensionless).

   In equation 84 capital equipment orders indicated by demand conditions CEOIDC is taken as the maximum of zero and indicated capital equipment orders ICEO. Equation 84 prevents cancellation and negative orders for capital equipment. Consequently capital equipment can only be reduced through scrappage.

$$CEOIDC.K = MAX(O,ICEO.K) \qquad\qquad 84, A$$

where
CEOIDC = capital equipment orders indicated by demand
          conditions (units/day/day)
ICEO   = indicated capital equipment orders (units/day/day).

   Equation 85 gives the policy governing indicated capital equipment orders ICEO. The policy is similar to the policies governing parts order rate and labor hiring. In equation 85 ICEO is set equal to the sum of average capital equipment scrappage ACES and the discrepancies between desired capital equipment DCE and capital equipment CE and between desired capital equipment on order DCEOO and capital equipment on order CEOO, corrected over the time to adjust capital equipment TACE. Time to adjust capital equipment is set to 240 days to reflect delays in drawing up expansion plans, having the plans approved, and releasing the orders.

$$ICEO.K = ACES.K + (DCE.K - CE.K + DCEOO.K$$
$$- CEOO.K)/TACE \qquad \text{85, A}$$
$$TACE = 240 \qquad \text{85.1, C}$$

where

ICEO   = indicated capital equipment orders (units/day/day)
ACES   = average capital equipment scrappage (units/day/day)
DCE   = desired capital equipment (units/day)
CE   = capital equipment (units/day)
DCEOO = desired capital equipment on order (units/day)
CEOO   = capital equipment on order (units/day)
TACE   = time to adjust capital equipment (days).

Average capital equipment scrappage ACES is represented in equation 86 as an exponential average of capital equipment scrappage CES. Time to average capital equipment scrappage TACES is set to 120 days.

$$ACES.K = SMOOTH(CES.JK,TACES) \qquad \text{86, A}$$
$$TACES = 120 \qquad \text{86.1, C}$$

where

ACES   = average capital equipment scrappage (units/day/day)
CES   = capital equipment scrappage (units/day/day)
TACES = time to average capital equipment scrappage (days).

Equation 87 defines desired capital equipment DCE as the sum of 1.0 plus capital equipment growth margin CEGM multiplied by forecast customer order rate for capital equipment FCORCE. FCORCE is an estimate of customer order rate based on historical growth rates. CEGM specifies how much capacity in excess of the forecast the company desires as a buffer against an inaccurate forecast.

$$DCE.K = (1 + CEGM.K) * FCORCE.K \qquad \text{87, A}$$

where

DCE   = desired capital equipment (units/day)
CEGM   = capital equipment growth margin (dimensionless)
FCORCE = forecast customer order rate for capital equipment
         (units/day).

Forecast customer order rate for capital equipment FCORCE is defined in equation 88. FCORCE equals the product of estimated average customer order rate EACOR and the sum of 1.0 plus capital equipment orders forecasting time CEOFT multiplied by observed customer order rate growth rate for capacity OCORGC. Equation 88 is the standard trend-forecasting equation developed in chapter 5. CEOFT is set equal to the sum of time to average customer order rate for capacity TACORC, time to acquire capital equipment TAQCE, and time to adjust capital equipment TACE.

$$FCORCE.K = EACOR.K * (1 + CEOFT * OCORGC.K) \qquad 88, A$$
$$CEOFT = TACORC + TAQCE + TACE \qquad 88.1, N$$

where

FCORCE = forecast customer order rate for capital equipment (units/day)
EACOR   = estimated average customer order rate (units/day)
CEOFT   = capital equipment orders forecasting time (days)
OCORGC = observed customer order rate growth for capacity (percent/day)
TACORC = time to average customer order rate for capacity (days)
TAQCE   = time to acquire capital equipment (days)
TACE   = time to adjust capital equipment (days).

Estimated average customer order rate EACOR is represented in equation 89 as an exponential average of estimated customer order rate ECOR. Time to average customer order rate for capacity TACORC is set to 240 days, on the assumption that most companies use yearly averages of orders in drawing up expansion plans.

$$EACOR.K = SMOOTH(ECOR.K, TACORC) \qquad 89, A$$
$$TACORC = 240 \qquad 89.1, C$$

where

EACOR   = estimated average customer order rate (units/day)
ECOR   = estimated customer order rate (units/day)
TACORC = time to average customer order rate for capacity (days).

Equation 90 states that estimated customer order rate ECOR equals customer order rate COR divided by the product of estimated effect of delivery delay on customer orders EEDDCO and estimated effect of price on customer orders EEPCO. ECOR gives an estimate of customer order rate if the company maintained a minimum delivery delay and competitive price.

$$ECOR.K = COR.K/(EEDDCO.K * EEPCO.K) \qquad 90, A$$

where

ECOR   = estimated customer order rate (units/day)
COR   = customer order rate (units/day)
EEDDCO = estimated effect of delivery delay on customer orders
          (dimensionless)
EEPCO   = estimated effect of price on customer orders
          (dimensionless).

Equation 91 defines estimated effect of delivery delay on customer orders EEDDCO. EEDDCO is a function of average delivery delay ADD. The logic behind and exact values of the function are discussed in section 11.4.

$$\text{EEDDCO.K} = \text{TABLE(TEEDDC,ADD.K/COMDD.K,}$$
$$0,4,.25) \hspace{3cm} \text{91, A}$$
$$\text{TEEDDC} = 1/1/1/1/1/1/1/1/1/1/1/1/1/1/1/1/1 \hspace{1.5cm} \text{91.1, T}$$

where

EEDDCO = estimated effect of delivery delay on customer orders
          (dimensionless)
TEEDDC = table for estimated effect of delivery delay on customer
          orders (dimensionless)
ADD   = average delivery delay (days)
COMDD   = competitor delivery delay (days).

Average delivery delay ADD is represented in equation 92 as an exponential average of delivery delay quoted by the company DDQC. ADD is the company's estimate of the delivery delay on which customers are acting. Time to average delivery delay TADD, here set to 60 days, is equal to the time for the market to perceive and act on delivery delay.

$$\text{ADD.K} = \text{SMOOTH(DDQC.K,TADD)} \hspace{2cm} \text{92, A}$$
$$\text{TADD} = 60 \hspace{5cm} \text{92.1, C}$$

where

ADD   = average delivery delay (days)
DDQC = delivery delay quoted by company (days)
TADD = time to average delivery delay (days).

Equation 93 defines estimated effect of price on customer orders EEPCO. EEPCO is a function of average price AVP relative to competitor price COMP. The logic behind and exact values for the function are discussed in section 11.4.

EEPCO.K = TABLE(TEEPCO,AVP.K/COMP.K,
    .75,1.25,.05)   93, A
TEEPCO = 1/1/1/1/1/1/1/1/1/1   93.1, T

where

EEPCO = estimated effect of price on customer orders
     (dimensionless)
TEEPCO = table for estimated effect of price on customer orders
     (dimensionless)
AVP = average price ($/unit)
COMP = competitor price ($/unit).

Average price AVP is represented in equation 94 as an exponential average of price P. AVP is the company's estimate of the price on which customers are acting. Time to average price TAVP, here set to 60 days, is equal to the time for the market to perceive and act on price.

AVP.K = SMOOTH(P.K,TAVP)   94, A
TAVP = 60   94.1, C

where

AVP = average price ($/unit)
P = price ($/unit)
TAVP = time to average price (days).

In equation 95 observed customer order rate growth rate for capacity OCORGC is calculated as a trend TRND of estimated average customer order rate EACOR. Time to observe order rate growth for capacity TOORGC is taken as 480 days. Although initial order rate growth rate for capacity IORGRC is given as 0, it is set to 20 percent per year in the runs of this chapter on the assumption that the growing company initially anticipates some growth in orders.

OCORGC.K = TRND(EACOR.K,TOORGC,IORGRC) 95, A
TOORGC = 480   95.1, C
IORGRC = 0   95.2, C

where

OCORGC = observed customer order rate growth for capacity
     (percent/day)
TRND = macro for detecting trends in input time series
     (percent/day)
EACOR = estimated average customer order rate (units/day)
TOORGC = time to observe order rate growth for capacity (days)
IORGRC = initial order rate growth rate for capacity (percent/day).

Equation 96 states that capital equipment growth margin CEGM is a function of observed customer order rate growth for capacity OCORGC (expressed in percent per year). The logic and values of the function are given in section 11.4.

$$\text{CEGM.K} = \text{TABLE(TCEGM,240 * OCORGC.K}, -1,1,.25) \quad \text{96, A}$$
$$\text{TCEGM} = 0/0/0/0/0/0/0/0/0 \quad \text{96.1, C}$$

where

CEGM   = capital equipment growth margin (dimensionless)
TCEGM = table for capital equipment growth margin
         (dimensionless)
OCORGC = observed customer order rate growth for capacity
         (percent/day).

In equation 97 desired capital equipment on order DCEOO is set equal to time to acquire capital equipment TAQCE multiplied by average capital equipment scrappage ACES. So defined, DCEOO equals the equilibrium value of capital equipment on order CEOO.

$$\text{DCEOO.K} = \text{TAQCE * ACES.K} \quad \text{97, A}$$

where

DCEOO = desired capital equipment on order (units/day)
TAQCE = time to acquire capital equipment (days)
ACES = average capital equipment scrappage (units/day/day).

Effect of Capital Equipment on Production Rate

As specified by equations 5 through 7, capital equipment introduces an additional constraint on production rate. In equation 5 production rate PR is defined to equal potential output from labor and capital POLC multiplied by effect of parts inventory level on production rate EPILPR. POLC represents the production rate achievable with the available labor, overtime, and capital equipment, assuming adequate parts inventory. Shortages of parts inventory cause PR to fall below POLC.

$$\text{PR.KL} = \text{POLC.K * EPILPR.K} \quad \text{5, R}$$
$$\text{PR} = \text{CCOR} \quad \text{5.1, N}$$

where

PR   = production rate (units/day)
POLC = potential output from labor and capital (units/day)

EPILPR = effect of parts inventory level on production rate
(dimensionless)
CCOR   = constant customer order rate (units/day).

Equation 6 similarly defines potential output from labor and capital POLC to equal potential output from labor POL multiplied by effect of capital equipment on production rate ECEPR. POL represents the production rate achievable with the available labor and overtime assuming adequate parts inventory and capital equipment. Shortages of capital equipment cause POLC to fall below POL.

$$POLC.K = POL.K * ECEPR.K \qquad\qquad 6, A$$

where
POLC = potential output from labor and capital (units/day)
POL   = potential output from labor (units/day)
ECEPR = effect of capital equipment on production rate
(dimensionless).

Equation 7 specifies the calculation of effect of capital equipment on production rate ECEPR. ECEPR is a nonlinear function of potential output from labor POL divided by capital equipment CE, as shown in figure 11.2. CE is defined in units per day of potential output; POL equals the potential output achievable with the available labor force and overtime. Consequently, if POL divided by CE is equal to or less than 1.4 (1.4 being the maximum overtime), the company has sufficient capital equipment to produce at POL, and ECEPR equals 1.0. Should POL divided by CE exceed 1.4, the company has insufficient capacity to produce at POL. Consequently ECEPR falls below 1.0 and thereby

Figure 11.2 Effect of capital equipment on production rate

reduces production rate. The values in TECEPR are such that POLC equals 1.4 multiplied by CE when POL exceeds CE by more than 1.4.

ECEPR.K = TABHL(TECEPR,POL.K/CE.K,.8,2,.2)   7, A
TECEPR = 1/1/1/1/.875/.777/.7   7.1, T

where

ECEPR   = effect of capital equipment on production rate
                (dimensionless)
TECEPR = table for effect of capital equipment on production rate
                (dimensionless)
POL   = potential output from labor (units/day)
CE   = capital equipment (units/day).

In chapter 7 shortages of parts inventory caused the company to cut back on the use of overtime and labor to avoid inefficient production. Shortages of capital equipment cause similar cutbacks. Because shortages of capital equipment also cause production rate to fall short of desired production rate, parts order rate is also reduced by such shortages.

11.3 Understanding the Causes of Loss of Market Share and Excess Capacity

Figure 11.3 illustrates the life-cycle-of-growth market demand pattern typical of product and company life cycles: an introductory phase of slow growth is followed by a period of rapid growth in demand; the rapid growth phase in turn gives way to a period of relatively stable demand, often referred to as market saturation or maturity; finally market demand declines. The fifteen-year life cycle may be more representative of a product line than a company. Many companies, however, have far shorter life spans than fifteen years while many products exceed this span. The pattern shown in figure 11.3 is used in the simulation runs of this chapter and chapter 12.

Figure 11.3 shows a typical market demand life cycle rather than an exact curve for some particular company. Ideally a company would like to design a capital equipment-ordering policy that gives sufficient capacity to meet any rapid growth in demand but also avoids large excesses of capacity when demand levels off and declines. Unfortunately in the absence of a perfect forecast the ideal cannot be achieved. Policy design must then trade off the cost of lost market

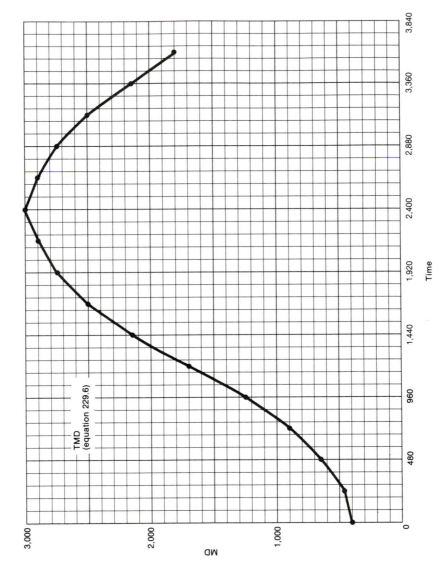

Figure 11.3   Life cycle of market demand

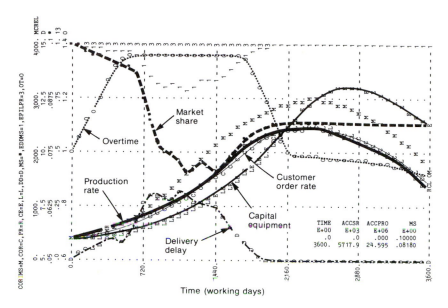

Figure 11.4 Model response to life cycle demand: capacity expansion based on forecast

share in the rapid growth phase against the cost of excess capacity in the saturation and decline phases.

The capital equipment-ordering policy described in section 11.2 has four features:

1. Orders equal the capacity necessary to meet forecast customer order rate.
2. The delay in adjusting capacity to desired capacity equals 240 days.
3. The forecast of customer order rate is an extrapolation, over the time to acquire and adjust capital equipment, of historical growth rates perceived over the last two years.
4. The company accurately anticipates an initial growth rate of 20 percent per year.

Figure 11.4 shows the consequences of such a policy under the life cycle market demand pattern of figure 11.3.[2]

During the introductory phase from day 0 to day 600 the company is

2. To focus exclusively on capital equipment effects on production, the company is assumed to follow the aggressive policy set with desired days supply parts inventory equal to 90 days.

able to match most of the growth in customer order rate with overtime. Consequently market share falls only slightly. During the rapid growth phase from day 600 to day 1200, however, market share falls sharply because delivery delay increases by 60 percent. Delivery delay increases because a capital equipment shortage prevents the company from increasing production rate sufficiently above customer order rate to build finished inventory (not shown). The shortage of capital equipment is evidenced by the fact that even with high overtime and no parts shortage the company cannot build enough finished inventory to reduce delivery delay.

A capital equipment shortage develops because the company is planning capacity on the basis of an inaccurate forecast, which did not predict that customer order rate growth rates would exceed historical growth rate during the rapid growth phase. Figure 11.5 demonstrates the problem. The perfect forecast gives market demand advanced by the time required to adjust and acquire capital equipment. The actual forecast falls significantly short of the perfect forecast because growth rates are increasing. Moreover, as delivery delay rises, growth in customer order rate is suppressed below growth in market demand. The company therefore is extrapolating a customer order rate suppressed

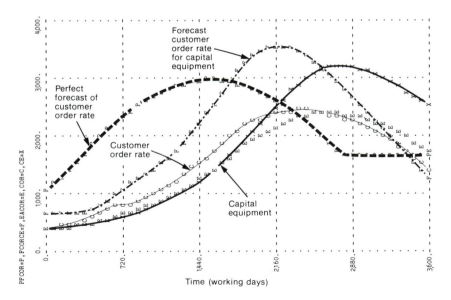

Figure 11.5   Forecast and capacity values from simulation of figure 11.4

by long delivery times, at a growth rate lagging true growth rates and suppressed below the growth rate in market demand.

The consequence of a forecast below market demand is that the forecast is self-validated. As shown in figure 11.5, capital equipment is acquired to match the forecast. But because market demand exceeds that forecasted, delivery delay increases. Delivery delay increases to pull down customer order rate to capital equipment. Customer order rate exceeds capital equipment only because the company works over-time. As capital equipment grows, so does customer order rate. In essence the growth in capital equipment governs the growth in cus-tomer order rate. Whatever capacity the company acquires, customer order rate adjusts to that capacity through changing delivery delay. The forecast is self-validated because the market adjusts orders to the capacity acquired on the basis of the forecast.

Self-validation can also occur if the forecast exceeds market demand at the company's traditional market share. The company with excess capacity is in a position to take market share from less aggressive competitors (as happens in figure 11.4—competitors of the model com-pany gain market share by having sufficient excess capacity to maintain a minimum delivery delay). Moreover, even if the market as a whole has excess capacity, market share can be gained by the company with a superior price/quality/service offering.

Of course there are limits to self-validation. Nevertheless, the con-cept is important enough for policy design to reflect it. The costs of some excess capacity will generally be more than outweighed by ben-efits that accrue from avoiding a loss of market share. Policies to achieve excess capacity are discussed in section 11.4.

Policy design guideline 11.1 A forecast of customer order rate, when used to acquire capital equipment or other production resources, tends to be self-validated by shifts in relative competitive position. To avoid loss of market share, and take market share from weaker competitors, ordering policies should reflect the concept of self-validation and strive for some excess capacity.

Figure 11.4 also demonstrates an important point about the risk as-sociated with capacity expansion. Some managers feels that a safe expansion plan is to wait for the market to develop before expanding capacity. By doing so, the company avoids the risk of excess capacity. In the model such a cautious expansion policy would not be extrapolat-ing customer order rate but instead setting desired capital equipment equal to estimated average customer order rate. Based on the behavior shown in figure 11.4, a substantial loss of market share might be expected to result from such a policy, although the risk of excess capacity would be reduced. Unfortunately the risk of lost market share is harder to measure than the risk of excess capacity.

Policy design guideline 11.2 Waiting for the market to develop before expanding is a risky strategy that can result in lost market share. The company should expand before the market develops.

Returning to the company that lost significant market share during the rapid growth phase, as growth slows after day 1200, market share recovers only slowly and rises only to approximately 8 percent (well below the company's original 10 percent). The slow recovery is again caused by the company's forecasting procedure. From day 1200 to day 1900 the company is extrapolating a customer order rate suppressed by long delivery delays. The company again does not order enough capacity to meet its true demand. Then, when delivery delay returns to normal around day 1900, market share levels off at 8 percent because the poor performance during the growth phase causes the company to lose some of its loyal customer base.

A final feature of the behavior shown in figure 11.4 is the excess of capacity that develops in the saturation and decline phases of the life cycle. The excess develops because the forecasting procedure lags the declining growth rate (see figure 11.5). Consequently the company is extrapolating at a higher growth rate than actually occurs. This is an inherent characteristic of trend forecasts.

The behavior exhibited in figure 11.4 is characteristic of that described in the introduction: a rapid loss of market share even as volume is growing; an excess of capacity as the market saturates and declines. The cause of the loss of market share is the failure to expand capacity sufficiently in anticipation of growth. Even trend forecasts suffer the loss of market share, although the loss would be much greater if the company did not follow a trend forecast but waited for orders to increase before expanding. Moreover, if the company used historical values of delivery delay in establishing goals, market share would continue to decline during the entire growth phase (as in chapter 8). Trend forecasting is also the cause of the excess capacity. It is human nature to extrapolate recent changes into the future. Excess capacity is the inevitable consequence.

11.4 Improving Behavior through Policy Design

Carry Extra Finished Product Inventory

In previous chapters extra finished product inventory was found to be an effective buffer against unanticipated increases in customer order rate. The increase in customer order rate is filled from finished inventory until sufficient resources are acquired to increase production rate. Finished inventory is a general buffer in the sense that it absorbs the consequences of shortages in any production resource—labor, parts inventory, or capital equipment.

Figure 11.6 shows model response to life cycle demand with capacity expansion based on forecast customer order rate and with desired days finished inventory increased from 30 to 45 days. For the life cycle demand extra finished inventory is not an effective buffer. While performance is improved somewhat in the introductory phase, rapid growth quickly overcomes the buffering capacity of the extra inventory.

Buffering capacity is overcome for two reasons: the rapid growth phase sees such an increase in customer order rate that the 45-day supply is quickly depleted, and the lead time on capital equipment is so long that production rate is slow to follow increases in customer order

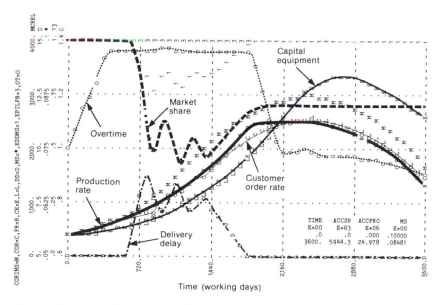

Time (working days)

Figure 11.6 Model response to life cycle demand: capacity expansion based on forecast and extra finished product inventory

rate. Consequently a 45-day supply of finished inventory cannot sufficiently absorb the life cycle growth in customer order rate, although it may be adequate for slower growth rates (as in the introductory phase).

Capacity Expansion Based on Adjusted Forecast

One of the problems with trend forecasts of customer order rate is that, as delivery delay increases, customer order rate is suppressed below demand. Then in extrapolating customer order rate rather than demand, the company plans capacity for a lower market share that is self-validated.

One method of extrapolating demand rather than customer order rate is to adjust customer order rate for the estimated effect of delivery delay on customer orders. Equation 90, described in section 11.2, performs such an adjustment by dividing customer order rate COR by estimated effect of delivery delay on customer orders EEDDCO. Figure 11.7 shows the EEDDCO used in subsequent simulation runs and gives an accurate estimate of the effect of delivery delay. Before adopting a policy containing such an adjustment, performance with inaccurate estimates should be checked. Nord (1963) and Swanson (1969) demonstrate, however, that such inaccuracies are generally insignificant.

Figure 11.8 shows model response to life cycle demand with capacity expansion based on an adjusted forecast and with extra finished product inventory (figure 11.8 should be compared to figure 11.6). While the policy of extra finished product inventory improves performance in the introductory phase, the policy of adjusting the forecast improves performance in the maturity phase. The improved performance is evidenced by the quicker and higher rise of market share between days 1200 and 1440.

A long delivery delay suppresses customer order rate below demand during the rapid growth phase. The lead time on capital equipment is such that expansion plans drawn up in the rapid growth phase affect capacity at the end of the rapid growth phase and into the maturity phase. Consequently the adjusted forecast does little to improve performance in the rapid growth phase but does help in the maturity phase. The effect of extrapolating a customer order rate suppressed by a long delivery delay can be clearly seen by comparing the forecasts with (figure 11.9) and without the adjustment (figure 11.5). With the

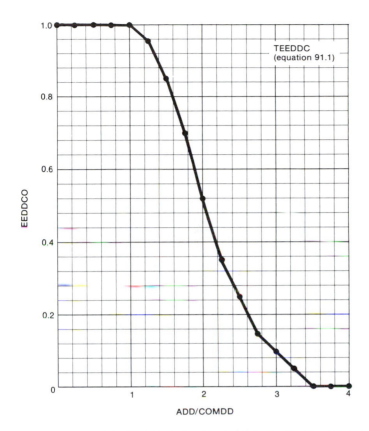

Figure 11.7 Estimated effect of delivery delay on customer orders

adjustment forecast customer order rate rises more quickly than without. Nevertheless, the forecast is still self-validating.

Policy design guideline 11.3 Planning based on customer order rate can lead to lost market share because customer order rate does not always equal demand. Planning should be based on customer order rate adjusted for delivery delay and other effects on market share.

Quicker Capacity Adjustments

One of the reasons an extra finished product inventory proved ineffective was the long delay in increasing capital equipment. This delay consists of the time to acquire capital equipment TACQE once it is ordered (360 days) and the time to adjust capital equipment TACE (240 days). TACE includes the time to perceive the need for additional capacity, the time to draw up plans for specific machinery and floor

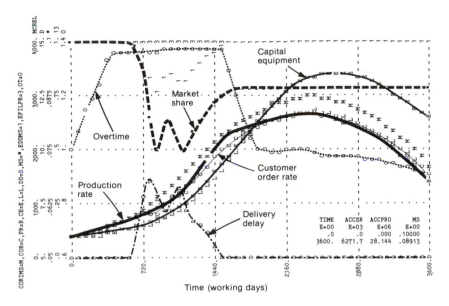

Figure 11.8   Model response to life cycle demand: capacity expansion based on
adjusted forecast and extra finished inventory

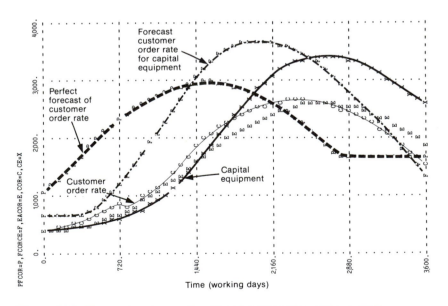

Figure 11.9   Forecast and capacity values for simulation of figure 11.8

space, and the time to approve the plans and let the contracts. What benefits might accrue to the company if this delay could be reduced, say, by drawing up plans in advance on the assumption of growth and shortening recognition and approval delays?

Figure 11.10 shows model response to life cycle demand with TACE reduced to 60 days (with capacity expansion based on an adjusted forecast and with extra finished inventory). Quicker adjustments reduce the loss of market share in the rapid growth phase without increasing the amount of excess capacity in the saturation and decline phases.

In an actual corporate study the costs of achieving such a reduction in TACE would be compared to the benefits. The model provides a means of calculating the benefits. The benefits of a shorter TACE should also be assessed in other market demand patterns that might affect the company. Short adjustment times may not be beneficial in, say, a CYCLICAL demand market.

Quicker Perception of Trends

As discussed in chapter 5, quick perception of trends is beneficial if the trends are long lasting. Life-cycle trends are long lasting, and figure

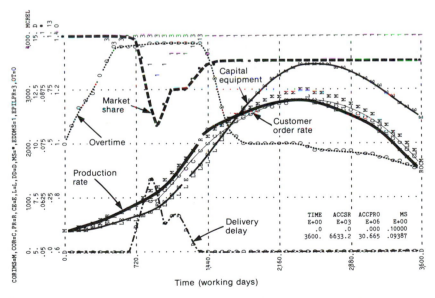

Time (working days)

Figure 11.10 Model response to life cycle demand: capacity expansion based on adjusted forecast with quick adjustments and extra finished inventory

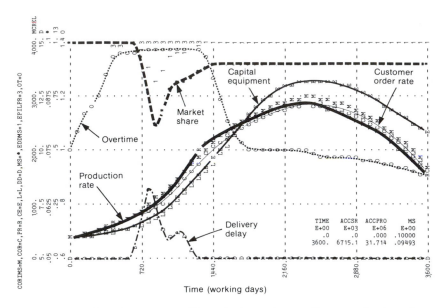

Figure 11.11   Model response to life cycle demand: capacity expansion based on adjusted forecast, quick adjustments, and shorter perception time of trends and with extra inventory

11.11 shows that reducing time to observe order rate growth for capacity TOORGC from 480 to 240 days improves performance. The improvement occurs primarily in the later stages of rapid growth and in maturity, where quicker perception of trends reduces the overshoot in capacity. Nevertheless, trend forecasts respond after the fact to changing conditions and therefore cannot cope with the rapid growth in demand.

Capital Equipment Growth Margin

Given the lead time on capital equipment and the likelihood of a capacity shortage the only way to avoid lost market share because of capacity shortage is to carry excess capacity. As given in equation 87, desired capital equipment equals forecast customer order rate for capital equipment multiplied by the sum of 1.0 and capital equipment growth margin CEGM. CEGM is a function of observed customer order rate growth rate for capacity OCORGC, as shown in figure 11.12. When OCORGC equals 0, CEGM is set to 10 percent as a buffer against increases in growth rate above forecast. The higher the OCORGC, the greater the buffer needed to guard against forecasting errors, given the

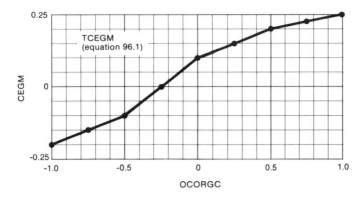

Figure 11.12 Capital equipment growth margin

long lead times (high growth rates suggest a developing market—one in which past growth rates provide little clue to future growth rates). As OCORGC falls, no excess capacity is needed.[3]

Figure 11.13 shows model response to a life cycle market demand pattern with capacity expansion based on an adjusted forecast and a growth margin (with quick adjustments, shorter perception of trend, and extra inventory). Performance, as measured by market share, shipments, and profits, is much improved over the unadjusted forecast policy. With the excess capacity, and overtime, the company is able to absorb the unanticipated growth in customer order rate without an increase in delivery delay and thus is prepared to take market share from less aggressive competitors.

However, the policy results in a larger excess of capital equipment during market saturation (by day 3600 the excess is proportionately the same as the excess for the policy with the unadjusted forecast). The excess is caused by the lagging nature of extrapolation coupled with a desire for excess capacity based on high growth rates in the past. Under the conditions of the simulation run the costs of the excess capacity are more than offset by the profits generated by increased market share.

Policy design guideline 11.4 The only way to avoid lost market share because of a shortage of capacity, given the lead time on capital equipment and the likelihood of inaccurate forecasts, is to carry excess capacity.

3. Note that even more extra capacity is available in the form of overtime.

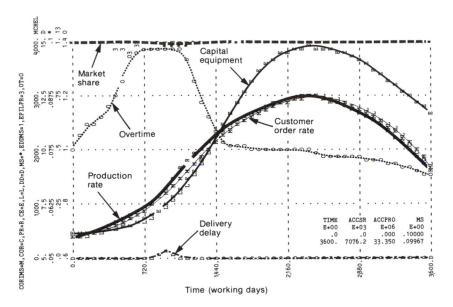

Figure 11.13 Model response to life cycle demand: capacity expansion based on adjusted forecast plus growth margin, quicker adjustments, shorter perception of trends and extra inventory

Summary

Company response to growth is facilitated by policies that

1. carry some extra finished inventory as a buffer against shortages of any production resource,
2. adjust customer order rate forecasts for any suppressing effects of long delivery delays,
3. adjust capital equipment to desired capital equipment quickly,
4. perceive long-term trends quickly,
5. carry a buffer of excess capital equipment because of the long lead time on this particular production resource.

11.5 Testing Scenarios in Policy Design

As discussed in previous chapters, an important part of the policy design process is testing policy performance under other than the most probable market demand pattern. If policy performance under these other patterns is undesirable, the company may need to adjust the policy should the likelihood of these other patterns warrant the change.

One such scenario test might include policy response to variations in the basic life cycle demand pattern. Figures 11.14 and 11.15 show policy response to more and less rapid growth phases. In the more rapid growth pattern market demand quadruples in four years. In the less rapid pattern the rise occurs over fifteen years.

The policy is unable to respond to the more rapid growth without loss of market share. In such a situation the company must ask: What is the probability of such a rapid rise? Will competitors be able to deliver if the company cannot? What are the policy changes required to meet the rapid rise and the costs of doing so? The answers affect selection of a policy. The less rapid pattern poses no difficulty for the policy.

A second type of scenario test might impose shorter-term changes on the life cycle pattern. One such shorter-term change would be the business cycle. This type of test is particularly important because some of the policy elements, shortened to give better response to growth, amplify shorter-term variations. Most likely, these shorter-term variations will be swamped in the rapid growth phase but become important in the maturity phase. A completely general policy might monitor underlying growth rates and adjust policy parameters as the underlying rate changes, giving quick response in the rapid growth phase and slower response in the maturity phase.

11.6 Summary

Many companies lose market share because capacity expansion plans fail to give the company sufficient capacity to follow rapid growth in demand. Forecasts are slow to respond to changing trends; in addition they are based on customer order rates suppressed by long delivery delays. But an inaccurate forecast is unavoidable. How the company handles the inaccuracies determines success or failure. The successful companies are those that buffer themselves against unanticipated changes in customer order rate.

A successful capacity expansion policy would include (1) an adjustment of customer order rate forecasts for any suppressing effects of long delivery delays and (2) a buffer of excess capacity. The company might also adjust capacity to respond to trends more quickly, although this would worsen performance for temporary variations. A buffer of excess finished product inventory guards against shortages of any production resource.

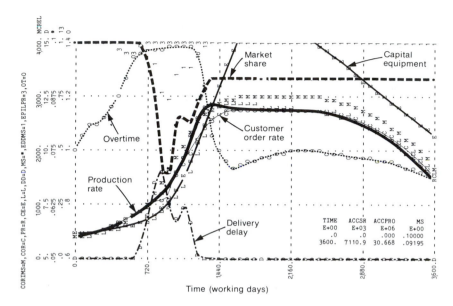

Figure 11.14 Policy response to more rapid growth

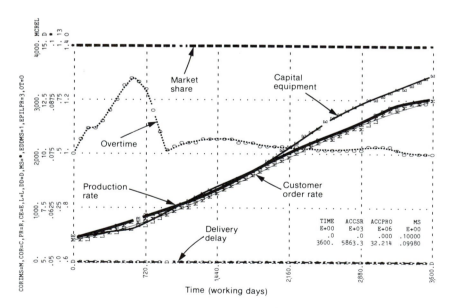

Figure 11.15 Policy response to less rapid growth

References

Forrester, Jay W. 1968. Market Growth as Influenced by Capital Investment. *Industrial Management Review*. 9:83–105.

Nord, Ole C. G. 1963. *Growth of a New Product: Effects of Capacity-Acquisition Policies*. Cambridge, Mass: The MIT Press.

Swanson, Carl V. 1969. Resource Control in Growth Dynamics, Ph.D. dissertation. Massachusetts Institute of Technology, Cambridge, Mass. Available from MIT Library-Microreproduction, 14–0551.

Dynamics Created by Financial Constraints

12.1 Introduction

Managers of growth companies often encounter a situation where available cash resources are not sufficient to finance investment in productive assets. Investment in production resources generally requires a relatively large, initial cash expenditure. The cash return on the investment, however, tends to be spread out over many years in the future. By exhausting both internal (profits from sales) and external (debt and stock) sources of funds, the pattern of a large initial cash expenditure and delayed cash return may strain a company's ability to make additional investments.

One accepted solution to a cash shortage is limiting investment to a level that can be supported by available funds. However, managers can take other actions besides control of investment expenditures to alleviate a shortage of cash, for example, increasing price or improving cash flow by reducing the collection period. Each of these actions has costs and benefits. Unfortunately a detailed comparison of the relative costs and benefits has not been performed by researchers or most companies. Instead managers have had to rely on intuition and experience to estimate the possible consequences of alternative actions.

But two factors complicate the design of financial policies. First, a multiplicity of factors and interrelationships influence a company's total cash flow. And second, the long-run effects of a policy change may differ from the short-run effects. Complex interactions are inherent in a company's accounting, debt-maturity-structure, and tax and dividend payments. Moreover a policy change often produces opposing effects on cash flow. For example, an increase in price increases the cash flow from a unit sale but reduces the number of unit sales. Interactions between sales and cash flow are even further complicated in reality because a company's rate of sales is determined not only by the product's price but also by its availability relative to the availability of competing products. Consequently the net effect of a change in price also depends on the change in relative product availability following the initial increase or decrease in unit sales caused by a price change.

The long-run effects of a policy change may differ from the short-run effects. For example, a reduction in investment reduces the current outflow of cash, thereby alleviating a cash shortage. In the long run, however, product availability is lower, and therefore unit sales and the cash flow from sales are reduced. As a second example, a price increase, even though it reduces unit sales, may so improve total cash flow that more investment in productive assets can be undertaken. The company thereby achieves an improvement in long-run product availability and sales, in exchange for a short-run decline in sales.

In view of the complexity of the feedbacks from financial policies to product attractiveness and hence to customer order rate, it is not surprising that many companies have taken actions that prevent a short-term financial crisis but lead to long-term difficulties. For example, during the credit shortages of the early seventies, many larger companies were unable to obtain sufficient external financing. In response, some took actions to eliminate the cash shortfall by reducing expenditures. These actions hindered company ability to compete several years later. One automobile manufacturer slowed development of a new size car and then was unable to compete in a rapidly growing segment of the market; a manufacturer of capital equipment reduced outlays for plant and equipment and then was unable to satisfy demand. In addition rapidly growing, new companies continually experience shortages of financial capital and are faced with the decision to cut expenditures or seek ways to improve cash flow.

The expedient method of solving a cash shortage is to reduce expenditures—it solves the short-term problem. Secondary effects tend to take years before they fully manifest themselves. Moreover the effects show up in areas that are difficult to trace back to the financial decision—for example, in the slow development of a product or lack of capacity.

The model developed thus far provides a vehicle for evaluating different financial policies. As described in chapter 9, the model incorporates the major determinants of the flow of funds within the financial sector of a company and between the financial sector and, respectively, the production sector of the company and the financial markets.

Moreover, because the model contains a representation of the production sector and of the market for a company's products, the effects of financial policies on market share can be analyzed. Such effects are direct, as from price, and indirect, as from lack of availability caused by the constraining effect of limited financial resources on investment. As a result expedient, costly decisions do not need to be taken.

12.2 Interactions among Financial Resources, Production Capability, and Market Share

Figure 12.1 shows the major interactions between production capability and market share contained in the model. Production capability, here termed production capacity, includes labor, parts inventory, and capital equipment. Production capacity determines production rate; production rate in turn depletes unfilled orders.

The negative feedback loop shown at the top of figure 12.1 strives to equate customer order rate and production capacity. Should customer order rate exceed capacity, unfilled orders decline, reducing delivery delay. A reduction in delivery delay increases customer order rate by increasing market share. Delivery delay continues to fall until customer order rate equals production capacity. The negative feedback loop works in the opposite direction, should customer order rate fall below capacity.

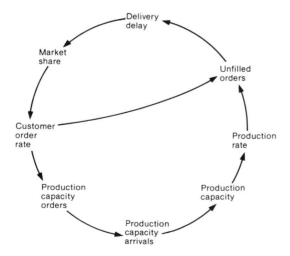

Figure 12.1   Major interactions between production capability and market share

In the absence of any financial constraints on ordering production capacity, customer order rate provides the driving force behind production capacity orders. After a delay that varies with the production resource, previous production capacity orders arrive and augment production capacity. In order to focus exclusively on the effects of financial policies on corporate growth, the set of capacity expansion policies that best followed the product life cycle in chapter 11 is employed throughout this chapter.

The financial sector of the model specifies the manner in which the firm borrows (debt financing), issues stock (equity financing), and pays dividends. Figure 12.2 shows the interactions among financial resources, production capability, and market share. The representation of the production sector shown in figure 12.1 is enclosed in the dashed rectangle in the upper left-hand side of the figure.

Production capacity arrivals increase investment expenditures which in turn increase indicated financing. Indicated financing, however, is reduced by cash flow from operations. Cash flow from operations is increased by production rate. In this simplified diagram production rate represents the production, shipment, and payment for an order so that, if the company is profitable, production rate increases cash flow from operations.

Indicated financing causes the company to use debt financing and equity financing, as determined by percent debt financing. The model assumes that the company first uses debt financing until target debt-equity is approached and then uses equity financing in the amount necessary for any remaining indicated financing.

Production rate increases earnings. Earnings minus dividends equals retained earnings. Since dividends are paid in proportion to earnings, an increase in earnings increases dividends. Retained earnings increases equity. Because the increase in equity decreases debt-equity ratio, the company is able to issue more debt.

In modeling limitations to financial resources, the assumption is made that the company cannot, or will not, issue new stock and that the company has a target debt-equity ratio beyond which debt is either not available or too costly to be practical. This assumption is consistent with the financial literature. Therefore the supply of financial resources available to a company is determined by cash flow from operations plus the unused debt capacity remaining until the company reaches target debt-equity ratio.

The dashed interactions shown in figure 12.2 represent possible in-

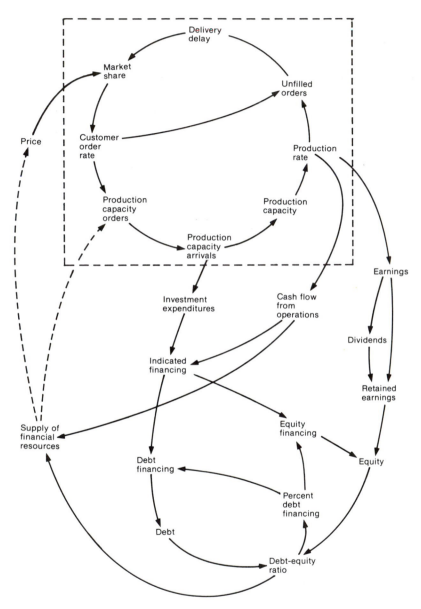

Figure 12.2 Interactions among financial resources, production capability, and market share

fluences of supply of financial resources on production capability and price. A limited supply of financial resources might reduce production capacity orders below those indicated by customer order rate. A likely consequence of such a capital-rationing policy is loss of market share as customer order rate is pulled down to production capacity by increasing delivery delays. Alternatively a limited supply of financial resources might cause the company to increase price, improving cash flow from operations and earnings (via influences not shown in figure 12.2) but also causing a loss of market share and lower customer orders. Details of these interactions are analyzed in sections 12.4 and 12.5. First, the behavior of the model assuming adequate financial resources is reviewed.

12.3 Dynamics Created under Conditions of Adequate Financial Resources

This section presents the behavior of the model with adequate financial resources, assuming adequate financing is always available. In the first simulation run, only cash flow from operations and debt financing is employed. In a second run, cash flow from operations, debt financing, and equity financing is used. Without feedback from limited financial resources, the financial sector passively monitors and provides the financing for production operation.

Debt Financing

Figures 12.3 (a and b) shows the simulated behavior of several important model variables under the assumption that the company has adequate financial resources. In the figure the company uses cash flow from operations and debt to finance investment expenditures. An equity issue is prohibited or avoided. Market demand follows the typical product life cycle described in chapter 11.

The behavior shown in figure 12.3 is identical to that described in chapter 11. Order rate grows with the growth in market demand (at initial market share, plotted as M but not highlighted). Investment in production capacity allows the company's production rate to match the growth in market demand. The variable ACCSR, accumulated shipment rate, given in the lower right-hand corner of figure 12.3a and all subsequent simulation runs, equals accumulated shipment rate over

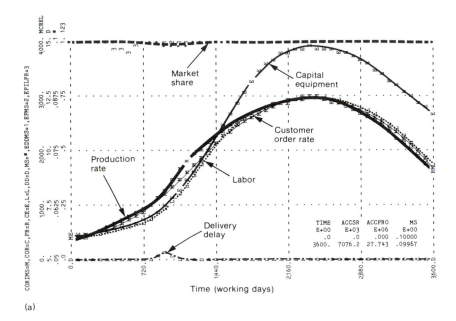

(a)

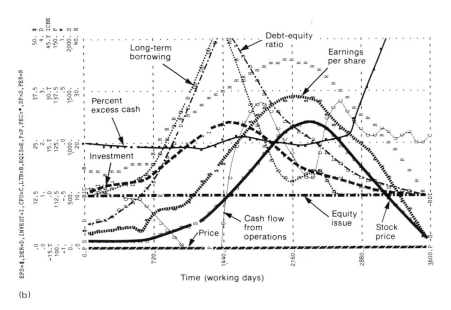

(b)

Figure 12.3 Model behavior with adequate financial resources: debt financing

the length of the simulation. ACCSR can be used in comparing growth rates under alternative policies. ACCPRO, accumulated profit, equals accumulated after tax profit over the length of the simulation.

The financial performance of the company is shown in figure 12.3b. Debt-equity ratio rises sharply between days 720 and 1440, peaks, and then declines steadily for the duration of the simulation run. Peak debt-equity ratio is approximately 4.0, a value well in excess of the target of most companies and probably in excess of the limits that would be imposed by the financial markets. Nevertheless, it is useful to analyze the factors that produce such a large demand for external financing.

Between days 216 and 1656 investment expenditures exceed cash flow from operations. As a result external debt financing is necessary, and the debt-equity ratio increases. Investment expenditures are large during this period because large capital equipment orders are required for production rate to match the growth in market demand. Cash flow from operations lags the growth in investment expenditures and even the growth in profits (represented by earnings per share which equals profits divided by shares outstanding). In fact cash flow from operations declines until day 1200. Cash flow declines because of the delay in collecting receivables and the cash drain caused by increases in parts and finished inventory. During the rapid growth phase, the company is investing in capital equipment, inventory, and receivables.

After day 1656 the growth rate of market demand slows. Consequently capital equipment orders and investment expenditures decline. Profits and cash flow from operations continue to grow, however. When growth slows, the company no longer needs cash to build inventory and accounts receivable. Consequently collections of accounts receivable far exceed cash outflows for labor and parts arrivals so that cash flow improves dramatically. As customer order rate declines after day 2400, reductions in inventory and accounts receivable cause cash flow to remain high. During maturity and decline the company earns a return on past investment.

In summary rapid growth requires large cash outlays for capital equipment during a period when receivables and inventory building drain cash flow. As a result, even though the company is highly profitable, large amounts of external financing are required. On the other hand, the maturity and decline phases see large cash flows but little demand for cash.

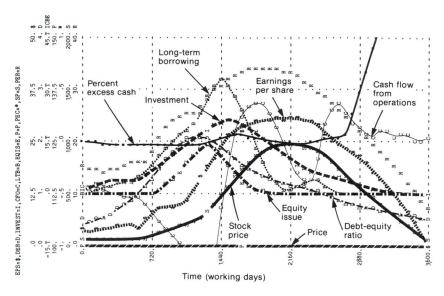

Figure 12.4 Model behavior with adequate financial resources: debt and stock financing

Debt and Stock Financing

Figure 12.4 shows simulated model behavior under the assumption that the company has adequate financial resources, as was the case in figure 12.3, but with the further assumption that the company uses cash flow from operations, debt, and equity to finance investment expenditures. In figure 12.4 then, the company uses cash flow and debt financing until its target debt-equity ratio (here 2.50) is reached.[1] Thereafter the company uses cash flow and equity financing (plus any debt allowed by the growth in equity).

Figure 12.4 shows only the financial performance of the company as the behavior of market share, delivery delay, and customer order rate is identical to that shown in figure 12.3a. In figure 12.4 debt-equity ratio rises to slightly over 2.0 at day 1200. As a result borrowing is constrained to that allowed by the growth in equity, and the company uses equity financing to finance the difference. Equity financing requires

1. Because of the magnitude of borrowing required to finance rapid growth, target debt-equity ratio was increased over that given in chapter 9 (from 1.25 to 2.5). In addition the ranges of all tables involving debt-equity ratio were extended.

that the company issue stock; consequently the number of shares outstanding (not shown) increases.

Because the number of shares outstanding increases, peak earnings per share fall from approximately \$36 to \$31 per share. Earnings per share fall less than might at first be anticipated, however, because with the reduced debt financing, debt-equity ratio, interest rate, and interest expenses (not shown) decrease. As a result net profit of the company is increased (accumulated profit under the equity-financing policy increases by 13 percent). Moreover increased profits and lower debt-equity ratio result in a higher stock price (during the growth period), and therefore relatively fewer shares need to be issued to raise a given amount of equity. The combination of all these factors causes earnings per share to fall less than might be anticipated.

Here a decreased reliance on debt improves profits, but at the expense of earnings per share. Experiments with other target debt-equity ratios may allow the company to find an acceptable trade-off.

12.4 Dynamics Created by Capital-Rationing Response to Limited Financial Resources

The simulations of section 12.3 assumed that the company had access to an unlimited supply of debt and equity. With a more realistic assumption of limited financial resources, the company must take actions to either raise cash inflow or reduce cash outflow. Otherwise the company will encounter a cash shortage during the rapid growth phase.

Effects of Capital Rationing on Production Capability

One common method for dealing with limited financial resources is to restrict investment in production capacity. Under capital rationing both a negative feedback loop (figure 12.5) and a positive feedback loop (figure 12.6) influence the investment process. The negative loop strives to keep investment expenditures equal to the supply of financial resources. The positive loop generates increased cash flow from investment and therefore an increased supply of financial resources for future investment.

In figure 12.5 an increase in production capacity orders leads to an increase in production capacity arrivals and therefore an increase in investment expenditures. The greater investment expenditure causes

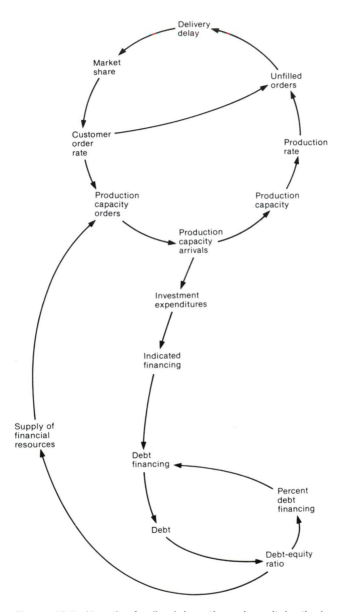

Figure 12.5 Negative feedback loop through capital-rationing policy

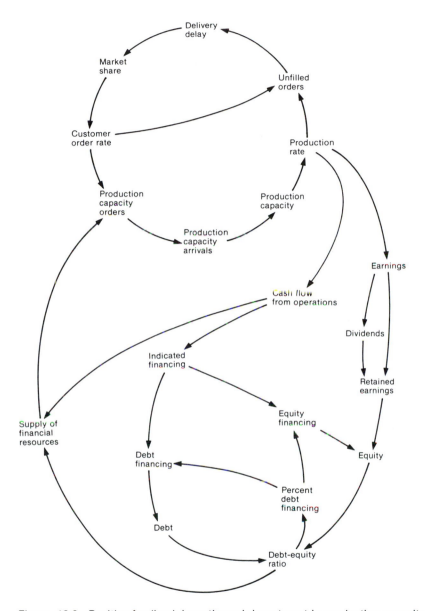

Figure 12.6 Positive feedback loop through investment in production capacity

the company to increase debt financing. Increased debt financing increases the level of debt outstanding and in turn reduces the company's
unused debt capacity by raising debt-equity ratio. The lower, unused
debt capacity constrains the supply of financial resources available for
future production capacity orders, completing the feedback loop.

Figure 12.6 shows the positive feedback loop associated with investment in production capacity. An increase in production capacity
orders increases production rate. An increase in production rate increases both cash flow from operations and earnings. An increase in
cash flow reduces indicated financing and therefore debt financing. As
less debt accumulates, the company has a larger reserve of unused debt
capacity for future investment. Moreover increased cash flow creates a
larger supply of financial resources for future investment. The increase
in the company's earnings brings about an increase in equity, reducing
debt-equity ratio and raising unused debt capacity. An increase in investment, working through the feedback loops shown in figure 12.6,
has the net effect of generating a greater supply of financial resources
for future investment.

Delays in the positive feedback loop associated with investment are
likely to be much longer than delays associated with the negative feedback loop. The acquisition of production capacity represents a current
cash expenditure; the flow of cash returns from this capacity may be
spread out over many years. Therefore during the company's growth
phase, when investment expenditures are high, the demand for cash is
likely to substantially exceed cash flow from operations. As growth
slows, returns from past investment should continue while the demand
for cash subsides.

Capital-rationing policies control the demand for cash by limiting the
production-capacity ordering. If demand exceeds capacity, order rate
is constrained by increase in the company's delivery delay. Through
capital rationing therefore the growth of the company is constrained to
the level supportable by the growth in cash flow and unused debt
capacity. Capital rationing equates the demand for cash generated by
the factors in figure 12.5 to the supply of cash provided by the factors in
figure 12.6.

In the model limitations on financial resources are imposed by pro-
hibiting the company from issuing stock and by the company taking
actions to prevent debt-equity ratio from exceeding a target value (here
2.50). These actions include

1. reducing capital equipment orders as target debt-equity ratio is approached,
2. reducing short-term borrowing as target debt-equity ratio is approached,
3. reducing employment as a shortage of cash develops,
4. reducing parts order rate as a shortage of cash develops,
5. reducing dividend payments as a shortage of cash develops,
6. delaying payments on accounts payable as a shortage of cash develops.

Equation 83 specifies the manner in which debt-equity ratio affects capital equipment orders. Capital equipment orders CEO equals capital equipment orders indicated by demand conditions CEOIDC multiplied by effect of debt-equity ratio on capacity expansion EDERCE. In other words the company prepares expansion plans on the basis of demand conditions and then, if necessary, reduces actual orders below desired by rationing the available financing.

$$CEO.KL = CEOIDC.K * EDERCE.K \qquad\qquad 83, R$$

where
CEO   = capital equipment orders (units/day/day)
CEOIDC = capital equipment orders indicated by demand
             conditions (units/day/day)
EDERCE = effect of debt-equity ratio on capacity expansion
             (dimensionless).

Effect of debt-equity ratio on capacity expansion EDERCE is a non-linear function of perceived debt-equity ratio for capacity expansion PDERCP, as shown in figure 12.7 and given in equation 98. Figure 12.7 indicates that, when the company experiences no debt limit, EDERCE remains at 1.0 (solid line). On the other hand, a debt limit requires that the company reduce expansion plans as the limit is approached. The dashed line in figure 12.7 indicates that, as PDERCP passes 1.0, EDERCE falls below 1.0, gradually at first but more quickly as the debt limit (here 2.5) is approached. When PDERCP exceeds 2.5, capital equipment orders are forced to 0 because of lack of financing.

$$EDERCE.K = TABHL(TEDERC,PDERCP.K,0,4,.25) \qquad 98, A$$
$$TEDERC = 1/1/1/1/1/1/1/1/1/1/1/1/1/1/1/1/1 \qquad\qquad 98.1, T$$

where
EDERCE = effect of debt-equity ratio on capacity expansion
             (dimensionless)

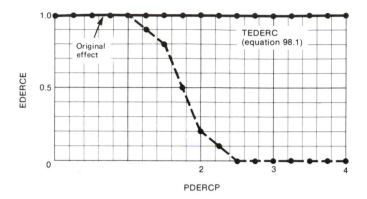

Figure 12.7   Effect of debt-equity ratio on capacity expansion

TEDERC = table for effect of debt-equity ratio on capacity
                expansion (dimensionless)
PDERCP = perceived debt-equity ratio for capacity (dimensionless).

Perceived debt-equity ratio for capacity expansion PDERCP is represented in equation 99 as an exponential average of committed debt-projected-equity ratio CDPER. Time to perceive debt-equity ratio for capacity expansion TPDERC, here set to 60 days, reflects the time required to assess the status of the company's debt position and negotiate with lenders.

PDERCP.K = SMOOTH(CDPER.K,TPDERC)   99, A
TPDERC = 60   99.1, C

where

PDERCP = perceived debt-equity ratio for capacity (dimensionless)
CDPER   = committed debt-projected-equity ratio (dimensionless)
TPDERC = time to perceive debt-equity ratio for capacity (days).

In assessing the availability of financing for capacity expansion, a company is concerned not with current debt-equity ratio but with the debt-equity ratio that reflects all of the company's outstanding obligations. Capital equipment on order represents one outstanding obligation. In arranging for financing, a company must include in debt such outstanding obligations, less financing available from operations.[2]

2. To the extent a company does not consider these obligations, whether due to lack of financial planning or its playing off different lenders in an effort to exceed what the lenders might consider a prudent debt limit, the possibility of

Committed debt-projected-equity ratio CDPER, equal to committed debt adjusted for equity CDAE divided by projected equity PEQ, incorporates these outstanding obligations (equation 100).

$$CDPER.K = CDAE.K/PEQ.K \qquad\qquad 100, A$$

where
CDPER = committed-debt-projected-equity ratio (dimensionless)
CDAE = committed debt adjusted for equity ($)
PEQ   = projected equity ($).

Committed debt adjusted for equity CDAE equals committed debt CDEBT less the cash flow from operations available to finance outstanding obligations—time to acquire capital equipment TAQCE multiplied by average cash flow from operations ACFO (equation 101).

$$CDAE.K = CDEBT.K - TAQCE * ACFO.K \qquad\qquad 101, A$$

where
CDAE = committed debt adjusted for equity ($)
CDEBT = committed debt ($)
TAQCE = time to acquire capital equipment (days)
ACFO = average cash flow from operations ($/day).

Equation 102 states that committed debt CDEBT equals total liabilities TL plus funding required for capital equipment on order—capital equipment on order CEOO multiplied by cost per unit of capital equipment CPUCE.

$$CDEBT.K = TL.K + CEOO.K * CPUCE.K \qquad\qquad 102, A$$

where
CDEBT = committed debt ($)
TL   = total liabilities ($)
CEOO = capital equipment on order (units/day)
CPUCE = cost per unit of capital equipment ($/unit/day).

Projected equity PEQ, defined in equation 103, is an estimate of the equity available when capital equipment on order must be paid for. PEQ equals equity EQ plus additions to equity over the time to acquire capital equipment TAQCE—TACQE multiplied by average retained earnings ARE.

$$PEQ.K = EQ.K + TAQCE * ARE.K \qquad\qquad 103, A$$

surpassing target debt-equity ratio increases, resulting in an inevitable crisis reduction in expenditures.

where
PEQ   = projected equity ($)
EQ   = equity ($)
TAQCE = time to acquire capital equipment (days)
ARE   = average retained earnings ($/day).

Average retained earnings ARE is represented in equation 104 as an exponential average of retained earnings RE. Time to average retained earnings TARE reflects the tendency to discount recent changes in retained earnings and to base plans on last year's earnings.

$$ARE.K = SMOOTH(RE.K, TARE) \qquad\qquad 104, A$$
$$TARE = 240 \qquad\qquad 104.1, C$$

where
ARE   = average retained earnings ($/day)
RE   = retained earnings ($/day)
TARE = time to average retained earnings (days).

As target debt-equity ratio is approached, a company has increasing difficulty arranging short-term borrowing as well as financing for capacity expansion. Consequently short-term borrowing STB, equation 185, incorporates effect of debt-equity ratio on short-term borrowing EDERSB.

$$STB.K = MAX(0, ICC.K) * ECRSTB.K * EDERSB.K \qquad 185, A$$

where
STB   = short-term borrowing ($/day)
ICC   = indicated change in cash ($/day)
ECRSTB = effect of current ratio on short-term borrowing
              (dimensionless)
EDERSB = effect of debt-equity ratio on short-term borrowing
              (dimensionless).

Effect of debt-equity ratio on short-term borrowing EDERSB, equation 189 and figure 12.8, is similar to effect of debt-equity ratio on capacity expansion in all but two respects. First, EDERSB depends on current debt-equity ratio rather than committed debt-projected-equity ratio because short-term borrowing does not finance longer-term commitments. And second, EDERSB does not fall to 0 until debt-equity ratio reaches 3.5, when the target is 2.5, because short-term borrowing is covered more by current assets so that debt-equity ratio is of secondary importance in the lending decision.

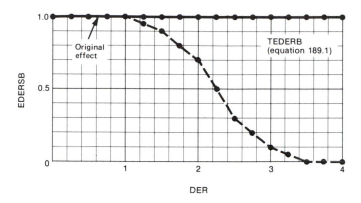

Figure 12.8   Effect of debt-equity ratio on short-term borrowing

EDERSB.K = TABHL(TEDERB,DER.K,0,4,.25)   189, A

TEDERB = 1/1/1/1/1/1/1/1/1/1/1/1/1/1/1/1/1   189.1, T

where

EDERSB = effect of debt-equity ratio on short-term borrowing
(dimensionless)

TEDERB = table for effect of debt-equity ratio on borrowing
(dimensionless)

DER   = debt-equity ratio (dimensionless).

Should debt-equity ratio approach target debt-equity ratio so that short-term borrowing is reduced, the company must rely on accumulated cash balances to finance operations. But as cash declines, actions must be taken to prevent cash from falling below zero. One such action is reducing employment by stopping hiring and laying off workers.

In equation 44 labor-hiring starts LHS incorporate effect of cash condition on hiring rate ECCHR. ECCHR, defined in equation 80 and shown in figure 12.9, is a nonlinear function of percent excess cash PEC. As PEC falls below 0, hiring is reduced, gradually at first but more rapidly as PEC approaches negative 0.8. A PEC value of negative 1.0 corresponds to a cash balance of 0.

LHS.KL = MAX(0,IHR.K) * ECCHR.K   44, R

where

LHS   = labor-hiring starts (persons/day)

IHR   = indicated hiring rate (persons/day)

ECCHR = effect of cash constraints on hiring rate (dimensionless);

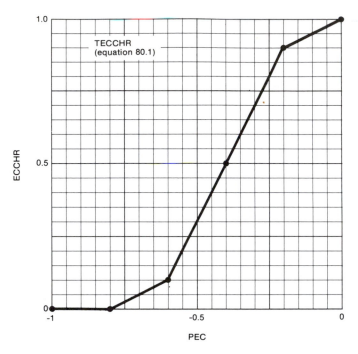

Figure 12.9   Effect on cash condition on hiring rate

ECCHR.K = TABHL(TECCHR,PEC.K, −1,0,.2)   80, A
TECCHR = 0/0/.1/.5/.9/1   80.1, T

where

ECCHR   = effect of cash constraints on hiring rate (dimensionless)
TECCHR = table for effect of cash constraints on hiring rate
               (dimensionless)
PEC   = percent excess cash (percent).

   Should cash balance fall too low, the company may have to lay off
workers. In equation 45 labor-firing rate LFR incorporates firings that
result from cash condition—fraction fired per month from cash condition FFMCC multiplied by labor L and divided by 20 days per month.
FFMCC is a function of percent excess cash PEC, as given in equation
81 and figure 12.10. FFMCC increases sharply as PEC approaches
negative 1.0.

LFR.KL = MIN(0,IHR.K) − FFMCC.K * L.K/20   45, R

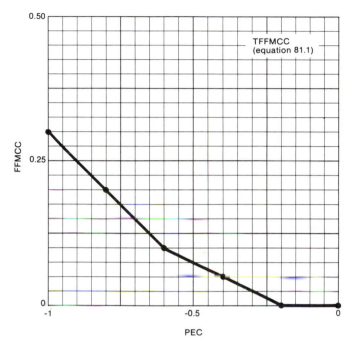

Figure 12.10   Fraction fired per month from cash condition

where
LFR   = labor-firing rate (persons/day)
IHR   = indicated hiring rate (persons/day)
FFMCC = fraction fired per month because of cash constraints
             (percent/month)
L   = labor (persons);

FFMCC.K = TABHL(TFFMCC,PEC.K, −1,0,.2)   81, A
TFFMCC = .3/.2/.1/.05/0/0   81.1, T

where
FFMCC   = fraction fired per month because of cash constraints
               (percent/month)
TFFMCC = table for fraction fired per month because of cash
               constraints (dimensionless)
PEC   = percent excess cash (percent).

A second action a company might take, should cash balance fall too
low, is to reduce parts order rate. In equation 63 indicated parts order
rate IPOR incorporates effect of cash condition on parts order rate
ECCPO. ECCPO is a function of percent excess cash PEC, as given in

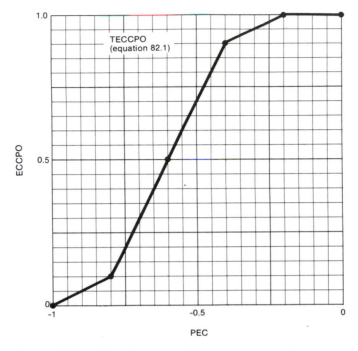

Figure 12.11   Effect of cash condition on parts ordering

equation 82 and figure 12.11. ECCPO acts to reduce POR as cash balances fall to zero.

$$IPOR.K = (BPR.K + PIC.K + POC.K)$$
$$* EFPPOR.K * ECCPO.K \qquad\qquad 63, A$$

where
IPOR   = indicated parts order rate (units/day)
BPR   = base production rate (units/day)
PIC   = parts inventory correction (units/day)
POC   = parts on order correction (units/day)
EFPPOR = effect of financial pressure on parts order rate
                (dimensionless)
ECCPO   = effect of cash constraints on parts ordering
                (dimensionless);

$$ECCPO.K = TABHL(TECCPO,PEC.K, -1,0,.2) \qquad 82, A$$
$$TECCPO = 0/.1/.5/.9/1/1 \qquad\qquad\qquad 82.1, T$$

where

ECCPO   = effect of cash constraints on parts ordering
           (dimensionless)
TECCPO = table for effect of cash constraints on parts ordering
           (dimensionless)
PEC   = percent excess cash (percent).

Dividend payments are also influenced by cash condition, as indicated in equation 225. Indicated dividend payout ratio IDPR responds to effect of cash condition on dividend payments ECCDP. As given in equation 227 and figure 12.12, dividends are reduced when the company is short of cash and increased when the company has extra cash.

$$IDPR.K = PRIROE.K * ECCDP.K \qquad\qquad 225,\ A$$

where

IDPR   = indicated dividend payout ratio (percent)
PRIROE = payout ratio indicated by return on equity (percent)
ECCDP   = effect of cash condition on dividend payments
           (dimensionless);

$$ECCDP.K = TABHL(TECCDP,APEC.K, -1,1,.2) \qquad 227,\ A$$
$$TECCDP = 0/.1/.5/.9/1/1/1/1.1/1.2/1.25/1.3 \qquad 227.1,\ C$$

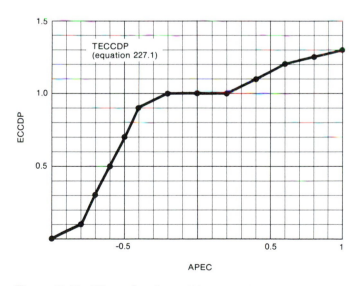

Figure 12.12 Effect of cash condition on dividend payments

where

ECCDP   = effect of cash condition on dividend payments
            (dimensionless)

TECCDP = table for effect of cash condition on dividend payments
            (dimensionless)

APEC   = average percent excess cash (percent).

Finally, a cash shortage can force the company to delay payments on accounts payable. In equation 157 time to pay accounts payable TPAP incorporates effect of cash condition on payment period ECCPP. As given in equation 158 and figure 12.13, payment period increases sharply as cash balance falls to 0. The model does not, however, incorporate any adverse effects on supplier deliveries from failure to pay bills.

$$TPAP.K = TPAPN * ECCPP.K \qquad\qquad\qquad 157, A$$
$$TPAPN = 30 \qquad\qquad\qquad\qquad\qquad\qquad\quad 157.1, C$$

where

TPAP   = time to pay accounts payable (days)

TPAPN = time to pay accounts payable, normal (days)

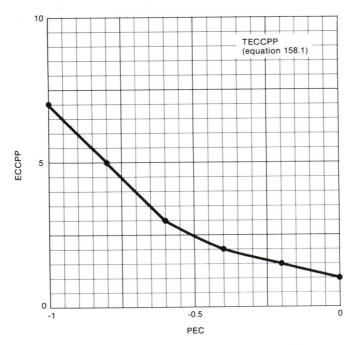

Figure 12.13 Effect of cash condition on payment period

ECCPP = effect of cash condition on payment period
              (dimensionless);

ECCPP.K = TABHL(TECCPP,PEC.K, −1,0,.2)   158, A
TECCPP = 7/5/3/2/1.5/1   158.1, T
where
ECCPP   = effect of cash condition on payment period
                (dimensionless)
TECCPP = table for effect of cash condition on payment period
                (dimensionless)
PEC   = percent excess cash (percent).

In summary limited financial resources can force a company to reduce cash outflows by cutting back orders for production resources and
by stretching payables and reducing dividends. In effect the company
rations available financial capital.

Response of Capital-Rationing Policy

Figure 12.14 (a and b) shows model behavior with limited financial
resources and a capital-rationing policy. Overall, company behavior is
worse than with adequate financial resources (figure 12.3): accumulated shipment rate is down by 13 percent; accumulated profits is down
by 40 percent; market share falls from 10 percent to 8.65 percent. As
will be described, the cause of the poor performance is an inability to
expand production resources in proportion to the growth of the market.

In figure 12.14b the increase in investment expenditures above cash
flow from operations causes debt-equity ratio to rise sharply beginning
around day 360. Debt-equity ratio approaches target debt-equity ratio
(2.5) at approximately day 1200. The approach to target debt-equity
ratio elicits the capital-rationing response.

Capital rationing is evidenced in figure 12.14a by the leveling of
capital equipment beginning around day 1200. Because capital equipment levels off, production rate falls below customer order rate at day
1296, such that finished inventory decreases (not shown). As finished
inventory declines, delivery delay increases to pull customer order rate
below market demand (plotted as M but not highlighted) down to production rate. The leveling of production rate slows the acquisition of
labor and parts inventory.

Because acquisition of production resources slows, the company
draws down finished and parts inventory. As a result cash outflows to

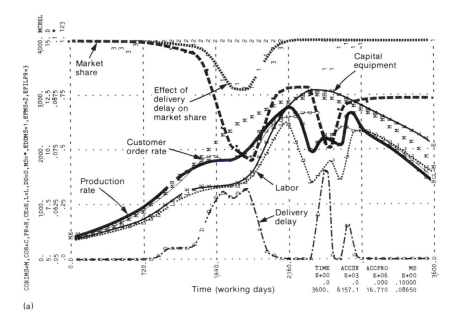

(a)

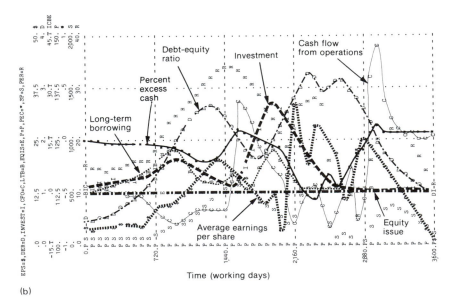

(b)

Figure 12.14   Model behavior with limited financial resources: capital rationing

pay for labor and parts fall, increasing cash flow from operations dramatically beginning at day 1440. Debt-equity ratio then declines, and the company can once again invest in production resources.

The investment occurs, and capital equipment rises again beginning at day 1656. As a result production rate increases and pulls up customer order rate through the reduction in delivery delay.

But the increase in investment expenditures to pay for the capital equipment and the drop in cash flow to build inventory and receivables cause long-term borrowing and debt-equity ratio to rise sharply again (day 1728). In fact debt-equity ratio exceeds target, and cash balances are drawn down.

The second cash crisis is more severe than the first particularly because the company now has sufficient capacity to build inventory. But the inventory building so drains cash flow that funds are insufficient for both capital equipment investment and inventory building. As a result the company must cut back on expenditures for capital equipment and other production resources—primarily labor.

As labor falls beginning at day 2160, production rate is pulled down. Consequently finished inventory (not shown) is depleted, and delivery delay rises. The increasing delivery delay reduces customer order rate.

Once again the reduction in inventory building improves cash flow so that debt-equity ratio falls. But by now the company has lost loyal customers, and market share stabilizes below its initial level.

Capital-rationing policies solve a financial problem by reducing cash outflows for the acquisition of production resources. But the ensuing lack of sufficient production resources reduces the availability of the company's products and thus causes a loss of market share. By the time financial position has improved to permit acquisition of production resources, the company has permanently lost market share.

12.5 Dynamics Created by Pricing Responses to Limited Financial Resources

Capital rationing is only one action available to the company for dealing with a limited supply of financial resources. As an alternative the company can raise price to balance the supply and demand for financial resources. Increasing price improves cash inflows and therefore does not constrain the acquisition of production resources. High price, not availability, causes loss of market share, and this in fact is the better way to lose market share, as will be proved in the simulation experiment that follows.

Pricing decisions are often made to obtain an adequate rate of return. The price in the model discussed here produces a rate of return on assets and a return on equity well above normal but within the range expected for a rapidly growing company. However, the company has no guarantee that the price, perhaps adequate or even exceptional by rate-of-return standards, will generate sufficient cash flow to support growth up to potential. If growth is restricted by lack of financial resources for investment in production capacity, the company ought to consider raising price rather than permitting product availability to deteriorate. At the same time the company can generate additional cash flow to support a higher rate of growth.

Effects of Price on Production Capability and Market Share

Figures 12.15 and 12.16 show the dominant feedback loops when pricing policy is used to deal with limited financial resources. The structure of the financial sector in figures 12.15 and 12.16 is analogous to that in figures 12.5 and 12.6. The only difference between these two sets of figures is that in figures 12.15 and 12.16 the company responds to changes in the supply of financial resources by changing price instead of reducing production capacity orders. Price changes influence the company's order rate and in turn the company's financial flows.

Figure 12.15 shows the negative feedback loops through pricing policy. In the figure an initial increase in price increases the company's cash flow from operations and earnings. The price increase also reduces order rate, lowering the required investment in production capacity. The supply of financial resources therefore tends to improve (through the financial sector mechanisms described previously), and price tends to decrease.

Figure 12.16 shows the positive feedback loops that oppose the actions of the negative feedback loops through pricing policy. A price increase lowers order rate and, by inducing a decrease in production rate, reduces cash flow and earnings. Therefore the supply of financial resources decreases, inducing a further increase in price.

When the loops shown in figures 12.15 and 12.16 are combined, the net effect of pricing policies depends on the relative strengths of the positive and negative loops. The relative strengths of these loops in turn depend primarily on the relationship defining the effect of price on

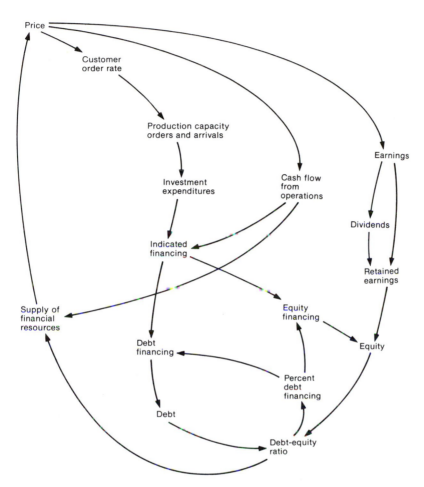

Figure 12.15   Negative feedback loops through pricing policy

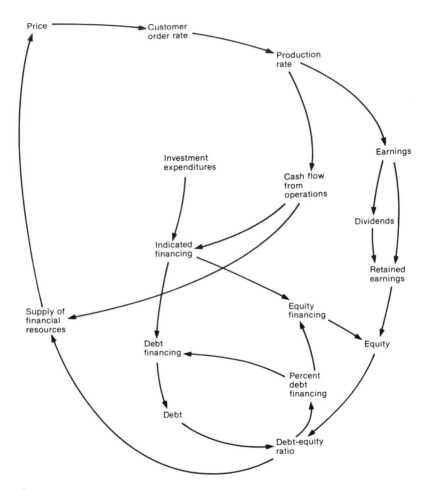

Figure 12.16 Positive feedback loops through pricing policy

order rate. The effect of price on order rate is determined not only by the direct relationship between price and order rate but also by the interaction between price and delivery delay in determining order rate. A decrease in price brings about a short-run decline in order rate. The decline in order rate, however, improves the company's delivery delay, increasing order rate. Therefore the direct impact of price on order rate is diminished by delivery delay and price interaction in determining order rate. Clearly, for all but very large elasticities of order rate with respect to price, pricing policies can improve the balance between the supply and demand for financial resources.

Figures 12.15 and 12.16 account for the relatively short-run effects of pricing policy. Longer-run effects of pricing policy manifest themselves through investment. The feedback loops through pricing tie into the feedback loops through investment policy via the effect of the supply of financial resources on investment. An increase in price that leads to an increased supply of financial resources may allow the company to undertake investment previously not feasible. Therefore the company's long-run delivery delay position may improve and order rate may increase. In other words the price increase may have different short-run and long-run effects on order rate.

A price response to limited financial resources is incorporated into the model by adjusting base price by the effect of debt-equity ratio on price. Equation 107 specifies the adjustment. Indicated price IP, to which price adjusts over the time to adjust price, equals base price BP multiplied by effect of debt-equity ratio on price EDERP (ERIP is initially inactive). BP is the price indicated by unit costs; BP is here a constant $100 per unit.

$$\text{IP.K} = \text{BP.K} * \text{ERIP.K} * \text{EDERP.K} \qquad\qquad 107, \text{A}$$

where
IP   = indicated price ($/unit)
BP   = base price ($/unit)
ERIP   = effect of relative inventory on price (dimensionless)
EDERP   = effect of debt-equity ratio on price (dimensionless).

Effect of debt-equity ratio on price EDERP is a function of perceived debt-equity ratio for capacity expansion PDERCP, as given in equation 112 and figure 12.17. When pricing policy does not respond to the financial condition, EDERP is set to 1.0 as indicated by the dashed line in figure 12.17. The solid line indicates how prices are increased as PDERCP rises. In practice a company would experiment with various

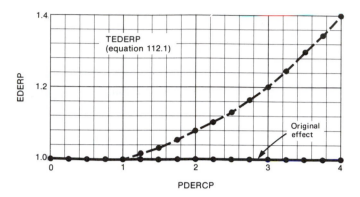

Figure 12.17   Effect of debt-equity ratio on price

TEDERP curves to determine which curve gives the best performance under a variety of market conditions and effect of price on market share curves.

EDERP.K = TABLE(TEDERP,PDERCP.K,0,4,.25)   112, A

TEDERP = 1/1/1/1/1/1/1/1/1/1/1/1/1/1/1/1/1   112.1, T

where

EDERP   = effect of debt-equity ratio on price (dimensionless)

TEDERP = table for effect of debt-equity ratio on price (dimensionless)

PDERCP = perceived debt-equity ratio for capacity (dimensionless).

Response of Pricing Policy

Figure 12.18 (a and b) shows model behavior with limited financial resources and pricing.[3] While the loss of market share is about the same as for the capital-rationing policy, accumulated profits are increased by 87 percent. Moreover the improved performance is achieved with a lower value of debt-equity ratio. Consequently less aggressive pricing might result in higher market share and still achieve target debt-equity ratio.

The reasons for the overall improvement in profits are evident. While price exceeds base price of $100 per unit between days 504 and 2448 and reduces order rate, delivery delay remains at its minimum value,

3. Debt-equity ratio and percent excess cash still affect short-term borrowing, labor, parts ordering, dividends, and payment period. Only the effect of debt-equity ratio on capacity expansion is neturalized.

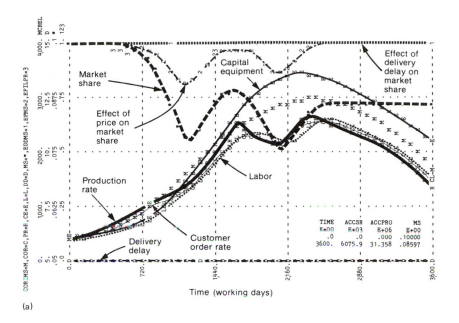

(a)

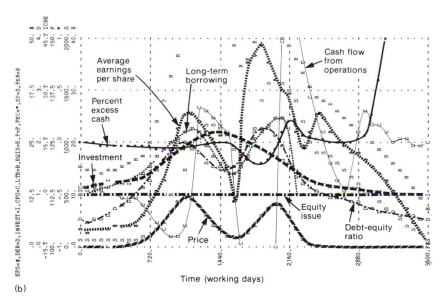

(b)

Figure 12.18 Model behavior with limited financial resources: pricing policy

well below the values attained in the capital-rationing policy simulations, and increases order rate. Delivery delay falls below these values because the price increases (1) reduce order rate, improving delivery delay in the short run, and (2) raise cash flow, enabling investment in production capacity to keep pace with growth in customer order rate. Consequently the company achieves the same total shipment rate but at a higher price per unit.

For example, the initial increase in investment expenditures above cash flow from operations, beginning at day 360 (figure 12.18b), causes debt-equity ratio to rise. The increase in debt-equity ratio induces the company to raise price in an effort to improve cash flow. Higher price between days 504 and 2448 raises cash flow from operations. Cash flow is no lower than in the capital-rationing simulation even though the company is able to build inventory as desired. However, the increased price also reduces market share, and consequently customer rate, during this period.

But by reducing customer order rate, the price rise beginning around day 504 shortens delivery delay. In effect the company has substituted a high price for a high delivery delay as the factor limiting order rate. Then, after day 2016 as price is reduced and debt-equity ratio improves, production resources are sufficient to allow production rate to match the growth in customer order rate. Consequently market share does not fall because of poor product availability.

In summary from a growth and profitability standpoint a pricing policy is superior to a capital-rationing policy. The interactions between price and delivery delay in determining order rate tend to mitigate the effect of the price increases. Consequently a price increase usually produces substantial financial resources to finance future growth. Reducing investment, on the other hand, limits the current demand for cash but does not increase, in fact may decrease, future cash flow.

Nevertheless, price increases in figure 12.18 occur after the increase in debt-equity ratio occurs. Performance might be improved if prices were increased in anticipation of the increase in debt-equity ratios. One of the major causes of the increase is the cash drain produced by building inventory. A forewarning of such a cash drain is an inventory shortage. One anticipatory policy is to base price changes on inventory discrepancies (as was done in chapter 8).

Figure 12.19 shows the response of such a pricing policy. As expected, prices rise sooner than in the previous simulation. Consequently debt-equity ratio rises more slowly. Moreover prices are

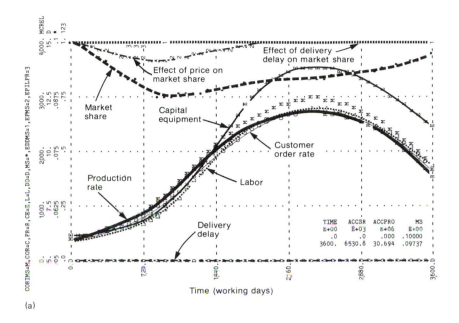

(a)

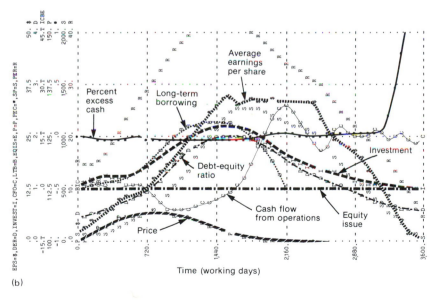

(b)

Figure 12.19 Model behavior with limited financial resources: pricing policy based on inventory discrepancy

highest in the middle of the rapid-growth phase when cash demands are highest. Rather than waiting for the cash demands to create a debt-equity ratio that warrants a price change, the pricing policy that responds to inventory shortages anticipates the cash drain.

The policy does not, however, control debt-equity ratio directly. If debt-equity ratio rises for some reason other than inventory building, the policy would not work. Some combination policy is probably desirable.

12.6 Summary

Shortages of financial resources are a common problem for all growing companies. Unfortunately the expedient solution to such a problem—capital rationing—is not the best solution.

Capital-rationing policies solve a financial problem by reducing cash outflows for the acquisition of production resources. But the ensuing shortage of production resources reduces the availability of the company's products and causes not only a loss of market share but also loyal customers.

Pricing policies, on the other hand, solve a financial problem by improving cash inflows. They do not constrain the acquisition of production resources, and therefore availability does not suffer. In effect loss of market share through high prices improves profits because the same, or greater, shipments are made at a higher price.

The following guideline summarizes the results of chapter 12:

Policy design guideline 12.1 When faced with limited financial resources, a higher-pricing response is superior to a capital-rationing response because sales lost by high prices rather than availability improve cash flow on sales made and thereby allow the investment in production resources which prevents availability delays from turning away customers permanently.

A more detailed treatment of financial policies can be found in Lyneis (1974).

Reference

Lyneis, James M. 1974. The Impact of Corporate Financial Policies On Corporate Growth and Profitability. Ph.D. dissertation. Graduate School of Business Administration, University of Michigan, Ann Arbor. Available from University Microfilms, Ann Arbor, Mich.

Dynamics Created by Professional Resource Expansion

13

13.1 Introduction

Professional resources are the manpower devoted to research and development, engineering, marketing, and management. Professional resources decide on the types of products to be manufactured; design and engineer these products; acquire production and financial resources; and organize, coordinate, and direct the many diverse functions carried out within a company.

Professional activities directly influence the attractiveness of a company's products, to the degree these products match the needs of the market, are of high quality, and are marketed effectively. The match between company products and market needs depends on the vision of professional resources and the ability of research and engineering to translate the vision into a usable product. Research and engineering determine the quality of the products. Marketing effort affects the way in which products are brought to the attention of customers. Professional resources therefore are responsible for the long-run competitive position of the company.

Professional activities also indirectly influence the attractiveness of a company's products through competitive variables such as delivery delay and price. Professional resources set the policies that guide the acquisition of production and financial resources and thereby influence delivery delay and price. Since professional resources manage the activities of the company, they inevitably influence all aspects of the competitive value of company products in the marketplace.

Understanding the effect of professional resources on corporate growth is much more difficult than understanding the effect of production and financial resources. Professional resources are allocated to a number of different functions within the company: research and engineering, marketing, finance, and management. Each functional area influences product attractiveness in a different way. Moreover the effects of "match to customer needs" and "quality" on market share are even less tangible than the effects of delivery delay and price. Consequently the relationship between professional resources and corporate growth is complex and difficult to study.

Nevertheless, professional resources as a class have some common behavioral characteristics. These common characteristics allow some generalization about the effect of professional resources on corporate growth and provide a framework within which more detailed studies of professional resources can be performed.

The three distinguishing characteristics of professional resources are

1. An assimilation delay to achieve peak productivity toward corporate goals. Newly hired professional employees may not become fully productive until they have been with a company for a substantial interval of time (perhaps six months to several years). Some of the assimilation delay results from training, learning communication channels, corporate goals, and policies, and generally moving up the learning curve. The remainder of the assimilation delay results from the time required to evaluate the strengths and weaknesses of new employees and place them in positions where their capabilities can be best utilized.

2. Training reduces the efficiency of existing professionals. The direct time spent in training reduces professional output. Moreover an organization with new employees tends to be less efficient because of the need to develop new communication links and to work new people into the operations of the present professionals.

3. Professional resources affect product attractiveness only after a long delay, in a less tangible manner than variables such as delivery delay. The lead time on developing products is several years. Consequently a company could operate for several years with inadequate professional staff before product attractiveness suffers. Moreover, because the effect of professional resources on attractiveness is nearly impossible to specify, professional budgets are easier to cut or hold to traditional levels in the face of cost pressures.

The effect of these characteristics on corporate growth is examined in this chapter. In addition section 13.5 identifies other dynamics created by professional resources and how the dynamics could be incorporated into the existing model.

13.2 Structure of Professional Resource Sector

Effect on Market Share

As a class professional resources determine a company's ability to service market demand. Market demand here represents the units sold per day in the company's general product line. Professional effort services demand by providing sales and technical support to customers, scanning customers for future needs, and designing products to meet these needs. The larger the market demand, the greater must be a company's professional resources.[1]

Traditional market share is therefore multiplied by effect of professional service level on market share EPSLMS (as well as by effects of delivery delay and price) to determine market share. Equation 155 specifies the revised calculation of market share.

$$MS.K = TMS.K * EDDMS.K * EPMS.K * EPSLMS.K \qquad 155, A$$

where
MS = market share (percent)
TMS = traditional market share (percent)
EDDMS = effect of delivery delay on market share (dimensionless)
EPMS = effect of price on market share (dimensionless)
EPSLMS = effect of professional service level on market share (dimensionless).

Equation 165 and figure 13.1 define effect of professional service level on market share EPSLMS. EPSLMS is a function of delayed professional service level DPRSL relative to competitor professional service level COMPSL. When DPRSL equals COMPSL, professional resources are sufficient to service the company's share of demand at the same level as competitors. Consequently EPSLMS equals 1.0. As DPRSL falls below 1.0, EPSLMS falls below 1.0: the company loses market share because it cannot provide the research, engineering, and marketing necessary to support its customers. Conversely, if DPRSL rises above 1.0, EPSLMS rises above 1.0: the company increases market share by marketing to new customers or introducing a new product that takes share from competitors.

1. Note that the absolute level of professional resources necessary to service a product depends on the nature of the product. It may take 10 professionals to service 100 units per day sales of automobiles, but 10 professionals may service 1,000 units per day sales of calculators.

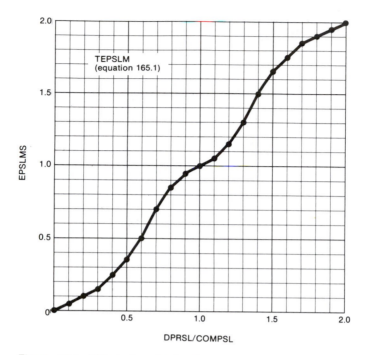

Figure 13.1   Effect of professional service level on market share

$$EPSLMS.K = TABLE(TEPSLM, DPRSL.K/COMPSL.K,$$
$$0,2,.1) \hspace{4cm} 165, A$$

$$TEPSLM = 0/.05/.1/.15/.25/.35/.5/.7/.85/.95/1/1.05/$$
$$1.15/1.3/1.5/1.65/1.75/1.85/1.9/1.95/2 \hspace{1cm} 165.1, T$$

where

EPSLMS = effect of professional service level on market share (dimensionless)

TEPSLM = table for effect of professional service level on market share (dimensionless)

DPRSL   = delayed professional service level (dimensionless)

COMPSL = competitor professional service level (dimensionless).

Delayed professional service level DPRSL is represented in equation 166 as an exponential average of professional service level PRSL. Time to average professional service level TAPRSL, here taken as 480 days, represents the delay with which marketing and research effort influences product attractiveness.

$$DPRSL.K = SMOOTH(PRSL.K, TAPRSL) \hspace{1.5cm} 166, A$$
$$TAPRSL = 480 \hspace{5cm} 166.1, C$$

where

DPRSL   = delayed professional service level (dimensionless)
PRSL   = professional service level (dimensionless)
TAPRSL = time to average professional service level (days).

Professional service level is defined in equation 167. Units per day serviceable by professional effort UDSPRE equals the current demand-supporting capacity of professionals. Market demand MD multiplied by traditional market share TMS equals the customer demand that normally looks to the company for such service. When UDSPRE and customer demand are equal, PRSL equals 1.0. Variations in either the output of the company's professional sector (UDSPRE) or market demand can cause professional service level to change.

$$PRSL.K = UDSPRE.K/(MD.K * TMS.K) \qquad\qquad 167, A$$

where

PRSL   = professional service level (dimensionless)
UDSPRE = units per day serviceable by professional effort
                (units/day)
MD   = market demand (units/day)
TMS   = traditional market share (percent).

Equation 168 states that units per day serviceable by professional effort UDSPRE equals normal units per day serviceable by professional effort NUDSPE multiplied by professional capability PRCAP. PRCAP is the effective professional effort devoted to servicing customer demand (as opposed to training). NUDSPE converts professional effort into the units that can be serviced by that effort. NUDSPE is an unknowable quantity. A value of 10.0, when taken with the company's normal ratio of professionals to customer orders, yields a professional service level of 1.0. In other words in equilibrium NUDSPE multiplied by PRCAP equals MD multiplied by TMS.

$$UDSPRE.K = NUDSPE * PRCAP.K \qquad\qquad 168, A$$
$$NUDSPE = 10 \qquad\qquad 168.1, C$$

where

UDSPRE = units per day serviceable by professional effort
                (units/day)
NUDSPE = normal units per day serviceable by professional effort
                (units/day/professional)
PRCAP   = professional capability (professionals).

Equation 169 defines competitor professional service level COMPSL to equal a constant 1.0.

COMPSL.K = 1   169, A

where

COMPSL = competitor professional service level (dimensionless).

Professional Effort and Resource Levels[2]

Figure 13.2 gives a flow diagram of the professional resource sector. Hiring professionals increases the level of professionals being assimilated; as professionals are assimilated, their number increases. The levels of professionals and professionals being assimilated determine professional effort available. Training and organizational inefficiencies reduce professional effort, thus professional capability.

Equation 115 defines professional capability PRCAP as professional effort allocated to marketing and research PREAMR multiplied by professional efficiency PREFF. PREAMR represents professional time allocated to marketing or research, as opposed to time allocated to recruiting or manufacturing. PREFF captures the negative effects of training and organizational inefficiencies on professional capability.

PRCAP.K = PREAMR.K * PREFF.K   115, A

where

PRCAP   = professional capability (professionals)

PREAMR = professional effort allocated to marketing and research (professionals)

PREFF   = professional efficiency (dimensionless).

Equation 116 and figure 13.3 define professional efficiency PREFF. PREFF is a nonlinear function of fraction of professionals being assimilated FRPRBA. FRPRBA is an indicator of the demands that expansion places on professional efficiency. If the fraction is high, many new employees are draining professional effort for training, evaluation, and remolding the organization structure. If no effort is being absorbed, efficiency is 1.0—denoting complete availability of professional effort for productive work. As the fraction rises, an increasing portion of the effort available goes to internal activities or is lost through inefficiencies, and professional efficiency drops. PREFF is assumed to level off at 0.6.

2. Much of this segment of the model is based on the work of Packer (1964).

PREFF.K = TABLE(TPREFF,FRPRBA.K,0,.4,.05)   116, A
TPREFF = 1/.975/.925/.85/.75/.675/.625/.6/.6   116.1, T

where
PREFF   = professional efficiency (dimensionless)
TPREFF = table for professional efficiency (dimensionless)
FRPRBA = fraction of professional being assimilated (percent).

Fraction of professionals being assimilated FRPRBA equals professionals being assimilated PRBA divided by total professionals TPR (equation 117). In equation 118 total professionals TPR is defined to equal the sum of professionals being assimilated PRBA and professionals PROF.

FRPRBA.K = PRBA.K/TPR.K   117, A

where
FRPRBA = fraction of professional being assimilated (percent)
PRBA   = professionals being assimilated (professionals)
TPR   = total professionals (professionals);

TPR.K = PRBA.K + PROF.K   118, A

where
TPR   = total professionals (professionals)
PRBA = professionals being assimilated (professionals)
PROF = professionals (professionals).

In equation 119 professional effort available for marketing and research PREAMR is set equal to professional effort available PREAVL. In the current model no professional effort is allocated to production activities or general management.

PREAMR.K = PREAVL.K   119, A

where
PREAMR = professional effort allocated to marketing and research
              (professionals)
PREAVL = professional effort available (professionals).

Professional effort available PREAVL sums the effort from professionals PROF and professionals being assimilated PRBA, less professional effort recruiting PRER (equation 120). Productivity of professionals PPROF is set arbitrarily to 1.0. Productivity of professionals being assimilated is set to a lower value of 0.25. While professionals being assimilated do some productive work, their work has less impact on the direct needs of customers.

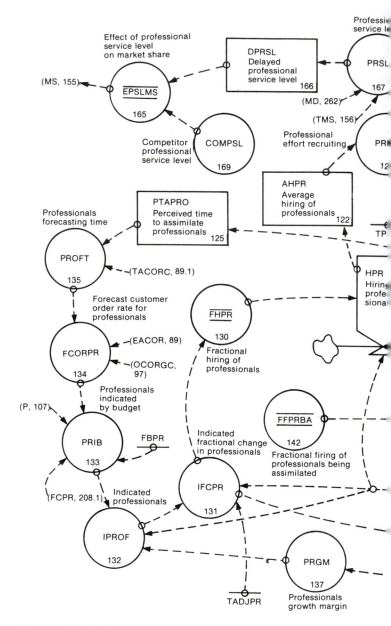

Figure 13.2 Professional resource sector

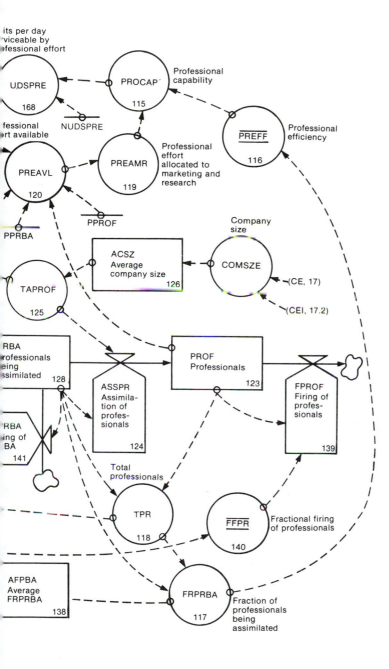

its per day
·viceable by
·fessional effort

UDSPRE

168

PROCAP·

115

Professional
capability

·fessional
·rt available

NUDSPRE

PREFF

116

Professional
efficiency

PREAVL

120

PREAMR

119

Professional
effort
allocated to
marketing and
research

PPROF

PPRBA

TAPROF

125

ACSZ
Average
company size

126

Company
size

COMSZE

—(CE, 17)

—(CEI, 17.2)

·RBA
·rofessionals
·eing
·ssimilated

128

ASSPR
Assimila-
tion of
profes-
sionals

124

PROF
Professionals

123

FPROF
Firing of
profes-
sionals

139

·RBA
·ing of
·BA

141

Total
professionals

TPR

118

FFPR

140

Fractional firing
of professionals

AFPBA
Average
FRPRBA

138

FRPRBA

117

Fraction of
professionals
being
assimilated

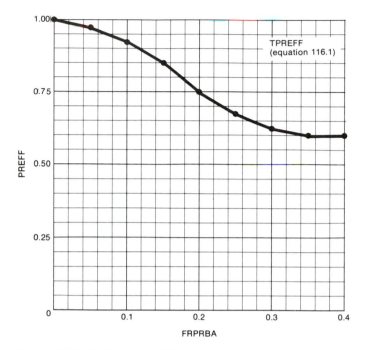

Figure 13.3 Professional efficiency

PREAVL.K = PROF.K * PPROF + PRBA.K * PPRBA
                  − PRER.K   120, A
PPROF = 1   120.1, C
PPRBA = .25   120.2, C

where

PREAVL = professional effort available (professionals)
PROF   = professionals (professionals)
PPROF = productivity of professionals (dimensionless)
PRBA   = professionals being assimilated (professionals)
PPRBA = productivity of professionals being assimilated
          (dimensionless)
PRER   = professional effort recruiting (professionals).

Equation 121 defines professional effort recruiting PRER to equal average hiring of professionals AHPR multiplied by time for professional
recruiting TPRR. TPRR is arbitrarily set to 0.025 professional per day
hired.

PRER.K = AHPR.K * TPRR   121, A
TPRR = .025   121.1, C

where
PRER = professional effort recruiting (professionals)
AHPR = average hiring of professionals (professionals/day)
TPRR = time for professional recruiting
(professionals/professionals/day).

In equation 122 average hiring of professionals AHPR is represented as an exponential average of hiring of professionals HPR. Because recruiting effort is tied directly to current hiring, time to average hiring of professionals TAHPR is set to a relatively short 20 days.

$$\text{AHPR.K} = \text{AHPR.J} + (\text{DT/TAHPR})(\text{HPR.JK} - \text{AHPR.J}) \quad \text{122, L}$$
$$\text{AHPR} = 0 \qquad\qquad\qquad\qquad\qquad\qquad\qquad\qquad\qquad \text{122.1, N}$$
$$\text{TAHPR} = 20 \qquad\qquad\qquad\qquad\qquad\qquad\qquad\qquad\quad \text{122.2, C}$$

where
AHPR   = average hiring of professionals (professionals/day)
DT   = delta time, simulation solution interval (days)
TAHPR = time to average hiring of professionals (days)
HPR   = hiring of professionals (professionals/day).

Professionals PROF is modeled as a level variable increased by assimilation of professionals ASSPR and decreased by firing of professionals FPROF (equation 123). The initial value of professionals is set equal to normal ratio of professionals to customer order rate NRPCOR multiplied by constant customer order rate CCOR. A value of 0.1 for NRPCOR yields a professional service level of 1.0 when normal units per day serviceable by professional effort is set to 10.0, as defined earlier.

$$\text{PROF.K} = \text{PROF.J} + (\text{DT})(\text{ASSPR.JK} - \text{FPROF.JK}) \quad \text{123, L}$$
$$\text{PROF} = \text{NRPCOR} * \text{CCOR} \qquad\qquad\qquad\qquad\qquad \text{123.1, N}$$
$$\text{NRPCOR} = .1 \qquad\qquad\qquad\qquad\qquad\qquad\qquad\quad \text{123.2, C}$$

where
PROF   = professionals (professionals)
DT   = delta time, simulation solution interval (days)
ASSPR   = assimilation of professionals (professionals/day)
FPROF   = firing of professionals (professionals/day)
NRPCOR = normal ratio of professionals to customer order rate
               (professionals/unit/day)
CCOR   = constant customer order rate (units/day).

Equation 124 defines assimilation of professionals ASSPR to equal professionals being assimilated PRBA divided by time to assimilate professionals TAPROF.

ASSPR.KL = PRBA.K/TAPROF.K   124, R

where
ASSPR   = assimilation of professionals (professionals/day)
PRBA   = professionals being assimilated (professionals)
TAPROF = time to assimilate professionals (days).

Equation 125 and figure 13.4 define time to assimilate professionals TAPROF. TAPROF is a nonlinear function of average company size ACSZ. Company size measures the current size of the company relative to its initial size. When company size remains small, time to assimilate professionals is assumed to be a relatively short 120 days. In a small company relatively experienced professionals can be hired through the personal contacts of present professionals. Consequently the assimilation delay is relatively short. As the company grows, however, the demand for new professionals exceeds the personal contacts of existing professionals, as does the supply of relatively experienced professionals decrease. Therefore less experienced professionals are hired, increasing the training delay.

TAPROF.K = TABLE(TTAPR,ACSZ.K,0,12,1)   125, A
TTAPR = 120/120/140/170/210/260/320/370/410/440/460/   125.1, T
             480/480

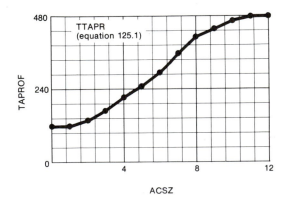

Figure 13.4   Time to assimilate professionals

where
TAPROF = time to assimilate professionals (days)
TTAPR = table for time to assimilate professionals (days)
ACSZ = average company size (dimensionless).

Average company size ACSZ is represented in equation 126 as an exponential average of company size COMSZE. Time to average company size TACSZ, here set to 240 days, reflects delay required for growth in the physical size of the company to affect professional hiring. Company size COMSZE simply equals current capital equipment CE divided capital equipment initial CEI (equation 127).

$$\text{ACSZ.K} = \text{SMOOTH(COMSZE.K,TACSZ)} \qquad 126, A$$
$$\text{TACSZ} = 240 \qquad 126.1, C$$

where
ACSZ = average company size (dimensionless)
COMSZE = company size (dimensionless)
TACSZ = time to average company size (days);

$$\text{COMSZE.K} = \text{CE.K/CEI} \qquad 127, A$$

where
COMSZE = company size (dimensionless)
CE = capital equipment (units/day)
CEI = capital equipment, initial (units/day).

Equation 128 defines professionals being assimilated PRBA as a level variable increased by hiring of professionals HPR and decreased by assimilation of professionals ASSPR and firing of professionals being assimilated FPRBA. PRBA is initially set to zero.

$$\text{PRBA.K} = \text{PRBA.J} + (\text{DT})(\text{HPR.JK} - \text{ASSPR.JK}$$
$$- \text{FPRBA.JK}) \qquad 128, L$$
$$\text{PRBA} = 0 \qquad 128.1, N$$

where
PRBA = professionals being assimilated (professionals)
DT = delta time, simulation solution interval (days)
HPR = hiring of professionals (professionals/day)
ASSPR = assimilation of professionals (professionals/day)
FPRBA = firing of professionals being assimilated
(professionals/day).

Expansion Policies

Hiring of professionals HPR, defined in equation 129, equals total
professionals TPR multiplied by fractional hiring of professionals
FHPR. FHPR is a function of indicated fractional change in professionals IFCPR, as defined in equation 130. In the current formulation
TFHPR merely constrains hiring of professionals from becoming negative. TFHPR might also be used to represent a maximum fractional
change in professionals.

$$\text{HPR.KL} = \text{TPR.K} * \text{FHPR.K} \qquad\qquad 129, R$$

where
HPR   = hiring of professionals (professionals/day)
TPR   = total professionals (professionals)
FHPR = fractional hiring of professionals (percent/day);

$$\text{FHPR.K} = \text{TABLE(TFHPR,IFCPR.K}, -.001,.004,.0005) \qquad 130, A$$
$$\text{TFHPR} = 0/0/0/.0005/.001/.0015/.002/.0025/.003/.0035/.004 \qquad 130.1, T$$

where
FHPR   = fractional hiring of professionals (percent/day)
TFHPR = table for fractional hiring of professionals (percent/day)
IFCPR = indicated fractional change in professionals (percent/day).

Equation 131 defines indicated fractional change in professionals
IFCPR. IFCPR adjusts professionals PROF and professionals being
assimilated PRBA to indicated professionals IPROF over the time to
adjust professionals TADJPR. The professionals per day adjustment
is divided by total professionals TPR to yield a fractional change.
A TADJPR value of 120 days reflects the long recruiting time for
professionals.

$$\text{IFCPR.K} = ((\text{IPROF.K} - \text{PROF.K}$$
$$- \text{PRBA.K})/\text{TADJPR})/\text{TPR.K} \qquad 131, A$$
$$\text{TADJPR} = 120 \qquad\qquad 131.1, C$$

where
IFCPR   = indicated fractional change in professionals (percent/day)
IPROF   = indicated professionals (professionals)
PROF   = professionals (professionals)
PRBA   = professionals being assimilated (professionals)
TADJPR = time to adjust professionals (days)
TPR   = total professionals (professionals).

Indicated professionals IPROF is defined in equation 132 to equal professionals indicated by budget PRIB multiplied by the sum of 1.0 and professionals growth margin PRGM. PRGM is similar to capital equipment growth margin defined in chapter 11.

$$IPROF.K = PRIB.K * (1 + PRGM.K) \qquad\qquad 132, A$$

where
IPROF = indicated professionals (professionals)
PRIB = professionals indicated by budget (professionals)
PRGM = professionals growth margin (dimensionless).

Equation 133 defines professionals indicated by budget PRIB. Total forecast budget is determined by multiplying forecast customer order rate for professionals FCORPR by price P. A fraction of that budget, fraction budget allocated to professionals FBPR, is used in setting PRIB. The budget allocation is then divided by fixed costs of professionals FCPR to determine PRIB.

$$PRIB.K = FBPR * FCORPR.K * P.K/FCPR \qquad 133, A$$
$$FBPR = .17 \qquad\qquad\qquad\qquad\qquad 133.1, C$$

where
PRIB   = professionals indicated by budget (professionals)
FBPR   = fraction budgeted to professionals (percent)
FCORPR = forecast customer order rate for professionals
        (units/day)
P   = price ($/unit)
FCPR   = fixed cost percentage (dimensionless).

Equation 134 calculates forecast customer order rate for professionals FCORPR. The company forecasts across the professionals-forecasting time PROFT.

$$FCORPR.K = EACOR.K * (1 + PROFT.K * OCORGC.K) \quad 134, A$$

where
FCORPR = forecast customer order rate for professionals
         (units/day)
EACOR   = estimated average customer order rate (units/day)
PROFT   = professionals-forecasting time (days)
OCORGC = observed customer order rate growth for capacity
         (percent/day).

Professionals-forecasting time PROFT, calculated in equation 135, equals the sum of perceived time to assimilate professionals PTAPRO and time to average customer order rate for capacity TACORC. In other words the company tries to hire professionals far enough in advance so that they are fully assimilated when needed.

PROFT.K = PTAPRO.K + TACORC   135, A

where

PROFT   = professionals-forecasting time (days)
PTAPRO = perceived time to assimilate professionals (days)
TACORC = time to average customer order rate for capacity (days).

Perceived time to assimilate professionals PTAPRO is represented in equation 136 as an exponential average of time to assimilate professionals TAPROF. Time to perceive time to assimilate professionals, here set to 480 days, reflects the time required to perceive the delay before new hires become fully productive.

PTAPRO.K = SMOOTH(TAPROF.K,TPTAPR)   136, A
TPTAPR = 480   136.1, C

where

PTAPRO = perceived time to assimilate professionals (days)
TAPROF = time to assimilate professionals (days)
TPTAPR = time to perceive time to assimilate professionals (days).

Professionals growth margin PRGM is defined in equation 137. PRGM is set to 0; different values for PRGM are explored in section 13.4. As also defined in that section, PRGM responds to average fraction of professionals being assimilated AFPBA (equation 138).

PRGM.K = TABLE(TPRGM,AFPBA.K,0,.4,.05)   137, A
TPRGM = 0/0/0/0/0/0/0/0/0   137.1, T

where

PRGM   = professionals growth margin (dimensionless)
TPRGM = table for professionals growth margin (dimensionless)
AFPBA   = average fraction of professionals being assimilated
                (percent);

AFPBA.K = SMOOTH(FRPRBA.K,TAFPBA)   138, A
TAFPBA = 480   138.1, C

where

AFPBA   = average fraction of professionals being assimilated
                (percent)
FRPRBA = fraction of professional being assimilated (percent)

TAFPBA = time to average fraction of professionals being assimilated (days).

Equations 139 through 142 define the firing of professionals FPROF and the firing of professionals being assimilated FPRBA. When indicated fractional change in professionals IFCPR is negative, professionals and professionals being assimilated are fired. The assumption is made that professionals being assimilated are more readily fired than professionals.

$$\text{FPROF.KL} = \text{PROF.K} * \text{FFPR.K} \qquad\qquad 139, R$$

where
FPROF = firing of professionals (professionals/day)
PROF = professionals (professionals)
FFPR = fractional firing of professionals (percent/day);

$$\text{FFPR.K} = \text{TABLE(TFFPR,IFCPR.K}, -.001,.001,.0005) \quad 140, A$$
$$\text{TFFPR} = .0005/.00025/0/0/0 \qquad\qquad 140.1, T$$

where
FFPR = fractional firing of professionals (percent/day)
TFFPR = table for fractional firing of professionals (percent/day)
IFCPR = indicated fractional change in professionals (percent/day);

$$\text{FPRBA.KL} = \text{PRBA.K} * \text{FFPRBA.K} \qquad\qquad 141, R$$

where
FPRBA = firing of professionals being assimilated (professionals/day)
PRBA   = professionals being assimilated (professionals)
FFPRBA = fractional firing of professionals being assimilated (percent/day);

$$\text{FFPRBA.K} = \text{TABLE(TFFPBA,IFCPR.K}, -.001,$$
$$.001,.0005) \qquad\qquad 142, A$$
$$\text{TFFPBA} = .00075/.00025/0/0/0 \qquad\qquad 142.1, T$$

where
FFPRBA = fractional firing of professionals being assimilated (percent/day)
TFFPBA = table for fractional firing of professionals being assimilated (percent/day)
IFCPR = indicated fractional change in professionals (percent/day).

13.3 Understanding Problem Behavior Created by Growth in Professional Resources

In a growing market a company must expand its professional resources to service the increasing customer demand. But in expanding professional resources, the company adds to the number of professionals being assimilated and causes a reduction in professional efficiency and ability to service demand. The reduction in efficiency increases with the size of the company (because assimilation delay increases) and with the growth rate. How do different expansion policies influence growth, given the decrease in efficiency with growth? For the purpose of illustration, market demand grows by a constant 20 percent per year in the runs of this chapter.

The expansion policy described in section 13.2 calculates indicated professionals on the basis of a budget for professionals. The budget in turn depends on a forecast of customer order rate. A constant fraction of forecast revenues is allocated to professionals. Figure 13.5 (a and b) shows the consequence of such a policy.

In figure 13.15a market share declines steadily over the length of the simulation. Market share falls because effect of professional service level falls. Figure 13.5b indicates why.

In figure 13.5b professional service level declines steadily over the length of the simulation. Professional service level declines for two reasons. From day 0 to day 1200 service level declines in large part because professional efficiency falls below its initial value of 1.0. The decline in efficiency is the inevitable consequence of the positive fraction of professionals being assimilated associated with the expansion of professional effort. Initially fraction of professionals being assimilated equals 0. But the company perceives growth in customer order rate and the need to expand professionals (high indicated fractional change in professionals). New professionals are hired, and fraction professionals being assimilated rises to a nearly stable level of 0.08. But this increase causes professional efficiency to fall from its initial value of 1.0 to a nearly stable value of 0.95. Because efficiency falls, professionals cannot devote enough effort to servicing customers. As a result service level and market share fall.

Service level also falls because the company is basing forecast orders not on true customer demand but on orders suppressed below demand because of low service levels. This behavior is particularly evident after day 1440: even though efficiency remains constant, service level

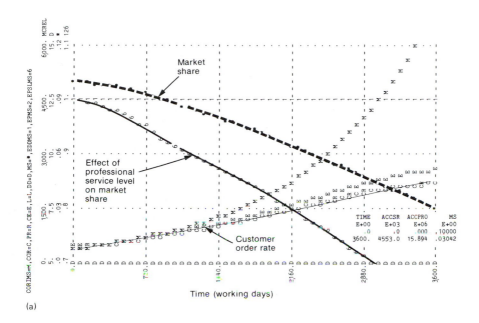

(a)

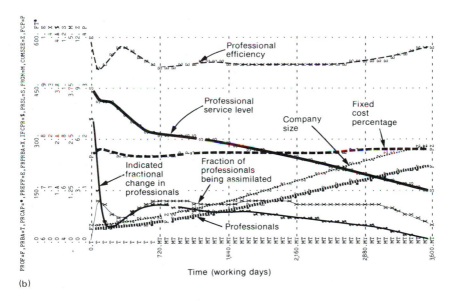

(b)

Figure 13.5   Model behavior with expansion budget based on forecast orders

falls. Service level falls because the company expands at a rate less than the rate of growth of the market. Customer order rate grows less than the market because service level is falling. In extrapolating customer order rate, the company budgets for professionals less than market requirements. Service level declines further in a downward spiral.

In summary a policy of professional expansion based on a fixed budget of forecast revenues leads to a continual erosion of market share. Any increase in growth rate causes professional efficiency to fall as more new professionals are hired. This results in a decline in service level and market share. Then the budgeting process causes a further loss of share when budgeting is conducted on the basis of a customer order rate suppressed, both in magnitude and growth rate, below demand by the decline in service level.

13.4 Improving Behavior through Policy Design

Budget Based on Adjusted Forecast

A solution to the problem of declining service levels is to adjust order rate for the estimated effect of professional service level on market share, as was done in chapter 11 for the estimated effect of delivery delay. Figure 13.6 shows the result of such an adjustment.[3]

The new policy is successful in stabilizing service level once efficiency levels off shortly after day 720. However, the policy introduces a new problem. Around day 1440 professional efficiency begins a steady decline. The cause of the decline is the increase in the fraction of professionals being assimilated. This fraction increases because the delay in assimilating professionals (not shown) increases with company size.

As the company grows, the expansion of professionals at a constant rate causes the fraction of professionals being assimilated to increase—with the increasing assimilation delay a constant growth rate causes a larger pool of professionals being assimilated. A similar problem did not occur in the prior simulation run, figure 13.5, because growth rate slowed (as indicated by indicated fractional change in professionals). But in figure 13.6 the company tries to grow as fast as the

3. Figure 13.6 assumes an accurate adjustment. In practice policy design would consider the consequences of inaccurate adjustments.

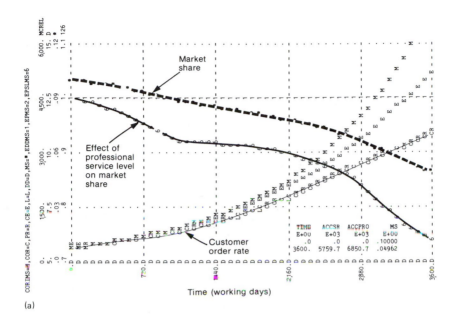

(a)

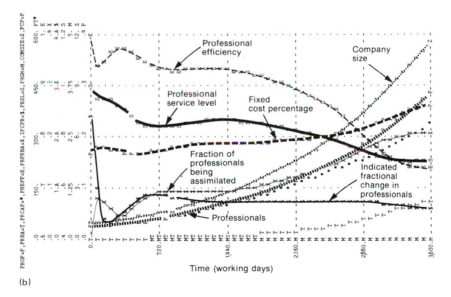

(b)

Figure 13.6   Model behavior with expansion budget based on adjusted forecast

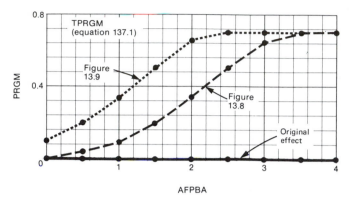

Figure 13.7   Professional growth margin

market. The attempt is unsuccessful because efficiency declines.[4] Moreover, as efficiency, service level, and market share decline, the fraction of the present budget allocated to professionals (fixed cost percentage) grows because the company is achieving proportionately less sales for the same professional staff.

The company is seemingly faced with a dilemma—to maintain efficiency (and profitability if prices are not increased), a company must slow its growth rate as size increases; attempts to grow at a constant rate eventually cause a decline in efficiency and market share anyway but with decreased profitability. Can the company continue to grow at a constant rate even though efficiency declines? As will be demonstrated, the answer is yes, but at a price.

Budget Based on Adjusted Forecast Plus Growth Margin

One way to offset the decline in efficiency is to hire enough extra professionals so that the decline is offset by sheer numbers. For example, professional growth margin can be tied to average fraction of professionals being assimilated, as shown in figure 13.7. Because efficiency depends on this fraction, the company can offset the decline by increasing professionals as the fraction increases.

Figure 13.8 shows model response with such a policy. In terms of market share and service levels the response is only marginally better than the last policy. In terms of costs the response is much worse—

4. An implicit assumption in the model is that other companies expand or new companies form to offer good professional services.

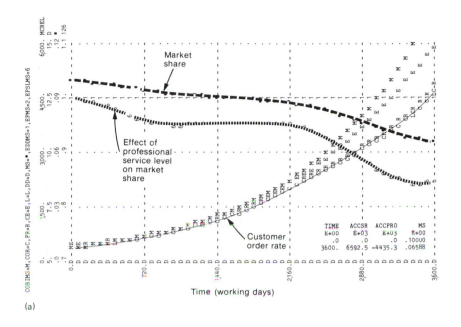

(a)

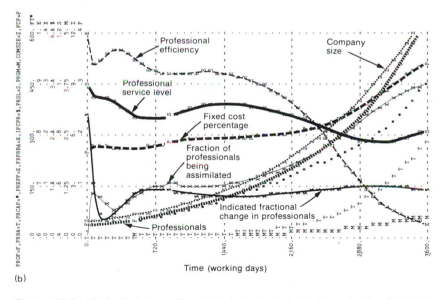

(b)

Figure 13.8   Model behavior with expansion budget based on adjusted forecast plus growth margin

professional efficiency is much lower, and as a result fixed cost percentage is higher. The company achieves a slightly higher service level and market share at much greater cost.

The reason that the improvement is so small is that the company waits for fraction of professionals being assimilated to increase before increasing the professionals growth margin. But given the one- to two-year delay in assimilating professionals, such a policy can only make matters worse in the short run: professionals being assimilated, not professionals, are in extra supply. As fraction of professionals being assimilated increases, the company hires more professionals to offset the unavoidable decline in efficiency. But hiring increases for one to two years the fraction being assimilated, further decreasing efficiency in the short run.

To implement effectively the extra professionals policy, the company must assimilate those professionals before they are needed. The dashed line in figure 13.7 represents a policy in which the company hires extra professionals before they are needed. Figure 13.9 shows the response of such a policy.

The policy is successful in maintaining market share. Although efficiency declines dramatically after day 1440, professional service level does not fall because of offsetting increases in the number of professionals.

The cost of such a policy is the cost of low efficiency and extra professionals. Implementation of the policy causes fixed cost percentage to increase. But such costs could be offset by price increases. Then the company faces the trade-off of losing market share due to high prices or low professional service level. Here the higher prices necessary to maintain profitability will cause loss of market share. On the other hand, not implementing the policy causes a loss of market share as a consequence of declining professional service levels. Simulation can provide a tool to assess the trade-off.

Summary

The results of section 13.4 lead to several conclusions about the relationship between professional resources and corporate growth:

1. Expansion policies based on historical growth rates and budget percentages can cause less than the growth in market demand because professional efficiency declines.

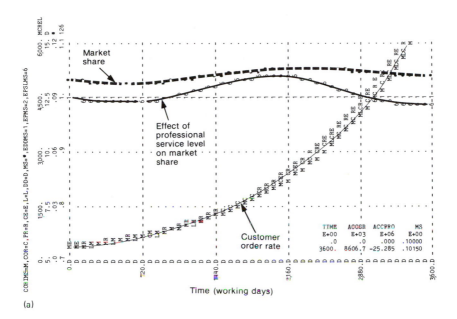

(a)

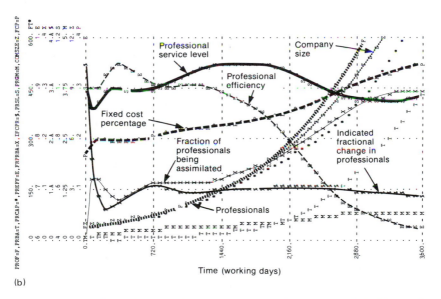

(b)

Figure 13.9   Model behavior with expansion budget based on adjusted forecast plus early assimilation of growth margin

2. Declining professional efficiency can be avoided by continually decreasing growth rates, but at the cost of lost market share.

3. Declining professional efficiency can be offset by assimilating extra professionals before the decline occurs, but at the cost of reduced profitability.

4. Market share can be lost with high prices or low service levels.

13.5 Other Dynamics Associated with Professional Resources

One purpose of this chapter is to introduce the complexities associated with professional resources. Several of these complexities are listed in this section.

Influence of Company Size on Efficiency

As the company grows, more professional resources must be devoted simply to managing the organization. Information must be collected, processed, and disseminated; the various functional areas must be coordinated. The management allocation becomes greater the larger the company.

Further, the larger the company, the more employee motivation is likely to decline. In the smaller company everyone sees a personal contribution to company success, but in the larger company the employee may feel like an insignificant part of the total organization.

For both these reasons professional efficiency can decline with company size. Unless compensating actions are taken, growth rate will fall.

Allocation of Professional Resources

Besides the allocation of professional resources among marketing, research and engineering, and management, there exists the additional allocation to production. Professional resources allocated to production perform tasks such as designing plants, working out production problems, scheduling work, writing service manuals, and working with customers. Professional resources are another input to the production function.

Allocation, as well as acquisition, is a policy problem. The tendency among companies is to allocate resources, whether they be financial or personnel, to the biggest problem areas. When one problem is solved, resources are shifted to the next problem. But such an allocation scheme can itself create problem cycles. For example, sales are falling, so management attention is diverted from production to marketing. After a delay sales respond. Because of lack of management input, however, production is unable to meet the rising sales. Management effort is redirected toward production. Once production problems are solved, management awakens to find sales once again falling. Forrester (1962) examines such an allocation problem in a corporate growth setting.

References

Forrester, Jay W. 1962. A Model for the Study of Corporate Growth. System dynamics group memorandum D-434. Massachusetts Institute of Technology, Cambridge, Mass.

Packer, David W. 1964. *Resource Acquisition in Corporate Growth*. Cambridge, Mass.: The MIT Press.

Appendix A: Equation Structure of System Dynamics Models

This appendix briefly outlines the equation format used in system dynamics modeling. The focus here is on explaining the mechanics of constructing a system dynamics model as a minimum basis for understanding the equations given in the text. The conceptual and theoretical foundations of system dynamics are presented in Forrester (1961, 1968) and Goodman (1974).

In formal mathematical terms, system dynamics models are systems of discrete difference equations. Such systems have the general form:

$$L_t = L_{t-\Delta t} + \Delta(L_{t-\Delta t}) \tag{A.1}$$

$$\Delta(L_{t-\Delta}) = f(L_{t-\Delta t}). \tag{A.2}$$

In equation (A.1) L_t is the value of variable L at time t.[1] Equation (A.1) then indicates that the present value of L, denoted L_t, equals the previous value of the variable Δt time units ago, $L_{t-\Delta t}$, plus the change in L occurring over the interval $(t - \Delta t)$ to t. Equation (A.2) states that the change in L, denoted $(L_{t-\Delta t})$, is some function f of $L_{t-\Delta t}$. As discussed in section A.1, the time interval between computations, Δt, is chosen sufficiently small so that the behavior of L over time approximates that of a continuous system.

A.1 Computation Sequence

The following section outlines the principle features of the DYNAMO computer language and the computation scheme used to trace the be-

Source: Appendixes A and B are taken from Nathaniel J. Mass, 1975, *Economic Cycles: An Analysis of Underlying Causes* (Cambridge, Mass.: Wright-Allen Press, Inc.), appendixes C and D, with permission of the author.

1. For readers with a background in matrix algebra, the variable L may be thought of as a vector of variables L_1 through L_n, with equations (A.1) and (A.2) describing the behavior of the entire vector defined by L.

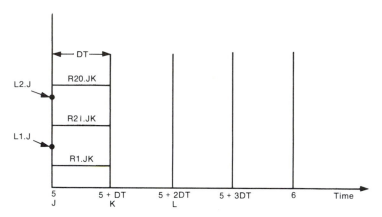

Figure A.1   Start of new computation sequence

havior of a system dynamics model.[2] The computation progresses in time steps as in Figure A.1. The figure assumes that the computations at time 5 have been completed, ready to begin computing the condition of the system at the next solution period, 5 + DT. The symbol DT, difference in time, is used for the length of the time interval between computations. The 5 and the 6 in the figure represent the units of time used in defining the system, for example, weeks or months, but the appropriate solution interval need not be the same as the unit of time measurement. The figure illustrates a situation where there are four computations of system condition in each unit of time.

As shown in figure A.1, the arbitrary convention has been adopted of using K to designate the point in time to which the current computation applies. The time 5 + DT is designated by the K as being the point in the time sequence now being evaluated. Correspondingly J is used to designate the time at which the preceding computation was made, and L to designate the next point in time. The equations are so structured that no other points in time need enter into the computation process. The computation is confined completely to the time J, the interval JK from J to K, the time K, and the interval KL.

At the start of the computations at time K, there are available from the previous computations the levels at time J and the rates of flow that existed over the interval JK. In figure A.1 the levels L1.J and L2.J

2. Most of the succeeding material is drawn from Forrester (1968), with permission of the author and publisher.

designate two values of levels (system states) at time J.[3] Also illustrated are three rates that existed over the time interval JK: the rate R1.JK flowed into level L1 and is the only rate that affected level L1; the rate R2I.JK flowed into level L2; and the rate R2O.JK flowed out of level L2.

The rates of flow are expressed in the time units of the system, such as dollars per week (in figure A.1 the time unit is from 5 to 6), not in terms of the solution interval DT. The selection of a solution interval DT is a technical matter to be discussed later and usually can be specified only after the model has already been constructed in terms of the time unit that is customarily used in the real system being represented.

In figure A.1 all the information is available that is needed to compute the new values of levels at time K. But the new values of rates for the KL interval cannot yet be computed because they depend on the not-yet-available levels at time K. The constant rates of flow during the JK interval acted on the levels beginning at time J and caused the levels to change at a uniform slope over the interval. The new values of levels are found by adding and subtracting the changes represented by the rates. The changes are found by multiplying the rates by the solution time interval. For example, the change in inventory in a one-quarter-month solution interval caused by production rate of 800 cartons per month would be 200 cartons added to inventory. All the levels can be computed. The sequence of computation does not matter because each level depends only on its own old value and on rates in the JK interval. No level depends directly on any other level. Finishing the computation of levels creates the situation in figure A.2, where the new levels for time K are now available. Although no values are actually computed except at the discrete solution intervals separated by DT, the nature of the rate and level equations implies that the constant rates have caused continuously changing levels, as shown by the dashed lines. Levels are continuous curves in the form of connected straight-line sections that can change slope at the solution times.

Only the present values of levels at time K are needed to compute the forthcoming rates that represent the action during the KL interval,

3. As discussed in section A.2, a "level" or a "stock" variable is an accumulation, such as a bank balance, an inventory of goods, or a level of employment. A "rate" is a flow that either increases or decreases a level. For example, a bank balance (a level) is increased by the rate of deposit of money (measured in dollars per unit time) and by the rate of accrual of interest. The bank balance is decreased through the withdrawal rate of money.

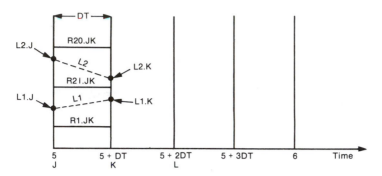

Figure A.2   After computation of levels

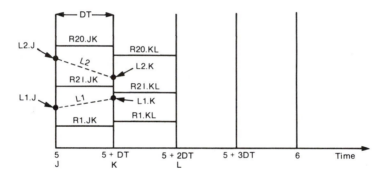

Figure A.3   After computation of rates

for the forthcoming action is based only on the currently available information at time K. Once all levels are computed, the rates can be computed. The order in which the rates are computed does not matter because they do not depend on one another. All the information needed for all the rates is available in the levels at time K.

The computation of the new rates brings the situation to that in figure A.3. The rates of flow are thought of as constant over a solution interval and change discontinuously to a new value at the solution time. The solution intervals are taken short enough that the stepwise discontinuities in rates are of no significance. Figure A.3 shows the completion of the computations at time K. The entire process is now repeated for the next point in time. To do this, the first step is to advance the time designators, J, K, and L, by one solution interval as shown in figure A.4. Relative to the new position of K, the conditions are the same as in figure A.1. The levels have become the J levels, and the KL rates have become the JK rates. The levels at time J and the rates for

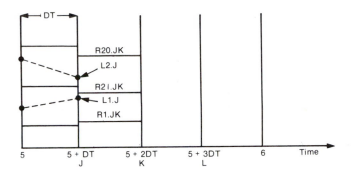

Figure A.4   Time designators advanced to next solution interval

the interval JK are available, and the new values of levels can be computed.

A variation from the level-rate sequence of computation occurs at the beginning time, $t = 0$, for a simulation series. The initial values of all levels must be given. The rates before time $= 0$ are immaterial. With the levels already available, the computation begins by computing the rates for the interval from time $= 0$ to time $= 0 + DT$. Thereafter the full cycle of computing first the levels and then the rates is followed.

A.2 Level Equations

A level equation represents a reservoir to accumulate the rates of flow that increase and decrease the content of the reservoir. The new value of a level is calculated by adding to or subtracting from the previous value the change that has occurred during the intervening time interval. The following format is used for a level equation:[4]

$$L.K = L.J + (DT)(RA.JK - RS.JK) \hspace{3cm} L$$

where

L   = level (units)
L.K   = new value of level being computed at time K (units)
L.J   = value of level from previous time J (units)
DT   = the length of the solution interval between time J and time
         K (time measure)
RA   = rate being added to level L (units/time measure)

4. An L at the right side of an equation denotes an equation defining a level variable.

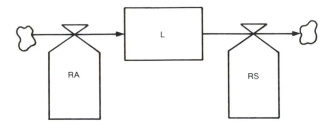

Figure A.5   A level variable with a single inflow and a single outflow

RA.JK = value of the rate added during the JK time interval
(units/time measure)

RS   = rate being subtracted from level L (units/time
measure)

RS.JK = value of the rate subtracted during the JK time interval
(units/time measure).

A flow diagram of the level L and rates RA and RS is shown in figure
A.5. The level is represented as a rectangle, and the rates of flow as
valves. The solid line through RA into L indicates that RA is an inflow
rate to L. The flow originates in a cloud. Such a cloud symbol represents a source. The designation of the source of the flow with a cloud
indicates that the flow originates outside the boundary of the system
studied.[5] Analogously the flow into the cloud at the right of figure A.5
represents a destination, or sink, lying outside the system boundary.[6]

Any number of rates, one or more, can be added to or subtracted
from a level. This is the only flexibility permissible in the standard level
equation. The right-hand side of the equation must contain the previous
value of the level being computed. It must also contain the solution
interval DT as a multiplier of the flow rates. The level equation is the
only equation type that properly contains the solution interval DT.

The solution interval DT is a parameter of the computing process,
not a parameter of the real system that the model represents. The flow
rates of the system, measured in units per time (for example, dollars
per year, or men per month) are accumulated in steps or batches over
the successive time intervals of DT in length. The solution interval DT,

5. See Forrester (1961) for a discussion of the criteria for selecting a model
boundary.

6. A flow between two levels within the system boundary would be represented by a solid line from the source level to the designation level.

measured in units of time, converts the flow rates to a quantity of the item flowing. It is this product of flow rate multiplied by time that creates the correct units of measure for adding to the value of the levels. The solution interval can be arbitrarily changed (if it does not become too long) without affecting the validity of the model.[7] All other equations in the model are formulated in terms of the basic unit of time used in the real system. The solution interval DT should not appear in any equation other than a level equation.

The level equation performs the process of integration. In the notation of calculus and differential equations, the preceding level equation would be written as follows:

$$L_t = L_0 + \int_0^t (\text{RA} - \text{RS})dt,$$

where

L_t = the value of the level at any time t (units)
L_0 = the initial value of the level at $t = 0$
$\int_0^t$ = the operator indicating integration or accumulation from time
        = 0 until time = t of the difference in flow rates ($\text{RA} - \text{RS}$)
RA = the flow rate being added
RS = the flow rate being subtracted
dt = the differential operator representing the infinitesimally small difference in time that multiplies the flow rates (corresponds to the coarser time steps represented by DT).

As described at the beginning of appendix A, a level equation is also known as a first-order difference equation in the branch of mathematics dealing with step-by-step integration.

A.3 Rate Equations

Rate equations state how the flows within a system are controlled. The output of a rate equation controls a flow to, from, or between levels.

Following the time notation of section A.2, the rate equation is computed at time K,using the information from levels at time K, to find the forthcoming flow rates for the KL interval.

The form of a rate equation is

$\text{R.KL} = f(\text{levels and constants}),$

7. See Forrester (1961, section 7.5 and appendix D), for a discussion of the criteria for selecting DT.

where the right-hand side implies any function, or relationship, of levels and constants that describes the policy controlling the rate.

The rate equations are policy statements that tell how decisions are made. The policy (rate equation) is the general statement of how the pertinent information is to be converted into a decision (or flow or present action stream, all being synonymous terms). The rate equations tell how the system controls itself.

The words policy and decision have broader meanings here than in common usage. They go beyond the usual human decisions and include the control processes that are implicit in system structure and in habit and tradition. A rate equation (or policy statement) might describe how the hiring rate in a firm depends on the level of vacancies and the level of available unemployed. A rate equation could also represent the subjective and intuitive responses of people to the social pressures within an organization; or a rate equation might represent the explicit policies that control inventory ordering on the basis of current inventory and the average sales rate.

The rate equations are more subtle than the level equations. The rate equations state our perception of how the real-system decisions respond to the circumstances surrounding the decision point.

A.4 Auxiliary Equations

Very often the clarity and meaning of a rate equation can be enhanced by dividing it into parts that are written as separate equations. These parts, called auxiliary equations, are algebraic subdivisions of the rates.

Suppose that desired inventory in an inventory-ordering equation is a variable that depends on the average sales rate. A flow diagram of the system appears in figure A.6.[8] The rate equation for ordering and the

8. In the flow diagram circles represent auxiliary variables. Information links, shown as dashed lines, are drawn from any level or auxiliary variable to each auxiliary and rate variable it affects. Thus, for example, in figure A.6 an information link is drawn from inventory I to order rate OR. Constants are shown in flow diagrams by short solid lines above or beneath the name; the lines are connected by information links to all rates or auxiliary variables that depend on the particular constant. Thus, for example, figure A.6 shows that desired inventory DI depends on the constant WID. Finally, in figure A.6 the average sales rate ASR is shown enclosed in parentheses with an information link to DI. The parentheses indicate that the determinants of ASR lie outside the flow diagram being considered.

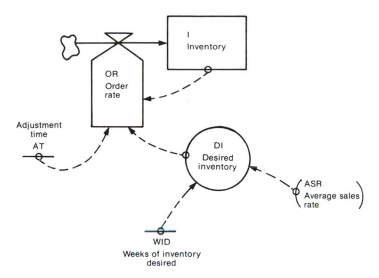

Figure A.6   A simple inventory control model

accompanying auxiliary equation for desired inventory could then be

$$OR.KL = \frac{1}{AT}(DI.K - I.K) \qquad\qquad R$$

$$DI.K = (WID)(ASR.K) \qquad\qquad A$$

where

OR = order rate (units per week)
DI   = desired inventory (units)
I   = inventory (units)
WID = weeks of inventory desired (weeks)
ASR = average sales rate (units per week).

In the preceding equation WID is a constant, the value of which states the desired inventory in terms of weeks of average sales. The expression for DI can be substituted into the rate equation to create the following rate equation that depends only on levels and constants:[9]

9. An average sales rate is a level variable. A simple test to distinguish levels and rates is the following. Suppose all action in the system halted. Then all rates of flow would be zero, but all level variables would continue to exist. Thus, for example, if all activity in a firm stopped, there would be no sales rate, but the average sales rate over the previous year or month would still exist. See Forrester (1961, 1968) for a further discussion of level and rate variables.

$$OR.KL = \frac{1}{AT}[(WID)(ASR.K) - I.K].$$ R

In this form the auxiliary equation has disappeared.

Auxiliary equations must be evaluated after the level equations on which they depend, and before the rate equations of which they are a part. When auxiliary equations exist—and they ordinarily will be numerous—the computation is in the sequence of levels, auxiliaries, and rates.

Unlike the levels and rates, auxiliary equations can depend on other auxiliary equations in a chain, so some groups of equations may have to be evaluated in a particular order. When there are interlinked chains of auxiliary equations, they must be evaluated in the sequence that permits successive substitution. Such a sequence will always exist in a properly formulated system.

A.5 Constant and Initial Value Equations

Constants

A constant, represented by a symbolic name, is given a numerical value in a constant equation. It carries the type designator C after the equation number. A constant has no time postscript because it does not change through time.

$$SY.K = (AB)(Z.K)$$ A

$$AB = 15.$$ C

The value of the constant AB is given in the preceding constant equation. In model listings the equation number of a constant will be given as a decimal subdivision of the primary equation number in which the constant first appears.

Initially Computed Constants

It is often convenient to specify one constant in terms of another constant when the two constants always bear a fixed relationship to each other. Suppose the constant CD is always to be 14 times the value of AB. CD would then be written as

$$CD = (14)(AB).$$ N

The type designator N (the same as for the initial value equations that give the initial values of levels) indicates that this equation need be evaluated only once at the beginning of the simulation computation, because the constants, by their very nature and definition, are values that are not to vary during any one simulation run.

Initial Value Equations

All level equations must be given initial values at the start of the simulation computation. These level variables represent the complete condition of the system necessary for determining the forthcoming flow rates. All system history that influences present action is represented by present values of appropriate level variables. It is the present version of history represented in the present values of system levels that governs present action. Initial values for rate variables need not and should not be given because they are fully determined by the initial values of the level variables.

From the initial values of level variables the rates of flow immediately following time zero can be computed, and with the initial values and the rates the new values of levels at the end of the first time step can be computed. The initial value equation will carry the type designator N after the equation number. No time postscripts are used. The right side of the initial value equation is written in terms of numerical values, symbolically indicated constants, and the initial values of other levels. An initial value equation is customarily written immediately following the corresponding level equation:

$$PT.K = PT.J + (DT)(M.JK - N.JK) \qquad\qquad L$$

$$PT = 8. \qquad\qquad N$$

The initial value equation above could also have been written in terms of constants as

$$PT = (3)(CD) \qquad\qquad N$$

or

$$PT = AB. \qquad\qquad N$$

It is unambiguous and permissible to state an initial value of one level equation in terms of the initial value of some other level as long as the latter is independent of the first. For example, the following initial value depends on the initial value of the variable PT.

$$RS.K = RS.J + (DT)(ML.JK - NL.JK) \qquad\qquad L$$

$$RS = PT. \qquad\qquad N$$

A.6 Table Equations

A table equation (table function) gives the numerical values of a dependent variable as a function of an independent variable over a specified range. Such equations represent a simple way of expressing relationships, particularly nonlinear relations, between variables. For example, suppose that the average lifetime of capital equipment in a firm is a function of the need for capital as measured by a variable called the capital ratio CR. A simple model of this process is given in the equations.

ALC.K = (NLC)(MCDLC.K)   71, A
NLC = 15   71.1, C

where
ALC   = average lifetime of capital (years)
NLC   = normal lifetime of capital (years)
MCDLC = multiplier from capital demand on lifetime of capital
              (dimensionless).

MCDLC.K = TABLE(TMCDLC,CR.K,∅,2,.5)   72, A
TMCDLC = 1.4/1.15/1/.85/.75   72.1, T

where
MCDLC   = multiplier from capital demand on lifetime of capital
              (dimensionless)
TMCDLC = table for multiplier from capital demand on lifetime of
              capital
CR   = capital ratio (dimensionless).

   In these equations the average lifetime of capital ALC equals a normal lifetime times a multiplier from capital demand on the lifetime of capital MCDLC. MCDLC, in turn, is specified as a table (TABLE) function of the capital ratio (figure A.7). The table TMCDLC gives the values of MCDLC for corresponding values of CR between 0 and 2 at intervals of 0.5. Thus, for example, if CR is 0, MCDLC has a value of 1.4; when CR is 0.5, MCDLC equals 1.15, and so on. If CR takes on a value intermediate between two points, say 0.2, a corresponding value of MCDLC is obtained by extrapolating linearly between the two values in the table function, here yielding a value of 1.3 [= 1.15 + (1.4 − 1.15)(0.2/0.5)]. If CR exceeds the specification range (say, it equals 4), MCDLC will assume the corresponding extreme value of the table

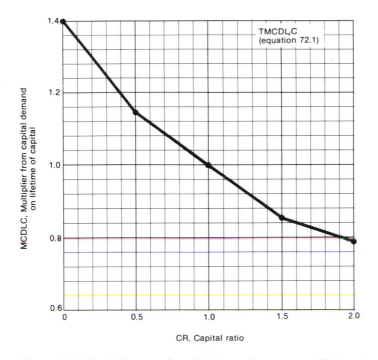

Figure A.7   The influence of capital demand on average lifetime of capital

function (here 0.75, meaning that the average lifetime of capital is never below 75 percent of its normal life).

A.7 Specification Cards

To simulate a model and plot the resulting output, several constants must be specified: the solution interval for the simulation (the DT), the total length of the simulation (denoted LENGTH), and the interval between successive plot-outs of a variable (denoted plot period or PLTPER); in addition, the variables to be plotted must be listed on plot cards. A sample set of specification cards could appear as

```
DT = .1                                                         C
LENGTH = 40                                                     C
PLTPER = 1                                                      C
PLOT HR = H(400,1200).
```

In these equations DT, LENGTH, and PLTPER are all defined as constants. The LENGTH of the simulation is 40 years and PLTPER is

1 year, so 40 values of each variable will be plotted. In the simple example above only one variable, hiring rate HR, is plotted. The PLOT statement designates that HR should be plotted with the symbol H on a scale of 400 to 1,200 men per year. If no range for a particular output variable is specified, the DYNAMO compiler will automatically set the vertical plot scales.

References

Forrester, Jay W. 1961. *Industrial Dynamics*. Cambridge, Mass.: The MIT Press.

Forrester, Jay W. 1968. *Principles of Systems*. Cambridge, Mass.: Wright-Allen Press.

Goodman, Michael R. 1974. *Study Notes in System Dynamics*. Cambridge, Mass.: Wright-Allen Press.

Appendix B: Delays

This appendix provides a brief introduction to the formulation and behavior of delays. "A delay," as described by Forrester,

is essentially a conversion process that accepts a given inflow rate and delivers a resulting flow rate at the output. The outflow may differ instant by instant from the inflow rate under dynamic circumstances where the rates are changing in value. This necessarily implies that the delay contains a variable amount of the quantity in transit. The content of the delay increases whenever the inflow exceeds the outflow, and vice versa.

A delay is a special, simplified category of the general concept of inventories or levels. All levels exist to permit the inflow rates to differ, over limited intervals, from the outflow rates.[1]

The delays typically used in system dynamics modeling belong to the class of exponential delays. These delays are simple in form and simulate real-world delay processes in a fairly realistic manner.[2] Section B.1 discusses the formulation of material delays. Section B.2 discusses information delays (exponential averages) and describes the basic relationships between information and material delays.

B.1 Material Delays

The first-order material delay consists simply of a level (which absorbs the difference between the inflow and outflow rates) and an outflow rate that depends on the level and on an average delay time. The

1. Forrester (1961), p. 86.

2. This appendix discusses only the simplest form of exponential delays, termed first-order delays. (See ibid., chapter 9 and appendix H for a discussion.) In the economic and econometric literature, first-order exponential delay formulations are frequently called Koyck transformations.

outflow rate of a material delay equals the level divided by the average delay time (which may in principle be either a constant or a variable):

$$\text{OUT.KL} = \text{LEV.K/DEL} \qquad\qquad\qquad\qquad\qquad\qquad \text{R}$$

where
OUT = outflow from delay
LEV = level measuring contents of delay
DEL = average delay time.

The representation of a material delay also includes an equation to generate the level representing the total amount of goods, money, or people in transit. Taken together, the level and overflow rate equations serve to convert an inflow rate IN into a delayed outflow OUT, as follows:

$$\text{LEV.K} = \text{LEV.J} + (\text{DT})(\text{IN.JK} - \text{OUT.JK}) \qquad\qquad\qquad \text{L}$$

where
LEV = level measuring contents of delay
IN = inflow to delay
OUT = outflow from delay.

As an example of a material delay, we might consider the response of a firm's hiring rate to its new vacancy creation rate. In figure B.1

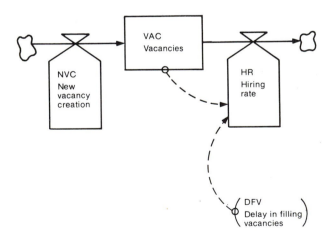

HR.KL = VAC.K/DFV.K   R
VAC.K = VAC.J + (DT) (NVC.JK - HR.JK)   L

Figure B.1 The hiring rate as a delayed version of vacancy creation

the rate of new vacancy creation NVC augments the level of vacancies VAC. The hiring rate HR is an outflow from the vacancy level and equals the level of vacancies VAC divided by the delay in filling vacancies DFV. Thus, for example, if DFV is 4 weeks, then one-quarter of all vacancies would be filled, on average, each week. The level of vacancies therefore represents a delay between new-vacancy creation (representing the decision to hire people) and the actual hiring rate.

A first-order delay, as in figure B.1, responds to a step increase in the inflow rate as shown in figure B.2. In figure B.2 the output of the delay gradually rises toward the input rate and eventually equals it. The delay characteristics of the system are represented by the interval during which the output variable lags behind the input.

In most industrial applications material delays are represented by third-order rather than first-order delays. A third-order delay consists of three cascaded first-order delays of delay time one-third the total delay, as shown in figure B.3a. Rather than writing out the equations for three first-order delays, however, DYNAMO has a built in function called DELAY3 which allows the modeler to write

OUT.KL = DELAY3(IN.JK,DEL).   R

In diagraming a model, a third-order delay is similarly abbreviated as in figure B.3b.

Figure B.4 compares the step response of a third-order delay to a first-order delay. The third-order delay starts with zero slope, rises

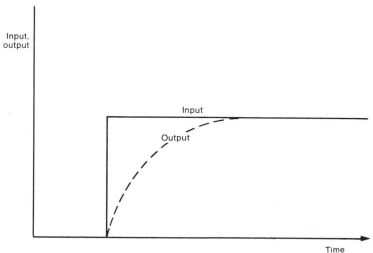

Figure B.2   Step response of a first-order material delay

(a)

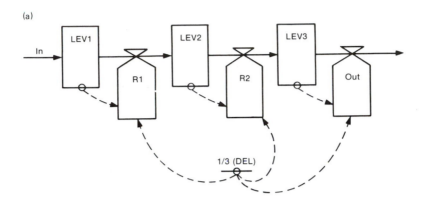

(b)

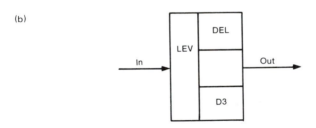

Figure B.3   Third-order exponential delay (from Forrester 1961)

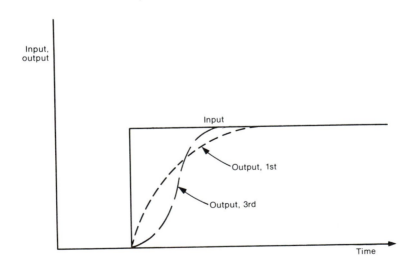

Figure B.4   Comparison of step response of first- and third-order material delay

more slowly at first, then rises more quickly around the average delay before tapering off. The response of a third-order delay more nearly approximates physical processes in which very little arrives just after the process is started, most arrives around the average delay, and some arrives after. Sharper responses can be achieved by cascading third-order delays.

B.2 Information Delays

Information delays, also called exponential averages, arise in any channel when data are smoothed or averaged in an effort to detect underlying trends. Smoothing or averaging necessarily introduces some delay in decision making, as decisions are normally deferred until persistent or stable patterns are detected; for example, increased orders for a firm's product may only lead to an expansion of output if the higher order rate persists for several weeks or months.

Information delays are represented in system dynamics models in the following manner:

$$OUT.K = OUT.J + (DT/DEL)(IN.JK - OUT.J) \qquad\qquad L$$

where
OUT = output of delay
DEL = average delay time
IN = input to the delay.

In the preceding equations, IN is the variable being smoothed; OUT is the smoothed value of IN. OUT equals its previous value (OUT.J) plus a correction term that is proportional to the difference between the input and output. Thus, if the input IN exceeds the output, OUT will gradually increase toward it over time. Analogously, if OUT exceeds IN, OUT will decline toward it. The delay time DEL measures the interval over which the adjustment takes place. A long delay time will produce a gradual adjustment, thereby heavily smoothing the data to filter out random noise from the observations of IN; analogously a short delay time will produce rapid adjustment and consequently low smoothing.[3]

3. The information delay can also be written in a simpler form:

$$OUT.K = SMOOTH(IN.JK,DEL). \qquad\qquad A$$

The DYNAMO compiler will automatically convert this notation into the equations given in the text.

The first-order information delay has the same time response as a first-order material delay with the same delay time. In fact the information and material delays are identical if the delay time DEL is constant over time. This equivalence can be seen by rewriting the equations in section B.1 to "solve" for the output OUT in terms of the input IN. Rewriting the output equation one time-period earlier:

OUT.JK = LEV.J/DEL.

Solving for LEV.J now yields

LEV.J = (OUT.JK)(DEL).

Substituting into the level equation,

LEV.K = (OUT.JK)(DEL) + (DT)(IN.JK − OUT.JK).

Finally, substituting for LEV.K and dividing by DEL yields

OUT.KL = OUT.JK + (DT/DEL)(IN.JK − OUT.JK).

The last equation is of the same form as the first-order information delay. The information and material delays differ only when the delay time DEL is in itself a variable. By analyzing the respective equations for information and material delays, the reader can verify that the output of an information delay is unaffected if its delay time is altered, while the output of a material delay is changed if its delay time changes.[4] The explanation for these results is stated by Forrester:

A material delay should not lose or create any units in the flow that is traveling through it. This means that in a material delay with a constant inflow rate the outflow will exhibit a transient change if the delay constant is changed. It is necessary that the output should differ from the input for a time long enough for the internal level stored in the delay to be adjusted. . . .

On the other hand, in delaying the flow of a constantly repeated value of information, this value should not change merely because the transmission delay is changed.[5]

Reference

Forrester, Jay W. 1961. *Industrial Dynamics*. Cambridge, Mass.: The MIT Press.

4. See Forrester (1961), appendix H, for a detailed discussion.

5. Ibid., p. 418.

Appendix C: Equation Listing and Rerun Control for Final Model

```
ITID13.DYNAMO
00001 *      ITID13
00002 NOTE
00003 NOTE     PRODUCTION INVENTORY SYSTEM MODEL
00004 NOTE        WITH VARIABLE SUPPLIER, LABOR, AND CAPITAL EQUIPMENT
00005 NOTE        AND MARKET SHARE DETERMINED BY DELIVERY AND PRICE
00006 NOTE        (ACCOUNTING AND FINANCE)
00007 NOTE
00008 NOTE     MODEL USED IN CHAPTER 13 OF
00009 NOTE     'INTRODUCTION TO INDUSTRIAL DYNAMICS'
00011 NOTE      BY JAMES M. LYNEIS
00012 NOTE
01001 MACRO PKNSE(MEAN,SDV,TC)
01010 L     PKNSE.K=PKNSE.J+(DT/TC)($G*NOISE()+MEAN-PKNSE.J)
01011 N     PKNSE=MEAN
01012 N     $G=SDV*SQRT(24*TC/DT)
01013 MEND
02001 MACRO TRND(INPUT,TOTRND,ITRND)
02010 A     TRND.K=($AIN1.K-$AIN2.K)/($AIN2.K*$TASI)
02020 L     $AIN1.K=$AIN1.J+(DT/$TSI)(INPUT.J-$AIN1.J)
02021 N     $AIN1=INPUT/(1+$TSI*ITRND)
02022 N     $TSI=.4*TOTRND
02030 L     $AIN2.K=$AIN2.J+(DT/$TASI)($AIN1.J-$AIN2.J)
02031 N     $AIN2=$AIN1/(1+$TASI*ITRND)
02032 N     $TASI=TOTRND-$TSI
02033 MEND
03001 MACRO DELAY3I(IN,DLY,PIPE,PIPEI)
03010 L     $LV1.K=$LV1.J+(DT)(IN.JK-$RT1.JK)
03011 N     $LV1=PIPEI/3
03020 R     $RT1.KL=$LV1.K/$DEL.K
03030 A     $DEL.K=DLY.K/3
03040 L     $LV2.K=$LV2.J+(DT)($RT1.JK-$RT2.JK)
03041 N     $LV2=$LV1
03050 R     $RT2.KL=$LV2.K/$DEL.K
03060 L     $LV3.K=$LV3.J+(DT)($RT2.JK-DELAY3I.J)
03061 N     $LV3=$LV1
03070 A     DELAY3I.K=$LV3.K/$DEL.K
03080 A     PIPE.K=$LV1.K+$LV2.K+$LV3.K
03081 MEND
03082 NOTE
03083 NOTE     PHYSICAL FLOWS
03084 NOTE
03085 NOTE
03086 NOTE          FINISHED INVENTORY
10020 L     FI.K=FI.J+(DT)(PCS.JK-SRS.JK)
10021 N     FI=DDFIN*CCOR
10022 NOTE          WORK-IN-PROCESS
10030 L     WIP.K=WIP.J+(DT)(PR.JK-PC.J)
10031 N     WIP=TCWIP*CCOR
```

```
10040 A     PC.K=DELAY3(PR.JK,TCWIP)
10041 C     TCWIP=20
10050 R     PR.KL=POLC.K*EP1LPR.K
10051 N     PR=CCOR
10060 A     POLC.K=POL.K*ECEPR.K
10070 A     ECEPR.K=TABHL(TECEPR,POL.K/CE.K,.8,2,.2)
10071 T     TECEPR=1/1/1/1/.875/.777/.7
10080 A     EP1LPR.K=TABHL(TEPIPR,DSPI.K,0,90.10)
10081 T     TEPIPR=0/.25/.5/.7/.85/.95/1/1/1
10090 A     DSPI.K=PI.K/(MAX(.001.POLC.K))
10100 A     POL.K=L.K*LPROD*OT.K
10101 C     LPROD=1
10102 NOTE            LABOR
10110 L     L.K=L.J+(DT)(LHR.JK+LFR.JK-LAR.JK)
10111 N     L=CCOR/LPROD
10120 R     LHR.KL=DELAY3(LHS.JK,LRD)
10121 C     LRD=20
10130 R     LAR.KL=L.K/ALE
10131 C     ALE=480
10140 L     LBR.K=LBR.J+(DT)(LHS.JK-LHR.JK)
10141 N     LBR=DLBR
10142 NOTE              PARTS INVENTORY
10150 L     PI.K=PI.J+(DT)(PAR.JK-PR.JK)
10151 N     PI=DDPI*CCOR
10152 NOTE              PARTS SUPPLIER PIPELINE
10160 L     POO.K=POO.J+(DT)(POR.JK-PAR.JK)
10161 N     POO=(PSPD+PSMSD)*CCOR
10162 NOTE            CAPITAL EQUIPMENT
10170 R     CES.KL=DELAY3I(CEA.JK,TSCE,CE.K,CEI)
10171 C     TSCE=2400
10172 N     CEI=CCOR*(1+CEGM)
10180 R     CEA.KL=DELAY3I(CEO.JK,TAQCE,CEOO.K,CEOO1)
10181 C     TAQCE=360
10182 N     CEOOI=(CEI/TSCE)*TAQCE
10183 NOTE            SHIPPING EQUATIONS
10190 R     SRS.KL=UOSS.K/TSS
10191 C     TSS=5
10200 L     UOSS.K=UOSS.J+(DT)(COSS.JK-SRS.JK)
10201 N     UOSS=TSS*CCOR
10210 R     COSS.KL=COR.K*FIOSS.K
10220 A     FIOSS.K=TABHL(TFIOSS.(UF1.K/ACORS.K),0,30.2.5)
10221 T     TFIOSS=0/.15/.3/.45/.55/.65/.725/.8/.875/.95/1/1/1
10230 A     UFI.K=FI.K-UOSS.K
10240 A     ACORS.K=SMOOTH(COR.K,20)
10250 R     PCS.KL=(1-FPRS.K)*PC.K
10260 R     SRP.KL=FPRS.K*PC.K
10270 A     FPRS.K=TABLE(TFPRS,DOSD.K/(TCWIP+TSS),0,1,.2)
10271 T     TFPRS=0/.3/.58/.8/.95/1
10280 A     DOSD.K=UOSD.K/PC.K
10290 L     UOSD.K=UOSD.J+(DT)(COSD.JK-SRP.JK)
10291 N     UOSD=0
10300 R     COSD.KL=COR.K*(1-FIOSS.K)
10310 A     UO.K=UOSS.K+UOSD.K
10311 NOTE
10312 NOTE    POLICIES
10313 NOTE
10314 NOTE            PRODUCTION RATE
10320 A     DPR.K=(BCOR.K+FIC.K+WIPC.K+UOC.K)*EFPDPR.K
10330 A     BCOR.K=(1+CORFT*OCORGR.K)*ACOR.K
10331 N     CORFT=TACOR+TCWIP
10340 A     OCORGR.K=TRND(COR.K,TOCORG,ICORGR)
10341 C     TOCORG=480
10342 C     ICORGR=0
10350 A     ACOR.K=SMOOTH(COR.K,TACOR)
10351 C     TACOR=60
10360 A     FIC.K=(FIG.K-FI.K)/TCFI
```

```
10361 C      TCFI=240
10370 A      FIG.K=DDFI.K*BCOR.K
10380 L      DDFI.K=DDFI.J+(DT/TDCT)((FI.J/ACORS.J)-DDFI.J)
10381 N      DDFI=DDFIN
10382 C      DDFIN=30
10383 C      TDCT=50000
10390 A      WIPC.K=(WIPG.K-WIP.K)/TCFI
10400 A      WIPG.K=TCWIP*BCOR.K
10410 A      UOC.K=(UO.K-DUO.K)/TCFI
10420 A      DUO.K=DDUO.K*BCOR.K
10430 A      DDUO.K=SMOOTH(DD.K,TDCT)
10431 N      DDUO=TSS
10432 NOTE             LABOR HIRING AND FIRING
10440 R      LHS.KL=MAX(0.IHR.K)*ECCHR.K
10450 R      LFR.KL=MIN(0,IHR.K)-FFMCC.K*L.K/12
10460 A      IHR.K=ALAR.K+(DL.K-L.K+DLBR.K-LBR.K)/TAL
10461 C      TAL=20
10470 A      ALAR.K=SMOOTH(LAR.JK,TALAR)
10471 C      TALAR=40
10480 A      DL.K=(DLS*SPR.K+(1-DLS)*BCORE.K*ECEDL.K)/LPROD
10481 C      DLS=0
10490 A      SPR.K=DPR.K*EPILSP.K*ECESPR.K
10491 N      SPR=CCOR
10500 A      EPILSP.K=TABHL(TEPlSP,PDSPI.K/DDSPIH,0,1,.1)
10501 T      TEPISP=0/.3/.5/.65/.75/.85/.9/.93/.96/.985/1
10502 C      DDSPIH=60
10510 A      PDSPI.K=SMOOTH(DSPI.K,TPDSPI)
10511 C      TPDSPI=20
10520 A      ECESPR.K=TABHL(TECESP.DPR.K/CE.K,.8,3,.2)
10521 T      TECESP=1/1/1/1/.875/.777/.7/.636/.58/.534/.5/.467
10530 A      DLBR.K=ALAR.K*LRD
10540 A      BCORE.K=(1+CORFTE*OCORGE.K)*ACORE.K
10541 N      CORFTE=TACORE+TCWIP+LRD
10550 A      ACORE.K=SMOOTH(COR.K,TACORE)
10551 C      TACORE=60
10560 A      OCORGE.K=TRND(COR.K,TOCORE,ICORGR)
10561 C      TOCORE=480
10570 A      ECEDL.K=TABHL(TECEDL,(LPROD*BCORE.K)/CE.K,.8.2,.2)
10571 T      TECEDL=1/1/.833/.714/.625/.555/.5
10572 NOTE             OVERTIME
10580 A      OT.K=TABHL(TOT,IOT.K,0,1.6,.2)*(1-DLS)+DLS
10581 T      TOT=0/.2/.4/.6/.8/1/1.2/1.35/1.4
10590 A      IOT.K=SPR.K/CNOTPR.K
10600 A      CNOTPR.K=L.K*LPROD
10601 NOTE             PARTS-ORDERING
10610 R      POR.KL=1POR.K*EMPO.K
10620 A      EMPO.K=TABHL(TEMPO,IPOR.K/PSPC.K,0,1,.2)
10621 T      TEMPO=0/.2/.4/.6/.8/1
10630 A      IPOR.K=(BPR.K+PIC.K+POC.K)*EFPPOR.K*ECCPO.K
10640 A      BPR.K=(1+PRFT.K*OPRGR.K)*APR.K
10650 A      PRFT.K=TAPRPO+PPSDT.K
10660 A      OPRGR.K=TRND(RPR.K,TOPRGR,IPRGR)
10661 C      TOPRGR=480
10662 C      IPRGR=0
10670 A      APR.K=SMOOTH(RPR.K,TAPRPO)
10671 C      TAPRPO=60
10680 A      RPR.K=(1-RPRSWT)*PR.JK+RPRSWT*DPR.K*ECESPR.K
10681 C      RPRSWT=1
10690 A      PIC.K=(PIG.K-Pl.K)/TCPI
10691 C      TCPI=240
10700 A      PIG.K=DDPI*BPR.K
10701 C      DDPI=60
10710 A      POC.K=(POOG.K-POO.K)/TCPI
10720 A      POOG.K=PPSDT.K*BPR.K
10730 A      PPSDT.K=SMOOTH(PSDT.K,TPPSDT)
10731 C      TPPSDT=60
```

```
10740 A     PSDT.K=PSPD.K+PSSD.K
10750 A     PSSD.K=PSOB.K/APSPS.K
10760 A     APSPS.K=SMOOTH(PSPS.JK,20)
10761 NOTE      FINANCIAL PRESSURES AND CONSTRAINTS
10770 A     EFPDPR.K=TABHL(TEFPPR,PAIT.K/AITG,0,2,.25)
10771 T     TEFPPR=1/1/1/1/1/1/1/1/1
10772 N     AITG=AIT
10780 A     EFPPOR.K=TABHL(TEFPPO,PAIT.K/AITG,0.2,.25)
10781 T     TEFPPO=1/1/1/1/1/1/1/1/1
10790 A     PAIT.K=SMOOTH(AIT.K,TPAIT)
10791 C     TPAIT=20
10800 A     ECCHR.K=TABHL(TECCHR,PEC.K,-1.0,.2)
10801 T     TECCHR=0/0/.1/.5/.9/1
10810 A     FFMCC.K=TABHL(TFFMCC,PEC.K,-1,0,.2)
10811 T     TFFMCC=.3/.2/.1/.05/0/0
10820 A     ECCPO.K=TABHL(TECCPO,PEC.K,-1,0,.2)
10821 T     TECCPO=0/.1/.5/.9/1/1
10822 NOTE      CAPACITY EXPANSION
10830 R     CEO.KL=CEOIDC.K*EDERCE.K
10840 A     CEOIDC.K=MAX(0,ICEO.K)
10850 A     ICEO.K=ACES.K+(DCE.K-CE.K+DCEOO.K-CEOO.K)/TACE
10851 C     TACE=60
10860 A     ACES.K=SMOOTH(CES.JK,TACES)
10861 C     TACES=120
10870 A     DCE.K=(1+CEGM.K)*FCORCE.K
10880 A     FCORCE.K=EACOR.K*(1+CEOFT*OCORGC.K)
10881 N     CEOFT=TACORC+TAQCE+TACE
10890 A     EACOR.K=SMOOTH(ECOR.K,TACORC)
10891 C     TACORC=240
10900 A     ECOR.K=COR.K/(EEDDCO.K*EEPCO.K*EEPSLM.K)
10910 A     EEDDCO.K=TABLE(TEEDDC,ADD.K/COMDD.K,0,4,.25)
10911 T     TEEDDC=1/1/1/1/1/.95/.85/.7/.5/.35/.25/.15/.1/.05/.025/.01/0
10920 A     ADD.K=SMOOTH(DDQC.K,TADD)
10921 C     TADD=60
10930 A     EEPCO.K=TABLE(TEEPCO,AVP.K/COMP.K,.75,1.25,.05)
10931 T     TEEPCO=1/1/1/1/1/1/1/1/1/1/1
10940 A     AVP.K=SMOOTH(P.K,TAVP)
10941 C     TAVP=60
10950 A     EEPSLM.K=TABLE(TEEPSM,APRSL.K,0,2,.1)
10951 T     TEEPSM=1/1/1/1/1/1/1/1/1/1/1/1/1/1/1/1/1/1/1/1/1
10960 A     APRSL.K=SMOOTH(PRSL.K,TAPRSL)
10970 A     OCORGC.K=TRND(EACOR.K,TOORGC,IORGRC)
10971 C     TOORGC=240
10972 C     IORGRC=.0008
10980 A     CEGM.K=TABLE(TCEGM,240*OCORGC.K,-1,1,.25)
10981 T     TCEGM=-.2/-.15/-.1/0/.1/.15/.2/.225/.25
10990 A     DCECO.K=TAQCE*ACES.K
11000 A     EDERCE.K=TABHL(TEDERC,PDERCP.K,0,4,.25)
11001 T     TEDERC=1/1/1/1/1/1/1/1/1/1/1/1/1
11010 A     PDERCP.K=SMOOTH(CDPER.K,TPDERC)
11011 C     TPDERC=60
11020 A     CDPER.K=CDAE.K/PEQ.K
11030 A     CDAE.K=CDEBT.K-TAQCE*ACFO.K
11040 A     CDEBT.K=TL.K+CEOO.K*CPUCE.K
11050 A     PEQ.K=EQ.K+TAQCE*ARE.K
11060 A     ARE.K=SMOOTH(RE.K,TARE)
11061 C     TARE=240
11062 NOTE      PRICING
11070 L     P.K=P.J+(DT)(CP.JK)
11071 N     P=PIN
11072 C     PIN=100
11080 R     CP.KL=PSWT*(IP.K-P.K)/TAP
11081 C     PSWT=0
11082 C     TAP=60
11090 A     IP.K=BP.K*ERIP.K*EDERP.K
11100 A     BP.K=PIN
11110 A     ERIP.K=TABLE(TERIP,ARFI.K,.5,1.5,.1)
```

```
11111 T      TERIP=1.25/1.2/1.15/1.1/1.05/1/.95/.9/.85/.8/.75
11120 A      ARFI.K=SMOOTH(RFI.K,TARFI)
11121 C      TARF1=60
11130 A      RFI.K=FI.K/FIG.K
11140 A      EDERP.K=TABLE(TEDERP,PDERCP.K,0,4,.25)
11141 T      TEDERP=1/1/1/1/1/1/1/1/1/1/1/1/1/1/1/1/1
11142 NOTE
11143 NOTE        PROFESSIONAL EFFORT
11144 NOTE
11150 A      PRCAP.K=PREAMR.K*PREFF.K
11160 A      PREFF.K=TABLE(TPREFF,FRPRBA.K,0,.4,.05)
11161 T      TPREFF=1/.975/.925/.85/.75/.675/.625/.6/.6
11170 A      FRPRBA.K=PRBA.K/TPR.K
11180 A      TPR.K=PRBA.K+PROF.K
11190 A      PREAMR.K=PREAVL.K
11200 A      PREAVL.K=PROF.K*PPROF+PRBA.K*PPRBA-PRER.K
11201 C      PPROF=1
11202 C      PPRBA=.25
11210 A      PRER.K=AHPR.K*TPRR
11211 C      TPRR=.025
11220 L      AHPR.K=AHPR.J+(DT/TAHPR)(HPR.JK-AHPR.J)
11221 N      AHPR=0
11222 C      TAHPR=20
11230 L      PROF.K=PROF.J+(DT)(ASSPR.JK-FPROF.JK)
11231 N      PROF=NRPCOR*CCOR
11232 C      NRPCOR=.1
11240 R      ASSPR.KL=PRBA.K/TAPROF.K
11250 A      TAPROF.K=TABLE(TTAPR,ACSZ.K,0,12,1)
11251 T      TTAPR=120/120/140/170/210/260/320/370/410/440/460/480/480
11260 A      ACSZ.K=SMOOTH(COMSZE.K,TACSZ)
11261 C      TACSZ=240
11270 A      COMSZE.K=CE.K/CEI
11280 L      PRBA.K=PRBA.J+(DT)(HPR.JK-ASSPR.JK-FPRBA.JK)
11281 N      PRBA=0
11290 R      HPR.KL=TPR.K*FHPR.K
11300 A      FHPR.K=TABLE(TFHPR,IFCPR.K,-.001,.004,.0005)
11301 T      TFHPR=0/0/0/.0005/.001/.0015/.002/.0025/.003/.0035/.004
11310 A      IFCPR.K=((IPROF.K-PROF.K-PRBA.K)/TADJPR)/TPR.K
11311 C      TADJPR=120
11320 A      IPROF.K=PRIB.K*(1+PRGM.K)
11330 A      PRIB.K=FBPR*FCORPR.K*P.K/FCPR
11331 C      FBPR=.17
11340 A      FCORPR.K=EACOR.K*(1+PROFT.K*OCORGC.K)
11350 A      PROFT.K=PTAPRO.K+TACORC
11360 A      PTAPRO.K=SMOOTH(TAPROF.K,TPTAPR)
11361 C      TPTAPR=480
11370 A      PRGM.K=TABLE(TPRGM,AFPBA.K,0,.4,.05)
11371 T      TPRGM=0/0/0/0/0/0/0/0/0/0
11380 A      AFPBA.K=SMOOTH(FRPRBA.K,TAFPBA)
11381 C      TAFPBA=480
11390 R      FPROF.KL=PROF.K*FFPR.K
11400 A      FFPR.K=TABLE(TFFPR,IFCPR.K,-.001,.001,.0005)
11401 T      TFFPR=.0005/.00025/0/0/0
11410 R      FPRBA.KL=PRBA.K*FFPRBA.K
11420 A      FFPRBA.K=TABLE(TFFPBA,IFCPR.K,-.001,.001,.0005)
11421 T      TFFPBA=.00075/.00025/0/0/0
11422 NOTE
11423 NOTE        PARTS SUPPLIER
11424 NOTE
11430 R      PAR.KL=DELAY3(PSPS.JK,PSPD.K)
11440 R      PSPS.KL=PSPC.K*PSPCUR.K
11441 N      PSPS=CCOR
11450 A      PSPCUR.K=TABHL(TPSCUR,PSDPR.K/PSPC.K,0,2,.25)
11451 T      TPSCUR=0/.25/.5/.75/1/1.15/1.25/1.3/1.3
11460 A      PSDPR.K=PSAPOR.K+PSOBC.K
```

```
11470 A      PSAPOR.K=SMOOTH(POR.JK,PSTAPO)
11471 C      PSTAPO=30
11480 A      PSOBC.K=(PSOB.K-PSDOB.K)/PSTCOB
11481 C      PSTCOB=60
11490 A      PSDOB.K=PSMSD*PSPC.K
11491 C      PSMSD=10
11500 L      PSOB.K=PSOB.J+(DT)(POR.JK-PSPS.JK)
11501 N      PSOB=PSMSD*CCOR
11510 L      PSPC.K=PSPC.J+(DT)(PSCPC.JK)
11511 N      PSPC=CCOR
11520 R      PSCPC.KL=(PSDPC.K-PSPC.K)/PSTAPC
11521 C      PSTAPC=480
11530 A      PSDPC.K=PSAPOR.K
11531 NOTE
11532 NOTE       MARKET SECTOR
11533 NOTE
11540 A      COR.K=MD.K*MS.K
11550 A      MS.K=TMS.K*EDDMS.K*EPMS.K*EPSLMS.K
11560 A      TMS.K=SMOOTH(MS.K,TDTMS)
11561 N      TMS=TMSI
11562 C      TMSI=.1
11563 C      TDTMS=960
11570 A      EDDMS.K=TABLE(TEDDMS,DDAC.K/COMDD.K,0,4,.25)
11571 T      TEDDMS=1/1/1/1/.95/.85/.7/.5/.35/.25/.15/.1/.05/.025/.01/0
11580 A      COMDD.K=TSS
11590 A      DDAC.K=SMOOTH(DDQC.K,TCADD)
11591 C      TCADD=60
11600 A      DDQC.K=SMOOTH(DD.K,TCPDD)
11601 C      TCPDD=20
11610 A      DD.K=UO.K/(SRS.JK+SRP.JK)
11620 A      EPMS.K=TABLE(TEPMS.PAC.K/COMP.K,.75.1.25,.05)
11621 T      TEPMS=1.6/1.4/1.25/1.15/1.05/1/.95/.85/.75/.6/.4
11630 A      COMP.K=PIN
11640 A      PAC.K=SMOOTH(P.K,TCAP)
11641 C      TCAP=60
11650 A      EPSLMS.K=TABLE(TEPSLM,DPRSL.K/COMPSL.K,0,2,.1)
11651 T      TEPSLM=0/.05/.1/.15/.25/.35/.5/.7/.85/.95/1/1.05/1.15/1.3/1.5/1.65
11652 X      /1.75/1.85/1.9/1.95/2
11660 A      DPRSL.K=SMOOTH(PRSL.K,TAPRSL)
11661 C      TAPRSL=480
11670 A      PRSL.K=UDSPRE.K/(MD.K*TMS.K)
11680 A      UDSPRE.K=NUDSPE*PRCAP.K
11681 C      NUDSPE=10
11690 A      COMPSL.K=1
11691 NOTE
11692 NOTE       FINANCIAL STATEMENTS AND POLICIES
11693 NOTE
11694 NOTE           BALANCE SHEET
11695 NOTE
11700 L      AR.K=AR.J+(DT)(DVS.J-COLL.J)
11701 N      AR=TCAR*DVS
11710 A      DVS.K=P.K*(SRS.JK+SRP.JK)
11720 A      COLL.K=AR.K/TCAR
11721 C      TCAR=40
11730 L      CASH.K=CASH.J+(DT)(NCF.J)
11731 N      CASH=DCASH
11740 A      NCF.K=CI.K-CO.K
11750 A      CI.K=COLL.K+STB.K+LTB.K+EQIS.K
11760 A      CO.K=APP.K+STP.K+LTP.K+INT.K+DIV.K+TAX.K+INVEST.K
11770 A      DVI.K=CFI.K*FI.K+CWIP.K*WIP.K+CPI.K*PI.K
11780 A      CFI.K=COSTP.K+VAASS.K
11790 A      VAASS.K=LC.K/APC.K
11800 A      APC.K=SMOOTH(PC.K,TAPCC)
11801 C      TAPCC=20
11810 A      CWIP.K=.5*COSTP.K+.5*CFI.K
```

```
11820 A      CPI.K=COSTP.K
11830 A      COSTP.K=COSTPI
11831 C      COSTPI=30
11840 A      CA.K=AR.K+CASH.K+DVI.K
11850 L      BVFA.K=BVFA.J+(DT)(INVEST.J-DEPR.J)
11851 N      BVFA=CE*CPUCE
11860 A      DEPR.K=BVFA.K/TDEPFA
11861 C      TDEPFA=2400
11870 A      TA.K=CA.K+BVFA.K
11871 NOTE
11880 L      AP.K=AP.J+(DT)(API.J APP.J)
11881 N      AP=TPAP*API
11890 A      API.K=CPAR.K+FC.K+LC.K
11900 A      CPAR.K=PAR.JK*COSTP.K
11910 A      APP.K=AP.K/TPAP.K
11920 A      TPAP.K=TPAPN*ECCPP.K
11921 C      TPAPN=30
11930 A      ECCPP.K=TABHL(TECCPP,PEC.K,-1,0..2)
11931 T      TECCPP=7/5/3/2/1.5/1
11940 L      STD.K=STD.J+(DT)(STB.J-STP.J)
11941 N      STD=(CA/CRI)-AP
11942 C      CRI=2.5
11950 A      CL.K=AP.K+STD.K
11960 L      LTD.K=LTD.J+(DT)(LTB.J-LTP.J)
11961 N      LTD=DERI*EQ-CL
11962 C      DERI=.5
11970 A      TL.K=CL.K+LTD.K
11980 L      EQ.K=EQ.J+(DT)(RE.J+EQIS.J)
11981 N      EQ=TA/(1+DERI)
11990 A      TLE.K=TL.K+EQ.K
11991 NOTE
11992 NOTE              INCOME STATEMENT
11993 NOTE
12000 A      RE.K=NPRO.K-DIV.K
12010 A      NPRO.K=GPRO.K-TAX.K
12020 A      TAX.K=GPRO.K*TR
12021 C      TR=.5
12030 A      GPRO.K=DVS.K-CMS.K-FC.K-DEPR.K-INT.K
12040 A      CMS.K=CFI.K*(SRS.JK+SRP.JK)
12050 A      LC.K=L.K*ASAL.K+MAX(OT.K-1,0)*L.K*1.5*ASAL.K+CLT.K
12060 A      ASAL.K=ASALN
12061 C      ASALN=40
12070 A      CLT.K=6*ASAL.K*(LHR.JK-LFR.JK)
12080 A      FC.K=FCPR*TPR.K
12081 C      FCPR=170
12090 A      INT.K=IR.K*(LTD.K+STD.K)/240
12100 A      IR.K=RFIR+RPDBT.K+AINFR.K
12101 C      RFIR=.02
12110 A      RPDBT.K=TABLE(TRPDBT,DER.K,0,4..5)
12111 T      TRPDBT=.015/.0175/.02/.0225/.025/.03/.04/.055/.075
12120 A      AINFR.K=SMOOTH(INFLR.K,TPINFI)
12121 C      TPINFI=240
12130 A      INFLR.K=INFLRI
12131 C      INFLRI=0
12132 NOTE
12133 NOTE              FINANCIAL RATIOS
12134 NOTE
12140 A      ROS.K=NPRO.K/DVS.K
12150 A      ROE.K=240*NPRO.K/EQ.K
12160 A      CR.K=CA.K/CL.K
12170 A      DER.K=TL.K/EQ.K
12180 A      AIT.K=240*DVS.K/DVI.K
12181 NOTE
12182 NOTE              FINANCING POLICIES
12183 NOTE
```

```
12190 A    STB.K=MAX(0,ICC.K)*ECRSTB.K*EDERSB.K
12200 A    ICC.K=(DCASH.K-CASH.K)/TACASH
12201 C    TACASH=10
12210 A    DCASH.K=DDDVSC*DVS.K
12211 C    DDDVSC=15
12220 A    ECRSTB.K=TABHL(TECRSB,CR.K,0,3,.5)
12221 T    TECRSB=0/.4/.7/.9/1/1/1
12230 A    EDERSB.K=TABHL(TEDERB,DER.K,0,4,.25)
12231 T    TEDERB=1/1/1/1/1/1/1/1/1/1/1/1/1/1/1/1/1
12240 A    STP.K=ISTP.K*ESTDP.K
12250 A    ISTP.K=(-1)*MIN(0,ICC.K)
12260 A    ESTDP.K=TABHL(TESTDP,STD.K/(MAX(.001,ISTP.K)).0.4,.5)
12261 T    TESTDP=0/.2/.4/.55/.7/.85/.95/1/1
12262 NOTE
12270 A    LTB.K=ILTF.K*PDF.K
12280 A    ILTF.K=MAX(0,INVEST.K+LTP.K-ACFO.K)
12290 A    INVEST.K=CEA.JK*CPUCE.K
12300 A    CPUCE.K=CPUCEN
12301 C    CPUCEN=6000
12310 A    ACFO.K=SMOOTH(CFO.K,TACFOB)
12311 C    TACFOB=240
12320 A    CFO.K=COLL.K-CO.K+INVEST.K+STP.K+LTP.K
12330 A    PDF.K=TABLE(TPDF,DER.K,0,4..25)
12331 T    TPDF=1/1/1/1/1/.95/.9/.8/.7/.5/.3/.2/.1/.05/0/0/0
12340 A    LTP.K=(LTD.K/ALTDM)*EECDP.K
12341 C    ALTDM=2400
12350 A    EECDP.K=TABHL(TEECDP,APEC.K,0,3..5)
12351 T    TEECDP=1/1.05/1.15/1.25/1.35/1.45/1.5
12360 A    APEC.K=SMOOTH(PEC.K,TAPEC)
12361 C    TAPEC=240
12370 A    PEC.K=(CASH.K-DCASH.K)/DCASH.K
12371 NOTE
12380 A    EQIS.K=ILTF.K*(1-PDF.K)*EQSWT
12381 C    EQSWT=1
12390 L    SP.K=SP.J+(DT)(CSP.JK)
12391 N    SP=ISP
12400 R    CSP.KL=(ISP.K-SP.K)/TASP
12401 C    TASP=20
12410 A    ISP.K=AEPS.K*PER.K
12420 A    AEPS.K=SMOOTH(EPS.K,TAEPS)
12421 C    TAEPS=240
12430 A    EPS.K=240*NPRO.K/SHARES.K
12440 L    SHARES.K=SHARES.J+(DT)(EQIS.J/SP.J)
12441 N    SHARES=100000
12450 A    PER.K=PERN*EROESP.K*EEGRSP.K*EDERSP.K
12451 C    PERN=10
12460 A    EROESP.K=TABLE(TEROES,AROE.K,0,.45,.05)
12461 T    TEROES=.1/1/1.85/2.6/3.25/3.75/3.85/3.95/4/4
12470 A    AROE.K=SMOOTH(ROE.K,TMAFV)
12471 C    TMAFV=480
12480 A    EEGRSP.K=TABHL(TEEGRS.AEGR.K,-.5,.7,.1)
12481 T    TEEGRS=.5/.6/.7/.8/.9/1/1.1/1.2/1.25/1.275/1.3/1.3/1.3
12490 A    AEGR.K=SMOOTH(EGR.K,TMAFV)
12500 A    EGR.K=240*TRND(NPRO.K,240.0)
12510 A    EDERSP.K=TABLE(TEDERS.ADER.K,0,4,.5)
12511 T    TEDERS=.9/.95/1/.95/.9/.85/.8/.75/.7
12520 A    ADER.K=SMOOTH(DER.K,TMAFV)
12521 NOTE
12530 L    DIV.K=DIV.J+(DT)(CDIV.JK)
12531 N    DIV=DIVPR*NPRO
12540 R    CDIV.KL=(IDIV.K-DIV.K)/TADIV
12541 C    TADIV=120
12550 A    IDIV.K=DIVPR.K*ANPRO.K
12560 A    ANPRO.K=SMOOTH(NPRO.K,240)
12570 L    DIVPR.K=DIVPR.J+(DT)(CDPR.JK)
12571 N    DIVPR=IDPR
```

```
12580 R     CDPR.KL=(IDPR.K-D1VPR.K)/TADPR
12581 C     TADPR=120
12590 A     IDPR.K=PRIROE.K*ECCDP.K
12600 A     PRIROE.K=TABHL(TPRIRE,ROE.K,0,.45,.05)
12601 T     TPRIRE=.75/.65/.55/.45/.35/.25/.15/.05/0/0
12610 A     ECCDP.K=TABHL(TECCDP,APEC.K,-1,1,.2)
12611 T     TECCDP=0/.1/.5/.9/1/1/1/1.1/1.2/1.25/1.3
12612 NOTE
12613 NOTE      TEST INPUTS
12614 NOTE
12615 NOTE          MARKET DEMAND
12620 A     MD.K=(CMD*(1+COGF.K))*(1+STEP(COSH.COST)+ACOS*SIN(6.28*TIME.K/PCOS
12621 X     )+ACOS2*SIN(6.28*TIME.K/PCOS2)+PKNSE(MCON,SDVCON,TCCON))*MDS
12622 X     +(1-MDS)*TABLE(TMD,TIME.K,0,3600,240)/TMSI
12623 C     MDS=1
12624 N     CMD=CCOR/TMSI
12625 C     CCOR=400
12626 C     COSH=0
12627 C     COST=60
12628 C     ACOS=0
12629 C     PCOS=240
12631 C     ACOS2=0
12632 C     PCOS2=960
12633 C     MCON=0
12634 C     SDVCON=0
12635 C     TCCON=10
12636 T     TMD=400/475/650/900/1250/1700/2150/2500/2750/2900/3000/
12637 X     2900/2750/2500/2150/1700
12640 A     COGF.K=COG.K-1
12650 L     COG.K=COG.J+(DT)(COGR*COG.J)
12651 N     COG=1
12652 C     COGR=0
12653 NOTE          PARTS SUPPLIER PRODUCTION DELAY
12660 A     PSPD.K=PSPDN*(1+STEP(PSPDSH,PSPDST)+STEP(PSSH2,PSST2)
12661 X     +PKNSE(MPSPDN,SDVPSN,TCPSN))
12662 C     PSPDN=50
12663 C     PSPDSH=0
12664 C     PSPDST=60
12665 C     PSSH2=0
12666 C     PSST2=180
12667 C     MPSPDN=0
12668 C     SDVPSN=0
12669 C     TCPSN=10
12671 NOTE
12672 NOTE      SIMULATION RUN EVALUATION
12673 NOTE
12680 L     ACCSR.K=ACCSR.J+(DT)(SRS.JK+SRP.JK)
12681 N     ACCSR=0
12690 L     ACCPRO.K=ACCPRO.J+(DT)(NPRO.J)
12691 N     ACCPRO=0
12700 A     CORIMS.K=MD.K*TMSI
12710 A     PFCOR.K=TABHL(TMD,TIME.K+CEOFT,0,3600,240)
12720 A     SR.K=SRS.JK+SRP.JK
12730 A     FCP.K=FC.K/DVS.K
12731 NOTE
12732 NOTE      SIMULATION RUN CONTROL CARDS
12733 NOTE
12734 C     DT=4
12735 C     LENGTH=0
12736 C     PLTPER=0
12737 C     PRTPER=0
12738 PLOT  CORIMS=M,COR=C,PR=R(350,550)/FI=F(4E3,20E3)/DD=D(5,15)
12739 X     /MS=*(.05,.1)/EDDMS=1,EPMS=2,EPILPR=3(.7,1.1)/P=$(75,125)
12741 PRINT ACCSR,ACCPRO,MS
12742 RUN COMPILE
READY
```

Appendix D: Definition File for Final Model

```
NAME      NO   T  DEFINITION
   WHERE USED

ACCPRO  269   L  ACCUMULATED PROFITS ($)
        269.1 N
   PRINT,274.1
ACCSR   268   L  ACCUMULATED SHIPMENT RATE (UNITS)
        268.1 N
   PRINT,274.1
ACES     86   A  AVERAGE CAPITAL EQUIPMENT SCRAPPAGE (UNITS/
                    DAY/DAY)
   ICEO,A,85/DCEOO,A,99
ACFO    231   A  AVERAGE CASH FLOW FROM OPERATIONS ($/DAY)
   CDAE,A,103/ILTF,A,228
ACOR     35   A  AVERAGE CUSTOMER ORDER RATE (UNITS/DAY)
   BCOR,A,33
ACORE    55   A  AVERAGE CUSTOMER ORDER RATE FOR EMPLOYMENT
                    (UNITS/DAY)
   BCORE,A,54
ACORS    24   A  AVERAGE CUSTOMER ORDER RATE FOR SHIPPING
                    (UNITS/DAY)
   FIOSS,A,22/DDFI,L,38
ACOS    262.8 C  AMPLITUDE OF CUSTOMER ORDERS SINE
                    (DIMENSIONLESS)
   MD,A,262
ACOS2   263.1 C  AMPLITUDE OF CUSTOMER ORDERS SINE TWO
                    (DIMENSIONLESS)
   MD,A,262
ACSZ    126   A  AVERAGE COMPANY SIZE (DIMENSIONLESS)
   TAPROF,A,125
ADD      92   A  AVERAGE DELIVERY DELAY (DAYS)
   EEDDCO,A,91
ADER    252   A  AVERAGE DEBT-EQUITY RATIO (DIMENSIONLESS)
   EDERSP,A,251
ADVS             AVERAGE DOLLAR VALUE OF SALES ($/DAY)
AEGR    249   A  AVERAGE EARNINGS GROWTH RATE (PERCENT/YEAR)
   EEGRSP,A,248
AEPS    242   A  AVERAGE EARNINGS PER SHARE ($/YEAR/SHARE)
   ISP,A,241
AFPBA   138   A  AVERAGE FRACTION OF PROFESSIONALS BEING
                    ASSIMILATED (PERCENT)
   PRGM,A,137
AHPR    122   L  AVERAGE HIRING OF PROFESSIONALS
        122.1 N    (PROFESSIONALS/DAY)
   PRER,A,121
AINFR   212   A  AVERAGE INFLATION RATE (PERENT/YEAR)
   IR,A,210
```

```
AIT      218   A  ANNUAL INVENTORY TURNS (1/YEAR)
    AITG,N,77.2/PAIT,A,79
AITG      77.2 N  ANNUAL INVENTORY TURNS GOAL (1/YEAR)
    EFPDPR,A,77/EFPPOR,A,78
ALAR      47   A  AVERAGE LABOR ATTRITION RATE (PERSONS/DAY)
    IHR,A,46/DLBR,A,53
ALE       13.1 C  AVERAGE LENGTH OF EMPLOYMENT (DAYS)
    LAR,R,13
ALTDM    234.1 C  AVERAGE LONG-TERM DEBT MATURITY (DAYS)
    LTP,A,234
ANPRO    256   A  AVERAGE NET PROFITS ($/DAY)
    IDIV,A,255
AP       188   L  ACCOUNTS PAYABLE ($)
         188.1 N
    APP,A,191/STD,N,194.1/CL,A,195
APC      180   A  AVERAGE PRODUCTION COMPLETIONS (UNITS/DAY)
    VAASS,A,179
APEC     236   A  AVERAGE PERCENT EXCESS CASH (PERCENT)
    EECDP,A,235/ECCDP,A,261
API      189   A  ACCOUNTS PAYABLE INCREASES ($/DAY)
    AP,L,188/AP,N,188.1
APP      191   A  ACCOUNTS PAYABLE PAYMENTS ($/DAY)
    CO,A,176/AP,L,188
APR       67   A  AVERAGE PRODUCTION RATE (UNITS/DAY)
    BPR,A,64
APRSL     96   A  AVERAGE PROFESSIONAL SERVICE LEVEL
                    (DIMENSIONLESS)
    EEPSLM,A,95
APSPS     76   A  AVERAGE PARTS SUPPLIER PRODUCTION STARTS
                    (UNITS/DAY)
    PSSD,A,75
AR       170   L  ACCOUNTS RECEIVABLE ($)
         170.1 N
    COLL,A,172/CA,A,184
ARE      106   A  AVERAGE RETAINED EARNINGS ($/DAY)
    PEQ,A,105
ARFI     112   A  AVERAGE RATIO OF FINISHED INVENTORY
                    (DIMENSIONLESS)
    ERIP,A,111
AROE     247   A  AVERAGE RETURN ON EQUITY (PERCENT/YEAR)
    EROESP,A,246
ASAL     206   A  AVERAGE SALARY ($/DAY/PERSON)
    LC,A,205/CLT,A,207
ASALN    206.1 C  AVERAGE SALARY, INITIAL ($/DAY/PERSON)
    ASAL,A,206
ASSPR    124   R  ASSIMILATION OF PROFESSIONALS
                    (PROFESSIONALS/DAY)
    PROF,L,123/PRBA,L,128
AVP       94   A  AVERAGE PRICE ($/UNIT)
    EEPCO,A,93
BCOR      33   A  BASE CUSTOMER ORDER RATE (UNITS/DAY)
    DPR,A,32/FIG,A,37/WIPG,A,40/DUO,A,42
BCORE     54   A  BASE CUSTOMER ORDER RATE FOR EMPLOYMENT
                    (UNITS/DAY)
    DL,A,48/ECEDL,A,57
BP       110   A  BASE PRICE ($/UNIT)
    IP,A,109
BPR       64   A  BASE PRODUCTION RATE (UNITS/DAY)
    IPOR,A,63/PIG,A,70/POOG,A,72
BVFA     185   L  BOOK VALUE OF FIXED ASSETS ($)
         185.1 N
    DEPR,A,186/TA,A,187
CA       184   A  CURRENT ASSETS ($)
    TA,A,187/STD,N,194.1/CR,A,216
```

```
CASH    173   L  CASH ($)
        173.1 N
   CA,A,184/ICC,A,220/PEC,A,237
CCOR    262.5 C  CONSTANT CUSTOMER ORDER RATE (UNITS/DAY)
   FI,N,2.1/WIP,N,3.1/PR,N,5.1/L,N,11.1/PI,N,15.1/POO,N,16.1
     CEI,N,17.2/UOSS,N,20.1/SPR,N,49.1/PROF,N,123.1/PSPS,N,
     144.1/PSOB,N,150.1/PSPC,N,151.1/CMD,N,262.4
CDAE    103   A  COMMITTED DEBT ADJUSTED FOR EQUITY ($)
   CDPER,A,102
CDEBT   104   A  COMMITTED DEBT ($)
   CDAE,A,103
CDIV    254   R  CHANGE IN DIVIDENDS ($/DAY/DAY)
   DIV,L,253
CDPER   102   A  COMMITTED-DEBT-PROJECTED-EQUITY RATIO
                     (DIMENSIONLESS)
   PDERCP,A,101
CDPR    258   R  CHANGE IN DIVIDEND PAYOUT RATIO (PERCENT/
                     DAY)
   DIVPR,L,257
CE                 CAPITAL EQUIPMENT (UNITS/DAY)
   ECEPR,A,7/CES,R,17/ECESPR,A,52/ECEDL,A,57/ICEO,A,85
     COMSZE,A,127/BVFA,N,185.1
CEA      18   R  CAPITAL EQUIPMENT ARRIVALS (UNITS/DAY/DAY)
   CES,R,17/INVEST,A,229
CEGM     98   A  CAPITAL EQUIPMENT GROWTH MARGIN
                     (DIMENSIONLESS)
   CEI,N,17.2/DCE,A,87
CEI      17.2 N  CAPITAL EQUIPMENT, INITIAL (UNITS/DAY)
   CES,R,17/CEOOI,N,18.2/COMSZE,A,127
CEO      83   R  CAPITAL EQUIPMENT ORDERS (UNITS/DAY/DAY)
   CEA,R,18
CEOFT    88.1 N  CAPITAL EQUIPMENT ORDERS FORECASTING TIME
                     (DAYS)
   FCORCE,A,88/PFCOR,A,271
CEOIDC   84   A  CAPITAL EQUIPMENT ORDERS INDICATED BY
                     DEMAND CONDITIONS (UNITS/DAY/DAY)
   CEO,R,83
CEOO               CAPITAL EQUIPMENT ON ORDER (UNITS/DAY)
   CEA,R,18/ICEO,A,85/CDEBT,A,104
CEOOI    18.2 N  CAPITAL EQUIPMENT ON ORDER, INITIAL (UNITS/
                     DAY)
   CEA,R,18
CES      17   R  CAPITAL EQUIPMENT SCRAPPAGE (UNITS/DAY/DAY)
   ACES,A,86
CFI     178   A  COST OF FINISHED INVENTORY ($/UNIT)
   DVI,A,177/CWIP,A,181/CMS,A,204
CFO     232   A  CASH FLOW FROM OPERATION ($/DAY)
   ACFO,A,231
CI      175   A  CASH INFLOWS ($/DAY)
   NCF,A,174
CL      195   A  CURRENT LIABILITIES ($)
   LTD,N,196.1/TL,A,197/CR,A,216
CLT     207   A  COST OF LABOR TURNOVER ($/DAY)
   LC,A,205
CMD     262.4 N  CONSTANT MARKET DEMAND (UNITS/DAY)
   MD,A,262
CMS     204   A  COST OF MATERIAL SHIPPED ($/DAY)
   GPRO,A,203
CNOTPR   60   A  CURRENT NO-OVERTIME PRODUCTION RATE (UNITS/
                     DAY)
   IOT,A,59
CO      176   A  CASH OUTFLOWS ($/DAY)
   NCF,A,174/CFO,A,232
COG     265   L  CUSTOMER ORDERS GROWTH (DIMENSIONLESS)
        265.1 N
   COGF,A,264
```

```
COGF    264   A  CUSTOMER ORDERS GROWTH FACTOR
                    (DIMENSIONLESS)
   MD,A,262
COGR    265.2 C  CUSTOMER ORDERS GROWTH RATE (PERCENT/DAY)
   COG,L,265
COLL    172   A  COLLECTIONS ($/DAY)
   AR,L,170/CI,A,175/CFO,A,232
COMDD   158   A  COMPETITOR DELIVERY DELAY (DAYS)
   EEDDCO,A,91/EDDMS,A,157
COMP    163   A  COMPETITOR PRICE ($/UNIT)
   EEPCO,A,93/EPMS,A,162
COMPSL  169   A  COMPETITOR PROFESSIONAL SERVICE LEVEL
                    (DIMENSIONLESS)
   EPSLMS,A,165
COMSZE  127   A  COMPANY SIZE (DIMENSIONLESS)
   ACSZ,A,126
COR     154   A  CUSTOMER ORDER RATE (UNITS/DAY)
   COSS,R,21/ACORS,A,24/COSD,R,30/OCORGR,A,34/ACOR,A,35
      ACORE,A,55/OCORGE,A,56/ECOR,A,90/PLOT,273.8
CORFT   33.1  N  CUSTOMER ORDER RATE FORECASTING TIME (DAYS)
   BCOR,A,33
CORFTE  54.1  N  CUSTOMER ORDER RATE FORECASTING TIME FOR
                    EMPLOYMENT (DAYS)
   BCORE,A,54
CORIMS  270   A  CUSTOMER ORDER RATE AT INITIAL MARKET SHARE
                    (UNITS/DAY)
   PLOT,273.8
COSD    30    R  CUSTOMER ORDERS TO BE SHIPPED DIRECT
                    (UNITS/DAY)
   UOSD,L,29
COSH    262.6 C  CUSTOMER ORDERS STEP HEIGHT (DIMENSIONLESS)
   MD,A,262
COSS    21    R  CUSTOMER ORDERS TO BE SHIPPED FROM STOCK
                    (UNITS/DAY)
   UOSS,L,20
COST    262.7 C  CUSTOMER ORDERS STEP TIME (DAYS)
   MD,A,262
COSTP   183   A  COST OF PARTS ($/UNIT)
   CFI,A,178/CWIP,A,181/CPI,A,182/CPAR,A,190
COSTPI  183.1 C  COST OF PARTS, INITIAL ($/UNIT)
   COSTP,A,183
CP      108   R  CHANGE IN PRICE ($/UNIT/DAY)
   P,L,107
CPAR    190   A  COST OF PARTS ARRIVAL RATE ($/DAY)
   API,A,189
CPI     182   A  COST OF PARTS INVENTORY ($/UNIT)
   DVI,A,177
CPUCE   230   A  COST PER UNIT OF CAPITAL EQUIPMENT ($/UNIT/
                    DAY)
   CDEBT,A,104/BVFA,N,185.1/INVEST,A,229
CPUCEN  230.1 C  COST PER UNIT OF CAPITAL EQUIPMENT, INITIAL
                    ($/UNIT/DAY)
   CPUCE,A,230
CR      216   A  CURRENT RATIO (DIMENSIONLESS)
   ECRSTB,A,222
CRI     194.2 C  CURRENT RATIO, INITIAL (DIMENSIONLESS)
   STD,N,194.1
CSP     240   R  CHANGE IN STOCK PRICE ($/SHARE/DAY)
   SP,L,239
CWIP    181   A  COST OF WORK IN PROCESS ($/UNIT)
   DVI,A,177
DCASH   221   A  DESIRED CASH ($)
   CASH,N,173.1/ICC,A,220/PEC,A,237
DCE     87    A  DESIRED CAPITAL EQUIPMENT (UNITS/DAY)
   ICEO,A,85
```

,198/SP,L,239/SHARES,L,244/DIV,L,253/DIVPR,L,257/COG,L,
265/ACCSR,L,268/ACCPRO,L,269
DUO   42   A DESIRED UNFILLED ORDERS (UNITS)
   UOC,A,41
DVI   177   A DOLLAR VALUE OF INVENTORY ($)
   CA,A,184/AIT,A,218
DVS   171   A DOLLAR VALUE OF SALES ($/DAY)
   AR,L,170/AR,N,170.1/GPRO,A,203/ROS,A,214/AIT,A,218/DCASH,
   A,221/FCP,A,273
EACOR   89   A ESTIMATED AVERAGE CUSTOMER ORDER RATE
                     (UNITS/DAY)
   FCORCE,A,88/OCORGC,A,97/FCORPR,A,134
ECCDP   261   A EFFECT OF CASH CONDITION ON DIVIDEND
                     PAYMENTS (DIMENSIONLESS)
   IDPR,A,259
ECCHR   80   A EFFECT OF CASH CONSTRAINTS ON HIRING RATE
                     (DIMENSIONLESS)
   LHS,R,44
ECCPO   82   A EFFECT OF CASH CONSTRAINTS ON PARTS
                     ORDERING (DIMENSIONLESS)
   IPOR,A,63
ECCPP   193   A EFFECT OF CASH CONDITION ON PAYMENT PERIOD
                     (DIMENSIONLESS)
   TPAP,A,192
ECEDL   57   A EFFECT OF CAPITAL EQUIPMENT ON DESIRED
                     LABOR (DIMENSIONLESS)
   DL,A,48
ECEPR   7   A EFFECT OF CAPITAL EQUIPMENT ON PRODUCTION
                     RATE (DIMENSIONLESS)
   POLC,A,6
ECESPR   52   A EFFECT OF CAPITAL EQUIPMENT ON SCHEDULED
                     PRODUCTION RATE (DIMENSIONLESS)
   SPR,A,49/RPR,A,68
ECOR   90   A ESTIMATED CUSTOMER ORDER RATE (UNITS/DAY)
   EACOR,A,89
ECRSTB   222   A EFFECT OF CURRENT RATIO ON SHORT-TERM
                     BORROWING (DIMENSIONLESS)
   STB,A,219
EDDMS   157   A EFFECT OF DELIVERY DELAY ON MARKET SHARE
                     (DIMENSIONLESS)
   MS,A,155
EDERCE   100   A EFFECT OF DEBT-EQUITY RATIO ON CAPACITY
                     EXPANSION (DIMENSIONLESS)
   CEO,R,83
EDERP   114   A EFFECT OF DEBT-EQUITY RATIO ON PRICE
                     (DIMENSIONLESS)
   IP,A,109
EDERSB   223   A EFFECT OF DEBT-EQUITY RATIO ON SHORT-TERM
                     BORROWING (DIMENSIONLESS)
   STB,A,219
EDERSP   251   A EFFECT OF DEBT-EQUITY RATIO ON STOCK PRICE
                     (DIMENSIONLESS)
   PER,A,245
EECDP   235   A EFFECT OF EXCESS CASH ON DEBT PAYMENTS
                     (DIMENSIONLESS)
   LTP,A,234
EEDDCO   91   A ESTIMATED EFFECT OF DELIVERY DELAY ON
                     CUSTOMER ORDERS (DIMENSIONLESS)
   ECOR,A,90
EEGRSP   248   A EFFECT OF EARNINGS GROWTH RATE ON STOCK
                     PRICE (DIMENSIONLESS)
   PER,A,245
EEPCO   93   A ESTIMATED EFFECT OF PRICE ON CUSTOMER
                     ORDERS (DIMENSIONLESS)
   ECOR,A,90

```
EEPSLM   95   A  ESTIMATED EFFECT OF PROFESSIONAL SERVICE
                    LEVEL ON MARKET SHARE (DIMENSIONLESS)
    ECOR,A,90
EFPDPR   77   A  EFFECT OF FINANCIAL PRESSURES ON DESIRED
                    PRODUCTION RATE (DIMENSIONLESS)
    DPR,A,32
EFPPOR   78   A  EFFECT OF FINANCIAL PRESSURE ON PARTS ORDER
                    RATE (DIMENSIONLESS)
    IPOR,A,63
EGR     250   A  EARNINGS GROWTH RATE (PERCENT/YEAR)
    AEGR,A,249
EMPO     62   A  EFFECT OF MINIMUM PARTS ORDERS
                    (DIMENSIONLESS)
    POR,R,61
EPILPR    8   A  EFFECT OF PARTS INVENTORY LEVEL ON
                    PRODUCITON RATE (DIMENSIONLESS)
    PR,R,5
EPILSP   50   A  EFFECT OF PARTS INVENTORY LEVEL ON
                    SCHEDULED PRODUCTION (DIMENSIONLESS)
    SPR,A,49
EPMS    162   A  EFFECT OF PRICE ON MARKET SHARE
                    (DIMENSIONLESS)
    MS,A,155
EPS     243   A  EARNINGS PER SHARE ($/YEAR/SHARE)
    AEPS,A,242
EPSLMS  165   A  EFFECT OF PROFESSIONAL SERVICE LEVLE ON
                    MARKET SHARE (DIMENSIONLESS)
    MS,A,155
EQ      198   L  EQUITY ($)
        198.1 N
    PEQ,A,105/LTD,N,196.1/TLE,A,199/ROE,A,215/DER,A,217
EQIS    238   A  EQUITY ISSUE ($/DAY)
    CI,A,175/EQ,L,198/SHARES,L,244
EQSWT   238.1 C  EQUITY SWITCH (DIMENSIONLESS)
    EQIS,A,238
ERIP    111   A  EFFECT OF RELATIVE INVENTORY ON PRICE
                    (DIMENSIONLESS)
    IP,A,109
EROESP  246   A  EFFECT OF RETURN ON EQUITY ON STOCK PRICE
                    (DIMENSIONLESS)
    PER,A,245
ESTDP   226   A  EFFECT OF SHORT-TERM DEBT ON PAYMENTS
                    (DIMENSIONLESS)
    STP,A,224
FBPR    133.1 C  FRACTION BUDGETED TO PROFESSIONALS
                    (PERCENT)
    PRIB,A,133
FC      208   A  FIXED COSTS ($/DAY)
    API,A,189/GPRO,A,203/FCP,A,273
FCORCE   88   A  FORECAST CUSTOMER ORDER RATE FOR CAPITAL
                    EQUIPMENT (UNITS/DAY)
    DCE,A,87
FCORPR  134   A  FORECAST CUSTOMER ORDER RATE FOR
                    PROFESSIONALS (UNITS/DAY)
    PRIB,A,133
FCP     273   A  FIXED COST PERCENTAGE (DIMENSIONLESS)
FCPR    208.1 C  FIXED COSTS PER PROFESSIONAL ($/DAY/
                    PROFESSIONAL)
    PRIB,A,133/FC,A,208
FFMCC    81   A  FRACTION FIRED PER MONTH BECAUSE OF CASH
                    CONSTRAINTS (PERCENT/MONTH)
    LFR,R,45
FFPR    140   A  FRACTIONAL FIRING OF PROFESSIONALS
                    (PERCENT/DAY)
    FPROF,R,139
```

```
FFPRBA   142   A   FRACTIONAL FIRING OF PROFESSIONALS BEING
                       ASSIMILATED (PERCENT/DAY)
    FPRBA,R,141
FHPR     130   A   FRACTIONAL HIRING OF PROFESSIONALS
                       (PERCENT/DAY)
    HPR,R,129
FI         2   L   FINISHED PRODUCT INVENTORY (UNITS)
             2.1 N
    UFI,A,23/FIC,A,36/DDFI,L,38/RFI,A,113/DVI,A,177/PLOT,
       273.8
FIC       36   A   FINISHED INVENTORY CORRECTION (UNITS/DAY)
    DPR,A,32
FIG       37   A   FINISHED INVENTORY GOAL (UNITS)
    FIC,A,36/RFI,A,113
FIOSS     22   A   FRACTION OF INCOMING ORDERS TO BE SHIPPED
                       FROM STOCK (DIMENSIONLESS)
    COSS,R,21/COSD,R,30
FPRBA    141   R   FIRING OF PROFESSIONALS BEING ASSIMILATED
                       (PROFESSIONALS/DAY)
    PRBA,L,128
FPROF    139   R   FIRING OF PROFESSIONALS (PROFESSIONALS/DAY)
    PROF,L,123
FPRS      27   A   FRACTION OF PRODUCTION RATE SPECIFIED
                       (DIMENSIONLESS)
    PCS,R,25/SRP,R,26
FRPRBA   117   A   FRACTION OF PROFESSIONAL BEING ASSIMILATED
                       (PERCENT)
    PREFF,A,116/AFPBA,A,138
GPRO     203   A   GROSS PROFITS ($/DAY)
    NPRO,A,201/TAX,A,202
HPR      129   R   HIRING OF PROFESSIONALS (PROFESSIONALS/DAY)
    AHPR,L,122/PRBA,L,128
ICC      220   A   INDICATED CHANGE IN CASH ($/DAY)
    STB,A,219/ISTP,A,225
ICEO      85   A   INDICATED CAPITAL EQUIPMENT ORDERS (UNITS/
                       DAY/DAY)
    CEOIDC,A,84
ICORGR  34.2  C   INITIAL CUSTOMER ORDER RATE GROWTH RATE
                       (PERCENT/DAY)
    OCORGR,A,34/OCORGE,A,56
IDIV     255   A   INDICATED DIVIDENDS ($/DAY)
    CDIV,R,254
IDPR     259   A   INDICATED DIVIDEND PAYOUT RATIO (PERCENT)
    DIVPR,N,257.1/CDPR,R,258
IFCPR    131   A   INDICATED FRACTIONAL CHANGE IN
                       PROFESSIONALS (PERCENT/DAY)
    FHPR,A,130/FFPR,A,140/FFPRBA,A,142
IHR       46   A   INDICATED HIRING RATE (PERSONS/DAY)
    LHS,R,44/LFR,R,45
ILTF     228   A   INDICATED LONG-TERM FINANCING ($/DAY)
    LTB,A,227/EQIS,A,238
IN                 INPUT TO THIRD-ORDER DELAY
    MACRO,.1/$LV1,L,1
INFLR    213   A   INFLATION RATE (PERCENT/YEAR)
    AINFR,A,212
INFLRI  213.1 C   INFLATION RATE, INITIAL (PERCENT/YEAR)
    INFLR,A,213
INPUT              INPUT TO TREND DETECTION MACRO ('UNITS')
    MACRO,.1/$AIN1,L,2/$AIN1,N,2.1
INT      209   A   INTEREST PAYMENTS ($/DAY)
    CO,A,176/GPRO,A,203
INVEST   229   A   INVESTMENT ($/DAY)
    CO,A,176/BVFA,L,185/ILTF,A,228/CFO,A,232
IORGRC  97.2  C   INITIAL ORDER RATE GROWTH RATE FOR CAPACITY
                       (PERCENT/DAY)
```

```
    OCORGC,A,97
IOT      59    A   INDICATED OVERTIME (DIMENSIONLESS)
    OT,A,58
IP      109    A   INDICATED PRICE ($/UNIT)
    CP,R,108
IPOR     63    A   INDICATED PARTS ORDER RATE (UNITS/DAY)
    POR,R,61/EMPO,A,62
IPRGR    66.2 C   INITIAL PRODUCTION RATE GROWTH RATE
                       (PERCENT/DAY)
    OPRGR,A,66
IPROF   132    A   INDICATED PROFESSIONALS (PROFESSIONALS)
    IFCPR,A,131
IR      210    A   INTEREST RATE (PERCENT/YEAR)
    INT,A,209
ISP     241    A   INDICATED STOCK PRICE ($/SHARE)
    SP,N,239.1/CSP,R,240
ISTP    225    A   INDICATED SHORT-TERM PAYMENTS ($/DAY)
    STP,A,224/ESTDP,A,226
ITRND             INITIAL TREND IN INPUT DATA TO TREND
                       DETECTION MACRO (PERCENT/DAY)
    MACRO,.1/$AIN1,N,2.1/$AIN2,N,3.1
L        11    L   LABOR (PERSONS)
         11.1 N
    POL,A,10/LAR,R,13/LFR,R,45/IHR,A,46/CNOTPR,A,60/LC,A,205
LAR      13    R   LABOR ATTRITION RATE (PERSONS/DAY)
    L,L,11/ALAR,A,47
LBR      14    L   LABOR BEING RECRUITED (PERSONS)
         14.1 N
    IHR,A,46
LC      205    A   LABOR COSTS ($/DAY)
    VAASS,A,179/API,A,189
LENGTH  273.5 C
LFR      45    R   LABOR FIRING RATE (PERSONS/DAY)
    L,L,11/CLT,A,207
LHR      12    R   LABOR HIRING RATE (PERSONS/DAY)
    L,L,11/LBR,L,14/CLT,A,207
LHS      44    R   LABOR HIRING STARTS (PERSONS/DAY)
    LHR,R,12/LBR,L,14
LPROD    10.1 C   LABOR PRODUCTIVITY (UNITS/DAY/PERSON)
    POL,A,10/L,N,11.1/DL,A,48/ECEDL,A,57/CNOTPR,A,60
LRD      12.1 C   LABOR RECRUITING DELAY (DAYS)
    LHR,R,12/DLBR,A,53/CORFTE,N,54.1
LTB     227    A   LONG-TERM BORROWING ($/DAY)
    CI,A,175/LTD,L,196
LTD     196    L   LONG-TERM DEBT ($)
        196.1 N
    TL,A,197/INT,A,209/LTP,A,234
LTP     234    A   LONG-TERM PAYMENTS ($/DAY)
    CO,A,176/LTD,L,196/ILTF,A,228/CFO,A,232
MCON    263.3 C   MEAN OF CUSTOMER ORDERS NOISE
                       (DIMENSIONLESS)
    MD,A,262
MD      262    A   MARKET DEMAND (UNITS/DAY)
    COR,A,154/PRSL,A,167/CORIMS,A,270
MDS     262.3 C   MARKET DEMAND SWITCH (DIMENSIONLESS)
    MD,A,262
MEAN              MEAN OF PINK NOISE VARIATION
    MACRO,.1/PKNSE,L,1/PKNSE,N,1.1
MPSPDN  266.7 C   MEAN OF PARTS SUPPLIER PRODUCTION DELAY
                       NOISE (DIMESNIONLESS)
    PSPD,A,266
MS      155    A   MARKET SHARE (PERCENT)
    COR,A,154/TMS,A,156/PLOT,273.8/PRINT,274.1
NCF     174    A   NET CASH FLOW ($/DAY)
    CASH,L,173
```

```
NPRO     201   A  NET PROFITS ($/DAY)
    RE,A,200/ROS,A,214/ROE,A,215/EPS,A,243/EGR,A,250/DIV,N,
     253.1/ANPRO,A,256/ACCPRO,L,269
NRPCOR  123.2 C  NORMAL RATIO OF PROFESSIONALS TO CUSTOMER
                      ORDER RATE (PROFESSIONALS/UNIT/DAY)
    PROF,N,123.1
NUDSPE  168.1 C  NORMAL UNITS PER DAY SERVICABLE BY
                      PROFESSIONAL EFFORT (UNITS/DAY/
                      PROFESSIONAL)
    UDSPRE,A,168
OCORGC   97   A  OBSERVED CUSTOMER ORDER RATE GROWTH FOR
                      CAPACITY (PERCENT/DAY)
    FCORCE,A,88/CEGM,A,98/FCORPR,A,134
OCORGE   56   A  OBSERVED CUSTOMER ORDER RATE GROWTH FOR
                      EMPLOYMENT (PERCENT/DAY)
    BCORE,A,54
OCORGR   34   A  OBSERVED CUSTOMER ORDER RATE GROWTH RATE
                      (PERCENT/DAY)
    BCOR,A,33
OPRGR    66   A  OBSERVED PRODUCTION RATE GROWTH RATE
                      (PERCENT/DAY)
    BPR,A,64
OT       58   A  OVERTIME (DIMENSIONLESS)
    POL,A,10/LC,A,205
P       107   L  PRICE ($/UNIT)
        107.1 N
    AVP,A,94/CP,R,108/PRIB,A,133/PAC,A,164/DVS,A,171/PLOT,
     273.8
PAC     164   A  PRICE ACTED ON BY CUSTOMERS ($/UNIT)
    EPMS,A,162
PAIT     79   A  PERCEIVED ANNUAL INVENTORY TURNS (1/YEAR)
    EFPDPR,A,77/EFPPOR,A,78
PAR     143   R  PARTS ARRIVAL RATE (UNITS/DAY)
    PI,L,15/POO,L,16/CPAR,A,190
PC        4   A  PRODUCTION COMPLETIONS (UNITS/DAY)
    WIP,L,3/PCS,R,25/SRP,R,26/DOSD,A,28/APC,A,180
PCOS    262.9 C  PERIOD OF CUSTOMER ORDERS SINE (DAYS)
    MD,A,262
PCOS2   263.2 C  PERIOD OF CUSTOMER ORDERS SINE TWO (DAYS)
    MD,A,262
PCS      25   R  PRODUCTION COMPLETIONS STOCKED (UNITS/DAY)
    FI,L,2
PDERCP  101   A  PERCEIVED DEBT-EQUITY RATIO FOR CAPACITY
                      (DIMENSIONLESS)
    EDERCE,A,100/EDERP,A,114
PDF     233   A  PERCENT DEBT FINANCING (PERCENT)
    LTB,A,227/EQIS,A,238
PDSPI    51   A  PERCEIVED DAYS SUPPLY PARTS INVENTORY
                      (DAYS)
    EPILSP,A,50
PEC     237   A  PERCENT EXCESS CASH (PERCENT)
    ECCHR,A,80/FFMCC,A,81/ECCPO,A,82/ECCPP,A,193/APEC,A,236
PEQ     105   A  PROJECTED EQUITY ($)
    CDPER,A,102
PER     245   A
    ISP,A,241
PERN    245.1 C  PRICE-EARNINGS RATIO, NORMAL ($/$/YEAR)
    PER,A,245
PFCOR   271   A  PERFECT FORECAST OF CUSTOMER ORDER RATE
                      (UNITS/DAY)
PI       15   L  PARTS INVENTORY (UNITS)
         15.1 N
    DSPI,A,9/PIC,A,69/DVI,A,177
PIC      69   A  PARTS INVENTORY CORRECTION (UNITS/DAY)
    IPOR,A,63
```

```
PIG      70   A  PARTS INVENTORY GOAL (UNITS)
   PIC,A,69
PIN      107.2 C  PRICE, INITIAL ($/UNIT)
   P,N,107.1/BP,A,110/COMP,A,163
PIPE      8   A  SUM OF LEVELS IN THIRD-ORDER DELAY
   MACRO,.1
PIPEI             INITIAL SUM OF LEVELS IN THIRD-ORDER DELAY
   MACRO,.1/$LV1,N,1.1
PKNSE     1   L  PINK (CORRELATED) NOISE VARIATION
          1.1 N
   MACRO,.1/MD,A,262/PSPD,A,266
PLTPER   273.6 C
POC      71   A  PARTS ON ORDER CORRECTION (UNITS/DAY)
   IPOR,A,63
POL      10   A  POTENTIAL OUTPUT FROM LABOR (UNITS/DAY)
   POLC,A,6/ECEPR,A,7
POLC      6   A  POTENTIAL OUTPUT FROM LABOR AND CAPITAL
                    (UNITS/DAY)
   PR,R,5/DSPI,A,9
POO      16   L  PARTS ON ORDER (UNITS)
          16.1 N
   POC,A,71
POOG     72   A  PARTS ON ORDER GOAL (UNITS)
   POC,A,71
POR      61   R  PARTS ORDER RATE (UNITS/DAY)
   POO,L,16/PSAPOR,A,147/PSOB,L,150
PPRBA    120.2 C  PRODUCTIVITY OF PROFESSIONALS BEING
                    ASSIMILATED (DIMENSIONLESS)
   PREAVL,A,120
PPROF    120.1 C  PRODUCTIVITY OF PROFESSIONALS
                    (DIMENSIONLESS)
   PREAVL,A,120
PPSDT    73   A  PERCEIVED PARTS SUPPLIER DELIVERY TIME
                    (DAYS)
   PRFT,A,65/POOG,A,72
PR        5   R  PRODUCTION RATE (UNITS/DAY)
          5.1 N
   WIP,L,3/PC,A,4/PI,L,15/RPR,A,68/PLOT,273.8
PRBA     128  L  PROFESSIONALS BEING ASSIMILATED
         128.1 N    (PROFESSIONALS)
   FRPRBA,A,117/TPR,A,118/PREAVL,A,120/ASSPR,R,124/IFCPR,A,
   131/FPRBA,R,141
PRCAP    115  A  PROFESSIONAL CAPABILITY (PROFESSIONALS)
   UDSPRE,A,168
PREAMR   119  A  PROFESSIONAL EFFORT ALLOCATED TO MARKETING
                    AND RESEARCH (PROFESSIONALS)
   PRCAP,A,115
PREAVL   120  A  PROFESSIONAL EFFORT AVAILABLE
                    (PROFESSIONALS)
   PREAMR,A,119
PREFF    116  A  PROFESSIONAL EFFICIENCY (DIMENSIONLESS)
   PRCAP,A,115
PRER     121  A  PROFESSIONAL EFFORT RECRUITING
                    (PROFESSIONALS)
   PREAVL,A,120
PRFT     65   A  PRODUCTION RATE FORECASTING TIME (DAYS)
   BPR,A,64
PRGM     137  A  PROFESSIONALS GROWTH MARGIN (DIMENSIONLESS)
   IPROF,A,132
PRIB     133  A  PROFESSIONALS INDICATED BY BUDGET
                    (PROFESSIONALS)
   IPROF,A,132
PRIROE   260  A  PAYOUT RATIO INDICATED BY RETURN ON EQUITY
                    (PERCENT)
   IDPR,A,259
```

```
PROF     123   L  PROFESSIONALS (PROFESSIONALS)
         123.1 N
  TPR,A,118/PREAVL,A,120/IFCPR,A,131/FPROF,R,139
PROFT    135   A  PROFESSIONALS FORECASTING TIME (DAYS)
  FCORPR,A,134
PRSL     167   A  PROFESSIONAL SERVICE LEVEL (DIMENSIONLESS)
  APRSL,A,96/DPRSL,A,166
PRTPER   273.7 C
PSAPOR   147   A  PARTS SUPPLIER AVERAGE PARTS ORDER RATE
                  (UNITS/DAY)
  PSDPR,A,146/PSDPC,A,153
PSCPC    152   R  PARTS SUPPLIER CHANGE IN PRODUCTION
                  CAPACITY (UNITS/DAY/DAY)
  PSPC,L,151
PSDOB    149   A  PARTS SUPPLIER DESIRED ORDER BACKLOG
                  (UNITS)
  PSOBC,A,148
PSDPC    153   A  PARTS SUPPLIER DESIRED PRODUCTION CAPACITY
                  (UNITS/DAY)
  PSCPC,R,152
PSDPR    146   A  PARTS SUPPLIER DESIRED PRODUCTION RATE
                  (UNITS/DAY)
  PSPCUR,A,145
PSDT     74    A  PARTS SUPPLIER DELIVERY TIME (DAYS)
  PPSDT,A,73
PSMSD    149.1 C  PARTS SUPPLIER MINIMUM SCHEDULING DELAY
                  (DAYS)
  POO,N,16.1/PSDOB,A,149/PSOB,N,150.1
PSOB     150   L  PARTS SUPPLIER ORDER BACKLOG (UNITS)
         150.1 N
  PSSD,A,75/PSOBC,A,148
PSOBC    148   A  PARTS SUPPLIER ORDER BACKLOG CORRECTION
                  (UNITS/DAY)
  PSDPR,A,146
PSPC     151   L  PARTS SUPPLIER PRODUCTION CAPACITY (UNITS/
         151.1 N  DAY)
  EMPO,A,62/PSPS,R,144/PSPCUR,A,145/PSDOB,A,149/PSCPC,R,152
PSPCUR   145   A  PARTS SUPPLIER CAPACITY UTILIZATION RATE
                  (PERCENT)
  PSPS,R,144
PSPD     266   A  PARTS SUPPLIER PRODUCTION DELAY (DAYS)
  POO,N,16.1/PSDT,A,74/PAR,R,143
PSPDN    266.2 C  PARTS SUPPLIER PRODCUTION DELAY NORMAL
                  (DAYS)
  PSPD,A,266
PSPDSH   266.3 C  PARTS SUPPLIER PRODUCTION DELAY STEP HEIGHT
                  (DIMENSIONLESS)
  PSPD,A,266
PSPDST   266.4 C  PART SUPPLIER PRODUCTION DELAY STEP TIME
                  (DAYS)
  PSPD,A,266
PSPS     144   R  PARTS SUPPLIER PRODUCTION STARTS (UNITS/
         144.1 N  DAY)
  APSPS,A,76/PAR,R,143/PSOB,L,150
PSSD     75    A  PARTS SUPPLIER SCHEDULING DELAY (DAYS)
  PSDT,A,74
PSSH2    266.5 C  PARTS SUPPLIER STEP HEIGHT TWO
                  (DIMENSIONLESS)
  PSPD,A,266
PSST2    266.6 C  PARTS SUPPLIER STEP TIME TWO (DAYS)
  PSPD,A,266
PSTAPC   152.1 C  PARTS SUPPLIER TIME TO ADJUST PRODUCTION
                  CAPACITY (DAYS)
  PSCPC,R,152
```

PSTAPO 147.1 C PARTS SUPPLIER TIME TO AVERAGE PARTS ORDERS
                     (DAYS)
     PSAPOR,A,147
PSTCOB 148.1 C PARTS SUPPLIER TIME TO CORRECT ORDER
                     BACKLOG (DAYS)
     PSOBC,A,148
PSWT   108.1 C PRICE SWITCH (DIMENSIONLESS)
     CP,R,108
PTAPRO 136   A PERCEIVED TIME TO ASSIMILATE PROFESSIONALS
                     (DAYS)
     PROFT,A,135
RE   200   A RETAINED EARNINGS ($/DAY)
     ARE,A,106/EQ,L,198
RFI   113   A RATIO OF FINISHED INVENTORY (DIMENSIONLESS)
     ARFI,A,112
RFIR   210.1 C RISK FREE INTEREST RATE (PERCENT/YEAR)
     IR,A,210
ROE   215   A RETURN ON EQUITY (PERCENT/YEAR)
     AROE,A,247/PRIROE,A,260
ROS   214   A RETURN ON SALES (DIMENSIONLESS)
RPDBT   211   A RISK PREMIUM OF DEBT (PERCENT/YEAR)
     IR,A,210
RPR   68   A REFERENCE PRODUCITON RATE (UNITS/DAY)
     OPRGR,A,66/APR,A,67
RPRSWT 68.1 C REFERENCE PRODUCITON RATE SWITCH
                     (DIMENSIONLESS)
     RPR,A,68
SDV   STANDARD DEVIATION OF PINK NOISE VARIATION
     MACRO,.1/$G,N,1.2
SDVCON 263.4 C STANDARD DEVIATION OF CUSTOMER ORDERS NOISE
                     (DIMENSIONLESS)
     MD,A,262
SDVPSN 266.8 C STANDARD DEVIATION OF PARTS SUPPLIER NOISE
                     (DIMENSIONLESS)
     PSPD,A,266
SHARES 244   L SHARES (SHARES)
        244.1 N
     EPS,A,243
SP   239   L STOCK PRICE ($/SHARE)
        239.1 N
     CSP,R,240/SHARES,L,244
SPR   49   A SCHEDULED PRODUCTION RATE (UNITS/DAY)
        49.1 N
     DL,A,48/IOT,A,59
SR   272   A
SRP   26   R SHIPMENT RATE FROM PRODUCTION (UNITS/DAY)
     UOSD,L,29/DD,A,161/DVS,A,171/CMS,A,204/ACCSR,L,268/SR,A,
     272
SRS   19   R SHIPMENT RATE FROM STOCK (UNITS/DAY)
     FI,L,2/UOSS,L,20/DD,A,161/DVS,A,171/CMS,A,204/ACCSR,L,268
       SR,A,272
STB   219   A SHORT-TERM BORROWING ($/DAY)
     CI,A,175/STD,L,194
STD   194   L SHORT-TERM DEBT ($)
        194.1 N
     CL,A,195/INT,A,209/ESTDP,A,226
STP   224   A SHORT-TERM PAYMENTS ($/DAY)
     CO,A,176/STD,L,194/CFO,A,232
TA   187   A TOTAL ASSETS ($)
     EQ,N,198.1
TACASH 220.1 C TIME TO ADJUST CASH (DAYS)
     ICC,A,220
TACE   85.1 C TIME TO ADJUST CAPITAL EQUIPMENT (DAYS)
     ICEO,A,85/CEOFT,N,88.1
TACES   86.1 C TIME TO AVERAGE CAPITAL EQUIPMENT SCRAPPAGE
                     (DAYS)

```
      ACES,A,86
TACFOB   231.1 C   TIME TO AVERAGE CASH FLOW FROM OPERATIONS
                     FOR BORROWING (DAYS)
      ACFO,A,231
TACOR     35.1 C   TIME TO AVERAGE CUSTOMER ORDER RATE (DAYS)
      CORFT,N,33.1/ACOR,A,35
TACORC    89.1 C   TIME TO AVERAGE CUSTOMER ORDER RATE FOR
                     CAPACITY (DAYS)
      CEOFT,N,88.1/EACOR,A,89/PROFT,A,135
TACORE    55.1 C   TIME TO AVERAGE CUSTOMER ORDER RATE FOR
                     EMPLOYMENT (DAYS)
      CORFTE,N,54.1/ACORE,A,55
TACSZ    126.1 C   TIME TO AVERAGE COMPANY SIZE (DAYS)
      ACSZ,A,126
TADD      92.1 C   TIME TO AVERAGE DELIVERY DELAY (DAYS)
      ADD,A,92
TADIV    254.1 C   TIME TO ADJUST DIVIDENDS (DAYS)
      CDIV,R,254
TADJPR   131.1 C   TIME TO ADJUST PROFESSIONALS (DAYS)
      IFCPR,A,131
TADPR    258.1 C
      CDPR,R,258
TADVSF             TIME TO AVERAGE DOLLAR VALUE OF SALES FOR
                     FIXED COSTS (DAYS)
TAEPS    242.1 C   TIME TO AVERAGE EARNINGS PER SHARE (DAYS)
      AEPS,A,242
TAFPBA   138.1 C   TIME TO AVERAGE FRACTION OF PROFESSIONALS
                     BEING ASSIMILATED (DAYS)
      AFPBA,A,138
TAHPR    122.2 C   TIME TO AVERAGE HIRING OF PROFESSIONALS
                     (DAYS)
      AHPR,L,122
TAL       46.1 C   TIME TO ADJUST LABOR (DAYS)
      IHR,A,46
TALAR     47.1 C   TIME TO AVERAGE LABOR ATTRITION RATE (DAYS)
      ALAR,A,47
TAP      108.2 C   TIME TO ADJUST PRICE (DAYS)
      CP,R,108
TAPCC    180.1 C   TIME TO AVERAGE PRODUCTION COMPLETIONS FOR
                     COSTING (DAYS)
      APC,A,180
TAPEC    236.1 C   TIME TO AVERAGE PERCENT EXCESS CASH (DAYS)
      APEC,A,236
TAPROF   125    A   TIME TO ASSIMILATE PROFESSIONALS (DAYS)
      ASSPR,R,124/PTAPRO,A,136
TAPRPO    67.1 C   TIME TO AVERAGE PRODUCTION RATE FOR PARTS
                     ORDERING (DAYS)
      PRFT,A,65/APR,A,67
TAPRSL   166.1 C   TIME TO AVERAGE PROFESSIONAL SERVICE LEVEL
                     (DAYS)
      APRSL,A,96/DPRSL,A,166
TAQCE     18.1 C   TIME TO ACQUIRE CAPITAL EQUIPMENT (DAYS)
      CEA,R,18/CEOOI,N,18.2/CEOFT,N,88.1/DCEOO,A,99/CDAE,A,103
        PEQ,A,105
TARE     106.1 C   TIME TO AVERAGE RETAINED EARNINGS (DAYS)
      ARE,A,106
TARFI    112.1 C   TIME TO AVERAGE RATIO OF FINISHED INVENTORY
                     (DAYS)
      ARFI,A,112
TASP     240.1 C   TIME TO ADJUST STOCK PRICE (DAYS)
      CSP,R,240
TAVP      94.1 C   TIME TO AVERAGE PRICE (DAYS)
      AVP,A,94
TAX      202    A   TAXES ($/DAY)
      CO,A,176/NPRO,A,201
```

```
TC                    TIME CONSTANT OF PINK NOISE VARIATION
     MACRO,.1/PKNSE,L,1/$G,N,1.2
TCADD     159.1 C   TIME FOR CUSTOMERS TO ACT ON DELIVERY DELAY
                       (DAYS)
     DDAC,A,159
TCAP      164.1 C   TIME FOR CUSTOMERS TO ACT ON PRICE (DAYS)
     PAC,A,164
TCAR      172.1 C   TIME TO COLLECT ACCOUNTS RECEIVABLE (DAYS)
     AR,N,170.1/COLL,A,172
TCCON     263.5 C   TIME CONSTANT OF CUSTOMER ORDERS NOISE
                       (DAYS)
     MD,A,262
TCEGM      98.1 T   TABLE FOR CAPITAL EQUIPMENT GROWTH MARGIN
                       (DIMENSIONLESS)
     CEGM,A,98
TCFI       36.1 C   TIME TO CORRECT FINISHED INVENTORY (DAYS)
     FIC,A,36/WIPC,A,39/UOC,A,41
TCPDD     160.1 C   TIME FOR COMPANY TO PERCEIVE DELIVERY DELAY
                       (DAYS)
     DDQC,A,160
TCPI       69.1 C   TIME TO CORRECT PARTS INVENTORY (DAYS)
     PIC,A,69/POC,A,71
TCPSN     266.9 C   TIME CONSTANT OF PARTS SUPPLIER NOISE
                       (DAYS)
     PSPD,A,266
TCWIP      4.1 C    TIME TO COMPLETE WORK-IN-PROCESS (DAYS)
     WIP,N,3.1/PC,A,4/FPRS,A,27/CORFT,N,33.1/WIPG,A,40/CORFTE,
     N,54.1
TDCT       38.3 C   TIME TO DEVELOP COMPANY TRADITIONS (DAYS)
     DDFI,L,38/DDUO,A,43
TDEPFA    186.1 C   TIME TO DEPRECIATE FIXED ASSETS (DAYS)
     DEPR,A,186
TDTMS     156.3 C   TIME TO DEVELOP TRADITIONAL MARKET SHARE
                       (DAYS)
     TMS,A,156
TECCDP    261.1 T   TABLE FOR EFFECT OF CASH CONDITON ON
                       DIVIDEND PAYMENTS (DIMENSIONLESS)
     ECCDP,A,261
TECCHR     80.1 T   TABLE FOR EFFECT OF CASH CONSTRAINTS ON
                       HIRING RATE (DIMENSIONLESS)
     ECCHR,A,80
TECCPO     82.1 T   TABLE FOR EFFECT OF CASH CONSTRAINTS ON
                       PARTS ORDERING (DIMENSIONLESS)
     ECCPO,A,82
TECCPP    193.1 T   TABLE FOR EFFECT OF CASH CONDITION ON
                       PAYMENT PERIOD (DIMENSIONLESS)
     ECCPP,A,193
TECEDL     57.1 T   TABLE FOR EFFECT OF CAPITAL EQUIPMENT ON
                       DESIRED LABOR (DIMENSIONLESS)
     ECEDL,A,57
TECEPR      7.1 T   TABLE FOR EFFECT OF CAPITAL EQUIPMENT ON
                       PRODUCTION RATE (DIMENSIONLESS)
     ECEPR,A,7
TECESP     52.1 T   TABLE FOR EFFECT OF CAPITAL EQUIPMENT ON
                       SCHEDULED PRODUCTION (DIMENSIONLESS)
     ECESPR,A,52
TECRSB    222.1 T   TABLE FOR EFFECT OF CURRENT RATIO ON SHORT-
                       TERM BORROWING (DIMENSIONLESS)
     ECRSTB,A,222
TEDDMS    157.1 T   TABLE FOR EFFECTO OF DELIVERY DELAY ON
                       MARKET SHARE (DIMENSIONLESS)
     EDDMS,A,157
TEDERB    223.1 T   TABLE FOR EFFECT OF DEBT-EQUITY RATIO ON
                       BORROWING (DIMENSIONLESS)
     EDERSB,A,223
```

TEDERC   100.1 T   TABLE FOR EFFECT OF DEBT-EQUITY RATIO ON
                   CAPACITY EXPANSION (DIMENSIONLESS)
  EDERCE,A,100
TEDERP   114.1 T   TABLE FOR EFFECT OF DEBT-EQUITY RATIO ON
                   PRICE (DIMENSIONLESS)
  EDERP,A,114
TEDERS   251.1 T   TABLE FOR EFFECT OF DEBT-EQUITY RATIO ON
                   STOCK PRICE (DIMENSIONLESS)
  EDERSP,A,251
TEECDP   235.1 T   TABLE FOR EFFECT OF EXCESS CASH ON DEBT
                   PAYMENTS (DIMENSIONLESS)
  EECDP,A,235
TEEDDC   91.1 T   TABLE FOR ESTIMATED EFFECT OF DELIVERY
                   DELAY ON CUSTOMER ORDERS (DIMENSIONLESS)
  EEDDCO,A,91
TEEGRS   248.1 T   TABLE FOR EFFECT OF EARNINGS GROWTH RATE ON
                   STOCK PRICE (DIMENSIONLESS)
  EEGRSP,A,248
TEEPCO   93.1 T   TABLE FOR ESTIMATED EFFECT OF PRICE ON
                   CUSTOMER ORDERS (DIMENSIONLESS)
  EEPCO,A,93
TEEPSM   95.1 T   TABLE FOR ESTIMATED EFFECT OF PROFESSIONAL
                   SERVICE LEVEL ON MARKET SHARE
                   (DIMENSIONLESS)
  EEPSLM,A,95
TEFPPO   78.1 T   TABLE FOR EFFECT OF FINANCIAL PRESSURE ON
                   PARTS ORDER RATE (DIMENSIONLESS)
  EFPPOR,A,78
TEFPPR   77.1 T   TABLE FOR EFFECT OF FINANCIAL PRESSURES ON
                   DESIRED PRODUCTION RATE (DIMENSIONLESS)
  EFPDPR,A,77
TEMPO   62.1 T   TABLE FOR EFFECT OF MINIMUM PARTS ORDERS
                   (DIMENSIONLESS)
  EMPO,A,62
TEPIPR   8.1 T   TABLE FOR EFFECT OF PARTS INVENTORY LEVEL
                   ON PRODUCTION RATE (DIMENSIONLESS)
  EPILPR,A,8
TEPISP   50.1 T   TABLE FOR EFFECT OF PARTS INVENTORY LEVEL
                   ON SCHEDULED PRODUCTION (UNITS/DAY)
  EPILSP,A,50
TEPMS   162.1 T   TABLE FOR EFFECT OF PRICE ON MARKET SHARE
                   (DIMENSIONLESS)
  EPMS,A,162
TEPSLM   165.1 T   TABLE FOR EFFECT OF PROFESSIONAL SERVICE
                   LEVEL ON MARKET SHARE (DIMENSIONLESS)
  EPSLMS,A,165
TERIP   111.1 T   TABLE FOR EFFECT OF RELATIVE INVENTORY ON
                   PRICE (DIMENSIONLESS)
  ERIP,A,111
TEROES   246.1 T   TABLE FOR EFFECT OF RETURN ON EQUITY ON
                   STOCK PRICE (DIMENSIONLESS)
  EROESP,A,246
TESTDP   226.1 T   TABLE FOR EFFECT OF SHORT-TERM DEBT ON
                   PAYMENTS (DIMENSIONLESS)
  ESTDP,A,226
TFFMCC   81.1 T   TABLE FOR FRACTION FIRED PER MONTH BECAUSE
                   OF CASH CONSTRAINT (FPERCENT/MONTH)
  FFMCC,A,81
TFFPBA   142.1 T   TABLE FOR FRACTIONAL FIRING OF
                   PROFESSIONALS BEING (ASSIMILATED
                   (PERCENT/DAY)
  FFPRBA,A,142
TFFPR   140.1 T   TABLE FOR FRACTIONAL FIRING OF
                   PROFESSIOANLS (PERCENT/DAY)
  FFPR,A,140

```
TFHPR    130.1 T   TABLE FOR FRACTIONAL HIRING OF
                      PROFESSIONALS (PERCENT/DAY)
    FHPR,A,130
TFIOSS    22.1 T   TABLE FOR FRACTION OF INCOMING ORDERS TO BE
                      SHIPPED FROM STOCK (DIMENSIONLESS)
    FIOSS,A,22
TFPRS     27.1 T   TABLE FOR FRACTION OF PRODUCTION RATE
                      SPECIFIED (DIMENSIONLESS)
    FPRS,A,27
TIME              TIME (DAYS)
    MD,A,262/PFCOR,A,271
TL        197   A   TOTAL LIABILITIES ($)
    CDEBT,A,104/TLE,A,199/DER,A,217
TLE       199   A   TOTAL LIABILITIES AND EQUITY ($)
TMAFV    247.1 C   TIME FOR MARKET TO AVERAGE FINANCIAL
                      VARIABLES (DAYS)
    AROE,A,247/AEGR,A,249/ADER,A,252
TMD      263.6 T   TABLE FOR MARKET DEMAND (UNITS/DAY)
    MD,A,262/PFCOR,A,271
TMS       156   A   TRADITIONAL MARKET SHARE (PERCENT)
          156.1 N
    MS,A,155/PRSL,A,167
TMSI     156.2 C   TRADITIONAL MARKET SHARE, INITIAL (PERCENT)
    TMS,N,156.1/MD,A,262/CMD,N,262.4/CORIMS,A,270
TOCORE    56.1 C   TIME TO OBSERVE CUSTOMER ORDER RATE GROWTH
                      FOR EMPLOYMENT (DAYS)
    OCORGE,A,56
TOCORG    34.1 C   TIME TO OBSERVE CUSTOMER ORDER RATE GROWTH
                      (DAYS)
    OCORGR,A,34
TOORGC    97.1 C   TIME TO OBSERVE ORDER RATE GROWTH FOR
                      CAPACITY (DAYS)
    OCORGC,A,97
TOPRGR    66.1 C   TIME TO OBSERVE PRODUCTION RATE GROWTH RATE
                      (DAYS)
    OPRGR,A,66
TOT       58.1 T   TABLE FOR OVERTIME (DIMENSIONLESS)
    OT,A,58
TOTRND            TIME TO OBSERVE TREND IN TREND DETECTION
                      MACRO (DAYS)
    MACRO,.1/$TSI,N,2.2/$TASI,N,3.2
TPAIT     79.1 C   TIME TO PERCEIVE ANNUAL INVENTORY TURNS
                      (DAYS)
    PAIT,A,79
TPAP      192   A   TIME TO PAY ACCOUNTS PAYABLE (DAYS)
    AP,N,188.1/APP,A,191
TPAPN    192.1 C   TIME TO PAY ACCOUNTS PAYABLE, NORMAL (DAYS)
    TPAP,A,192
TPDERC   101.1 C   TIME TO PERCEIVE DEBT-EQUITY RATIO FOR
                      CAPACITY (DAYS)
    PDERCP,A,101
TPDF     233.1 T   TABLE FOR PERCENT DEBT FINANCING (PERCENT)
    PDF,A,233
TPDSPI    51.1 C   TIME TO PERCEIVE DAYS SUPPLY PARTS
                      INVENTORY (DAYS)
    PDSPI,A,51
TPINFI   212.1 C   TIME TO PERCEIVE INFLATION FOR INTEREST
                      RATES (DAYS)
    AINFR,A,212
TPPSDT    73.1 C   TIME TO PERCEIVE PARTS SUPPLIER DELIVERY
                      TIME (DAYS)
    PPSDT,A,73
TPR       118   A   TOTAL PROFESSIONALS (PROFESSIONALS)
    FRPRBA,A,117/HPR,R,129/IFCPR,A,131/FC,A,208
TPREFF   116.1 T   TABLE FOR PROFESSIONAL EFFICIENCY
                      (DIMENSIONLESS)
```

```
      PREFF,A,116
TPRGM     137.1 T  TABLE FOR PROFESSIONALS GROWTH MARGIN
                      (DIMENSIONLESS)
      PRGM,A,137
TPRIRE   260.1 T  TABLE FOR PAYOUT RATIO INDICATED BY RETURN
                      ON EQUITY (PERCENT)
      PRIROE,A,260
TPRR     121.1 C  TIME FOR PROFESSIONAL RECRUITING
                      (PROFESSIONALS/PROFESSIONALS/DAY)
      PRER,A,121
TPSCUR   145.1 T  TABLE FOR PARTS SUPPLIER CAPACITY
                      UTILIZATION RATE (PERCENT)
      PSPCUR,A,145
TPTAPR   136.1 C  TIME TO PERCEIVE TIME TO ASSIMILATE
                      PROFESSIONALS (DAYS)
      PTAPRO,A,136
TR       202.1 C  TAX RATE (DIMENSIONLESS)
      TAX,A,202
TRND       1   A  MACRO FOR DETECTING TRENDS IN INPUT TIME
                      SERIES (PERCENT/DAY)
   MACRO,.1/OCORGR,A,34/OCORGE,A,56/OPRGR,A,66/OCORGC,A,97
      EGR,A,250
TRPDBT   211.1 T  TABLE FOR RISK PREMIUM OF DEBT (PERCENT/
                      YEAR)
      RPDBT,A,211
TSCE      17.1 C  TIME TO SCRAP CAPITAL EQUIPMENT (DAYS)
   CES,R,17/CEOOI,N,18.2
TSS       19.1 C  TIME TO SHIP FROM STOCK (DAYS)
      SRS,R,19/UOSS,N,20.1/FPRS,A,27/DDUO,N,43.1/COMDD,A,158
TTAPR    125.1 T  TABLE FOR TIME TO ASSIMILTAE PROFESSIONALS
                      (DAYS)
      TAPROF,A,125
UDSPRE    168   A  UNITS PER DAY SERVICABLE BY PROFESSIONAL
                      EFFORT (UNITS/DAY/PROFESSIONAL)
      PRSL,A,167
UFI        23   A  UNCOMMITTED FINISHED INVENTORY (UNITS)
      FIOSS,A,22
UO         31   A  UNFILLED ORDERS (UNITS)
      UOC,A,41/DD,A,161
UOC        41   A  UNFILLED ORDER CORRECTION (UNITS/DAY)
      DPR,A,32
UOSD       29   L  UNFILLED ORDERS TO BE SHIPPED DIRECT
           29.1 N     (UNITS)
      DOSD,A,28/UO,A,31
UOSS       20   L  UNFILLED ORDERS TO BE SHIPPED FROM STOCK
           20.1 N     (UNITS)
      SRS,R,19/UFI,A,23/UO,A,31
VAASS     179   A  VALUE ADDED IN ASSEMBLY ($/UNIT)
      CFI,A,178
WIP         3   L  WORK-IN-PROCESS (UNITS)
            3.1 N
      WIPC,A,39/DVI,A,177
WIPC       39   A  WORK-IN-PROCESS CORRECTION (UNITS/DAY)
      DPR,A,32
WIPG       40   A  WORK-IN-PROCESS GOAL (UNITS)
      WIPC,A,39
$AIN1       2   L  AVERAGE INPUT ONE IN TREND MACRO ('UNITS')
            2.1 N
      TRND,A,1/$AIN2,L,3/$AIN2,N,3.1
$AIN2       3   L  AVERAGE INPUT TWO IN TREND MACRO ('UNITS')
            3.1 N
      TRND,A,1
$DEL        3   A
      $RT1,R,2/$RT2,R,5/DELAY3I,A,7
$G          1.2 N
      PKNSE,L,1
```

```
$LV1        1   L
            1.1 N
   $RT1,R,2/$LV2,N,4.1/$LV3,N,6.1/PIPE,A,8
$LV2        4   L
            4.1 N
   $RT2,R,5/PIPE,A,8
$LV3        6   L
            6.1 N
   DELAY3I,A,7/PIPE,A,8
$RT1        2   R
   $LV1,L,1/$LV2,L,4
$RT2        5   R
   $LV2,L,4/$LV3,L,6
$TASI       3.2 N  TIME TO AVERAGE SECOND INPUT IN TREND MACRO
                       (DAYS)
   TRND,A,1/$AIN2,L,3/$AIN2,N,3.1
$TSI        2.2 N  TIME TO SMOOTH INPUT IN TREND MACRO (DAYS)
   $AIN1,L,2/$AIN1,N,2.1/$TASI,N,3.2
                       PRICE-EARNINGS RATIO ($/$/YEAR)


READY
```

Problems

The five problems require students either to analyze the behavior of or to perform policy experiments on an existing model of industrial activity. The problems enhance the student's understanding of the use of system dynamics models in planning and policy design: in particular the importance of structure in creating behavior and the concept of designing policies to improve behavior.

A suggested sequencing of the text and problems is

1. problem 1 in conjunction with chapters 1 and 2,
2. problem 2 in conjunction with chapters 3 and 4,
3. problem 3 in conjunction with chapter 7,
4. problems 4 and 5 in conjunction with chapters 11, 12, and 13.

Problem 1: Inventory Simulation Game

Purpose: To illustrate that a systems behavior is largely determined by its internal structure.

Assignment: The inventory simulation game is played in class with at least four participants per game. In preparation for the game read the instructions and develop an inventory-ordering rule. During the game you will have approximately 30 seconds to calculate your order. Therefore use a simple ordering rule and/or bring a calculator. At the end of the game plot the behavior of each sector's order rate and inventory as a function of time.

Source: An early version of this game appeared in Jarmain (ed.), *Problems and Cases In Industrial Dynamics,* Cambridge, Mass.: The MIT Press.

Instructions for Inventory Simulation Game

System Dynamics is founded upon two notions: a system's behavior arises from its internal structure, and this internal structure consists of feedback loops. The inventory simulation game provides a tangible means of experiencing these theorizations in the form of role-playing. Participants function as decision-makers in a four-tiered production-distribution system. The first component in the chain is the retailer, who sells to the public and receives goods from a wholesaler. The wholesaler in turn gets its supply of goods from a distributor who relies upon a manufacturer for its supply of goods. This chain of relationships is depicted in figure 1a.

Imagine that the retailer in this chain is none other than your school bookstore. Have you ever marveled at the errant inner workings of the bookstore when, after much searching through piles of textbooks for that one book your professor said you needed right away, you find that it is "out of stock!"? If you have, you may have concluded that a little intelligent planning is surely all that is needed to prevent such disastrous events. The following exercise will provide you with an opportunity to test this hypothesis.

The Simulation The class should divide up into teams, with one or more team member(s) assigned to each of the four components of the production-distribution chain. Each player will be responsible for filling orders for the component immediately preceding it in the chain and placing orders with the component following it in the chain. These order and shipping decisions will be made in every period of the simulated operation of the system.

Orders received from customers by the retailer (for example, the bookstore) arrive at one-period intervals. These are predetermined by the instructor, but the retailer has no knowledge of future orders. You

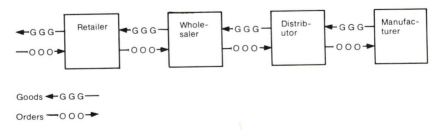

Figure 1a   A production–distribution chain

can assume that past orders have an average value equal to the first-period order rate and a standard deviation of 25 percent of the average. Each policy-maker is free to determine an individual ordering policy subject to the following restrictions designed to make the simulation more realistic:

1. All orders must be filled as long as there is inventory to do so.
2. To prevent the adoption of an obvious, but unrealistic, policy for avoiding "Out of stocks" (say, keeping unlimited inventory), a realistic cost structure must be imposed. As managers, of the bookstore and other components within the chain, you are certainly interested in minimizing your costs of operation. In any inventory system there are basically two costs: carrying and out-of-stock costs. Carrying costs arise when a unit is carried in inventory, the money that was used to buy the unit is not earning the interest that it could have earned had it been invested. This cost will be taken as $.50 per unit/period. Out-of-stock costs occur whenever there is insufficient inventory to meet demand. This cost should reflect a double loss. The loss of revenue from potential sales lost (for example, if students go elsewhere to purchase, or make arrangements to do without) and a loss of goodwill. This stock-out cost will be set at $2.00 per unit/period.

To minimize total costs, each sector in the system should attempt to hold its inventory at the lowest level sufficient to meet unexpected changes in demand. If inventory falls below this desired level, extra units should be ordered above the sales rate to rebuild inventory. If inventory begins to accumulate above desired levels, the order rate should be decreased below the existing sales rate. Your success at the end of the simulation will be measured by the total cost of operation summed for each period over the length of the game or simulation.

Each policy-maker must therefore answer two questions. The first is a question of fact: Do I have sufficient inventory to meet demand? The second is a policy question: How much should I order from the sector supplying me so as to maintain the smallest level of inventory necessary to avoid stock-outs?

Prior to playing the game familiarize yourself with the instructions for the simulation. Then work out the ordering policy you will use to control your inventory. Write it down to hand in to your instructor, and be prepared to discuss it after the simulation. You may of course change your ordering policy during the simulation.

General Instructions and Initialization

1. Each decision-maker will perform all of the necessary actions for the period determined by the group simulation coordinator.

2. All orders for goods will be transmitted only on slips of paper; poker chips or pennies represent physical entities.

3. An identical set of customer orders will be supplied to each retailer.

4. Each sector begins with an inventory of 12 units. There are 4 units in the left half of each shipping delay (refer to sample game board in figure 1b), 4 in the right half of each mail delay, and orders for 4 units in each order backlog.

5. The factory sector is sketched in figure 1c. Orders from the distributor pass through the mail delay into a goods-in-process delay of 3 weeks, and then through the shipping delay to the distributor. The factory is assumed to have unlimited capacity. The top and bottom portions of the goods-in-process box, each representing a 1-week delay, are initialized with 4 units. Both halves of the shipping delay are also initialized with 4 units apiece.

Specific Instructions   During each time period of the simulation you will go through the following sequence of steps (refer to figure 1b), as they are called out by the group coordinator:

1. Fill from inventory any order in the unfilled order backlog by placing the total requested number of units in the right half of the shipping delay to the sector at your left. If zero units are shipped, place a piece of paper in the delay to occupy the place of the shipment as it is moved through the delay. If the order was completely filled, remove it from backlog, and discard it. If it was not completely filled, subtract the units shipped from the units requested, and leave the slip in the backlog.

2. Record your effective inventory on the chart provided. Effective inventory is equal to actual inventory minus any order backlog, and can be either positive or negative. (Negative effective inventory indicates "out of stock.")

3. Advance the units from the left half of the shipping delay to your inventory.

4. Advance the units from the right half of the shipping delay to the left. (Factory people also advance the goods in the goods-in-process box.)

5. Decide how many units you wish to order, and place your order to

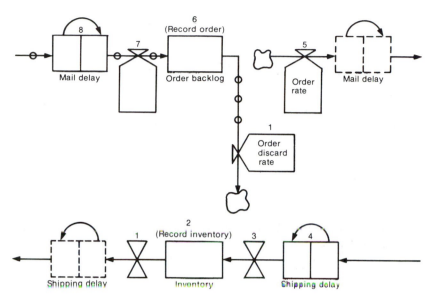

Figure 1b   Sequence of steps in one component of the hand simulation

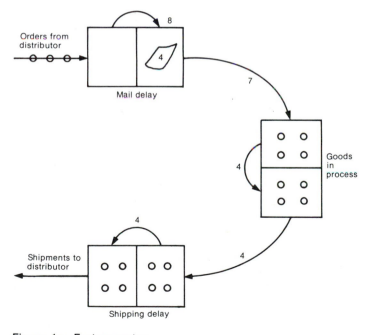

Figure 1c   Factory sector

your supplier *face down* in the left half of the mail delay in the sector at
your right.
6. Record on the chart the number of units that you ordered.
7. Take the order in the right half of the mail delay, and place it in your
backlog. (Retailers take a card from the "orders deck"; factory people
remove the order from the right half of your mail delay, and introduce
an equivalent number of goods in the top portion of the goods-in-
process box.)
8. Advance the order slip from the left half of the mail delay to the
right. The simulation of one week's activities is now completed, and
the sequence begins again at step 1.

Problem 2: Computer Simulation of the Inventory Simulation Game

Purpose:

1. To show that a dynamic system can be modeled on the computer
and that the model exhibits behavior characteristics of the system.
2. To illustrate the process of designing policies to improve behavior
and the effectiveness of a system-wide solution as opposed to solutions
by system parts.

Assignment: Review the structure and equations for the hand simulation game model. Answer the questions in the exercises about the
model.

Exercises

1. Sketch a flow diagram of the major flows in the model; develop a
detailed diagram of one sector. Simulate the basic model. In what ways
does model output agree (differ) with the behavior of the system observed in class? Would you say this is a valid model?
2. Can changes in parameter values improve the performance of the
system? Specifically, can reductions in physical delays such as delay in
mailing orders (DMO, equation 75) improve performance? Can increases in action delays such as time to adjust inventory (TAI, equation
77.03) improve performance? Why or why not?
3. Show that the addition of a supply line correction improves system
performance. (Be sure to describe how you evaluate system performance.) Why does this improvement occur? (A supply line correction
can be switched in by setting CSLC to 1.0 in RERUN mode.)

4. Can changes in parameter values further improve the performance of the system? (Do not try more than 2 or 3 changes.)
5. Devise a policy that shares information among the four stages. Does policy design using a system-wide perspective improve performance?
6. Are structural (new information inputs) or parameter changes more effective in improving performance? If so, why do you think this is true?

Documenter Listing of Inventory Simulation Game Model

```
------------------------------

NAME      - HAND SIMULATION GAME MODEL
PURPOSE   - TO PROVIDE A MODEL OF THE
            FOUR-TIERED DISTRIBUTION SYSTEM
            IN THE HAND SIMULATION GAME
AUTHOR    - DALE RUNGE
SOURCE    -
DATE      - 11 JUN 77


------------------------------


------------------------------
   RETAIL SECTOR
------------------------------

   SECTOR STRUCTURE FOR RETAILER
```

```
BR.K=BR.J+(DT)(OC.JK-SC.JK)                                      L,1
BR=IB                                                           N,1.01
   BR      - BACKLOG OF RETAILER (UNITS) <1>
   DT      - DELTA TIME, THE TIME STEP FOR COMPUTATION (WEEKS) <80>
   OC      - ORDERS FROM CONSUMERS (UNITS/WEEK) <2>
   SC      - SHIPMENTS TO CONSUMERS (UNITS/WEEK) <5>
   IB      - INITIAL VALUE OF BACKLOG (UNITS) <74>


OC.KL=OMC.K/DMO                                                  R,2
   OC      - ORDERS FROM CONSUMERS (UNITS/WEEK) <2>
   OMC     - ORDERS IN MAIL FROM CONSUMERS (UNITS) <3>
   DMO     - DELAY IN MAILING ORDERS (WEEKS) <75>


OMC.K=OMC.J+(DT)(OPC.JK-OC.JK)                                   L,3
OMC=IOM                                                         N,3.01
   OMC     - ORDERS IN MAIL FROM CONSUMERS (UNITS) <3>
   DT      - DELTA TIME, THE TIME STEP FOR COMPUTATION (WEEKS) <80>
   OPC     - ORDERS PLACED BY CONSUMERS (UNITS/WEEK) <4>
   OC      - ORDERS FROM CONSUMERS (UNITS/WEEK) <2>
   IOM     - INITIAL VALUE OF ORDERS IN THE MAIL (UNITS) <74>


OPC.KL=COPC+STEP(SOPC,STOP)+RAMP(SIIO,STOP)                      R,4
   OPC     - ORDERS PLACED BY CONSUMERS (UNITS/WEEK) <4>
   COPC    - CONSTANT ORDERS PLACED BY CONSUMERS (UNITS/WEEK) <79>
   STEP    - FUNCTION TO PROVIDE STEP CHANGE
   SOPC    - STEP IN ORDERS PLACED BY CONSUMERS (UNITS/WEEK) <79>
   STOP    - STEP TIME FOR ORDERS PLACED (WEEKS) <79>
   SIIO    - SLOPE INCREASE IN INCOMING ORDERS (UNITS/WEEK/WEEK) <79>


SC.KL=MIN(BR.K,IR.K)/DFO                                         R,5
   SC      - SHIPMENTS TO CONSUMERS (UNITS/WEEK) <5>
   MIN     - FUNCTION TO SELECT MINIMUM VALUE
   BR      - BACKLOG OF RETAILER (UNITS) <1>
```

```
IR     - INVENTORY OF RETAILER (UNITS) <6>
DFO    - DELAY IN FILLING ORDERS (WEEKS) <75>


IR.K=IR.J+(DT)(AW.JK-SC.JK)                                              L,6
IR=II                                                                   N,6.01
     IR     - INVENTORY OF RETAILER (UNITS) <6>
     DT     - DELTA TIME, THE TIME STEP FOR COMPUTATION (WEEKS) <80>
     AW     - ARRIVALS FROM WHOLESALER (UNITS/WEEK) <7>
     SC     - SHIPMENTS TO CONSUMERS (UNITS/WEEK) <5>
     II     - INITIAL VALUE OF INVENTORY (UNITS) <74>


AW.KL=SMW.K/DMG                                                         R,7
     AW     - ARRIVALS FROM WHOLESALER (UNITS/WEEK) <7>
     SMW    - SHIPMENTS IN THE MAIL FROM WHOLESALER (UNITS) <8>
     DMG    - DELAY IN MAILING GOODS (WEEKS) <75>


SMW.K=SMW.J+(DT)(SR.JK-AW.JK)                                           L,8
SMW=ISM                                                                 N,8.01
     SMW    - SHIPMENTS IN THE MAIL FROM WHOLESALER (UNITS) <8>
     DT     - DELTA TIME, THE TIME STEP FOR COMPUTATION (WEEKS) <80>
     SR     - SHIPMENTS TO RETAILER (UNITS/WEEK) <23>
     AW     - ARRIVALS FROM WHOLESALER (UNITS/WEEK) <7>
     ISM    - INITIAL VALUE OF SHIPMENTS IN THE MAIL (UNITS) <74>


          ORDERING POLICY FOR RETAILER


OPR.KL=TABLE(TORD,DOPR.K,0,200,25)                                      R,9
     OPR    - ORDERS PLACED BY RETAILER (UNITS/WEEK) <9>
     TORD   - TABLE FOR ORDERS -- PREVENTS NEGATIVE ORDERS (UNITS/
              WEEK) <77>
     DOPR   - DESIRED ORDERS PLACED BY RETAILER (UNITS/WEEK) <10>


DOPR.K=AOC.K+COPR.K/TAI                                                 A,10
     DOPR   - DESIRED ORDERS PLACED BY RETAILER (UNITS/WEEK) <10>
     AOC    - AVERAGE ORDERS FROM CONSUMERS (UNITS/WEEK) <16>
     COPR   - CORRECTION ORDERS PLACED BY RETAILER (UNITS/WEEK) <11>
     TAI    - TIME TO ADJUST INVENTORY (WEEKS) <77>


COPR.K=(CIC)(DIR.K-IR.K)+(CBC)(BR.K-DBR.K)+(CSLC)(DSLR.K-SLR.K)         A,11
     COPR   - CORRECTION ORDERS PLACED BY RETAILER (UNITS/WEEK) <11>
     CIC    - COEFFICIENT FOR INVENTORY CORRECTION (DIMENSIONLESS) <77>
     DIR    - DESIRED INVENTORY OF RETAILER (UNITS) <15>
     IR     - INVENTORY OF RETAILER (UNITS) <6>
     CBC    - COEFFICIENT FOR BACKLOG CORRECTION (DIMENSIONLESS) <77>
     BR     - BACKLOG OF RETAILER (UNITS) <1>
     DBR    - DESIRED BACKLOG OF RETAILER (UNITS) <12>
     CSLC   - COEFFICIENT FOR SUPPLY LINE CORRECTION (DIMENSIONLESS)
              <77>
     DSLR   - DESIRED SUPPLY LINE OF RETAILER (UNITS) <13>
     SLR    - SUPPLY LINE OF RETAILER (UNITS) <14>


DBR.K=AOC.K*NBC                                                         A,12
     DBR    - DESIRED BACKLOG OF RETAILER (UNITS) <12>
     AOC    - AVERAGE ORDERS FROM CONSUMERS (UNITS/WEEK) <16>
     NBC    - NORMAL BACKLOG COVERAGE (WEEKS) <76>


DSLR.K=AOC.K*(DMO+DFO+DMG)                                              A,13
     DSLR   - DESIRED SUPPLY LINE OF RETAILER (UNITS) <13>
     AOC    - AVERAGE ORDERS FROM CONSUMERS (UNITS/WEEK) <16>
     DMO    - DELAY IN MAILING ORDERS (WEEKS) <75>
     DFO    - DELAY IN FILLING ORDERS (WEEKS) <75>
     DMG    - DELAY IN MAILING GOODS (WEEKS) <75>


SLR.K=OMR.K+BW.K+SMW.K                                                  A,14
     SLR    - SUPPLY LINE OF RETAILER (UNITS) <14>
     OMR    - ORDERS IN THE MAIL FROM RETAILER (UNITS) <22>
     BW     - BACKLOG OF WHOLESALER (UNITS) <20>
     SMW    - SHIPMENTS IN THE MAIL FROM WHOLESALER (UNITS) <8>
```

```
DIR.K=AOC.K*NIC                                                             A,15
    DIR    - DESIRED INVENTORY OF RETAILER (UNITS) <15>
    AOC    - AVERAGE ORDERS FROM CONSUMERS (UNITS/WEEK) <16>
    NIC    - NORMAL INVENTORY COVERAGE (WEEKS) <76>

AOC.K=AOC.J+(DT/TAO)(OC.JK-AOC.J)                                           L,16
AOC=OC                                                                     N,16.01
    AOC    - AVERAGE ORDERS FROM CONSUMERS (UNITS/WEEK) <16>
    DT     - DELTA TIME, THE TIME STEP FOR COMPUTATION (WEEKS) <80>
    TAO    - TIME TO AVERAGE ORDERS (WEEKS) <77>
    OC     - ORDERS FROM CONSUMERS (UNITS/WEEK) <2>



            RETAIL ACCOUNTING

TCR.K=TCR.J+(DT)(OCR.JK)                                                    L,17
TCR=0                                                                      N,17.01
    TCR    - TOTAL COSTS OF RETAILER (DOLLARS) <17>
    DT     - DELTA TIME, THE TIME STEP FOR COMPUTATION (WEEKS) <80>
    OCR    - OPERATING COSTS OF RETAILER (DOLLARS/WEEK) <18>

OCR.KL=(CCI)(MAX(EIR.K,0))-(OSC)(MIN(EIR.K,0))                             R,18
    OCR    - OPERATING COSTS OF RETAILER (DOLLARS/WEEK) <18>
    CCI    - COST OF CARRYING INVENTORY (DOLLARS/UNIT-WEEK) <78>
    MAX    - FUNCTION TO SELECT MAXIMUM VALUE
    EIR    - EFFECTIVE INVENTORY OF RETAILER (UNITS) <19>
    OSC    - OUT-OF-STOCK COST (DOLLARS/UNIT-WEEK) <78>
    MIN    - FUNCTION TO SELECT MINIMUM VALUE

EIR.K=IR.K-BR.K                                                            A,19
    EIR    - EFFECTIVE INVENTORY OF RETAILER (UNITS) <19>
    IR     - INVENTORY OF RETAILER (UNITS) <6>
    BR     - BACKLOG OF RETAILER (UNITS) <1>


        --------------------------------
            WHOLESALE SECTOR
        --------------------------------

        SECTOR STRUCTURE FOR WHOLESALER

BW.K=BW.J+(DT)(OR.JK-SR.JK)                                                L,20
BW=IB                                                                      N,20.01
    BW     - BACKLOG OF WHOLESALER (UNITS) <20>
    DT     - DELTA TIME, THE TIME STEP FOR COMPUTATION (WEEKS) <80>
    OR     - ORDERS FROM RETAILER (UNITS/WEEK) <21>
    SR     - SHIPMENTS TO RETAILER (UNITS/WEEK) <23>
    IB     - INITIAL VALUE OF BACKLOG (UNITS) <74>

OR.KL=OMR.K/DMO                                                            R,21
    OR     - ORDERS FROM RETAILER (UNITS/WEEK) <21>
    OMR    - ORDERS IN THE MAIL FROM RETAILER (UNITS) <22>
    DMO    - DELAY IN MAILING ORDERS (WEEKS) <75>

OMR.K=OMR.J+(DT)(OPR.JK-OR.JK)                                             L,22
OMR=IOM                                                                    N,22.01
    OMR    - ORDERS IN THE MAIL FROM RETAILER (UNITS) <22>
    DT     - DELTA TIME, THE TIME STEP FOR COMPUTATION (WEEKS) <80>
    OPR    - ORDERS PLACED BY RETAILER (UNITS/WEEK) <9>
    OR     - ORDERS FROM RETAILER (UNITS/WEEK) <21>
    IOM    - INITIAL VALUE OF ORDERS IN THE MAIL (UNITS) <74>

SR.KL=MIN(BW.K,IW.K)/DFO                                                   R,23
    SR     - SHIPMENTS TO RETAILER (UNITS/WEEK) <23>
    MIN    - FUNCTION TO SELECT MINIMUM VALUE
```

```
    BW      - BACKLOG OF WHOLESALER (UNITS) <20>
    IW      - INVENTORY OF WHOLESALER (UNITS) <24>
    DFO     - DELAY IN FILLING ORDERS (WEEKS) <75>

IW.K=IW.J+(DT)(AD.JK-SR.JK)                                             L,24
IW=II                                                                  N,24.01
    IW      - INVENTORY OF WHOLESALER (UNITS) <24>
    DT      - DELTA TIME, THE TIME STEP FOR COMPUTATION (WEEKS) <80>
    AD      - ARRIVALS FROM DISTRIBUTOR (UNITS /WEEK) <25>
    SR      - SHIPMENTS TO RETAILER (UNITS/WEEK) <23>
    II      - INITIAL VALUE OF INVENTORY (UNITS) <74>


AD.KL=SMD.K/DMG                                                        R,25
    AD      - ARRIVALS FROM DISTRIBUTOR (UNITS /WEEK) <25>
    SMD     - SHIPMENTS IN THE MAIL FROM DISTRIBUTOR (UNITS) <26>
    DMG     - DELAY IN MAILING GOODS (WEEKS) <75>


SMD.K=SMD.J+(DT)(SW.JK-AD.JK)                                          L,26
SMD=ISM                                                                N,26.01
    SMD     - SHIPMENTS IN THE MAIL FROM DISTRIBUTOR (UNITS) <26>
    DT      - DELTA TIME, THE TIME STEP FOR COMPUTATION (WEEKS) <80>
    SW      - SHIPMENTS TO WHOLESALER (UNITS/WEEK) <41>
    AD      - ARRIVALS FROM DISTRIBUTOR (UNITS /WEEK) <25>
    ISM     - INITIAL VALUE OF SHIPMENTS IN THE MAIL (UNITS) <74>


            ORDERING POLICY FOR WHOLESALER


OPW.KL=TABLE(TORD,DOPW.K,0,200,25)                                     R,27
    OPW     - ORDERS PLACED BY WHOLESALER (UNITS/WEEK) <27>
    TORD    - TABLE FOR ORDERS -- PREVENTS NEGATIVE ORDERS (UNITS/
                WEEK) <77>
    DOPW    - DESIRED ORDERS PLACED BY WHOLESALER (UNITS/WEEK) <28>


DOPW.K=AOR.K+COPW.K/TAI                                                A,28
    DOPW    - DESIRED ORDERS PLACED BY WHOLESALER (UNITS/WEEK) <28>
    AOR     - AVERAGE ORDERS FROM RETAILER (UNITS/WEEK) <34>
    COPW    - CORRECTION ORDERS PLACED BY WHOLESALER (UNITS/WEEK) <29>
    TAI     - TIME TO ADJUST INVENTORY (WEEKS) <77>


COPW.K=(CIC)(DIW.K-IW.K)+(CBC)(BW.K-DBW.K)+(CSLC)(DSLW.K-SLW.K)        A,29
    COPW    - CORRECTION ORDERS PLACED BY WHOLESALER (UNITS/WEEK) <29>
    CIC     - COEFFICIENT FOR INVENTORY CORRECTION (DIMENSIONLESS) <77>
    DIW     - DESIRED INVENTORY OF WHOLESALER (UNITS) <33>
    IW      - INVENTORY OF WHOLESALER (UNITS) <24>
    CBC     - COEFFICIENT FOR BACKLOG CORRECTION (DIMENSIONLESS) <77>
    BW      - BACKLOG OF WHOLESALER (UNITS) <20>
    DBW     - DESIRED BACKLOG OF WHOLESALER (UNITS) <30>
    CSLC    - COEFFICIENT FOR SUPPLY LINE CORRECTION (DIMENSIONLESS)
                <77>
    DSLW    - DESIRED SUPPLY LINE OF WHOLESALER (UNITS) <31>
    SLW     - SUPPLY LINE OF WHOLESALER (UNITS) <32>


DBW.K=AOR.K*NBC                                                        A,30
    DBW     - DESIRED BACKLOG OF WHOLESALER (UNITS) <30>
    AOR     - AVERAGE ORDERS FROM RETAILER (UNITS/WEEK) <34>
    NBC     - NORMAL BACKLOG COVERAGE (WEEKS) <76>


DSLW.K=AOR.K*(DMO+DFO+DMG)                                             A,31
    DSLW    - DESIRED SUPPLY LINE OF WHOLESALER (UNITS) <31>
    AOR     - AVERAGE ORDERS FROM RETAILER (UNITS/WEEK) <34>
    DMO     - DELAY IN MAILING ORDERS (WEEKS) <75>
    DFO     - DELAY IN FILLING ORDERS (WEEKS) <75>
    DMG     - DELAY IN MAILING GOODS (WEEKS) <75>
```

```
SLW.K=OMW.K+BD.K+SMD.K                                                          A,32
    SLW    - SUPPLY LINE OF WHOLESALER (UNITS) <32>
    OMW    - ORDERS IN THE MAIL FROM WHOLESALER (UNITS) <40>
    BD     - BACKLOG OF DISTRIBUTOR (UNITS) <38>
    SMD    - SHIPMENTS IN THE MAIL FROM DISTRIBUTOR (UNITS) <26>

DIW.K=AOR.K*NIC                                                                 A,33
    DIW    - DESIRED INVENTORY OF WHOLESALER (UNITS) <33>
    AOR    - AVERAGE ORDERS FROM RETAILER (UNITS/WEEK) <34>
    NIC    - NORMAL INVENTORY COVERAGE (WEEKS) <76>

AOR.K=AOR.J+(DT/TAO)(OR.JK-AOR.J)                                               L,34
AOR=OR                                                                         N,34.01
    AOR    - AVERAGE ORDERS FROM RETAILER (UNITS/WEEK) <34>
    DT     - DELTA TIME, THE TIME STEP FOR COMPUTATION (WEEKS) <80>
    TAO    - TIME TO AVERAGE ORDERS (WEEKS) <77>
    OR     - ORDERS FROM RETAILER (UNITS/WEEK) <21>

              WHOLESALE ACCOUNTING

TCW.K=TCW.J+(DT)(OCW.JK)                                                        L,35
TCW=0                                                                          N,35.01
    TCW    - TOTAL COSTS OF WHOLESALER (DOLLARS) <35>
    DT     - DELTA TIME, THE TIME STEP FOR COMPUTATION (WEEKS) <80>
    OCW    - OPERATING COSTS OF WHOLESALER (DOLLARS/WEEK) <36>

OCW.KL=(CCI)(MAX(EIW.K,0))-(OSC)(MIN(EIW.K,0))                                  R,36
    OCW    - OPERATING COSTS OF WHOLESALER (DOLLARS/WEEK) <36>
    CCI    - COST OF CARRYING INVENTORY (DOLLARS/UNIT-WEEK) <78>
    MAX    - FUNCTION TO SELECT MAXIMUM VALUE
    EIW    - EFFECTIVE INVENTORY OF WHOLESALER (UNITS ) <37>
    OSC    - OUT-OF-STOCK COST (DOLLARS/UNIT-WEEK) <78>
    MIN    - FUNCTION TO SELECT MINIMUM VALUE

EIW.K=IW.K-BW.K                                                                 A,37
    EIW    - EFFECTIVE INVENTORY OF WHOLESALER (UNITS ) <37>
    IW     - INVENTORY OF WHOLESALER (UNITS) <24>
    BW     - BACKLOG OF WHOLESALER (UNITS) <20>


          --------------------------------
            DISTRIBUTOR SECTOR
          --------------------------------

          SECTOR STRUCTURE OF DISTRIBUTOR

BD.K=BD.J+(DT)(OW.JK-SW.JK)                                                     L,38
BD=IB                                                                          N,38.01
    BD     - BACKLOG OF DISTRIBUTOR (UNITS) <38>
    DT     - DELTA TIME, THE TIME STEP FOR COMPUTATION (WEEKS) <80>
    OW     - ORDERS FROM WHOLESALER (UNITS/WEEK) <39>
    SW     - SHIPMENTS TO WHOLESALER (UNITS/WEEK) <41>
    IB     - INITIAL VALUE OF BACKLOG (UNITS) <74>

OW.KL=OMW.K/DMO                                                                 R,39
    OW     - ORDERS FROM WHOLESALER (UNITS/WEEK) <39>
    OMW    - ORDERS IN THE MAIL FROM WHOLESALER (UNITS) <40>
    DMO    - DELAY IN MAILING ORDERS (WEEKS) <75>

OMW.K=OMW.J+(DT)(OPW.JK-OW.JK)                                                  L,40
OMW=IOM                                                                        N,40.01
    OMW    - ORDERS IN THE MAIL FROM WHOLESALER (UNITS) <40>
    DT     - DELTA TIME, THE TIME STEP FOR COMPUTATION (WEEKS) <80>
    OPW    - ORDERS PLACED BY WHOLESALER (UNITS/WEEK) <27>
    OW     - ORDERS FROM WHOLESALER (UNITS/WEEK) <39>
    IOM    - INITIAL VALUE OF ORDERS IN THE MAIL (UNITS) <74>
```

```
SW.KL=MIN(BD.K,ID.K)/DFO                                              R,41
    SW    - SHIPMENTS TO WHOLESALER (UNITS/WEEK) <41>
    MIN   - FUNCTION TO SELECT MINIMUM VALUE
    BD    - BACKLOG OF DISTRIBUTOR (UNITS) <38>
    ID    - INVENTORY OF DISTRIBUTOR (UNITS) <42>
    DFO   - DELAY IN FILLING ORDERS (WEEKS) <75>

ID.K=ID.J+(DT)(AF.JK-SW.JK)                                           L,42
ID=II                                                                 N,42.01
    ID    - INVENTORY OF DISTRIBUTOR (UNITS) <42>
    DT    - DELTA TIME, THE TIME STEP FOR COMPUTATION (WEEKS) <80>
    AF    - ARRIVALS FROM FACTORY (UNITS/WEEK) <43>
    SW    - SHIPMENTS TO WHOLESALER (UNITS/WEEK) <41>
    II    - INITIAL VALUE OF INVENTORY (UNITS) <74>

AF.KL=SMF.K/DMG                                                       R,43
    AF    - ARRIVALS FROM FACTORY (UNITS/WEEK) <43>
    SMF   - SHIPMENTS IN THE MAIL FROM FACTORY (UNITS) <44>
    DMG   - DELAY IN MAILING GOODS (WEEKS) <75>

SMF.K=SMF.J+(DT)(SD.JK-AF.JK)                                         L,44
SMF=ISM                                                               N,44.01
    SMF   - SHIPMENTS IN THE MAIL FROM FACTORY (UNITS) <44>
    DT    - DELTA TIME, THE TIME STEP FOR COMPUTATION (WEEKS) <80>
    SD    - SHIPMENTS TO DISTRIBUTOR (UNITS/WEEK) <59>
    AF    - ARRIVALS FROM FACTORY (UNITS/WEEK) <43>
    ISM   - INITIAL VALUE OF SHIPMENTS IN THE MAIL (UNITS) <74>


              ORDERING POLICY FOR DISTRIBUTOR

OPD.KL=TABLE(TORD,DOPD.K,0,200,25)                                    R,45
    OPD   - ORDERS PLACED BY DISTRIBUTOR (UNITS/WEEK) <45>
    TORD  - TABLE FOR ORDERS -- PREVENTS NEGATIVE ORDERS (UNITS/
            WEEK) <77>
    DOPD  - DESIRED ORDERS PLACED BY DISTRIBUTOR (UNITS/WEEK) <46>

DOPD.K=AOW.K+COPD.K/TAI                                               A,46
    DOPD  - DESIRED ORDERS PLACED BY DISTRIBUTOR (UNITS/WEEK) <46>
    AOW   - AVERAGE ORDERS FROM WHOLESALER (UNITS/WEEK) <52>
    COPD  - CORRECTION ORDERS PLACED BY DISTRIBUTOR (UNITS/WEEK) <47>
    TAI   - TIME TO ADJUST INVENTORY (WEEKS) <77>

COPD.K=(CIC)(DID.K-ID.K)+(CBC)(BD.K-DBD.K)+(CSLC)(DSLD.K-SLD.K)       A,47
    COPD  - CORRECTION ORDERS PLACED BY DISTRIBUTOR (UNITS/WEEK) <47>
    CIC   - COEFFICIENT FOR INVENTORY CORRECTION (DIMENSIONLESS) <77>
    DID   - DESIRED INVENTORY OF DISTRIBUTOR (UNITS) <51>
    ID    - INVENTORY OF DISTRIBUTOR (UNITS) <42>
    CBC   - COEFFICIENT FOR BACKLOG CORRECTION (DIMENSIONLESS) <77>
    BD    - BACKLOG OF DISTRIBUTOR (UNITS) <38>
    DBD   - DESIRED BACKLOG OF DISTRIBUTOR (UNITS) <48>
    CSLC  - COEFFICIENT FOR SUPPLY LINE CORRECTION (DIMENSIONLESS)
            <77>
    DSLD  - DESIRED SUPPLY LINE OF DISTRIBUTOR (UNITS) <49>
    SLD   - SUPPLY LINE OF DISTRIBUTOR (UNITS) <50>

DBD.K=AOW.K*NBC                                                       A,48
    DBD   - DESIRED BACKLOG OF DISTRIBUTOR (UNITS) <48>
    AOW   - AVERAGE ORDERS FROM WHOLESALER (UNITS/WEEK) <52>
    NBC   - NORMAL BACKLOG COVERAGE (WEEKS) <76>

DSLD.K=AOW.K*(DMO+DFO+DMG)                                            A,49
    DSLD  - DESIRED SUPPLY LINE OF DISTRIBUTOR (UNITS) <49>
    AOW   - AVERAGE ORDERS FROM WHOLESALER (UNITS/WEEK) <52>
    DMO   - DELAY IN MAILING ORDERS (WEEKS) <75>
    DFO   - DELAY IN FILLING ORDERS (WEEKS) <75>
    DMG   - DELAY IN MAILING GOODS (WEEKS) <75>
```

```
SLD.K=OMD.K+BF.K+SMF.K                                               A,50
    SLD   - SUPPLY LINE OF DISTRIBUTOR (UNITS) <50>
    OMD   - ORDERS IN THE MAIL FROM DISTRIBUTOR (UNITS) <58>
    BF    - BACKLOG OF FACTORY (UNITS) <56>
    SMF   - SHIPMENTS IN THE MAIL FROM FACTORY (UNITS) <44>

DID.K=AOW.K*NIC                                                      A,51
    DID   - DESIRED INVENTORY OF DISTRIBUTOR (UNITS) <51>
    AOW   - AVERAGE ORDERS FROM WHOLESALER (UNITS/WEEK) <52>
    NIC   - NORMAL INVENTORY COVERAGE (WEEKS) <76>

AOW.K=AOW.J+(DT/TAO)(OW.JK-AOW.J)                                    L,52
AOW=OW                                                              N,52.01
    AOW   - AVERAGE ORDERS FROM WHOLESALER (UNITS/WEEK) <52>
    DT    - DELTA TIME, THE TIME STEP FOR COMPUTATION (WEEKS) <80>
    TAO   - TIME TO AVERAGE ORDERS (WEEKS) <77>
    OW    - ORDERS FROM WHOLESALER (UNITS/WEEK) <39>


            ACCOUNTING FOR DISTRIBUTOR

TCD.K=TCD.J+(DT)(OCD.JK)                                             L,53
TCD=0                                                               N,53.01
    TCD   - TOTAL COSTS OF DISTRIBUTOR (DOLLARS) <53>
    DT    - DELTA TIME, THE TIME STEP FOR COMPUTATION (WEEKS) <80>
    OCD   - OPERATING COSTS OF DISTRIBUTOR (DOLLARS/WEEK) <54>

OCD.KL=(CCI)(MAX(EID.K,0))-(OSC)(MIN(EIW.K,0))                       R,54
    OCD   - OPERATING COSTS OF DISTRIBUTOR (DOLLARS/WEEK) <54>
    CCI   - COST OF CARRYING INVENTORY (DOLLARS/UNIT-WEEK) <78>
    MAX   - FUNCTION TO SELECT MAXIMUM VALUE
    EID   - EFFECTIVE INVENTORY OF DISTRIBUTOR (UNITS) <55>
    OSC   - OUT-OF-STOCK COST (DOLLARS/UNIT-WEEK) <78>
    MIN   - FUNCTION TO SELECT MINIMUM VALUE
    EIW   - EFFECTIVE INVENTORY OF WHOLESALER (UNITS ) <37>

EID.K=ID.K-BD.K                                                      A,55
    EID   - EFFECTIVE INVENTORY OF DISTRIBUTOR (UNITS) <55>
    ID    - INVENTORY OF DISTRIBUTOR (UNITS) <42>
    BD    - BACKLOG OF DISTRIBUTOR (UNITS) <38>


        --------------------------------
            FACTORY SECTOR
        --------------------------------

        SECTOR STRUCTURE OF FACTORY

BF.K=BF.J+(DT)(OD.JK-SD.JK)                                          L,56
BF=IB                                                              N,56.01
    BF    - BACKLOG OF FACTORY (UNITS) <56>
    DT    - DELTA TIME, THE TIME STEP FOR COMPUTATION (WEEKS) <80>
    OD    - ORDERS FROM DISTRIBUTOR (UNITS/WEEK) <57>
    SD    - SHIPMENTS TO DISTRIBUTOR (UNITS/WEEK) <59>
    IB    - INITIAL VALUE OF BACKLOG (UNITS) <74>

OD.KL=OMD.K/DMO                                                      R,57
    OD    - ORDERS FROM DISTRIBUTOR (UNITS/WEEK) <57>
    OMD   - ORDERS IN THE MAIL FROM DISTRIBUTOR (UNITS) <58>
    DMO   - DELAY IN MAILING ORDERS (WEEKS) <75>

OMD.K=OMD.J+(DT)(OPD.JK-OD.JK)                                       L,58
OMD=IOM                                                            N,58.01
    OMD   - ORDERS IN THE MAIL FROM DISTRIBUTOR (UNITS) <58>
    DT    - DELTA TIME, THE TIME STEP FOR COMPUTATION (WEEKS) <80>
    OPD   - ORDERS PLACED BY DISTRIBUTOR (UNITS/WEEK) <45>
```

```
    OD      - ORDERS FROM DISTRIBUTOR (UNITS/WEEK) <57>
    IOM     - INITIAL VALUE OF ORDERS IN THE MAIL (UNITS) <74>

SD.KL=MIN(BF.K,IF.K)/DFO                                                       R,59
    SD      - SHIPMENTS TO DISTRIBUTOR (UNITS/WEEK) <59>
    MIN     - FUNCTION TO SELECT MINIMUM VALUE
    BF      - BACKLOG OF FACTORY (UNITS) <56>
    IF      - INVENTORY OF FACTORY (UNITS) <60>
    DFO     - DELAY IN FILLING ORDERS (WEEKS) <75>

IF.K=IF.J+(DT)(PG.JK-SD.JK)                                                    L,60
IF=II                                                                         N,60.01
    IF      - INVENTORY OF FACTORY (UNITS) <60>
    DT      - DELTA TIME, THE TIME STEP FOR COMPUTATION (WEEKS) <80>
    PG      - PRODUCTION OF GOODS (UNITS/WEEK) <61>
    SD      - SHIPMENTS TO DISTRIBUTOR (UNITS/WEEK) <59>
    II      - INITIAL VALUE OF INVENTORY (UNITS) <74>

PG.KL=GIP.K/DPG                                                                R,61
    PG      - PRODUCTION OF GOODS (UNITS/WEEK) <61>
    GIP     - GOODS IN PRODUCTION (UNITS) <62>
    DPG     - DELAY IN PRODUCING GOODS (WEEKS) <75>

GIP.K=GIP.J+(DT)(OPF.JK-PG.JK)                                                 L,62
GIP=IGIP                                                                      N,62.01
    GIP     - GOODS IN PRODUCTION (UNITS) <62>
    DT      - DELTA TIME, THE TIME STEP FOR COMPUTATION (WEEKS) <80>
    OPF     - ORDERS PLACED BY FACTORY (UNITS/WEEK) <63>
    PG      - PRODUCTION OF GOODS (UNITS/WEEK) <61>
    IGIP    - INITIAL VALUE OF GOODS IN PRODUCTION (UNITS) <74>


            ORDERING POLICY FOR FACTORY

OPF.KL=TABLE(TORD,DOPF.K,0,200,25)                                             R,63
    OPF     - ORDERS PLACED BY FACTORY (UNITS/WEEK) <63>
    TORD    - TABLE FOR ORDERS -- PREVENTS NEGATIVE ORDERS (UNITS/
              WEEK) <77>
    DOPF    - DESIRED ORDERS PLACED BY FACTORY (UNITS/WEEK) <64>

DOPF.K=AOD.K+COPF.K/TAI                                                        A,64
    DOPF    - DESIRED ORDERS PLACED BY FACTORY (UNITS/WEEK) <64>
    AOD     - AVERAGE ORDERS FROM DISTRIBUTOR (UNITS/WEEK) <69>
    COPF    - CORRECTION ORDERS PLACED BY FACTORY (UNITS/WEEK) <65>
    TAI     - TIME TO ADJUST INVENTORY (WEEKS) <77>

COPF.K=(CIC)(DIF.K-IF.K)+(CBC)(BF.K-DBF.K)+(CSLC)(DGIP.K-GIP.K)                A,65
    COPF    - CORRECTION ORDERS PLACED BY FACTORY (UNITS/WEEK) <65>
    CIC     - COEFFICIENT FOR INVENTORY CORRECTION (DIMENSIONLESS) <77>
    DIF     - DESIRED INVENTORY OF FACTORY (UNITS) <68>
    IF      - INVENTORY OF FACTORY (UNITS) <60>
    CBC     - COEFFICIENT FOR BACKLOG CORRECTION (DIMENSIONLESS) <77>
    BF      - BACKLOG OF FACTORY (UNITS) <56>
    DBF     - DESIRED BACKLOG OF FACTORY (UNITS) <66>
    CSLC    - COEFFICIENT FOR SUPPLY LINE CORRECTION (DIMENSIONLESS)
              <77>
    DGIP    - DESIRED GOODS IN PRODUCTION (UNITS) <67>
    GIP     - GOODS IN PRODUCTION (UNITS) <62>

DBF.K=AOD.K*NBC                                                                A,66
    DBF     - DESIRED BACKLOG OF FACTORY (UNITS) <66>
    AOD     - AVERAGE ORDERS FROM DISTRIBUTOR (UNITS/WEEK) <69>
    NBC     - NORMAL BACKLOG COVERAGE (WEEKS) <76>
```

```
DGIP.K=AOD.K*DPG                                                               A,67
     DGIP   - DESIRED GOODS IN PRODUCTION (UNITS) <67>
     AOD    - AVERAGE ORDERS FROM DISTRIBUTOR (UNITS/WEEK) <69>
     DPG    - DELAY IN PRODUCING GOODS (WEEKS) <75>

DIF.K=AOD.K*NIC                                                                A,68
     DIF    - DESIRED INVENTORY OF FACTORY (UNITS) <68>
     AOD    - AVERAGE ORDERS FROM DISTRIBUTOR (UNITS/WEEK) <69>
     NIC    - NORMAL INVENTORY COVERAGE (WEEKS) <76>

AOD.K=AOD.J+(DT/TAO)(OD.JK-AOD.J)                                              L,69
AOD=OD                                                                        N,69.01
     AOD    - AVERAGE ORDERS FROM DISTRIBUTOR (UNITS/WEEK) <69>
     DT     - DELTA TIME, THE TIME STEP FOR COMPUTATION (WEEKS) <80>
     TAO    - TIME TO AVERAGE ORDERS (WEEKS) <77>
     OD     - ORDERS FROM DISTRIBUTOR (UNITS/WEEK) <57>


              ACCOUNTING FOR FACTORY

TCF.K=TCF.J+(DT)(OCF.JK)                                                       L,70
TCF=0                                                                         N,70.01
     TCF    - TOTAL COSTS OF FACTORY (DOLLARS) <70>
     DT     - DELTA TIME, THE TIME STEP FOR COMPUTATION (WEEKS) <80>
     OCF    - OPERATING·COSTS OF FACTORY (DOLLARS/WEEK) <71>


OCF.KL=(CCI)(MAX(EIF.K,0))-(OSC)(MIN(EIF.K,0))                                 R,71
     OCF    - OPERATING COSTS OF FACTORY (DOLLARS/WEEK) <71>
     CCI    - COST OF CARRYING INVENTORY (DOLLARS/UNIT-WEEK) <78>
     MAX    - FUNCTION TO SELECT MAXIMUM VALUE
     EIF    - EFFECTIVE INVENTORY OF FACTORY (UNITS) <72>
     OSC    - OUT-OF-STOCK COST (DOLLARS/UNIT-WEEK) <78>
     MIN    - FUNCTION TO SELECT MINIMUM VALUE

EIF.K=IF.K-BF.K                                                               A,72
     EIF    - EFFECTIVE INVENTORY OF FACTORY (UNITS) <72>
     IF     - INVENTORY OF FACTORY (UNITS) <60>
     BF     - BACKLOG OF FACTORY (UNITS) <56>

TC.K=TCR.K+TCW.K+TCD.K+TCF.K                                                   A,73
     TC     - TOTAL COSTS (DOLLARS) <73>
     TCR    - TOTAL COSTS OF RETAILER (DOLLARS) <17>
     TCW    - TOTAL COSTS OF WHOLESALER (DOLLARS) <35>
     TCD    - TOTAL COSTS OF DISTRIBUTOR (DOLLARS) <53>
     TCF    - TOTAL COSTS OF FACTORY (DOLLARS) <70>


         ----------------------------------
              PARAMETERS
         ----------------------------------


              INITIAL VALUES

IB=4                                                                          C,74
IOM=DMO*COPC                                                                  N,74.01
ISM=8                                                                         C,74.02
II=12                                                                         C,74.03
IGIP=24                                                                       C,74.04
     IB     - INITIAL VALUE OF BACKLOG (UNITS) <74>
     IOM    - INITIAL VALUE OF ORDERS IN THE MAIL (UNITS) <74>
     DMO    - DELAY IN MAILING ORDERS (WEEKS) <75>
     COPC   - CONSTANT ORDERS PLACED BY CONSUMERS (UNITS/WEEK) <79>
     ISM    - INITIAL VALUE OF SHIPMENTS IN THE MAIL (UNITS) <74>
     II     - INITIAL VALUE OF INVENTORY (UNITS) <74>
     IGIP   - INITIAL VALUE OF GOODS IN PRODUCTION (UNITS) <74>
```

DELAY TIMES

```
DMO=2                                                                        C,75
DMG=2                                                                        C,75.01
DPG=6                                                                        C,75.02
DFO=1                                                                        C,75.03
    DMO    - DELAY IN MAILING ORDERS (WEEKS) <75>
    DMG    - DELAY IN MAILING GOODS (WEEKS) <75>
    DPG    - DELAY IN PRODUCING GOODS (WEEKS) <75>
    DFO    - DELAY IN FILLING ORDERS (WEEKS) <75>
```

COVERAGES

```
NIC=3                                                                        C,76
NBC=1                                                                        C,76.01
    NIC    - NORMAL INVENTORY COVERAGE (WEEKS) <76>
    NBC    - NORMAL BACKLOG COVERAGE (WEEKS) <76>
```

ORDERING POLICY PARAMETERS

```
CIC=1                                                                        C,77
CBC=1                                                                        C,77.01
CSLC=0                                                                       C,77.02
TAI=8                                                                        C,77.03
TAO=4                                                                        C,77.04
TORD=0/25/50/75/100/125/150/175/200                                          T,77.05
    CIC    - COEFFICIENT FOR INVENTORY CORRECTION (DIMENSIONLESS) <77>
    CBC    - COEFFICIENT FOR BACKLOG CORRECTION (DIMENSIONLESS) <77>
    CSLC   - COEFFICIENT FOR SUPPLY LINE CORRECTION (DIMENSIONLESS)
              <77>
    TAI    - TIME TO ADJUST INVENTORY (WEEKS) <77>
    TAO    - TIME TO AVERAGE ORDERS (WEEKS) <77>
    TORD   - TABLE FOR ORDERS -- PREVENTS NEGATIVE ORDERS (UNITS/
              WEEK) <77>
```

ACCOUNTING PARAMETERS

```
CCI=0.5                                                                      C,78
OSC=2.0                                                                      C,78.01
    CCI    - COST OF CARRYING INVENTORY (DOLLARS/UNIT-WEEK) <78>
    OSC    - OUT-OF-STOCK COST (DOLLARS/UNIT-WEEK) <78>
```

TEST INPUT CHARACTERISTICS

```
COPC=4                                                                       C,79
SOPC=4                                                                       C,79.01
SIIO=0                                                                       C,79.02
STOP=5                                                                       C,79.03
    COPC   - CONSTANT ORDERS PLACED BY CONSUMERS (UNITS/WEEK) <79>
    SOPC   - STEP IN ORDERS PLACED BY CONSUMERS (UNITS/WEEK) <79>
    SIIO   - SLOPE INCREASE IN INCOMING ORDERS (UNITS/WEEK/WEEK) <79>
    STOP   - STEP TIME FOR ORDERS PLACED (WEEKS) <79>
```

```
    ----------------------------------
             CONTROL CARDS
    ----------------------------------
```

```
DT=0.125/LENGTH=120/PLTPER=2/PRTPER=120                                      C,80
    DT     - DELTA TIME, THE TIME STEP FOR COMPUTATION (WEEKS) <80>
```

```
PRINT (3,3)TCR,TCW,TCD,TCF,TC                                                81
    TCR    - TOTAL COSTS OF RETAILER (DOLLARS) <17>
    TCW    - TOTAL COSTS OF WHOLESALER (DOLLARS) <35>
    TCD    - TOTAL COSTS OF DISTRIBUTOR (DOLLARS) <53>
    TCF    - TOTAL COSTS OF FACTORY (DOLLARS) <70>
    TC     - TOTAL COSTS (DOLLARS) <73>


PLOT OPC=C,OPR=R,OPW=W,OPD=D,OPF=F                                           82
    OPC    - ORDERS PLACED BY CONSUMERS (UNITS/WEEK) <4>
    OPR    - ORDERS PLACED BY RETAILER (UNITS/WEEK) <9>
    OPW    - ORDERS PLACED BY WHOLESALER (UNITS/WEEK) <27>
    OPD    - ORDERS PLACED BY DISTRIBUTOR (UNITS/WEEK) <45>
    OPF    - ORDERS PLACED BY FACTORY (UNITS/WEEK) <63>

PLOT EIR=R,EIW=W,EID=D,EIF=F                                                 82.01
    EIR    - EFFECTIVE INVENTORY OF RETAILER (UNITS) <19>
    EIW    - EFFECTIVE INVENTORY OF WHOLESALER (UNITS ) <37>
    EID    - EFFECTIVE INVENTORY OF DISTRIBUTOR (UNITS) <55>
    EIF    - EFFECTIVE INVENTORY OF FACTORY (UNITS) <72>

RUN                                                                         82.02
```

Problem 3: Value of Information

Purpose:

1. To show how a system dynamics model can be used to solve a practical management problem.
2. To provide a framework for evaluating the design of a management information system.

Assignment: Complete the attached exercise. You will observe that, in contrast to earlier problems, Exercise 3 leaves the design of simulation experiments to the student.

Background

This exercise provides the student with a simple model that can be used to investigate the impact of information changes on corporate decision making and control. This general subject area is an important one since each year corporations make sizable investments in equipment and personnel to improve data processing capability. For example, in 1975, $35 billion were spent on data-processing activities in the United States, 2.3 percent of the GNP.

The justification for introducing a new information system usually lies on comparative cost-saving grounds, How much does it cost to obtain the information with the new system by comparison with the old? This is certainly an important criterion, and one that can usually be expressed and realized in concrete dollar amounts. However, the criterion fails to attach importance to the impact the new information may have on decision making and control. Information has a value to the company independent of the cost of obtaining it. This value is related to the effects the information has on company performance, which is often very difficult to estimate in advance and for this reason often goes unestimated. As Forrester states,

better information is worth the value we attach to the improved industrial performance which results when better information is available. Unless we can determine the change in system performance that will result from a changed information flow we cannot determine its value. The value of information has usually been determined by highly subjective means that necessarily include an estimate of what the information will do to the dynamic behavior of the system. Our ability to estimate the characteristics of information-feedback systems is poor. It is to be expected that one of the weakest areas of managerial judgment is in placing a dollar value on an information source.[1]

Model Description

The model used in the exercise is a workforce-inventory model.[2] A DYNAMO flowchart of the model is shown in figure 3a; an equation listing is given at the end of the exercise.

The basic model has been modified to include two typical information sources used in production planning. The changes form the basis for experimentation and analysis in the exercise, so they will be discussed in some detail.

Order-Processing System The order-processing system is represented as a first-order delay of the shipment rate SR, shown in figure 3b. The time constant associated with the delay represents the time taken by the information system to detect a change in the shipment rate.

The output of the order-processing system has two applications. The first is in determining the inventory goal (desired inventory) and the second in determining changes in the workforce, the only factor of

1. See Jay W. Forrester, 1961, *Industrial Dynamics* (Cambridge, Mass.: The MIT Press), appendix J.

2. In this model the order and shipment rates are synonymous (there is no backlog). Throughout the text they are used interchangeably.

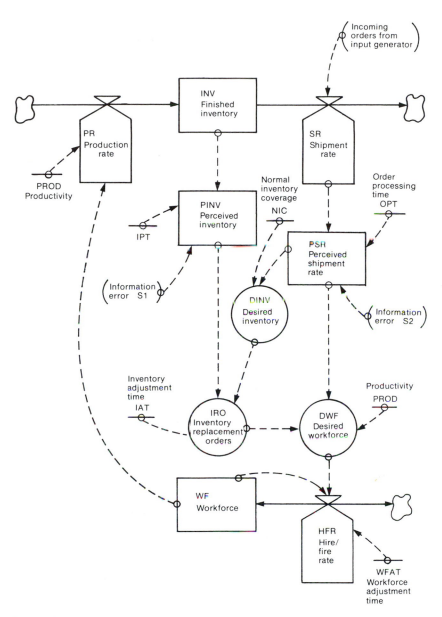

Figure 3a Simple workforce-inventory model modified to show explicit information systems

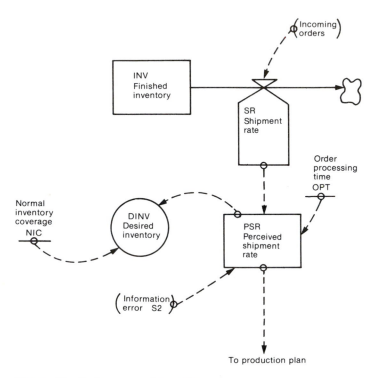

Figure 3b   Order-processing system

production in the model. More timely information on orders can be represented by simply reducing the order-processing time OPT. For example, if a step input in orders occurs the output of the order-processing system, for different order-processing times, would be as sketched in figure 3c.

The effects of variations in the accuracy of information processing can be represented by changes in the noise input to the perceived shipment rate.

In the aggregate the formulation is a much simplified version of order-processing systems widely used in industry. The newcomer to system dynamics may question where the true parallel lies between the model and reality. After all, there is no attempt to capture any of the detail that any normal information system handles. The formulation is not concerned with the intricacies of data processing, nor the details of product line, product mix or option offtake. Although the real system may deal with such low-level information, the collective effects are of interest and importance in system dynamics, effects such as the time

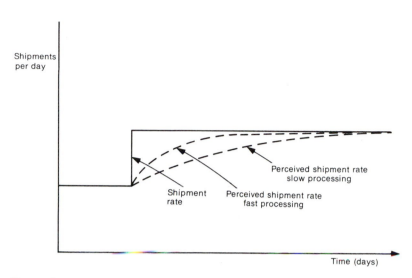

Figure 3c   Comparison of slow and fast order-processing times (OPT)

delay before management is fully aware of changes in the business volume, or the trust placed in the accuracy of the reports the information system produces. These are the information qualities included in the model.

Inventory-Tracking System   The inventory-tracking system is modeled exactly like the order-processing system. The assumption is made that the inventory of finished units is sufficiently large and varied that it is impossible to know at any one time the exact number of items in inventory. The delay in recognizing changes in the inventory level corresponds to the information-processing time associated with making an inventory count. Error in the observation can be represented by noise.

The output of the inventory-tracking system is used in deriving the second component in the production-planning policy, inventory replacement orders IRO.

This simple formulation can be linked to the more complex information processing that occurs, for example, in the full-scale production-planning system of a durable goods manufacturer. Such systems usually operate on a biweekly or monthly basis and are used for scheduling production and ordering the many thousands of parts required in assembly. To do this, they need as input the production rate planned by model and option and a record of all the finished inventories, work in process, parts inventories, and orders placed with suppliers. Clearly both for manual and computer systems a vast amount of data is required to monitor the changes in product stored at each stage of production. The formulation in the model merely captures at an aggregate level the delay required to gather, process, and distribute such information.

Details of the Exercise

The exercise is designed to look at three different ways of relating information to the stability of production:

1. through the impact of more timely information,
2. through trade-off between more timely and more accurate information,
3. through feedback from information accuracy to policy response time.

For each of these several simulation runs should be made based on simple parameter changes (no structural changes are required in any of the experiments. The entire analysis can be conducted in re-run mode.). The student chooses which parameters to change and, after making the runs, carries out a detailed analysis that explains why the observed response took place.

The Impact of More Timely Information   There are two aspects of information timeliness that may have differing impacts on production control and stability. One is related to the intuitive argument that says, "Give me more up-to-date information, and I can control the system better." The other is related to the argument that slower information filters rapid change and can be used, for example, to smooth a noisy demand stream.

The student should find parameters to change within the model to illustrate and explain these opposing viewpoints. NOISE and STEP inputs are recommended as test inputs to the model during the analysis.

The Trade-off between More Timely and More Accurate Information
All information sources within organizations are subject to error. The error is closely related to the amount of time taken to compile the information. For any given information source the possibility always exists that, as more time is spent in preparing information to increase its accuracy, its timeliness is reduced.[3] The object of this

3. To take a statistical example, larger samples from a random population take longer to collect but give more reliable information on the population.

section is to investigate the potential trade-off by selecting suitable combinations of timeliness and accuracy for the two information systems in the model. It is suggested that a STEP input be used as a test to compare the short-term, transient response of the system with its long-run, equilibrium behavior.

The Feedback from Information Accuracy to Policy Response Time

The exercise so far has concentrated on the purely mechanical aspects of substituting information flows, with differing characteristics, under the assumption that there is no overall change in the policies using the information. For example, in the inventory-tracking system it was assumed that changes in the accuracy and timeliness of the information did not influence the speed of inventory corrections or the size of the inventory goal. In many real instances it is quite possible that policies actually depend on the information they use. In the case of inventory control it is not difficult to imagine that, when inventory data is inaccurate, there is little point in exerting strong control to keep inventory close to a specified goal. As more accurate information becomes available, the possibility of taking stronger action is greater, if only because discrepancies are more noticeable. However, as the detailed analysis of the workforce-inventory model shows, more rapid correction of inventory discrepancies usually induces greater production instability. It is therefore possible that a new information system, which is more accurate than its predecessor, could result in an overall decrease in production stability.

In this part of the exercise the student should aim to identify the model parameters that are involved in the feedback from information accuracy to policy response time. Two alternatives are then possible: the analysis of simulation runs for meaningful combinations of the parameters, or the addition of structure to model the dynamic relationships of the parameters.

Program Listing

```
NOTE       INFORMATION SYSTEM MODEL                                  00000001
NOTE                                                                 00000002
MACRO      PKNSE(MEAN,SDV,CORRT)                                     00000003
L          PKNSE.K=PKNSE.J+(DT/CORRT)($G*NOISE()+MEAN-PKNSE.J)       00000010
N          PKNSE=MEAN                                                00000011
N          $G=SDV*SQRT(24*(CORRT/DT))                                00000012
MEND                                                                 00000013
NOTE                                                                 00000014
NOTE       DEMAND GENERATOR                                          00000015
NOTE                                                                 00000016
R          SR.KL=400*FIFGE(PKNSE(1,SIG,CORRT),1,TIME.K,STNOISE)      00010010
X          *SINE.K*RAMP.K*STEP.K                                     00010011
C          SIG=0/CORRT=5                                             00010012
C          STNOISE=20    TH DAY                                      00010013
```

```
A       SINE.K=1+AMP*SIN(6.283*TIME.K/PER)                        00010020
C       AMP=0/PER=240                                             00010021
A       RAMP.K=1+RAMP(RS1/240,RT1)                                00010030
C       RS1=0/RT1=20                                              00010031
A       STEP.K=1+STEP(SH,ST)                                      00010040
C       SH=0/ST=20   TH DAY                                       00010041
NOTE                                                              00010042
NOTE                                                              00010043
NOTE    WORKFORCE-INVENTORY MODEL MODIFIED TO INCLUDE MIS         00010044
NOTE                                                              00010045
L       INV.K=INV.J+(DT)(PR.JK-SR.JK)                             00010050
N       INV=INVI                                                  00010051
C       INVI=10000   UNITS OF OUTPUT                              00010052
A       PSR.K=SMOOTH(SR.JK,OPT)*FIFGE(PKNSE(1,S2,CT2),1           00010060
X       ,TIME.K,STNOISE)*BIAS2                                    00010061
C       OPT=20/S2=0/CT2=10/BIAS2=1                                00010062
A       PINV.K=SMOOTH(INV.K,IPT)                                  00010070
X       *FIFGE(PKNSE(1,S1,CT1),1,TIME.K,STNOISE)*BIAS1            00010071
C       IPT=10/S1=0/CT1=10/BIAS1=1                                00010072
R       PR.KL=WF.K*PROD                                           00010080
C       PROD=1   UNIT/MAN-DAY                                     00010081
L       WF.K=WF.J+(DT)(HFR.JK)                                    00010090
N       WF=WFI                                                    00010091
C       WFI=400   MEN                                             00010092
R       HFR.KL=(DWF.K-WF.K)/WFAT                                  00010100
C       WFAT=20   DAYS                                            00010101
A       DWF.K=DPR.K/PROD                                          00010110
NOTE                                                              00010111
NOTE                                                              00010112
NOTE    PRODUCTION-PLANNING POLICY WITH TWO COMPONENTS            00010113
NOTE                                                              00010114
A       DPR.K=IRO.K+PSR.K                                         00010120
A       IRO.K=(DINV.K-PINV.K)/IAT                                 00010130
C       IAT=10   DAYS                                             00010131
A       DINV.K=FIFGE(FINVG,VINVG.K,IPSW,1)                        00010140
C       FINVG=10000   UNITS                                       00010141
C       IPSW=0                                                    00010142
A       VINVG.K=PSR.K*NIC                                         00010150
C       NIC=25   DAYS                                             00010151
A       ASR.K=SMOOTH(PSR.K,ORAVT)                                 00010160
C       ORAVT=60   DAYS                                           00010161
NOTE                                                              00010162
NOTE    CONTROL CARDS                                             00010163
C       LENGTH=0                                                  00010164
C       DT=1                                                      00010165
C       PLTPER=10   DAYS                                          00010166
PLOT    SR=S,PSR=*,PR=P(200,600)/IRO=2(-200,200)/                 00010167
X       PINV=+,INV=I,DINV=D(8000,12000)                           00010168
RUN     ANALYSIS OF INFORMATION                                   00010169
```

Problem 4: Analysis of Market Growth Model

Purpose:

1. To illustrate some important principles of dynamic system behavior: structure is more important than parameters in determining behavior,

Source: This problem explores in detail the structure and behavior of feedback loops described in Jay W. Forrester, 1968, "Market Growth as Influenced by Capital Investment," *Industrial Management Review 9* (winter):83–105. Reprinted in Jay W. Forrester, 1975, *Collected Papers of Jay W. Forrester* (Cambridge, Mass.: Wright-Allen Press).

and only a few feedback loops determine behavior over a period of time (loop dominance).

2. To present a technique for analyzing complex system dynamics models.

Assignment: Review the flow diagrams and equations of the market growth model. A reading of Jay W. Forrester's article, "Market Growth as Influenced by Capital Investment (see source note), is strongly recommended. Then read the description of the analysis technique used in this assignment. Answer the questions regarding the behavior of the model.

Structure of Market Growth Model

The market growth model consists of three major feedback loops, as illustrated in figure 4a: a positive salesmen loop, a negative market loop, and a negative capacity expansion loop. Flow diagrams of each of the loops are given in figures 4b, 4c, 4d. DYNAMO equations for the market growth model are given in figure 4e, with plots of two table functions provided in figures 4f and 4g.

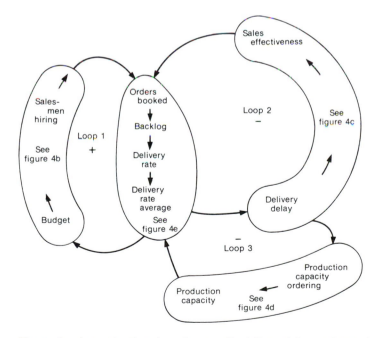

Figure 4a   Loop structure for sales growth, delivery delay, and capacity expansion

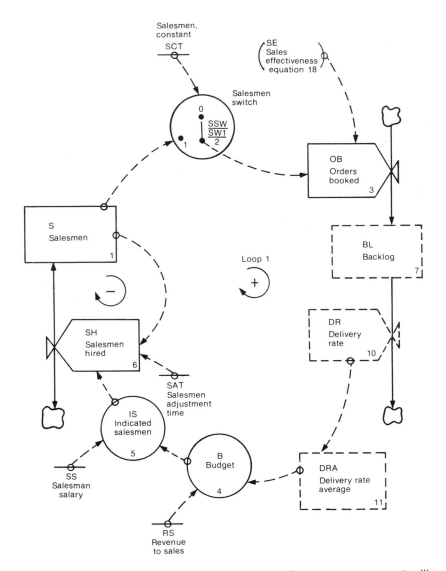

Figure 4b   Salesmen-hiring loop with sales generating revenue to support selling effort

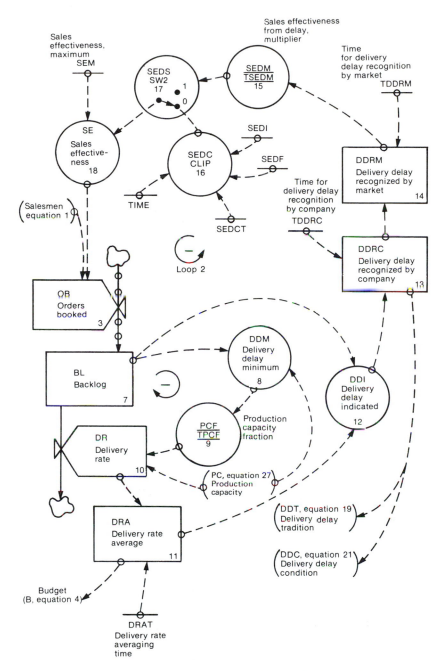

Figure 4c   Market loop with delivery delay determining product attractiveness

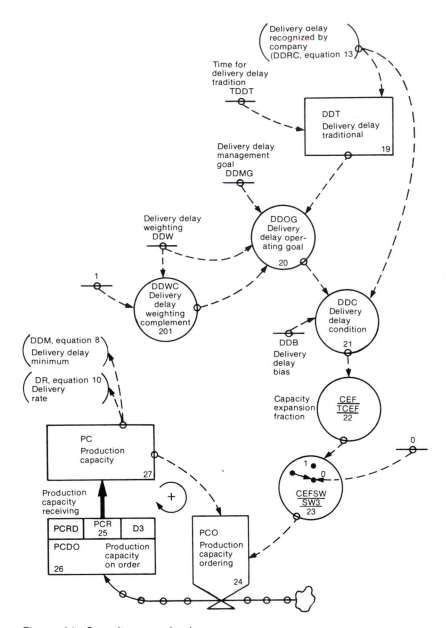

Figure 4d Capacity expansion loop

Figure 4e   DYNAMO equations

```
*       MARKET GROWTH AS INFLUENCED BY CAPITAL INVESTMENT
NOTE
NOTE        POSITIVE LOOP -- SALESMEN
NOTE
L       S.K=S.J+(DT)(SH.JK)
N       S=SN
C       SN=10
A       SSW.K=SWITCH(SCT,S.K,SW1)
C       SCT=60
C       SW1=0
R       OB.KL=SSW.K*SE.K
A       B.K=DRA.K*RS
C       RS=12
A       IS.K=B.K/SS
C       SS=2000
R       SH.KL=(IS.K-S.K)/SAT
C       SAT=20
NOTE
NOTE        NEGATIVE LOOP -- MARKET
NOTE
L       BL.K=BL.J+(DT)(OB.JK-DR.JK)
N       BL=BLN
C       BLN=8000
A       DDM.K=BL.K/PC.K
A       PCF.K=TABHL(TPCF,DDM.K,0,5,.5)
T       TPCF=0/.25/.5/.67/.8/.87/.93/.95/.97/.98/1
R       DR.KL=PC.K*PCF.K
L       DRA.K=DRA.J+(DT/DRAT)(DR.JK-DRA.J)
N       DRA=DR
C       DRAT=1
A       DDI.K=BL.K/DRA.K
L       DDRC.K=DDRC.J+(DT/TDDRC)(DDI.J-DDRC.J)
N       DDRC=DDI
C       TDDRC=4
L       DDRM.K=DDRM.J+(DT/TDDRM)(DDRC.J-DDRM.J)
N       DDRM=DDRC
C       TDDRM=6
A       SEDM.K=TABHL(TSEDM,DDRM.K,0,10,1)
T       TSEDM=1/.97/.87/.73/.53/.38/.25/.15/.08/.03/.02
A       SEDC.K=CLIP(SEDF,SEDI,TIME.K,SEDCT)
C       SEDF=1
C       SEDI=1
C       SEDCT=36
A       SEDS.K=SWITCH(SEDC.K,SEDM.K,SW2)
C       SW2=0
A       SE.K=SEDS.K*SEM
C       SEM=400
NOTE
NOTE        CAPITAL INVESTMENT
NOTE
L       DDT.K=DDT.J+(DT/TDDT)(DDRC.J-DDT.J)
N       DDT=DDRC
C       TDDT=12
A       DDOG.K=(DDT.K)(DDW)+(DDMG)(DDWC)
N       DDWC=1-DDW
C       DDW=0
C       DDMG=2
A       DDC.K=(DDRC.K/DDOG.K)-DDB
C       DDB=.3
A       CEF.K=TABHL(TCEF,DDC.K,0,2.5,.5)
T       TCEF=-.07/-.02/0/.02/.07/.15
A       CEFSW.K=SWITCH(0,CEF.K,SW3)
C       SW3=0
R       PCO.KL=PC.K*CEFSW.K
```

```
R      PCR.KL=DELAY3(PCO.JK,PCRD)
C      PCRD=12
L      PCOO.K=PCOO.J+(DT)(PCO.JK-PCR.JK)
N      PCOO=PCO*PCRD
L      PC.K=PC.J+(DT)(PCR.JK)
N      PC=PCI
C      PCI=12000
NOTE
NOTE       CONTROL CARDS
NOTE
PLOT   OB=*,PC=C,DR=D(0,24000)/S=S(0,80)/SE=E(0,400)/BL=B(0,120000)/DDRM=
X      R,DDOG=G(2,6)/CEF=F(-.06,.18)
SPEC   DT=.5/LENGTH=0/PLTPER=2
RUN    COMPILE
CP     LENGTH=100
CP     SW1=1
C      PCI=100000
RUN    UNLIMITED EXPONENTIAL GROWTH
C      SEDF=.25
C      PCI=100000
RUN    GROWTH AND DECLINE
C      SW1=0
CP     SW2=1
RUN    NEGATIVE LOOP OSCILLATION
CP     SW1=1
RUN    SALES STAGNATION
C      RS=13.6
RUN    INCREASED SALES BUDGET ALLOCATION
CP     SW3=1
RUN    CAPACITY EXPANSION
C      DDW=1
RUN    GOAL=TRADITION
C      DDW=.5
RUN    GOAL=.5*TRADITION+.5*ABSOLUTE
/*EOJ ********

R; T=0.05/0.30 12:09:31
```

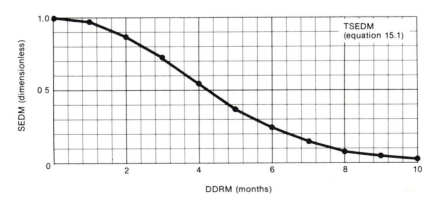

Figure 4f Table for sales effectiveness from delay multiplier as it depends on DDRM

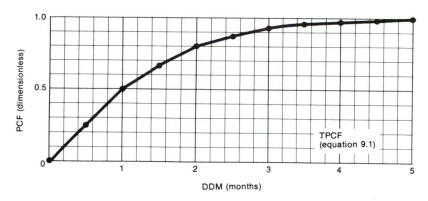

Figure 4g Table for production capacity fraction as it depends on delivery delay minimum

Overview of Analysis Technique

Each major feedback loop is analyzed first in isolation and then in combination. Each loop exhibits a characteristic behavior mode. Analysis of each loop focuses on understanding the cause of that mode and the effect of parameter values on the behavior mode. A detailed understanding of each loop facilitates analysis of the model as a whole.

Analysis of the loops in combination focuses on understanding how structural additions—the combination of loops—alter behavior. Structure, rather than parameters, is then seen to determine the model's characteristic behavior mode.

Analysis of Salesmen Loop (Loop 1)

The salesmen loop is a positive feedback loop—changes within the loop are self-reinforcing. Positive feedback loops determine the growth characteristics of system behavior. The exercises that follow seek to identify the elements of positive loops that affect growth.

Exercises

1. Figure 4h shows the behavior of loop 1 in isolation. What behavior mode does the loop display? What is the role of the minor negative loop? What does the run imply about PC?
2. Identify the delay times (or time constants) around loop 1. Note whether the values remain constant during the model run.

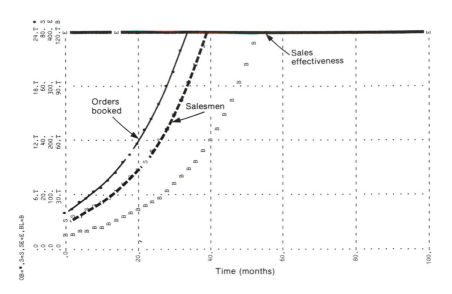

Figure 4h   Behavior of loop 1 in isolation

3. What impact do these delay times have on the behavior of loop 1? Can changes in delay times alter the behavior mode?

4. Assume that a broken link between delivery rate DR and delivery rate average DRA makes loop 1 an open loop. Then put a STEP input of 10,000 units per month in orders booked OB. Plot BL and DR as functions of time on the grid in figure 4i. BL is initially zero.

5. Define *gain* as the value of the output divided by the value of the input. Define *steady-state gain* as the gain when the system reaches equilibrium. What is the steady-state gain from OB to DR?

6. What is the steady-state gain across each of the other elements in loop 1? Find the total loop gain by multiplying the individual element gains.

7. What happens to system behavior when the open-loop gain is greater than 1? Less than 1? Equal to 1? Can the parameters that determine loop gain affect loop behavior mode?

Analysis of Market Loop (Loop 2)

The market loop is a negative feedback loop. All negative loops are goal seeking. Negative loops can cause system behavior to shift from growth to stagnation.

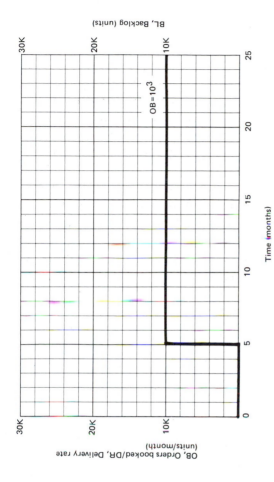

Figure 4i

Exercises

8. What is the goal of loop 2? How does the loop accomplish its goal?
9. Figure 4j shows the behavior of loop 2 in isolation. Explain why the system oscillates.
10. What would be the impact of making DDPM and DDPC a first-order delay with the same total delay time? Explain why the behavior change occurs.
11. What would be the impact of increasing delay times? Of eliminating delay times? Why?
12. What is the impact of changing the slope of the SEDM relationship? What happens if SEDM is flat at 1.0? What does this imply about the appropriateness of including a largely unmeasurable relationship such as SEDM in a model?
13. Comment on the relative importance of structure and parameters in determining the behavior of Loop 2.

Analysis of Loops 1 and 2 Combined

Loops 1 and 2 consist of both a positive and negative feedback loop. A system with more than one feedback loop has the potential for a shift in behavior mode as time passes.

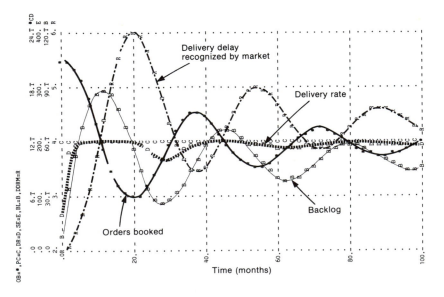

Figure 4j Behavior of loop 2 in isolation

Exercises

14. Figure 4k shows the behavior of loops 1 and 2 combined. Explain the cause of the shift in behavior mode. How does loop 2 cause the positive loop, with gain initially greater than 1, to stop growing? Why does S continue to rise, even though at, say, month 40 there are enough salesmen to keep orders booked equal to production capacity.

15. Is there a change in the feedback loop that dominates system behavior?

16. What effect will changes in loop 1 parameters have on behavior? Loop 2 parameters?

17. Is the model thus far insensitive to parameters? Why or why not?

Analysis of Loops 1, 2, and 3 Combined

Loops 1, 2, and 3 together constitute the market growth model. Loop 3 adds a negative feedback loop and therefore introduces another source of instability.

Exercises

18. Figure 4l shows the behavior of loops 1, 2, and 3 combined. Explain why the system exhibits growth instability.

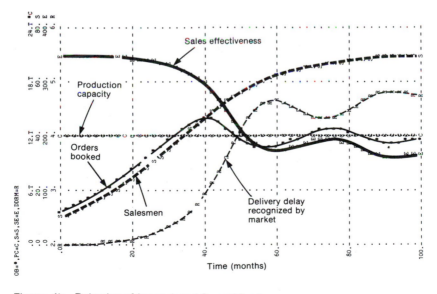

Figure 4k Behavior of loops 1 and 2 combined

19. Over the course of figure 4l does any shift in loop dominance occur?

20. Can parameter changes alter the observed behavior mode, particularly loop 3 parameters?

21. Comment on the relative importance of structure and parameters in determining behavior.

22. Figure 4m shows model behavior with delivery delay weight DDW set equal to 1.0. DDW determines the goal structure of the capacity expansion loop. What causes the system collapse? Which loops dominate system behavior?

Problem 5: Policy Design on Market Growth Model

Purpose: To extend the analysis of problem 4 to show that structural changes in the market growth model can eliminate the decline periods.

Assignment: Review problem 4, and then do the three exercises.

Exercises

1. With the company's present capacity expansion policy, a capacity shortage develops before the company expands. A better policy might be to expand before the shortage develops. Implement such a policy

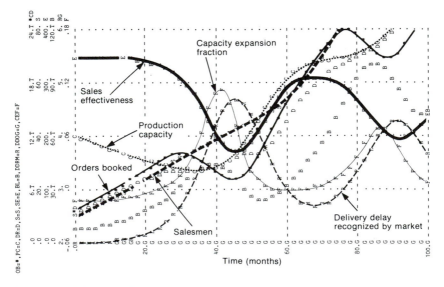

Figure 4l   Behavior of loops 1, 2, and 3 combined

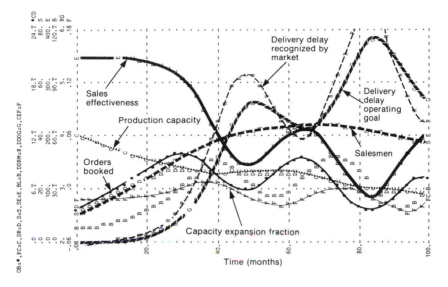

Figure 4m   Model behavior with DDW = 1.0

using different values for capacity expansion fraction CEF. Is the policy successful in averting periods of decline? Is sales effectiveness at a
maximum? Why or why not? What are the disadvantages of a policy
based on a concept like the capacity expansion fraction that responds
to delivery delay?

2. Develop a capacity expansion policy that explicitly adjusts capacity
to the capacity necessary to meet forecast orders. Does the policy yield
smooth growth? Are salesmen fully effective? If not, why not? Is the
forecast self-validated; that is, does it always come true as a consequence of company actions?

3. How can the company expand capacity to achieve full sales effectiveness? How does the company deal with forecasting inaccuracies?

Cases

The four cases require students to construct and analyze a model from a description of a company problem and structure. The cases can be used in courses that place some emphasis on model construction. Cases 1 and 2 are suitable as introductory modeling assignments. Cases 3 and 4 are more advanced.[1]

Students get the most out of the cases if they are required to hand in their work in parts, with instructor feedback on each part before they proceed to the next part. The four parts to a model analysis and construction are

1. Write down a problem statement and dynamic hypothesis. The problem statement identifies the behavior mode of interest; the dynamic hypothesis gives a preliminary statement of the feedback loops and policies that might produce the behavior mode. Causal loop diagrams are often useful in developing the dynamic hypothesis.
2. Devise a flow diagram and preliminary model equations. If time is short, instructor comments on gross equation errors can often save valuable time for beginning students.
3. Examine the model behavior and verify or alter the dynamic hypothesis. The analysis techniques developed in the text should be helpful here.
4. Develop policies that improve model behavior.

Case 1: Resource Allocation in a Small Company

Problem Statement

Instead of acquiring new resources, some managers shift resources within the organization to wherever they are needed most at any mo-

1. The association between the companies mentioned in these cases and any real company is purely coincidental.

ment in time. The motivation for such an action ranges from financial pressures to the belief of some managers that this is a good policy. It seems to make the best use of available resources. The situation described concerns a rather typical production problem.

In a small company the production rate is rising slightly higher than the sales rate so that inventories start to pile up. In an effort to induce sales, production is reduced by transferring available resources from production to marketing. Not realizing the delay between sales effort and incoming customer orders, the firm continues transferring resources until the customer order rate increases to the point where it exceeds production, and inventories are depleted. To correct this inventory shortage, the firm finds itself transferring available resources from marketing back to production. After some delay this decrease of resources in marketing leads to a decrease in sales, and inventories start piling up again. At this point resources have to be shifted back to marketing in order to induce sales, and a new cycle begins.

Case 2: Future Electronics Company

Problem Statement

The Future Electronics Company is a medium-sized firm producing a line of integrated circuits. Integrated circuits are single pieces of semiconductor material that perform the functions of entire complex electronic circuits (amplifiers, oscillators, and so on). Because of the delicate production processes involved, only 70 to 90 percent of the items produced prove usable. Therefore all units produced must undergo testing before sale.

The management of Future has for some time been worried about their quality image. From time to time they have heard such statements from customers as, "We are generally quite satisfied with your quality, and consider you one of our highest quality suppliers, but are bothered by some of the variations that occur. Every so often, we receive a series of poor shipments from you. These create a disruption of our production, and we are forced to find a supplier whose quality is more

Source: Earlier modeling exercises dealing with the Future case are available as System Dynamics Group memorandum D-1599, and in M. R. Goodman, 1974, *Study Notes in System Dynamics* (Cambridge, Mass.: Wright-Allen Press). This case has been extensively revised from these earlier versions.

dependable, even if their best is not as good as yours.'' While customers are not always so outspoken, Future has noticed that at times customers return many defective units, but at other times customers return very few defectives.

The management of Future is quite sensitive to this situation and, upon noticing increased complaints, they respond aggressively to increase the thoroughness of the testing procedure. Discussions with Mr. Watson, manager of quality control, provided insight into how Future responds.

Watson stated that while Future monitors testing rate per man, the company was unsure what quality the market demanded. Complaints provided an index of company performance relative to demand. ''When complaints are low, I assume we are providing quality equal to or better than market requirements. Consequently I try to get more testing out of each tester. You see, the company has a policy against laying off testers. We have difficulty getting good testers, and it takes several months to train them. So we like to hold on to the testers we've trained. But we're also reluctant to hire new testers because of the investment in training and the no-layoff policy. When complaints are low, my boss sits on approvals for new testers—it can take up to six months to get his okay. So I try to shade a little bit on quality.

''But when complaints start pouring in, we move fast. There's nothing like a fourfold increase in complaints to get my boss moving on new personnel requests. And I also get flak on the poor quality; so I try to improve that. I suppose I overreact a little, but its easier to get the testers I might need later when management is under pressure from customers.''

Testing integrated circuits is a difficult and chancy operation. Whether a unit is good or bad is often a matter of degree. The circuits can be tested under a wide range of test and operating conditions. Meeting specification requires passing several basic tests. But the more tests performed, the higher the probability of catching a unit that might break down in certain uses. And the longer the tests are performed, the higher the probability of catching early failures. Longer testing means higher quality units are shipped to customers.

The quite difficult testing procedure requires several months training, although some trainees learn faster than others. The testers in training do not test parts for shipment, since Future does not wish to take the chance that inexperienced testers might let bad units get through. The new people are trained by experienced employees. An experienced tester assigned to the training of a new man must spend about half his time in this capacity and thus take time away from actual testing.

Because of the investment in training and the historically tight labor market, Future has a policy against laying off testers but lets attrition reduce an apparent excess. After becoming fully trained, a tester remains with Future an average of 40 months.

Future's production policies are such that demand forces testers to keep up with production—Future maintains a constant delivery delay, even if variations in quality result. If the volume of incoming orders and production vary, the time spent testing each unit varies also.

While Future's hiring policies are intended to reduce fluctuations in quality, they have not accomplished their purpose. At times, Future is short of testers so that testing time per unit and quality falls. Then Future encounters a period of excess testers so that testing time per unit increases. On average, Future detects 90 percent of the defective units. If time spent testing a unit falls by 20 percent, Future estimates 25 percent of the defective units get through testing.

Future does not know a great deal about the policies of customers, but the company feels that an appreciable amount of time often passes before customers detect defects in the quality of units they receive. Many defective units are not returned for six months. Moreover, after a customer decides to switch suppliers, it can take as much as six months before Future's units can be designed out of the customer's equipment.

Case 3 Fashionwear Clothes Company

Problem Statement

Fashionwear Clothes Company is a metropolitan chain of retail clothing stores. Each store is relatively small and specializes in trendy medium-priced women's clothing. Fashionwear is controlled from a single central location. Central management organizes each store as a profit center with a revenue and a unit margin target for each outlet's activities.

Over the last few years Fashionwear has experienced short-term fluctuations of eight to ten months duration in revenue (measured as dollar sales) and unit margin (measured as the average dollar margin across all items sold). Central management has discerned that the fluctuations exist independent of any seasonal variations in sales, because they do not seem to recur during particular months of the year. Further, during informal discussion with major competitors, management found that no similar pattern of revenue flows was experienced elsewhere in the industry. Consequently they wonder if they might take any actions to eliminate the fluctuations.

Central management sets the revenue and unit margins for each store. The revenue target is set according to past performance on a store-by-store basis. The margin is based on a traditional average unit margin that experience has shown to be sufficient to support each store in a healthy financial condition, given its expected sales volume.

The local store manager is directly responsible for achieving the revenue goal and is pressured by central management to meet the margin goal. Local management can control revenue inflow to a store by use of specials. A special sale on a particular selection of clothes leads to a net increase in revenue despite the lower unit price. Naturally the use of specials causes a reduction in unit margin. Interviews with local store managers showed that specials are also used to reduce revenue inflow whenever revenue exceeds the target. This action is primarily taken to safeguard future performance against target. Since store managers know their target sales revenue is set on the basis of recent past trends, they wish to prevent any temporary increase in demand leading to an excessive target in the future.

Every quarter the store managers analyze their books and prepare a report showing revenue and average unit margin. Central management reviews the figures and takes action when discrepancies appear. Two frequently used avenues of action are available. If stores are reporting shortfalls in their revenue target, media advertising and promotion are undertaken in an attempt to restore sales volume. The costs of advertising are deducted, on a sales-weighted basis, from the unit margin reported by local management. If stores are reporting deviations from their margin target, central management raises or lowers list prices to restore the margin. When margins are low, central management feels the need to protect store profitability. When margins are high, list prices are adjusted to prevent overpricing. Deviations from the margin target also prompt central management to pressure the store managers into curbing or expanding their program of specials. When margins are low, pressure is applied to reduce specials, somewhat minimizing the margin problem.

Hints and Guidelines

Identifying Level Variables   This case study is unique because there is
no clear evidence of physical accumulations common in most industrial
dynamics models, such as inventories, backlogs, workforce, or capital
equipment. The model deals with the intangibles of price, advertising
expenditures, and specials. Nevertheless, the important physical levels
(as opposed to information levels representing information delays) are
easily identified because they correspond to the rates that represent the
control policies of the system. The three control policies—pricing, advertising, and specials—can be viewed in terms of three level
variables—price level, advertising expenditure level, and number of
specials. A typical configuration for the pricing policy and the price level
is shown in the figure that follows.

One technique many modelers find useful is applying normals and
multipliers. For example, indicated price IP, to which price level is adjusted, might equal normal price NP multiplied by the effect of revenue
discrepancy ERDP and the effect of margin discrepancy EMDP.

$$\text{IP.K} = \text{NP} * \text{ERDP.K} * \text{EMDP.K}.$$

The multipliers ERDP and EMDP would equal 1.0 when the discrepancies equal 0. Price would thus equal normal price.

Parameter Selection   Parameter selection is a difficult task that only
becomes easier with practice. It is not an arbitrary process as many
critics of system dynamics suppose. With some thought, basically common sense and experience, any parameter can be confined within quite a
narrow range. When personal experience is not sufficient, interviews
with people familiar with the system can provide working estimates, a

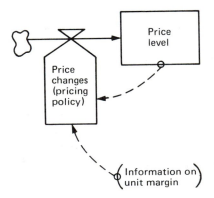

technique always used by consultants. In this exercise we are confined to common sense and personal experience.

Important parameters are likely to be the length of information delays, the responsiveness of control policies, and the sensitivity of demand to price and advertising changes. As an example, consider the pricing control policy's effect on demand. If the unit margin of store sales drops, the pricing policy should initiate a price increase. However, before any policy action can be taken, central management must first be apprised of the margin discrepancy. This involves reporting and information-processing delays. Once the margin discrepancy is known, central management must decide on an appropriate price change to correct the discrepancy and how quickly to introduce the change; both are aspects of pricing policy. The timing of a price change represents the sensitivity of the pricing policy. How should it be estimated? Everyday experience suggests that prices rarely change by more than 1 percent per month, and often less. Incorporating this information in the model will give a plausible pricing policy. Finally, it is necessary to include an estimate of customer response to price changes. We already know from the background information that a price decrease generates an increase in sales revenue, despite the drop in unit revenue. This is a useful starting point. It means that a 10 percent price change produces a change in sales volume greater than 10 percent. From this base we can now think about plausible extremes of price elasticity that could exist in this industry. Since the clothes industry is quite competitive, it is reasonable to expect a price elasticity considerably greater than one (a 10 percent price change might cause a 15 or 20 percent volume change).

The example illustrates that, by using existing knowledge in a structured manner, it is possible to make plausible and accurate informed guesses of parameter values. One word of warning, however: the estimation of delay times is always difficult. There is a strong natural tendency to underestimate the time it takes to get things done. This is a common failing not just in system dynamics modeling but virtually in every planning process. Initial estimates have a habit of being only one-half or one-third of their true value, simply because it is difficult to visualize all the detailed steps in the completion of a particular activity.

The foregoing guidelines should be useful for arriving at a workable specification of the model. In later behavior testing these first estimates are considerably refined. The process of refinement should always be tied back to reality. Very often through this process a clearer understanding of the real system emerges.

Case 4: Digitronics Company

Problem Statement

Digitronics, Inc., is a medium-sized producer of electronic equipment whose products are extremely intricate and require specialized development, manufacturing, and marketing efforts. Over the years Digitronics has acquired extensive expertise in the design and production of electronic equipment and has successfully introduced new products to meet new needs.

Since its founding in the early 1950s, Digitronics has experienced rapid but erratic sales growth. Typically sales will rise rapidly for five or six years and then will slow. Sometimes sales decline for periods of one to three years. A period of slow growth is followed by a period of rapid growth.

The company is worried about this erratic sales growth and wants to understand the cause of its behavior because it is currently experiencing little sales growth.

Background Information   The electronics industry is highly competitive in research and development and product performance. The state of the art in instrumentation technology advances rapidly. The firm that does not continually develop new products in line with technological advances soon finds itself with a declining product line. Further, the nature and uses of electronic equipment require high product performance. Because of the complexity of the products, substantial engineering effort must be allocated to manufacturing and marketing electronic equipment. Product reliability requires that the manufacturing and testing processes be carried out under the supervision of competent engineering personnel. Similarly substantial engineering effort is allocated to demonstrating, explaining, selling, and setting up products for customer use.

The electronics industry has experienced rapid growth. In large part the rapid growth is due to (1) the increased market for traditional electronic equipment and (2) the application of electrical engineering to new areas such as medicine. Industry spokesmen expect that the electronics industry will continue to grow rapidly in the future as new applications continue to surface.

Information from Interviews with Digitronics Personnel Mr. Stone, president of Digitronics, provided historical information about company orders, products, and engineering staff. He pointed out the erratic sales growth pattern from historical data. According to him the past president of Digitronics felt that the erratic sales growth was in large part due to exogenous economic factors. Mr. Stone, however, felt that the sales growth pattern could be the result of internal management practice.

When asked what he felt causes the periods of rapid increases in sales, Mr. Stone explained that new products seemed to catch on and produce the sales growth. He went on to explain that about two or three years after a new product was introduced, competition would capture some of the market.

When asked about delivery delays and quality of the company's products, the president replied that both were competitive. He explained that Digitronics had a reputation for high quality products and that he felt this reputation to be an important contributor to the company's success. After some prodding, the president did admit that delivery delay was occasionally high and that this did cause the firm to lose potential sales. This was particularly true for mature products. For new products the company had little if any competition. High delivery delays, however, tended to induce potential customers to stay with an old method of doing the job. In summary the president felt that sales of new products, while affected by delivery delay, were less sensitive to delivery delay than mature products.

Mr. Stone went on to point out that when delivery delay was high, Digitronics acted to correct the problem. For the most part Digitronics production capacity was determined by production engineers. Physical production capacity had never been a constraint to filling orders. The nature of Digitronics product line required a substantial engineering effort merely to produce and market the products. Production engineers were needed to work out bugs in the complex production process. Further, these same engineers very often had to work with customers to install and debug the new products in actual use. Very often after new products caught on, Digitronics was short of production engineers. The president said that at such times they would hire mostly production engineers so as to alleviate the delivery delay problem.

The president explained that in his opinion the success of the organization lay in its technical capability to introduce new products and solve difficult production problems. Even now, when sales are stagnant, he felt that engineering expenditures should be slightly expanded rather than cut back. However, he admitted that this commitment to engineering excellence might conflict with internal financial pressures to keep professional expenditures within a strict professional budget.

Interviews with operation managers yielded further insights into company operations.

Acquisition of Professionals   The firm's desired number of professionals (both research and development engineers and production engineers) is defined by a professional sector budget. Digitronics allocated a fraction of average sales to this area. The policy variable—percent sales to professional activities—has been set at 10 percent. The vice-president of R & D thought Digitronics might be induced to spend 15 percent of average sales, but no more, in this area.

The estimated monthly cost per engineer was $2,500 per month. Also, on the average, it takes 6 months to find, select, and hire an engineer and an additional 9 months to train him.

The vice-president confirmed the president's statement regarding the relative hiring of product development and production engineers. He said that in the past, when delivery delays were low, the company tended to employ approximately twice as many engineers in product development as in production. During such periods Digitronics hired about 30 percent production engineers and 70 percent R & D engineers. When delivery delays were high, they hired 90 to 95 percent production engineers. Unfortunately, the vice-president told us, it usually took 3 months to shift hiring policies because the two types of engineers were recruited by different departments and often at different schools or professional societies.

Research and Development   Product development engineers at Digitronics worked individually on the development of new electronic equipment. Occasionally small teams were formed. The vice-president of R & D said, "Individual work on a product results in high morale among Digitronics engineers. An engineer working on a new product can feel that the product is 'his baby.' As a result engineers take a great deal of pride in developing a superior product." Later on the vice-president stated that, while team research might improve the speed with which new products are developed, he felt the overall quality of the product and morale of engineers would decline. At any rate, he thought, the average 14 to 18 months from project initiation to production and the one out of two project success ratio (ratio of products produced to projects initiated) were acceptable. He also noted that 6 months often passed between the time when an engineer completed one project and began a second, during which time the engineer often became involved in the initial stages of producing the new product as well as in the planning of future products. He further noted that some competitors were changing to the team approach, perhaps because this allows them to develop competing products more quickly.

Production   Assembly of Digitronics products is carried out both on assembly lines and by individuals working on a particular product or component. Some stages of the production process are extremely complex and require extensive engineering. Neither physical production capacity nor assembly labor has been a constraint to filling orders in the past.

After assembly each product is tested for quality by production engineers. Defective units are set aside for potential future repair.

Finally, products are shipped to fill orders. Some products require that Digitronics' engineers work with customer engineers in setting up and debugging the products in the customer's application.

Marketing   The vice-president for marketing provided information about product demand. He said that new products faced little direct competition. After about one to three years, new products would mature as competitors entered. Then in this market, even with good deliveries, demand was much lower than for new products. Products lasted in the mature category for about another two to three years before becoming obsolete.

Average product price, the vice-president said, was $14,000 per unit.

When asked about market perception of the company's performance, he said that the nature of electronic equipment made for long perception delays. Long lead times were required to review and evaluate products. As a result it was difficult to shift manufacturers on short notice.

Index